In Defence of Conspiracy Theories

with examples from Irish and International
History and Politics

Corstown – MMVIII

Dedicated to St Patrick and St Oliver Plunkett

22 November 2009.

ISBN 978-0-9556812-2-6

CONTENTS

PREFACE

This is a book compiled from various articles, most of them hosted at indymedia.ie whom I'd like to thank, on the general subject of conspiracy theories. In some ways its probably not a particularly useful categorisation but it seems to be applied to virtually every case of involved or complicated state corruption in modern times and hence seems to apply to all these articles. I apologise that I use an internet writing style that is a lot different to normal academic styles but hopefully the points raised are clear enough. Similarly I hope too that I will be forgiven for using standard internet abbreviations like afaik – as far as I know, lol and :-) – lots of laughter, and imho – in my humble opinion.

I'd like to thank my family and all the research institutions and libraries that I used, which I list in the book 'Shakespeare is Irish', and many many thanks also to the many commentators that contributed to indymedia. This would get like the Oscars if I was to list them all :-), but I beg forgiveness from those that I have left out and plead lack of space, memory, sheer exhaustion after proof reading this book (and yes I know there are no doubt still piles of errors, they'll just have to do!lol) etc etc.

I hope too that the many victims of the groups listed in these pages will take heart and one day see better days.

Brian Nugent B.A.(Hons)
Co.Meath
26 March 2008

CHAPTER 1

In Defence of Conspiracy Theories

This chapter attempts to answer some of the criticism levelled at 'conspiracy theorists', by showing inter alia that factors in modern society make it all too possible for conspiracies to exist and difficult for them to be exposed.

Modern Mé Féin Culture

I think a lot of people would agree with Fred Johnston when he says that:
> "This is not the age of principles, as commentators
> keep telling us; we live in a fallen, mé-fhéin [selfish]
> epoque, when nothing matters."[1]

The thing is that this kind of general atmosphere has implications for the question of whether or not conspiracies flourish. Clearly if people don't care about their fellow citizens then they won't bother exposing conspiracies and are much more likely to participate in them for their own financial or career advancement.

Another way of looking at it is that formerly the morals of society were set by the church, particularly by the Catholic Church in Ireland, and probably by the public school and university systems in places like the UK, and this influence led to a personal morality which, in theory anyway, certainly proscribed getting involved in any duplicitous practices:

- The Church. I know its perfectly true to say that some of those Christian Brothers, and others, in the later 20th century have not exactly lived up to the ideals they taught but I still wonder if its not fair to say that they impressed upon their students a code of morality, and an 'informed conscience', which encouraged their pupils not to get involved in 'conspiratorial' practices. Like obviously if you emerged believing in the 10 Commandments, which they drilled into people, with its requirements not to lie, steal, or kill etc then you really would be useless as a conspirator! Also the Irish Catholic Church was always traditionally critical of Secret Societies and under that pressure those societies often wilted, so again maybe that particular 'conspiracy theory', that those societies are all powerful, would be truer in the period when the church is in decline.

- Universities and Public Schools. During most of the 19th and early 20th century these institutions used to boast of turning out a 'gentleman' who had a high standard of morality and learning. This certainly involved keeping your word, not stealing, and being well informed and educated about the world around you. Within that code incidentally they also tended to praise a kind of semi leisure existence, certainly working all the time to the detriment of expanding your mind was considered the ultimate social faux pas! (As Oscar Wilde once said "Work is the curse of the drinking classes!") Anyway this 'gentleman' type would also never tolerate the goings on that are described in the usual 'conspiracy theories'.

Obviously this education and code of morality was not followed by all who were brought up in it, plenty of Christian Brothers pupils, and teachers unfortunately, turned out to be perfectly evil and many of those 'gentlemen' were anything but. That being said you could surely make the case that people existing in a society which cherishes those kind of values are somewhat less likely to get involved in 'conspiracies' than a society where the pursuit of money, and even sex, are held up as the end all and be all of human existence. For example its well known that intelligence agencies are only too willing to provide those last two commodities for anybody wishing to participate in their 'conspiracies' so its natural to assume that they will have more influence on a society where they are glorified than in one where they are not.

I think as well that there are two other factors here which impinge on the question of conspiracy theories. One is that if the general public are selfish or deliberately uniformed, because they might consider work to be more important than being informed or educated about society, then they might not do very much to expose and crush conspiracies that might have been brought to their attention. The other issue is that this mé féin culture is permeating each of the various areas of civic life, leading to a climate of at least low level corruption, which again makes it difficult to expose and close down conspiracies.

On that first point I thought I would quote from Rodney Stich, a former pilot with a lot of experience in dealing with whistleblowers and various conspiracies in all areas of the US government. At first, in 1978, he enthusiastically tried to engage with the general public trying to get them motivated to deal with the huge conspiracies that he described, very soberly and intelligently with all sources noted, on over 3,000 TV and radio shows and numerous books. But now he is very depressed at the level of selfishness and apathy that he sees in the general public, and regrets bothering to sacrifice all in trying to inform them about what

6

was happening. He clearly now regards this apathy on the part of the general public as one of the main factors in preventing 'conspirators' from being stopped in their tracks. He would say that even when the general public know what's going on they don't attempt to get it stopped, either through the political system or when they serve on Juries etc. Its the ordinary American that he has given up on, he has even got depressed in dealing with relatives of people who lost their lives as part of these conspiracies, many of the latter being more interested in compensation payments than justice. He goes so far as to talk about the "public's complicity in corruption and tragedies", which he describes as follows:

> "The widespread public ignorance, apathy, denial, about the corrupt activities detailed and documented in the books written by government insiders has made possible an endless series of tragedies. This information has been made available to the people if they would only look, show an interest, and read.
>
> ...
>
> Next in line for blame is the apathy, cowardice, or low morality, of the American public. Information has been available for years revealing this misconduct and the tragedies inflicted upon the American people. A culture of filthy songs, "music," drugs, has changed the morality in the United States.
>
> In the books written by former government agents, there are such major factual matters stated, by people such as the former heads of secret CIA operations, that should have resulted in major media articles and public concern. Instead: nothing!
>
> For instance: ...[Describes some of the activities highlighted in his books like murders and drug smuggling by the US government, and notes the 'no response' by the general public]...
>
> The list goes on and on. The problems are numerous, including:
>
> - Certain people are not sophisticated enough to contemplate anything more complex than the ball games or their grand children.
> - Certain people don't care to hear about these matters, and could care less. It doesn't directly affect them.
> - Certain people are so involved in corrupt activities themselves that they could care less or do not want to

voice opposition to the corruption in government for fear of exposing themselves.

- The large numbers of immigrants reduces their interest, or ability to understand, the corruption in government (possibly due to the fact that government personnel from where they came from were also corrupt and that it was an accepted culture).

- Certain people feel there is nothing that they can do about it, so why try.

- Certain people rant and rave about misconduct in government, focusing on some relatively minor matter, and refuse to address the hardcore corruption brought to their attention; or that the hardcore corruption involves confrontation, while complaining about some obscure matter doesn't result in any confrontation or requires any efforts.

- The culture in the United States has deteriorated to such a low level that there is no interest in attacking corruption.

- The culture in the United States, and its morals, have deteriorated to such a low level that there is no outrage about the harm done to others or to the nation.

- The person who is too scared to speak out, afraid of what government officials can do to them.

- Hear no evil, see no evil, and speak no evil—the in-denial American!

- In all fairness, it is possible that many who do nothing would show some semblance of character and integrity if media people did not cover-up for the misconduct.

...

Ball game fanatics with a gluttonous passion for sports (children games), while too cowardly, or too lazy, to address the corruption that inflicts such great tragedies upon so many people. Fiddling while Rome burns may be a good parallel. Flag-waving "patriot" who does nothing to learn or to react to corruption in government. With similarities to Pontius Pilate and the crucifixion of Jesus Christ, most Americans wash their hands of the tragic consequences of their inactions.

...

What better example can there be than their support for the invasion and murder of tens of thousands of Iraqis on the obvious serial lying of their smooth-talking political leaders."[2]

The fed up Stich is now writing books talking about the 'Ugly Americans'! I think one of the reasons he focuses on this is because his experiences go back to WWII, in which he fought for the US although he in fact is of Austrian ancestry. My guess is that he relates the atmosphere in the US today to the great tragedy that afflicted the German people in that war. Clearly your ordinary German didn't know that much about what their leaders were up to in the 30s and 40s but they must have known something and yet they turned a blind eye, preoccupied with working hard, as they always do, and enjoying the economic benefits that the Nazis had brought at that time. They didn't know what was around the corner and as it turned out they paid a high price for their indifference. Meanwhile it is obvious from Stich's comments that he sees the US public being indifferent about the guilt of launching an aggressive invasion (and you could add things like Guantanamo Bay - surely a second cousin to a concentration camp - and jokes being made about CIA 'snow boarding' practices) and is saying that the US public is similarly well enough informed and doing nothing to stop these things. Many people are saying now that Ireland is becoming a lot like America and might end up suffering from the same sort of apathy. This then obviously impacts on the question of whether widespread 'conspiracies' exist, because if people are so indifferent when the facts about such 'conspiracies' are put before them then clearly the conspiracies can keep on flourishing.

The other point about this mé féin culture is that it means less people will come forward in the first place. Obviously if your morality is based on the next paycheck, the pension, career advancement, paying the mortgage etc then you aren't likely to bother whistleblowing about anything. It also doesn't help particularly if your morality is based on the law, because a lot of this corruption is committed by the State and they usually have some obscure legal opinion ready which justifies what they do. An example of that would be the legal opinion which the US government sought and used to justify their torture practices in Iraq and Guantanamo Bay.

What seems to be happening as well is that people quickly adapt themselves to the prevailing culture existing in all the different walks of life in Ireland, and abide by that 'code' of morality rather than any other of these older codes of ethics which used to come from the church or the universities or whatever. Unfortunately if these institutions have become corrupt then the new people who work there also become corrupt - to an extent - very quickly. I think you can see this in a lot of areas in

Ireland right now, where the prevailing culture in these professions allows conspiracies to happen:

Police
An example could be the culture that has come across from evidence given to the Morris Tribunal. Its clear from that that perjury is not considered such a big crime on the part of many Gardaí, and yet that has disastrous implications for the justice system considering the huge reliance that is placed there on the word of the Gardaí, and trust in their control over evidence and contact with witnesses.[3] In fact you can be jailed in Ireland for quite a long sentence purely on the word of a senior member of the Gardaí given in court.[4] Obviously with that kind of corruption conspiracies can flourish easier than if they always told the truth in court.

As regards the atmosphere in the US maybe these comments by Gerard MacManus, from the MacManus pub in Dundalk, might be of interest. He spent over a quarter of a century in two different police departments in the US, and was also an Irish army military policeman and later attached to the police in the Philippines. Furthermore he was involved in intelligence as the founder of the FNEOA, set up to share intelligence among narcotic enforcement officers across Florida, and was head of the Atlanta Criminal Information Network which involved coordinating intelligence with other police forces across the US. He was also involved in intelligence in the Philippines while in Ireland he had plenty of experience that way, but from the other side of the fence!:-) (MacManus' was a Republican pub in Dundalk.) This is his account of the kind of atmosphere that exists behind the scenes within law enforcement in the US:

> "Then the favourite theory [a theory about the murder of Martin Luther King] of all bloomed. An unknown southern businessman had put up $50,000 for the hit. I thought that was far-fetched. While a wealthy businessman would have access to forged passports and money, there is no way they would have been able to navigate the myriad local police agencies from Memphis to Atlanta to 'plant' the rifle and the Mustang. [The car that James Earl Ray was supposed to have used to go from Memphis to Atlanta, Gerard MacManus found that car himself while working for the police in Atlanta.] It definitely was not an elaborate civilian hit job with local law enforcement involvement because it had to go much higher in the American

10

government.

My rationale is simple and based on a lifetime around the law enforcement community. The murder of Martin Luther King was a complex and convoluted conspiracy that could not have been executed by any person or group other than the government of the United States. They had the motive, which is central to any murder investigation: fear.

...

At the head of the FBI there was no more qualified man to organise the conspiracy than J. Edgar Hoover...Hoover held all politicians in contempt. To protect himself and his organisation he ordered his agents to place all powerful politicians under close surveillance, including the president and vice president. He amassed a vast array of damaging information on these politicians and by doing so assured himself of a lifetime of job security and immense power. Should a politician resist his many budget increase requests, Hoover would show up on that politician's doorstep with the politician's dirty laundry packaged in an FBI file...To this day the FBI remains the most incompetent and corrupt law enforcement agency in America. It is also not trusted by any other American or foreign law enforcement agency in the world. [Although it actually trains most of the senior Gardaí.] This reputation is well-deserved...I personally have worked with agents on cases from bank robbery to terrorism.

...

A very senior black woman administrator in the detective division was caught on a television newscast wearing a burglary victim's expensive jewellery. When the victim went to the media and complained, the administrator became an invisible person. She was protected from all enquiries, and nothing happened...When the victims arrive to sign out their valuable jewellery, and protest that it is not theirs, all they get is a shrug and an explanation that the criminal must have replaced the real jewellery with fakes. What are they to do? There is nowhere to go because the police themselves were the perpetrators.

...

Since its inception the Atlanta Organised Crime Unit had not investigated organised crime in the city nor had it made a single organised crime arrest. The upper echelons of the department had to be involved in this obvious cover-up of a crooked relationship between the two: organised crime and the organised crime squad itself. How else could such inactivity exist or be explained?...The mob never likes to draw attention to themselves because they have found it easier over the years to just grease the palms of corrupt cops, and they have apparently been very successful in that endeavour.

...

Cops make peanuts compared to the billion-dollar profits raked in by the drug barons. It is a simple matter of economics versus morality. Certainly there are pockets of honesty - not all cops are dishonest. However those honest cops who protest my contentions in this book are naive and, I guarantee you, ineffective. They do not understand the big picture because they are just pawns and are used to making a few 'big' phoney busts to satisfy the media and the unaware public. The drug barons feed their handlers in the police department what they call 'loss leaders'. These are drug dealers who work for the barons, who are suspected of stealing from their operation, or of working for a competitor. For the barons there is no loss, and in essence the police end up doing their dirty work for them, knowingly or unknowingly.

Sometimes the drug barons even throw in a few kilos of heavily cut cocaine just to make the police look good. Then you get headlines like 'Biggest Cocaine Bust in Years', and everybody is happy. For the drug barons its a cheap price for keeping the politicians and the public placated. It's all in the cost of doing business, as a drug dealer once explained to me. Honest cops are the drug dealers greatest asset because they use them like pawns in a chess game. And crooked cops, working on the inside, guide things along nicely, keeping everybody happy."

Maybe the 'unaware public' is the issue here, people are making their calculations on how the police would react to a given 'conspiracy theory' based on a naive view of what is really going on in many police forces?

Legal Profession
The legal profession is another area where there is widespread suspicion of a culture of coverup and fraud, as exposed by the VLPS group and the website www.rate-your-solicitor.com. Disillusionment with the professions is brought to the stage where:

> "the solicitor who declines to take your case is probably doing you a better turn than the one who accepts your case". That is a fact." [5]

This VLPS group is even saying that:

> "...We have a message from a decent High Court Registrar who told us there are only about five NON-CORRUPT judges operating in the Four Courts and we are highlighting this on the world wide web.A Fianna Fáil TD from the Midlands believes that this is the case..." [6]

Pretty shocking details are also coming out from the above website, like this from Kerry:

> "They are noted for this..,[legal corruption, stealing property from vulnerable people] ...'Victim Farming & Harvesting' they call it in the trade...my late dad was a judge..." [7]

At their meetings they are saying that collusion, to the detriment of the client, between defence legal teams and Judges and Gardaí is totally endemic all across Ireland. All other kinds of corruption is also rife behind the scenes apparently like bribery of solicitors. I wonder if the story of the Carey family in Waterford reflects some of these dubious practices. The Sunday Independent some time ago carried some curious quotes from an internal IDA memo, signed by an IDA executive, referring to the elderly Carey family living in the outskirts of Waterford City on land coveted by the IDA:

> "We must bear in mind that the Careys did not want to move from their existing house and it was only because of representations made to them by Waterford County Council that they agreed to enter into discussions with the IDA...I did indicate [to the solicitor for the Careys] that I would recommend that the IDA use his firm for the conveyancing of the two pieces of land - Careys to IDA and IDA to Carey. The reason for making that suggestion was to try and 'encourage' him to make a decision in IDA favour." [8]

The upshot was that the family, threatened with a compulsory purchase order, eventually moved onto new land that proved to be much smaller than the IDA had contracted to give them. Meanwhile in the US its actually alleged that about half of the Federal Judges are secretly taking bribes from the CIA! What's even more surprising is that this is apparently done through an Irish company, registered in Dublin.[9]

This situation looks so bad that you'd wonder if one of the above mentioned points by Stich has a particular relevance in this area:

> "Certain people are so involved in corrupt activities themselves that they could care less or do not want to voice opposition to the corruption in government for fear of exposing themselves."

Hence the conspiracies will flourish unchecked.

Academia

The atmosphere in Universities does not seem so great either these days, see for example the experiences of climatologist Timothy Ball:

> "No doubt passive acceptance yields less stress, fewer personal attacks and makes career progress easier. What I have experienced in my personal life during the last years makes me understand why most people choose not to speak out; job security and fear of reprisals. Even in University, where free speech and challenge to prevailing wisdoms are supposedly encouraged, academics remain silent... Sadly, my experience is that universities are the most dogmatic and oppressive places in our society. This becomes progressively worse as they receive more and more funding from governments that demand a particular viewpoint.
>
> ...
>
> Until you have challenged the prevailing wisdom you have no idea how nasty people can be. Until you have re-examined any issue in an attempt to find out all the information, you cannot know how much misinformation exists in the supposed age of information." [10]

He is trying to get across the fact that to his knowledge global warming is not caused by any man made activity, but is dependent on sun spot activity and other factors. In fact he can remember a time when there was huge international panic about global cooling! Actually David Bellamy, the well known botanist and author of 35 books, has much the same story to tell about the realities of life for a dissenting academic:

> "Yet for more than 10 years he has been out of the limelight, shunned by bosses at the BBC where he

made his name, as well as fellow scientists and environmentalists.

His crime? Bellamy says he doesn't believe in man-made global warming.

Here he reveals why – and the price he has paid for not toeing the orthodox line on climate change.

When I first stuck my head above the parapet to say I didn't believe what we were being told about global warming I had no idea what the consequences would be.

I am a scientist and I have to follow the directions of science but when I see that the truth is being covered up I have to voice my opinions.

According to official data, in every year since 1998 world temperatures have been getting colder, and in 2002 Arctic ice actually increased. Why, then, do we not hear about that?

The sad fact is that since I said I didn't believe human beings caused global warming I've not been allowed to make a TV programme.

...

At that point I was still making loads of television programmes and I was enjoying it greatly. Then I suddenly found I was sending in ideas for TV shows and they weren't getting taken up. I've asked around about why I've been ignored but I found that people didn't get back to me.

...

And my opinion is that there is absolutely no proof that carbon dioxide is anything to do with any impending catastrophe. The science has, quite simply, gone awry. In fact, it's not even science any more, it's anti-science.

There's no proof, it's just projections and if you look at the models people such as Gore use, you can see they cherry pick the ones that support their beliefs.

To date, the way the so-called Greens and the BBC, the Royal Society and even our political parties have handled this smacks of McCarthyism at its worst.

Global warming is part of a natural cycle and there's nothing we can actually do to stop these cycles. The world is now facing spending a vast amount of money in tax to try to solve a problem that doesn't actually exist." [11]

Politics.
The behind the scenes atmosphere in politics in Ireland is also worth looking at I think. Say you were to test that atmosphere against one of the familiar 'conspiracy theories' that is floating around. You will often hear it said that political parties are so corrupt, and collude so much at a high level, that the party system operates as a control mechanism in society. The allegation is that the powers that be control the upper ranks, HQ and the party leader maybe, of the political parties but yet encourage the lower ranks to have all kinds of quietly pointless or toothless arguments among themselves, in order to keep divided the political activists in the country. In otherwords its alleged to be a kind of 'divide and rule' tactic by the powers that be. Some claim, like I think the Tipperary priest Fr Denis Fahey, that this is done by exploiting the necessity political parties have for large sums of money:

> "This domination is permanent irrespective of the party in office. All parties require money, it often becomes profitable to the Money Power to finance all alike...turned legislatures into a marionette show with puppets moved on wires behind the scenes." [12]

Then the standard reply to such a theory is that there are thousands of people involved in political parties, even just in Ireland, and they are hardly all involved in, or could keep quiet, this massive conspiracy? So that ok the number of party political leaders, and in the know HQ people, are pretty few, small enough to keep a secret, but then that group would have to have an iron grip on the thousands of party political activists scattered around the country, in order for such a conspiracy to succeed. Of course party policy is set by up to thousands of members attending Ard Fheiseanna, election candidates are selected by often quite well attended Conventions etc., so how could this conspiracy take place without this large group knowing about it? Again the answer might lie in the practical behind the scenes atmosphere within the polit-

16

ical party system in Ireland. I think its fair to say that in modern times a few people in the party HQs do dominate these parties behind the scenes, and the local activists have actually no say at all in what their party does. If democracy is the standard that you feel these parties should abide by, then my contention would be that they are mostly corrupt, democratic they just ain't! Some examples of that:

- In Fianna Fail Royston Brady has revealed quite a bit about what its like behind the scenes. He says that running for that party is just like setting up a franchise operation, you get the logos and posters from party HQ and all that but as regards influencing policy, as a candidate you can forget it.[13] He described that when he was asked at one point to speak on an important matter, while he was Lord Mayor of Dublin, he was just given a script by the officials in party HQ and when he didn't like what it said he found his only option was to walk out. He was simply not permitted to offer his own opinions. And in fact conventions are dying out as a way of selecting Dail candidates in Fianna Fail, and other parties, candidates are now being selected by the unelected officials in the party HQs.[14]

- Afaik at the last Fine Gael ard fheis no speaker spoke against any of the motions, and, generally speaking, nobody even voted against them. This is because the motions were all uncontroversial, a small group from HQ vet all the motions and speakers and I would say simply don't allow any divisive subjects to be debated.

- In the case of the special Sinn Fein conference that decided to recognise the PSNI many knowledgeable commentators have speculated that this was only the window dressing for a decision that had already been taken in secret by the IRA, with the latter operating as a kind of secret society within Sinn Fein.

- Amazingly it came out after the recent leadership election in the Green party that, unknown to the beaten candidate, the returning officer was secretly allowing some kind of telephone voting by party members in an election everybody thought was by secret paper ballot. This brought out some other stories from behind the scenes in the Green party:

> "The Greens have a long history of fraud in selection
> conventions. The most egregious was that defrauding
> the late, great Vincent MacDowell. In that case, the
> rules and procedures committee was abolished in order
> to further the interests of one Mr Cuffe. What infuriated

many of us about it was to see Vincent's obituary including the statement that he left the party after losing to Cuffe, giving the impression that this stalwart of Irish political life for half a century went off in a huff. As I recall, the RO was one John Gormley.

A second trick was to tell a soon-to-be-defrauded candidate objecting at the convention that the vote was to be rerun, and then going ahead once (s)he had left to declare a winner. This happened in DSE in 2003, and the result was that all 3 council seats were lost. The DSE group up to that point were integrated enough to get all 3 elected; in fact, we used to be the last out of the Dail bar, itself surely a Green first.

What is intriguing in retrospect is to look at the whole GP set-up as simply an undemocratic congeries to further the political ambitions of several individuals. As someone who served on the National council 1997-2003, which determines policy, it was hilarious to hear talk from the TD's about "we must go into coalition to implement our policies". Fact; none of these guys came to NC more than once every year, in some cases far less, and in Gormley's case he did not even cycle the one mile to get there. Then, of course, it became clear; policies that they didn't agree with could be rescinded at national convention, or in extremis simply binned at main office. The GM policy suffered both fates."[15]

Hence you can see that the reality on the ground in the party system is such that the above 'conspiracy theory' is just possible. It is only a small - and maybe secretive - group anyway that is calling the shots in the political parties, the large mass of party members are really only canvassing fodder for the party machine, they have no say in the policies of their parties.

Diplomacy

Behind the scenes in the world of diplomacy you see the same sort of ongoing corruption is routinely tolerated, this is from Conor Cruise O'Brien describing the UN in the 50s:

"To digress on the subject of "arm-twisters": this was a term very little heard in public discussions of the UN, and little used in academic examinations of the work-

18

ings of the world body. But the concept was absolutely central from about 1948-1958 to the actual workings of the UN. Arm-twisters, of which there was invariably at least one on each of the seven main committees, were American delegates, usually of middle rank, whose function was to influence crucial votes, and make sure the United States got the necessary two-thirds support for whatever proposition might appear, at any given moment, required by American interests. The modus operandi of the arm-twister varied according to circumstances. Often, in the case of delegates who had been through the mill, a mere recital of what the United States wanted would do the trick. But the main function of the arm-twister was to smell out possible recalcitrance, and deal with it. "Dealing with it" could include bribery or blackmail or both together. If these techniques failed, in relation to an individual delegate, they would sometimes be employed directly on governments which were weak, dependent on American subsidies, or corrupt. Most of the world's governments fell into at least one, if not all, of these categories.

...[Referring to the 1948 vote on the recognition of the state of Israel:]

Some delegates were bribed, some of those who could not be bribed personally were recalled by their bribed or intimidated governments and replaced by suitably-instructed people. The necessary number of "unsuitable" delegates were replaced by an equal number of "suitable" ones. Several careers were ended and several new ones promoted. In the end the General Assembly passed the required resolution and the United States could bask once more, for a time, in the approval of the "moral conscience of mankind".[16]

Therefore some of the 'conspiracy theories' that people might have and which some might imagine would be exposed by diplomats, are not highlighted because for them this is just the normal experiences of their profession. Maybe another example of this behind the scenes cynicism is related here by Dr Paul Roberts who was Assistant Secretary of the US Treasury in the Reagan Administration, formerly Associate Editor of the Wall Street Journal, holder of numerous professorships across the US etc etc:

"Back during the Nixon years, my Ph.D. dissertation

chairman, Warren Nutter, was Assistant Secretary of Defense for International Security Affairs. One day in his Pentagon office I asked him how the US government got foreign governments to do what the US wanted. "Money," he replied.

"You mean foreign aid?" I asked.

"No," he replied, "we just buy the leaders with money."

It wasn't a policy he had implemented. He inherited it and, although the policy rankled with him, he could do nothing about it. Nutter believed in persuasion and that if you could not persuade people, you did not have a policy.

Nutter did not mean merely third world potentates were bought. He meant the leaders of England, France, Germany, Italy, all the allies everywhere were bought and paid for.

They were allies because they were paid. Consider Tony Blair. Blair's own head of British intelligence told him that the Americans were fabricating the evidence to justify their already planned attack on Iraq. This was fine with Blair, and you can see why with his multi-million dollar payoff once he was out of office.
...
Nothing real issues from the American media. The media is about demonizing Russia and Iran, about the vice presidential choices as if it matters, about whether Obama being on vacation let McCain score too many points.

The mindlessness of the news reflects the mindlessness of the government, for which it is a spokesperson.

The American media does not serve American democracy or American interests. It serves the few people who exercise power."

The overall point then is that if you are a person who believes that

Gardaí never lie, that the legal profession is bubbling with practitioners always anxious to ferret out the truth, that political parties draw up their policies after nice democratic debates, and that those fine debates are also what lie behind decisions at the UN and advice given by academics, then you would naturally believe that those great 'conspiracy theories' couldn't possibly be true. You might think that there are just too many good people out there in these various areas of civic life that conspiracies would be easily exposed and stopped in their tracks. But I think the reality is that this mé féin keep-your-head-down type of era, that we live in, permeates these professions, where a kind of behind the scenes low level corruption is tolerated, which in turn makes these conspiracies possible. In many cases they just don't care enough about the public's rights and interests to bother getting involved in exposing conspiracies.

Possibly too this type of atmosphere is worst at the higher levels, for example in the state system. Complete heartlessness and ruthlessness I think is often encountered at the high end of the power, and pay level, structure in any country and this should be factored in when people are considering whether conspiracies can exist or not. For example during the troubles of 1919-21 in Ireland many people were talking about a 'conspiracy theory' that the state was involved in reprisal action against totally innocent Irish people, as punishment for various IRA operations. This 'conspiracy theory' was hotly denied by the state, for example by Hamar Greenwood in the House of Commons, and the question arises as to how could this be kept a secret, since it must have involved many people in the security and state apparatus in Ireland at the time. Of course they did know but they just couldn't care less about the fate of those Irish people who lost their homes and lives to this policy. You can see this from the diary of a high up Dublin Castle official, Mark Sturgis, writing in 1920 on the sacking by the British forces of Balbriggan:

> "Still worse things can happen than the firing up of a
> sink like Balbriggan and surely the people who say
> 'stop the murders before all our homes go up in smoke'
> must increase."[17]

Obviously he was hoping that the effect would be to turn people off the IRA. And of course at this level they have other ways of dealing with the few people in that circle who might develop a conscience, e.g. its a curious statistic that five people committed suicide in de Winter's, the intelligence head in Dublin Castle, office during the year 1920-21! [18]

Media response to Whistleblowers

So OK say we get someone coming forward, breaking through the pre-vailing selfishness, and willing to expose a given 'conspiracy'. What does he do to blow this conspiracy wide open? Naturally he goes to the media, they expose it and all is right again, theoretically. The point is that the media does not react this way to whistleblowers, as a general rule the media does not 'do' conspiracies, most of the time they simply don't report what whistleblowers say irrespective of how much evidence they might have. Because this is the reality of the modern media it means that conspiracies flourish nowadays more than in the past.

Films like "All the Presidents Men" have given maybe a falsely romantic view of modern journalism. The general public thinks that there are small armies of investigative journalists out there just itching to get the truth out to the general public, but the reality might be a bit more mundane. I wonder if in fact there is only ever about 1 or 2 really fear-less - not secretly police agents - investigative journalists in Ireland des-pite the large number of journalists in general. Most people would cer-tainly put the late Martin O'Hagan in that category, and look what happened to him. During his life it wasn't the case at all that his skills and courage were nurtured in Irish journalistic circles, as his friend Paul Larkin relates:

> "One must ask where the job offers were from the qual-ity newspapers or the TV industry for possibly the only journalist in Ireland who made it his business not just to write tittle tattle about paramilitaries but also to seri-ously confront the question of state cooperation with loyalist killers? O'Hagan increasingly regarded the Bel-fast offices of the Sunday World as a cold house...Put simply the courageous controversialist had very few outlets for his stories, some of which were of major im-portance."[19]

John Pilger, who served as a reporter in Vietnam, emerged with a some-what jaundiced view of the modern media:

> "There were 649 reporters in Vietnam on March 16, 1968 - the day that the My-Lai massacre happened - and not one of them reported it." [20]

In contrast in the US in 1994 some courageous journalists from York-shire Television did try and expose paedophile rings among the political elite in Nebraska but their resulting documentary ("Conspiracy of Si-lence", which is available on youtube) was pulled before it could be broadcast. They described in the documentary that when a number of these victims came forward talking about the paedophile ring operating among senior politicians, police, and media figures in Nebraska and Washington they found that the media set out to belittle them and as far as possible bury the story: "The whole purpose of the newspaper [articles] was to destroy" the credibility of the witnesses according to Foster Care director Carol Stitt with particular reference to the 'Omaha World Herald'.

Fred Holroyd describes in his book his huge efforts to expose what was going on in Ulster. Starting from the early 80s to I guess the present he has tramped the highways and byways of the UK and Irish media and at the end of that experience has found himself compiling a long list of 'journalists' that he hinted are probably just government agents.[21] (Incidentally its often said that government agents are very active among security/defence/justice correspondents, diplomatic correspondents, and Northern Irish correspondents among others of course.) After trying every avenue on Fleet St for years he only managed to interest about 2 or 3 journalists in his startling revelations, despite being clearly well qualified to talk about these subjects.[22] Even the smaller publications proved to be keen on dismissing those allegations as just the fertile imagination of lunatics. For example it was Holroyd who rescued Wallace from jail, having read a letter by him that was discarded in one of the magazine offices as just one of the usual lunatic letters! The Belfast based journalist Paul Larkin has described how some of his highly 'respected' colleagues in Belfast suspiciously went out of their way to rubbish Holroyd and Wallace's revelations, and that pattern continues:

> "one would have thought that his [Wallace's] rehabilitation would have been complete by Oct 1996 when his conviction for manslaughter was quashed. Wallace and Holroyd, however, are effectively shunned by most media outlets both in Ireland and Britain." [23]

So this then is the real reception that your average whistleblower experiences in the mass media. It naturally follows from this that there are a lot more whistleblowers out there than the general public are aware of. And crucially there are a lot of 'conspiracies' which are proven by people coming forward to explain what is happening but the general public do not have ready access to their testimony because of this media silence. Just to take this one example, clearly if Wallace and Holroyd's story had been highlighted properly from the beginning then nobody would have spent the last two decades disparaging the 'conspiracy theory' that strong links existed between the security forces and loyalist paramilitaries, a 'theory' which is only now accepted after a report on this was published earlier this year by the Ombudsman's office in Belfast.

I think this all adds up a situation where many whistleblowers end up in a kind of glass cage, where they are desperately trying to tell people what is really going on but cannot get the word out through an Orwellian media which puts much greater store on sport or sex than it does on this kind of serious political corruption. Then because the general public have no idea of the kind of practices that are going on, because the media never tells them, these whistleblowers become classed are 'cranks' or nutcases when they explain their case in the few fora, like on the internet, that is still open to them. To give a simple example of this take Hugh Murphy who is trying to highlight the fact that the big Irish unions cooperated with employers in shafting some Belfast dockers who had handled asbestos. He has been through the usual experiences with the media:

> "I have tried them all, from The Irish Times, down.
> I have told Vincent Brown, Fintan O'Toole and Kevin
> Myers, when he was with Irish Times..."

and in general about some media he concludes that "they are quelling a good story for political objectives." [24] Then in trying to explain this to the chattering classes he discovers that:

> "Why is it that when someone speaks the TRUTH - to
> SOME people, they are either drunk or a lunatic.
> ...
> What is crazy about the corruption of ITGWU and the
> cover-up by SIPTU is that a so-called Left Wing union
> collaborated with the employers to SACK its own
> members! And that the so-called Free Thinking people
> in the South, when told of it, don't believe it." [25]

So I think a big factor in the growth of this 'conspiracy theory' accusation is the increasing power of the modern mass media. It is creating the agenda for what is or isn't plausible or feasible in the minds of many people, and it is doing that while systematically locking out facts and people that might challenge the prevailing viewpoint.

That the mass media in Ireland has never been the clean conduit for information that the general public thinks they are can be seen from the pages of history. For example as long ago as the Irish rebellion of 1641 Charles I was undermined by a flood of pamphlets that painted a false account of that rebellion. One contemporary commentator talking about these early newspapers said it was "..incredible what mischief they do."![26] And I suppose it is but it is even more incredible to what extent the state in Ireland secretly controlled the media over the centuries, totally unknown to the Irish people most of whom thought they were living in a country which, to a certain extent, cherished free speech.

Looking at that kind of picture I will begin with a letter the Chief Secretary of Ireland wrote back to London in 1781:

> "We have hitherto, by the force of good words and with some degree of private expense, preserved an ascendancy over the press not hitherto known here, and it is of an importance equal to 10,000 times its cost..." [27]

Some of this secret world began to leak in the mid 19th century, especially with the revelations concerning the spy ring run by the editor of the Freeman's Journal during the 1798 rebellion period. It became a popular subject at that time to try and hunt down the British government's moles in the Irish media, as you can read in the 'Sham Squire', a book that quotes this from the Dublin Evening Post of the time:

> "This payment [the regular secret payments to the Freeman's Journal] may have been on account of proclamations inserted as advertisements; but the Duke of Wellington's correspondence, when Irish Secretary, makes no disguise that all money paid on such grounds was for purposes of corruption. This arrangement was partially relinquished from the death of Pitt; but in 1809, on the restoration of the old Tory regime, we find a Dublin journalist petitioning for a renewal. Sir A. Wellesley, addressing Sir Charles Saxton, the under-secretary, alluded to "the measures which I had in contemplation in respect to newspapers in Ireland. It is quite impossible to leave them entirely to themselves; and we have probably carried our reforms in respect to publishing proclamations as far as they will go, excepting only that we might strike off from the list of those permitted to publish proclamations in the newspapers, both in town and country, those which have the least extensive circulation, and which depend, I believe, entirely upon the money received on account of proclamations. I am one of those, however, who think that it will le [be] very dangerous to allow the press in Ireland to take care of itself, particularly as it has so long been in leading strings. I would, therefore, recommend that in proportion as you will diminish the profits of the better kind of newspapers, such as the Correspondent and the Freeman's Journal, on account of proclamations, you shall increase the sum they are allowed to charge on account of advertisements and other publications.

[Meaning presumably other types of government advertisements, which would be more of a disguise than the obvious proclamations.] It is absolutely necessary, however, to keep the charge within the sum of ten thousand pounds per annum, voted by Parliament, which probably may easily be done when some newspapers will cease to publish proclamations, and the whole will receive a reduced sum on that account, even though an increase should be made on account of advertisements to the accounts of some. It will also be very necessary that the account of this money should be of a description always to be produced before Parliament. – Ever, yours, &c., - Arthur Wellesley." [28]

Some Secret Service papers leaked around that time show how much the British government controlled Irish newspapers all those years, this is from some preface written I think by Major Sirr describing these Secret Service receipts:

"100 original documents ...The several suborned proprietors or editors of venal newspapers and magazines of "The Correspondent", "The Patriot", "The Belfast Newsletter", "The Milesian Magazine" (Dr John Brennan), The "bought up" [these are his quotes!] "Irish Magazine" (of the "bought off" Walter Cox cum multis aliis [with many others]..." [29]

These papers include a letter from the aforementioned Walter Cox (dated Dublin 9 Jan 1815) where he says he was obliged to submit to the government to avoid another dreary imprisonment (which the Attorney General threatened would be in some remote jail). He is now to be paid £400 in America and expresses gratitude that at least his magazine didn't collapse through dullness but rather from "the overwhelming power of the British government." [30] He was actually paid an allowance by the British government on condition that he wouldn't start any more publications, this was stopped by Peel in 1835.[31]

In 1836 a row broke out over the sale of the Derry Journal newspaper, during which it was revealed that the newspaper had always been in receipt of a secret government payment ever since it had been clandestinely purchased with government money in 1797. (By a Captain Ryan who then perished in the rebellion.) When it was sold in 1829 one of the contract clauses said that it was being purchased:

"together with all claims which the Parties aforesaid have to a certain allowance heretofore annually paid by

Government to the said newspaper."

On 13 May 1837 the government decided that yes they would continue to pay the money secretly to the new owners of the paper.[32]

As you get into the late 19th century, and early 20th, you find that the big newspapers like the Freeman's Journal and the Independent were the subject of endless intrigues by the different factions of the Irish Parliamentary Party. They in practice controlled the Freeman through much of this time and in a way died with it. You can read a lot of the intrigues at http://www.chaptersofdublin.com/books/THealy/healy29.htm , http://www.chaptersofdublin.com/books/THealy/healy43.htm , and other chapters of that book. From that last reference you can read how £10,000 given to the Freeman before its collapse came from the US Secret Service, via T.P. O'Connor. Btw the 'suave' T.P., one of the big IPP 'bosses', was "known to be on friendly terms with the Prime Minister." [33]

More on the Freeman from Captain Sheehan MP:

> "To show the veritable depths of baseness to which the so-called National Movement had fallen [the Irish Parliamentary Party under the secret control of the Ancient Order of Hibernians c.1909] it need only be stated that it was charged against their official organ --'The Freeman's Journal'-- that no less than eighteen members of its staff had obtained positions of profit under the Crown, including a Lord Chancellorship, an Under-secretaryship, Judgeships, Crown Prosecutorships, University Professorships, Resident Magistracies, Local Government Inspectorships, etc. In this connection it is also worthy of mention that when the premises of this concern were burnt out in the course of the Easter Week Rebellion it was reendowed for "national" purposes, with a Treasury grant of L60,000, being twice the amount which the then directors of the 'Freeman' confessed to be the business value of the property." [34]

The Irish Independent was famously owned by Tim Healy's close friend William Martin Murphy and Healy clearly had a big influence on this newspaper, and he in turn was always close to the centre of power in the UK. The paper also reflected Healy's estrangement from the IPP from about 1916 on, so it tended to follow an anti-IPP course, including attempting to crush the IPP's Freeman and backing Healy's close friend Michael Collins.[35]

Later the wine merchant Martin Fitzgerald, a friend of both Collins and Griffith, bought the Freeman's Journal and Piaras Beaslai became the leader writer for it and at that point "a good deal of publicity was given to Mick Collins" in the paper.[36] This Martin Fitzgerald, who also had a say in the Independent later ("he controlled, I think, the Irish Independent") was in close communication with George Duggan, a banker and the father of George Chester Duggan of Dublin Castle.[37] George Chester was involved it seems in the intelligence department of the Castle, going by the fact that he audited Colonel de Winter's intelligence apparatus at one point.[38]

Of course the Secret Societies, powerful in every area of Irish life, also controlled a large swathe of the media. For example M. O'Hanlon, effectively the AOH's candidate in the East Cavan bye election, was the proprietor of the Anglo-Celt,[39] and Gaynor, the editor of the Evening Telegraph, was a prominent AOH member.[40] The IRB of course exercised its considerably muscle in this department too. 'Irish Freedom' and 'Nationality' were in fact, secretly, official IRB organs;[41] the "'Irish World' and 'Saoghail Gael' ..[were] directly under their [IRB] influence."[42]; while in the Enniscorthy Echo the editor, sub editor, and most of the staff were IRB men.[43] One of these IRB papers, The Irish World, reprinted in 1917 an interesting speech entered into the Congressional Record of the US by Mr Callaway of Texas, later highlighted by Hon. J. Hampton Moore of Pennsylvania:

> "In March 1915, the J. P. Morgan interests, the steel, shipbuilding and powder interests, and their subsidiary organisations, got together twelve men high up in the newspaper world and employed them to select the most influential newspapers in the United States and sufficient number of them to control generally the policy of the daily press of the United States.
>
> These twelve men worked the problem out by selecting 179 newspapers, and then began, by an elimination process, to retain only those necessary for the purpose of controlling the general policy of the daily press throughout the country. They found it was only necessary to purchase the control of twenty-five of the greatest papers. The twenty-five papers were agreed upon; emissaries were sent to purchase the policy, national and international, of these papers; an agreement was reached; the policy of the papers was bought, to be paid for by the month; an editor was furnished for each paper, to properly supervise and edit information regarding the question of preparedness, militarism, financial policies, and the other things of national and inter-

national nature considered vital to the interests of the purchasers.

This contract is in existence at the present time, and it accounts for the news columns of the daily press of the country being filled with all sorts of preparedness arguments and misrepresentations as to the present condition of the United States army and navy, and the possibility and probability of the United States being attacked by foreign foes.

This policy also included the suppression of everything in opposition to the wishes of the interests served. The effectiveness of this scheme has been conclusively demonstrated by the character of the stuff carried in the daily press throughout the country since March 1915. They have resorted to anything necessary to commercialise public sentiment and sandbag the National Congress into making extravagant and wasteful appropriations for the army and navy under the false pretense that it is necessary. Their stock argument is that it is 'patriotism.' They are playing on every prejudice and passion of the American people."[44]

These forces which controlled the media of course abused that position, hence these influences in turn meant that Irish people many times came away with completely inaccurate views of important events. For example Sean Farrelly called the long time editor (1919-1960) of the Meath Chronicle, Patrick Quilty, "that irresponsible scribe" [45] in whose "ill informed journal" they printed a glowing nationalistic obituary on a guy who was actually a member of the Black Hand Gang which was a gang of criminals linked to the state.[46] And the secret to that particular mystery might lie in the fact that, according to General Sean Boylan TD, Quilty was all along a British agent.[47] Incidentally the previous editor of the Meath Chronicle, Hugh Smith, was involved in some mysterious effort to set up a fake Volunteer company in the Drumbaragh area, presumably to cause confusion in Volunteer ranks which, one could speculate, might have also been in the British government's interest at that time.[48] So in practice all kinds of manipulation of facts and information were going on all this time unknown I think to the vast majority of Irish people. This even included printing completely fictitious newspaper interviews.[49] Publicity lockouts were very common, where people or groups could get no say whatsoever for their case in any organ of the media. Even the Archbishop of Dublin complained in 1919 that "none of our newspapers dare publish the fact that I had subscribed to the Dail fund." [50] William O'Brien's party it is said got virtually no publicity for its viewpoint outside of Munster - a reference to the Cork Examiner no doubt. One of these MPs noted sadly that alongwith the Irish in the US most Irish people were very ill informed:

"In Ireland, as I have said, outside Munster the truth was never allowed to reach the people." [51]

Also of course the cabal who controlled the media used that to condition the people to accept their long term political strategies. Maybe you can see a glimpse of that kind of grand strategy in the episode in 1918 when W.B. Yeats proposed to P.J. Little, the owner of the 'New Ireland' newspaper, that:

"if I would turn the policy of the paper to a 'moderate, but passionate advocacy of Dominion Home Rule', Lord Wimborne would be prepared to subsidise it, to the amount of £2000." [52]

And nothing much has changed since those days imho!

Police response to Whistleblowers

So our mythical whistleblower guy gets nowhere in dealing with the media, instead maybe he just goes to the proper authorities and everything is sorted out and the 'conspirators' get their legal comeuppance etc? He contacts the FBI or police forces who take it from there, blowing apart any nascent 'conspiracy' in its tracks? Frankly this again is presuming upon a naive view of state agencies, especially the police. In practice the police as well do not 'do' conspiracy theories, generally speaking you will find that they are not interested in complaints about complex corruption say. I'm sorry but that's what I think you will find when you look into these cases.

As regards the FBI you can see the experiences of the victims in the Omaha paedophile scandal mentioned above. According to a Nebraska State Senator the FBI and the police in that case "in fact...turned the witnesses... into the offenders so to speak," referring to the aggressive way they demanded proof in backing up their assertions.[53]

You can read in the whistleblowing experiences of Major Holroyd how early on he gave detailed accounts of intelligence agency corruption to two police forces in England as well as to the RUC and to the Gardaí and none of these investigations went anywhere. He even had physical evidence, including diaries and photographs, to back up his assertions but it did no good, they just weren't interested. One example was about the murder of an elderly man in Armagh which Holroyd had investigated and had written statements to back up his assertions, but:

> "I had attempted to give the statement [that describes the case] to the Essex police who informed me as the crime had been committed outside their area, it was not their responsibility. As I know from bitter experience that the RUC have engaged in many cover-ups of these events, this case apparently will never be investigated, even though the informant identified himself in the statement." [54]

When Channel 4 broadcast serious allegations of a conspiracy that the RUC and loyalist paramilitaries were pretty much joint organisations, the RUC Chief Superintendent, James Nesbitt, put in charge of investigating these claims was actually involved in covering the whole thing up, according to the programmes producer:

> "..the subsequent Nesbitt enquiry had been primarily interested in suppressing the truth and in limiting the damage we had inflicted on the RUC." [55].

A somewhat war weary Major Colin Wallace explained at a meeting of' 'Justice for the Forgotten' in Dublin on the 27th June 2003, that he had been through something like, I think, nine enquiries into his allegations but left the distinct impression that these proved to be nearly all whitewashes and coverups. (He harboured some hope though for the Saville tribunal in Derry and the Barron investigations in Dublin.)

You can also follow the experiences of the two whistleblowers in the RUC and the Garda Special Branch, Johnston Brown and John White respectively. Brown has written a book on his experiences of trying to investigate the links between the state and the killing of Pat Finucane - based on evidence that came his way - and his account outlines how his superiors and colleagues were either indifferent or anxious to get him killed! [56]

Det Sgt John White, meanwhile, was asked some time ago at the Morris Tribunal why he didn't blow the whistle earlier about the extensive illegal bugging by the Gardaí. He replied:

> "Because I knew exactly what would happen. The senior Garda authorities would turn on me like a team of dogs, if I was serious about making such a report. You look after your own. It's a big family and even when you retire you still look after your own. That is the situation and you know it." [57]

So in practice I think the depressing truth is that the police, and most state agencies, are much more interested in protecting their employer, their own colleagues, and some would say even big businesses, rather than trying to genuinely investigate any 'conspiracy'. This obviously means again that 'conspiracies' can flourish that bit easier in our modern society, because the powers that be are so disinterested in bringing the perpetrators to justice.

Possibly another issue involved in labelling people 'conspiracy theorists' involves a very naive attitude that sometimes the general public have about state agencies. It seems to this observer anyway that virtually any serious criticism of the police, for example, is treated as ipso facto a conspiracy theory. The general public in Western countries seem almost to be brainwashed with a feeling that the police are there to investigate crime and catch the bad guys and that's it, the feeling that they could be the bad guys committing the crime is a view that is simply not tolerated in some quarters. This is partly because the media drill this concept into people constantly. An instance of this occurred on the Duffy show on RTE radio some time ago. During a discussion one of his guests said that she went to the Gardaí asking them to intervene to protect her son who was being threatened by some drug dealers over money that he owed them. The Gardaí simply told the mother to pay the debt and were entirely disinterested in knowing about the drug dealers who the mother was able to name. For her pains Joe Duffy simply shouted at her "I don't believe you", because apparently Joe Duffy knew for certain that police forces are incapable of such an act.[58] There are plenty of examples of that in the Irish media, local and national. When P J Brogan, one of the Donegal victims of the Gardaí, tried to tell his story to the local press in Donegal he was simply told by one of the leading reporters on the local newspaper that they never carry stories like his critical of the Gardaí.[59] It follows then that people who have grown up with this media silence naturally enough find it difficult to believe anyone who tries to articulate a completely different version of events.

Maybe another factor here is the big influence that a generation of TV programs have had on people. Clearly your average Western citizen has probably viewed thousands of hours of the Sweeney, Kojak, Hill Street Blues, Morse, Frost, Law and Order etc etc and has subconsciously absorbed these fictional accounts as being representative of how police forces normally operate. But in fact they are fictional and the large companies that control this output have no interest in allowing people to get a more 'conspiratorial' view of events. For instance the writer of the Sweeney, Troy Kennedy-Martin, realised how corrupt the system was but couldn't reflect this accurately because

"we were getting a little bit of pressure from on high.

The Metropolitan police was part of a structure then
which was almost impervious to any kind of criticism."
In fact it was later found out that that unit in the Metropolitan Police
was completely corrupt, taking a cut of all armed robberies committed
in the area etc etc. So the TV program is a sanitised view of the reality,
the reality being a lot more corrupt, this is what the writer really thought
was going on:

> "I went, as we all did, to some of the do's. And there
> was this, I thought, rather unhealthy alliance between
> 'the bar', barristers that worked at the criminal bar, and
> judges and senior police officers, you know it was, to
> no small extent, masonic. Certainly a freemasonry in
> terms of the way they reacted and related to each other.
> We did hint at that from time to time. I think we pushed
> it as far as we could." [60]

The powers that be in Ireland are particularly keen on keeping a close
eye on what is permitted in fictional TV dramas, as this account in the
Sunday Times about the RTE drama 'Proof' shows:

> "Somebody evidently decided to cut this material from
> the final version in order to make the show more palat-
> able. But to whom: viewers or politicians?
> Thanks to a series of fortuitous circumstances, the ori-
> ginal scripts for the four-part series have landed in my
> possession. Offering an intriguing glimpse of what the
> show might have looked like, they make fascinating
> reading.
> ...the storyline revolved around an all-guns-blazing
> hunt for a stolen computer disc.
> The disc was eagerly sought — by its owners and an in-
> vestigative journalist among others — because it con-
> tained information linking a sex-slave racket and an in-
> ternational bank in a conspiracy to divert 25m euro in
> laundered funds into the election campaign of Myles
> Carrick, a charismatic Irish opposition leader played by
> Bryan Murray.
>
> ...
> [In the revised script:] "This portrait of a noble states-
> man who is exposed as a victim of circumstance rather
> than a wilful wrongdoer will no doubt have comforted
> the numerous Irish politicians currently facing allega-
> tions of malfeasance at Dublin Castle or the Four
> Courts, and their numerous colleagues who fear they

could be next.

In the original script, a somewhat more plausible scenario was envisaged. The central conspiracy is no less fanciful but, crucially, Carrick is the taoiseach. He is acutely aware of the fact that he has been bought and paid for by big business, because he agreed the deals personally. His only concern is that nobody else discovers the terms and conditions under which he is contracted to his generous sponsors.

[The original writer left in frustration and the last two episodes were rewritten by new writers]...

The otherwise inexplicable neutering of the shows original script suggests that the price RTE is prepared to pay for extra resources is to adopt a meek and docile attitude towards its political masters.

Editorial calls made on a lightweight thriller like Proof may seem peripheral to lofty questions of broadcasting policy, but they are indicative of a wider mindset. If RTE bosses are afraid to ruffle political feathers through fiction, what's the likelihood of them doing so through current affairs coverage?" [61]

So this deliberately sanitised version of the truth, which is what we are getting in the media even in fiction, is the version that is in most peoples heads right now, and it is this mindset which prints out 'conspiracy theory' whenever a different view of the police or the political system is put forward. For all we know the reality could be a lot worse, after all if you think about the current era, as regards drug smuggling say, it is much the same as the Prohibition era in the US, and yet no self respecting gangster of that time survived very long without having the Chief of Police in his pocket.

To find out what's really going on you sometimes have to wait for regimes to fall, even the fall of the Royal Irish Constabulary in Ireland in 1922 threw up a few interesting facts. It turned out that the RIC (and the Dublin Metropolitan Police) were by no means just involved in gathering evidence to use in court (which was obviously the posture they put on for public consumption) they had their own ways of dealing with people they disliked. Whenever a person came into their radar as a Sinn Fein suspect they immediately endeavoured to get them sacked from their employment,[62] and approached everybody else in the 'suspects' orbit in order to put the squeeze on their targets, using

"all kinds of intimidation on the men [of the Volunteers] through approach to parents, employers, even to the clergy." [63]

It was also a routine practice for the RIC to blackmail any publican who looked as if he might lose his vintners license because of repeated breaches of the licensing laws. The RIC identified such businesses, which were hanging on by a 'cobweb' to use their phrase, and of course promised never to raid them if they agreed to pass on any information that might be overheard there.[64] I think this is an important precedent because obviously in modern times the state has a great capacity for closing businesses using much more onerous tax, health and safety, and planning laws than existed at that time, which leaves a great potential for this kind of blackmail in our own era.

Agent provocateurs were quite heavily used by the RIC it seems:

> "...the police in Ireland were part of the British military establishment. They were armed with rifles and revolvers. Their policy was to promote crime and, as often happened to commit crime and have the blame placed on some unfortunate local person. There are many cases of this kind on record, but the House of Commons would not make them public...[Proportionally the number of agent provocateurs in the RIC were few] but they were to be found in every area of Ireland." [65]

They also dabbled in the odd conspiracy. The writer of the above quotes, Captain Lawrence Nugent, relates that when his group had seized back - in an armed raid - the HQ of the National Volunteers from the AOH (c.1918 I think) he was approached by an Inspector of the RIC with a proposition. The Inspector asked him to launch a similar raid on AOH headquarters in Dublin, the bargain being that they could keep everything they seized except the register which the RIC wanted. This was obviously to remain an entirely secret mutually beneficial arrangement, which as it happens Nugent declined.[66] The police, I think particularly the DMP, at the time were very heavily infiltrated by the AOH, which was anti-conscription among other things. This meant that the powers that be would have wanted to weed them out in order to take back control of the police.[67]

This was nothing when you compare it to what British army intelligence were doing in Ireland during the same period. Not long before the Truce the head of the Auxiliaries came forward to reveal something of what was going on, as reported in the New Statesman in May 1921:

> "According to General Crozier, the whole system of military government in Ireland is a vast conspiracy of

silence and lies, in which everyone from top to bottom is involved. ...[As an example of that atmosphere he said that often times expelled army cadets were let back in a short time later because of the blackmail information they had on their superiors.]...

Take, for example, the case of the "Drumcondra shootings" when two men, Kennedy and Murphy, admittedly innocent of any crime were taken out and shot in cold blood. General Crozier tells us that, at a subsequent enquiry at a military court, the evidence in favour of the officer accused of the crime was deliberately "manufactured" by the military authorities in Dublin Castle. It was all arranged and rehearsed, and he himself was present at one of the "rehearsals", which took place before a prominent officer of the Intelligence Department." [68]

Another scheme the RIC indulged in during the troubles was to sponsor criminal gangs, in County Meath anyway, presumably to create a lawless type of atmosphere, which would then be blamed on the IRA and justify harsher security measures against them. Also it might have been done just to scare the populace, encouraging them to go the police with information. Anyway this was the kind of conversation that the Duc de Stacpoole found himself having with General Sean Boylan, the head of the IRA in Meath of course, when Boylan's men were returning all his stolen possessions. Boylan explained that the police were disinterested in finding them and that in fact it was more likely that the RIC were linked to the robbers.[69] I think as well that this kind of huge agent provocateur thing might have been behind the famous Black Hand gang that terrorised north Meath during the troubles. This was a large criminal gang that contained AOH and Sinn Fein members, ex British soldiers, and even some IRA members which indulged in such amazing exploits as blowing up labourers cottages at the same time as the whole county was swarming with British military and the Black and Tans. It isn't therefore much of a surprise to find that the gang seemed to have some connection to the security forces. I say that because one IRA Volunteer, Joseph Martin, was given a warning notice by the Black and Tans which was signed by the Black Hand Gang.[70] In any case they were eventually put out of business by the IRA after they had murdered a Mr Clinton near Moynalty.[71]

But that's not the half of it, some other RIC practices were a lot worse. Eugene Bratton, an RIC Constable based in Navan during the Troubles, tells a tale which involves his own RIC colleagues in the station murdering one of the few decent Black and Tans and even their own Sergeant Keighery. Also three senior local RIC members, including District Inspector Egan and his brother County Inspector Egan, personally murdered the Postmaster in Navan called Hodgett. Hodgett had refused a position in the post office to the daughter of the RIC Head Constable Queenan, and it was because of that he was killed, even though he had no connection whatsoever to the IRA. Of course the murderers were then placed in charge of the 'investigation' into the crime and proceeded to scrape away blood stains etc. The RIC in Meath also planted false evidence on, and then charged, the Crown Prosecutor in the county, Lord Dunsany who again had no connection to the IRA, because he was inclined to question police witnesses too closely. In short the RIC considered themselves "kings in their own area" and really did whatever they liked,[72] knowing of course that it was easy for them to cover up their tracks considering the power of the police in the justice system.

The RIC then were certainly up to no good a lot of the time, but evenso I think there is some evidence that the powers that be were deliberately setting up the RIC for a fall in the 1916-21 period. After all it was manned almost entirely by Irishmen and the British government seemed to feel no great care towards them when the going got hot in Ireland. I think one of their tricks was, after a certain point, to make the RIC deliberately unpopular and the focus of the IRA's efforts and the public's encomium to a degree that actually seems unfair. Maybe the government was afraid of their loyalty and wanted the conflict to develop into a nationalist v. RIC clash before nationalist and patriotic sympathies could develop within the RIC itself. Lawrence Nugent, at this time heavily involved in IRA intelligence work in Dublin, stated that:

> "By every means in their power the Dublin Castle authorities tried to cause conflicts between the people and the police." [73]

How they did this he doesn't say but I think it is interesting that the Irish Volunteers in the 1920-21 period - which perchance might have been infiltrated at a high level by the Castle - issued an instruction that all operations had to be passed by HQ with the exception that the RIC were to be shot on sight, which presumably then deliberately spared the British military.[74] De Winter's impression was that "everything was done to vilify and calumniate the police," which again seems to surprisingly leave out the British government and the military in these insults.[75] Maybe as well it is worth considering this passage in a circular sent out by Dublin Castle to the various RIC Head Constables around Ireland, outlining the methods to be employed in dealing with Ginnell's cattle driving campaign: "It was essential that people should be roughly handled."[76] By these means they deliberately landed the RIC in it I think.

Hence I respectfully submit that when you look at real history, and the experience of other countries, you have to come to the conclusion that police forces can become incredibly corrupt, and the centre of huge byzantine conspiracies, which you will never see if your horizons remains fixed on the standard role of the village policeman in the justice system.

Technology

Obviously on the internet and elsewhere there is a lot of speculation that intelligence agencies, and other groups, have access to very advanced technology which may be harming the health of dissidents using high tech gadgetry like even microwave weapons. Most of the people who then talk about those things are of course in turn laughed at as 'conspiracy theorists', or even the 'tin foil hat brigade' etc etc! But the thing is that there is, in my opinion anyway, pretty compelling information out there, from pretty respected sources, on this that cannot be laughed off so easily? As an example recently Pravda in Russia published an article which was actually illustrated with a picture of a person wearing a 'tin-foil hat' and yet they did not see any humour in that whatsoever. The article was a very serious short survey of the kind of advanced technologies that it seems are being used against dissidents today. A few bits and pieces from it:

> "Major-general of the reserve of the Russian Federal Custodial Service Boris Ratnikov tells that Russia and other countries work on making special devices that turn humans into zombies.
>
> It was already twenty years ago that mass media first mentioned the strange word combination 'psychotronic weapon'. All information about such weapons arrived from military men transferred to the reserve and from researchers that were not officially recognized by the Russian Academy of Sciences. They usually told about some generators that could make people muddleheaded even when they were distanced at hundreds of kilometers.
>
> Such devices were said to be able to control people's behaviour, seriously impair psyche and even drive

people to death...

Boris Ratnikov says that Russia has been working on the psychotronic impact upon humans since the 1920s. ...Thousands of brilliant researchers were working on the problem in the twenty secret centers.

...

At the same time, the official science still insists that psychotronic is mere charlatanry. Boris Ratnikov is sure however that in less than ten years psychotronic weapons will grow more dangerous than nuclear and atomic weapons.

It is known that several researchers are still investigating the problem in Russia.

...

In North Korea, the Service for Security and Control of Foreign Policy conducts experiments with special oscillators that can modify functions of human organs.

In Pakistan, special services can use a special device that can cause dysfunctions of human organs and physiological systems and even cause people's death.

The Spanish intelligence finances studies of the effect of physical factors on human organs and human brain with the view of making devices to cause dysfunctions of organs and mental transformations.

...

Many countries possess information about secret use of a distance impact upon individuals and large groups of people. And these are not at all mere experiments but also practical application of technologies for various political and military purposes. Such technologies grow more perfect thanks to scientific and technological innovations.

Boris Ratnikov says that he once saw a KGB's classified document about potential threats and a psychotronic generator. The document said that the mechanism of a psychotronic generator is based upon the resonance of response functions of human organs, the heart, liver, kidneys and brain."[77]

Clearly a lot of dissidents have been alleging this for years and the standard reply has been that while things like microwave devices might have been developed, and used, in the former USSR yet in the West there is no question of those governments developing or using such technologies. But of course they'd say that wouldn't they!, such denials don't mean very much :-). For decades the citizens of the West were assured that the huge Western nuclear arsenal was of course never used in operational combat, it was only there as a deterrent in case the Communist Bloc used it against them. This of course was a very necessary piece of reassurance when you consider the long term effect of releases of radioactivity and all that. Then after the first Gulf War it was revealed that the West had indeed used a type of nuclear weapon in that conflict, Depleted Uranium in ammunition, which went on to cause all the nightmarish injuries that radiation releases are famous for. It then slowly leaked out that the US had been contemplating DU weaponry since 1943, had deployed them in weapons systems since 1968,[78] test fired them on US soil in the 60s,[79] and they had been used extensively in combat in the 1973 Arab-Israeli War.[80] Hence its remarkable to what extent the powers that be in the West can successfully keep secret over a long number of years its, what might be called, reckless enthusiasm to use these horrific weapons against their enemies. So now we find that in this latest war it is coming to the fore, and accepted in the mainstream media, that they are extensively using these mysterious microwave weapons.[81] So how can we be sure that US intelligence agencies, for example, have not used those things before? Is it not usually the case that the US would deploy these weapons in secret within those agencies long before their use would be publicly acknowledged in open warfare?

As I see it anyway the fact is that there is a huge time lag involved here, like in the case of DU it seems to take about 30 years before the civilian world gets up to speed on the kind of technologies in use in the military/ intelligence field, especially in the US. Dr Robert Duncan, a "Ph.D. in Artificial Intelligence from Harvard University & Formerly Defence Scientist with the US government", has interviewed personally some 650 people in his research on the use of these esoteric technologies on US citizens and he has found that there is "at least a 35 year gap between civilian and military technology in this area."[82] We seem to live in a world where in civilian technology, in some areas anyway, precious little seems to change or improve all that much, say in medicine for example, but in the world of the US military budgets the skies the limit! Look at aircraft speeds for example. The fastest civilian aircraft now flying is the Cessna Citation X which travels at a top speed of Mach 0.92,[83] while the fastest acknowledged military aircraft is usually said to be the SR-71 Blackbird travelling at Mach 3.35. Note too that that Cessna was first rolled out in 1996 [84] while the Blackbird dates from 1964 [85] showing again this huge military-civilian technology gap. Btw the Blackbird has officially retired, and as such some might say I should compare it then to Concorde in the civilian sphere but while the latter has certainly gone it is generally felt that the Blackbird has been replaced by an aircraft that flies as fast as Mach 6 [86] or even Mach 8,[87] so comparing like with like would give you an even greater disparity. As time goes on this gap seems to widen all the time, the gap between the white acknowledged civilian technologies and the classified military technologies. For instance as far as I know this aircraft speed gap would have been much narrower at the time Concorde was rolled out in the 70s, and much narrower again at the time of the civilian flying boats flying into Foynes in the 30s.

Surely the logic of it then is that people should be nervous about dismissing specific allegations about the use of advanced technology? And should acknowledge that history shows that the governments in the West are extremely good at keeping these things secret over very long periods of time, but yet are surprising ruthless and irresponsible in the way that they deploy them? As such maybe there is something to the allegations about the use of those weapons against dissidents, maybe even about the deployment of microchips in people (to track and maybe to influence peoples health slightly, I'm not saying they can control a person that way!), and certainly it is perfectly clear that many of the big Western intelligence agencies, and maybe even some cults, have the capacity to implant and erase memories and even create split personalities in people using hypnosis, drugs and contrived episodes of physical and psychological trauma (described later in Chapter 6). Not a nice thought I know but the world we live in I think! [88]

Secret Societies

Another issue that crops up in this 'conspiracy theory' criticism is the role of Secret Societies. Obviously whenever anybody mentions them, particularly the Freemasons, a 'conspiracy theory' alert goes off and you might as well be discussing alien landings! But this is surely unfair, there are and have always been Secret Societies, and in Ireland at any rate, they have frequently exercised great power over our political destiny, so it seems unfair not to be able to speculate about the role they might play nowadays. For example in the tumultuous 1770-1800 period in Ireland the Freemasons seemed to have if anything the dominant role in the Volunteers,[89] Defenders,[90] and United Irishmen [91] and as such must have exercised a crucial role in Irish politics at that time. This role seemed to have continued afterwards as Larry Conlon writes in Riocht na Mídhe:

>"Freemasonry has had a significant if not always obvious influence on Irish history and society...[later, after the 1798 period] it became an increasingly powerful and influential organisation. It is not surprising, therefore, to find that many of the influential figures in Irish society and indeed internationally were Freemasons." [92]

Irish historical sources contain much gossip about what the Freemasons were allegedly up to which for some reason does not tend to be written about or reflected on by most modern Irish historians. Maud Gonne for example, commenting on events leading up to WWI in France, where she was then living, said that King Edward reconciled the UK's Scottish rite of Freemasonry with the French Grand Orient rite, the secret back drop to the Entente Cordiale, which in her opinion "made war inevitable".[93]

If talking about Freemasonry makes you automatically a 'conspiracy theorist' then there seems to be a lot of the latter in Irish history! :-) Even Sean Lemass, the future Taoiseach of course, speaking in 1929 claimed that Mexico "fell into the hands of the Freemasons" at the same time "that foreign capitalists went into Mexico to exploit the resources of the country in their own interests." He went on to talk about a similar scenario here:

>"Col Claude Cane Grand High Master of the Freemasons in Ireland announced the fact that Masonry was booming here; that Freemasons held positions of power in government departments and enterprises that seriously affected the countries interests. Some time ago the official organ of Cumann na nGaedhal launched an attack on the Knights of Columbanus, because, it said, they wanted to become a second Freemason organisation. The 'Irish Times' next day reminded Mr Cosgrave that he was dependent for his position as President on a majority in the Dail that was composed of six Freemasons. If there was likely to be a situation here as in Mexico, in which Freemasons would dominate the country, he [Lemass] hoped the Irish people would show to it the same attitude as the people of Mexico had done." [94]

But obviously there are other Secret Societies that have had a great bearing on modern Irish history. The Ancient Order of Hibernians was one such society that is said to have completely dominated the Irish scene from around 1906-1916 say. It is reported to have been "a secret sectarian society that had the country in its vicious grip" during those years.[95]

However the big beast of the Secret Societies in Ireland was soon to be the Irish Republican Brotherhood. This 'Brotherhood' - a word that is usually used in a certain context internationally - had huge influence over the Irish Labour Movement, for example, with members like James Connolly,[96] William O'Brien [97] and P.T. Daly etc. Also the IRB had set up a special unit to infiltrate Irish labour unions in order

> "to get hold of men in important positions such as Power Stations, Railways and Transport Dock workers etc, ...[in order] to undermine the Cross Channel Unions" etc.[98]

The IRB had considerable influence over Irish arts, numbering among their members such luminaries as W.B.Yeats,[99] Sean O'Casey,[100] Charles Kickham, Ernest Blythe, and Piaras Beaslai, not to mention the obvious people like Pádraig Pearse.

Then an incredible number of Irish nationalist politicians of the period were in the IRB including Joseph Biggar [101] and Tim Healy (also apparently in the Invincibles [102]) from the Irish Parliamentary Party; Michael Davitt (a Supreme Council member of the IRB), Frank Byrne, Secretary, and Patrick Egan, Treasurer, of the Land League (Dr Hamilton Williams and other Land Leaguers were high officials in the Invincibles.[103] The Invincibles of course were an offshoot of the IRB.); Arthur Griffith ("at one time fairly high up in the councils of that organisation",[104] he apparently left fed up with its toleration of senior informers in its ranks.[105]) and nearly all the other big Sinn Fein names of the 1916-24 period like de Valera, Cathal Brugha (those last two were at least at one time quite senior IRB people), the future Irish President Sean T O'Kelly (always a key IRB man and later an important member of the Knights of Columbanus), Liam Lynch, and obviously Michael Collins (of course President of the Supreme Council of the IRB), Bulmer Hobson, Dr Patrick MacCartan, Mulcahy, Sean McKeon etc etc.

This meant that a lot of the history of the time was in turn fashioned by the clandestine machinations involving this secret society. For instance the Irish Parliamentary Party tried to get control of the IRB at one time and it was at that point that the Invincibles broke off.[106] When relations between France and the UK were strained c.1900 it is said that the French government maintained contact with the IRB with a view to diverting UK military resources into Ireland.[107] Also it is obvious now that the Redmondite takeover of the Irish Volunteers in 1914 was in fact "merely a gloss for the continuance of the old duel between the A.O.H. and the I.R.B." [108] This secret duel even extended to the IRB infiltrating the AOH in the c.1916-17 period. These IRB moles then later aggravated the collapse of the AOH's power which happened a little later, c.1920:

> "The members of the IRB who had joined the AOH were now able to bring the greater number of branches in their districts into line with the general breakaway."
> [109]

Obviously then the Irish Civil War took off on the back of a split in the IRB - with Liam Lynch opposing the Treaty in the Supreme Council of that body which otherwise was mostly pro-Treaty - and in the opinion of some exacerbated the divisions at that time. One such commentator, Frank Henderson of the Dublin IRA, ruefully remarked in after years:

> "We decided that [the] IRB had done the real damage.
> It had split the army. They now saw the reason for the Church condemning Secret Societies." [110]

The story of Irish Secret Societies and the modern Irish state doesn't end with the IRB either, a number of other secret organisations appear on the scene with apparently the same behind the scenes influence. This is a report of a debate held at the 1933 Fianna Fail Ard Fheis on the reported influence of the Knights of Columbanus:

> "Mr James Comyn contended that the Knights of Columbanus and the Freemasons were a menace to the State.
>
> ...
>
> He personally had been more affected by the machinations of the Knights than anybody else. Patronage in the Courts was bestowed on the Knights.
>
> Not one brief had been given by the Attorney General except to Knights of Columbanus and there was not one of those Knights to whom he gave patronage who had not been an active enemy of the Movement from 1916 to 1923.
> ...[De Valera denied that there was any such influence and claimed that for example no member of the Executive was a Knight]...
> Mr Comym: I say it is a fact.
> Mr de Valera: I say it is not a fact.
> Mr Comyn: I maintain it as a fact.
>
> Mr O'Connor, said that as a Secret Society, the Knights of Columbanus, they must presume, wanted to get con-

trol of the Fianna Fail organisation. It was to be pre-
sumed also that they had in fact got control of the Civil
Service, and "since the mutiny many officers in the
Free State army are now connected with it." If they got
hold of FF they would control the whole state absolutely.

It was generally believed that the Knights of Columbanus were working determinedly to get control of
every department of the Civil Service, and it was also
said that almost every Catholic member of the legal
profession was a member. (cries "No.")

Mr P.T. MacGinley ('Cu Uladh') seconding, said he
was convinced that the knights aimed at getting control
of affairs of the State.

Mr E McGawran (Dublin) stated that he had evidence
that at a place where he worked, which came under the
direction of the Minister for Industry and Commerce,
and in which 458 people were employed, all the people
who held good positions did so not because of their
ability or national outlook, but because they were
Knights of Columbanus.

Mr Lemass (Minister for Industry and Commerce):
name the department.

Mr McGauran: The ESB.

Mr Lemass: I have nothing to do with employment
there." [111]

Clearly these delegates, having been through the mill of the Civil War
period, were extremely interested and nervous about the role of Secret
Societies, rather than dismissing such influence as unlikely or unimportant as many modern commentators do. Its like the more they knew
about Irish politics the more they guessed that these societies were running the show. That the FF bigwigs seemed to have something to hide
on this score was shown by Frank O'Connor writing in 1942:

"Every year that has passed, particularly since de
Valera's rise to power, has strengthened the grip of the
gombeen man, of the religious Secret Societies like

Knights of Columbanus..." [112]

So going by this history I cannot see how people can be so dismissive of allegations of widespread influence held by Secret Societies, I mean anything is possible?

Underestimating the Complexity of Politics

"There are very rarely coincidences, very rarely simple fortunate (or unfortunate) accidents in matters of state. Most things are arranged and managed, with varying degrees of success, often by those organisations with centuries of experience at this sort of thing."
- Vincent MacDowell

In the case of 'conspiracy theories' in modern politics my contention here is that politics is simply more complicated and has more twists and turns - and duplicity - attached to it than the general public sometimes gives it credit for. What I mean is that often a particular 'theory' automatically becomes a 'conspiracy theory' because what it entails is seen as complicated and therefore politicians couldn't possibly be that clever to pull off this particular 'theory' or plot say. I know all types are involved in politics, and it would be only fair to say that not all of them are that brainy or whatever, but some people at a high level of the political/security apparatus can, I respectfully submit, act very cleverly in the way that they manipulate people, and can pull off long term political stunts and goals. To give you an example of what I mean here is a fascinating quote from Jean Monnet, one of the great European 'statesmen' behind the creation of the EU:

"Europe's nations should be guided towards the superstate without their peoples realising what is happening. This can be accomplished by successive steps, each described as having an economic purpose, but which will eventually and irreversibly lead to federation." [113]

So what people imagine are random or confused acts are, often enough, skilfully planned long term political manoeuvres. Of course there are errors and confusion too but my guess is that people generally under, rather than over, estimate the degree to which they are being conned by their political leaders. Some of these leaders are simply cleverer than people give them credit for, and the political game in your average Western democracy is right now more a matter of manipulating large numbers of people than it is anything else.

To give you another example consider the agreement reached between the British and Irish governments at their mysterious conference at Baldonnel aerodrome in c.1974. In 2003 Major Fred Holroyd, formerly of British army intelligence of course and relying in this instance on later contacts, revealed that the two governments had jointly agreed to criticize each other in the media with respect to their handling of the IRA. Specifically it was agreed that the British government would criticize the Irish government's supposedly lax attitude in cracking down on the IRA. The beauty of this is that it would strengthen the Irish government's position, and all these politicians knew this of course, because the Irish public would rally round their government when it was being attacked like this by the old enemy. This then would nicely disguise the fact that the Irish government had sold out to the British, at the same meeting, with respect to their control over Irish intelligence matters.[114] Also, I would contend that it provided a nice explanation that the UK government could sell to their own electorate for their failure to stop the IRA campaign. They obviously blamed the presence of a porous border and the provision of safe houses in the South, while in fact its possible that the British government, at some high level, was actually supporting rather than crushing the IRA campaign, for its own reasons.[115]

That they often have such reasons you can see from these comments by the 71 year old English MEP Ashley Mote, speculating on the real causes of some recent airport security scares:

> "We all know modern governments welcome, perhaps even contrive, what are known as "beneficial crises". Once an apparent threat arises, they can then introduce legislation and regulations which would not otherwise be tolerated by the general public...We have to ask ourselves this: who is fighting against democracy? The terrorists? The British government? Or both of them?...There is undeniable evidence to support claims of such a sub-plot here. The British government is allowing a level of terrorist threat to continue – presumably believing it can be kept under control – so that it can complete a programme of draconian legislation to control all the rest of us.
> The ultimate purpose is obvious. Previously legitimate peaceful protest and dissent will become much more difficult, if not impossible, in the future." [116]

When you consider political practices like that doesn't it sometimes look as if the general public are more like hamsters spinning around on these evil geniuses' caged playground rather than anything else? And they obviously rely upon the fact that the general public don't realize how conspiratorial and manipulative these politicians can be?

In fact I would suggest that it is frequently a very complex affair trying to unravel the true goings on in your average political drama. So complex in fact that I think sometimes it helps to understand what is going on by dividing up the actors in a given drama into various stages, say three, with a different explanation of the truth being given at each stage. I know that sounds awfully wafflish but after you read the next two chapters maybe you can see where I am coming from. Possibly it might be instructive to take a simple example, I will take the question of the British government's now pretty obvious support for Loyalist paramilitary groups during the recent troubles. I would suggest that there are maybe three different explanations given here, with the last one being nearest the truth:

a) The general public were of course told all that time that the British Army were there as honest brokers, trying to keep separated two groups of paramilitaries who were constantly at each others throats, and if it wasn't for their supposedly heroic defence of law and order there would have been a civil war. This is the line the general public got, and was followed virtually without fail by the mass media, and was of course the normal pack of lies that you expect from an advanced Western democracy. I'm sorry to be so cynical but I doubt if that simple first explanation, the one the general public gets at the time, is ever a truthful explanation in modern times.

b) But then the question arises how could they have kept the truth a secret? Thousands of army and police personnel, not to mention politicians North and South and in London, must have known that the standard public explanation was a lie. We know now that many, possibly all, Loyalist paramilitary attacks were facilitated by the army and police 'freezing' areas to allow the paramilitaries to do their stuff unmolested by the security forces. But clearly then there must have been huge numbers of military and police who could see perfectly well that these attacks coincided with helpful enabling security arrangements that their superiors were instructing them to undertake. Bear in mind now we are talking about mostly completely innocent targets, taxi men, musicians etc etc, it really is amazing the low numbers that spoke out against this is it not? Again you have to factor in the huge number of people nowadays that hear nothing and see nothing that could jeopardise their pension etc. But the interesting thing here is the compartmentalisation of the real information and the spreading around of a false explanation of what was going on. Obviously you couldn't tell these personnel that there were no links between the army and the Loyalist paramilitaries, the explanation the general public was getting, instead they were encouraged to think, I suspect, that the Loyalist paramilitaries were secretly supported as proxy armies of the British government fighting against the IRA. Then the security force personnel were happy enough to follow their orders and keep quiet, anything to hit back at the IRA which was seen to be the real enemy.

c) So hence you have two explanations spread around simultaneously, one for the general public, and one for the security personnel, the latter needing a different explanation because they had access to information which meant they wouldn't believe version (a). But I think that this is only stage 2, the security force personnel were lied to as well. Imagine if those personnel had known at the time that the IRA's security section, the 'nutting squad', was all along run by the British army, a fact that is now widely acknowledged? [117] Only a tiny number of them knew secrets like that and if they did know I'm thinking that they would have begun posing some serious questions about what the whole business was about. At the really high level in London it looks now that they were playing all sorts of political games, similar I think to the 'Strategy of Tension' tactic, the support of the security services for both sides in a paramilitary conflict, which was being played out in Italy at the same time.

So that is maybe a model to apply to understand some of these conspiracies? Various groups know a portion of the truth, and they are then given different explanations, a process helped by a powerful compartmentalisation of information. After all, if you think about it, when you organise information on a 'need to know' basis you make it very easy to organise a conspiracy! I hope to show two other examples of this, Hungary in 1956 and the German Plot in Ireland in 1918, divided again into three stages or explanations of what was happening:

Soviet invasion of Hungary in 1956
a) The Soviet Union obviously invaded Hungary in 1956 and although the US actually never did anything to stop the Soviets, naturally they were seen to be appalled at the USSR's action. They blamed the UN for their inaction, as explained here by Conor Cruise O'Brien, working at that time as a leading Irish diplomat:
> "Eisenhower, though rejecting any military reaction,
> was under pressure to find forms of reaction which

would be showy and moralistic, but safe. ...To suggestions that the United States should intervene in Eastern Europe after the Russian intervention, Eisenhower's spokesman replied that the United States, unlike the Soviet Union, was a law-abiding power, bound to act only under the constraints of the Charter of the UN. In fact, as those who talked in those terms well knew, there are no such constraints. The Charter allows a power which feels threatened by the actions of another power, to act in legitimate self-defence: as the United States had been prepared to do over Korea, whatever the UN might have done. Still the picture of the United States as constrained by inaction by the UN Charter lent dignity to a policy of inaction and was highly congenial to the popular mood, both in the United States and Western Europe. ...

The matter was first brought before the Security Council and a resolution ordering the Soviet Union to withdraw its forces from Hungary was duly vetoed by the Soviet Union. Western spokesmen then spoke of the parlous condition of the UN "paralysed by the Soviet veto" and this was much healthier, from the point of view of the United States, than a public discussion of the position of the United States could have been. ...

[The United States publicly] deplored the failure of the Security Council to bring the aggression to an end. The Security Council had been "paralysed by the Soviet veto" and there was vague talk about the need to bring about "Charter revision".

The point of the whole exercise was, of course, to shift the blame for letting down the Hungarians away from the United States and on to the UN, which has in reality no material power to take any action at all...[which amounted to] the shabby and dishonest series of transactions directed by the Americans but supported by the Europeans through which the sacrifice of the Hungarians had been achieved. "

b) The interesting thing is that among the diplomats at the UN they well knew that the public were told a pack of lies about all this. So they get a completely different explanation from the US, as O'Brien also describes:

"He [the US arm-twister at the UN] offered no bribes, nor did he use any threats. He simply offered me an analysis of the situation in Hungary in this brief period, when Imre Nagy was apparently seeking to extricate his country from the Warsaw Pact and trying to enlist the support of the United States. My arm-twister told me that Imre Nagy deserved absolutely no support or encouragements from any democratic country. He was as bad a communist as any other. Whether he was left in charge or replaced by some other communist would make absolutely no difference to anyone.

I was quite surprised by this discussion. Virtually the entire Western press was highly supportive of Nagy, at this time, and wished him well in his efforts to liberate his country from the communist yoke. Nobody in the West was anything but supportive of Imre Nagy *in public*. But my little arm-twister was telling me something different and what he was telling me was correct in that it reflected the substance, as distinct from the style, of United States policy at this point.

...[The US Republican administration made very warlike noises in Eastern Europe and elsewhere but] The Republicans did not really expect to roll back any part of it [the Iron Curtain]. But they did want to give the impression that the Republicans, unlike the Democrats, had a policy for ending communist rule and were actively engaged in promoting it. This message would be highly congenial to many Americans of Eastern European origins, and more vaguely agreeable to many other Americans. In other words, it was a foreign policy for internal consumption. ...

Eisenhower seems to have decided very early on that no material encouragement was to be given to the Hungarians. Whatever those broadcasts might have encouraged them to hope, their hopes must now be dashed. ...

Letting down the Hungarians was a tricky business, in the light of previous propaganda, but the letting-down was accomplished in stages with considerable skill. While the fate of Imre Nagy and his colleagues remained in doubt, the United States government professed to see the situation as troubling but unclear. Privately and to friendly governments, the message was the same as that conveyed by my own arm-twister: Nagy, not to be trusted, as bad a communist as any of them. Reading the American signals correctly, the Russians decided on military intervention in Hungary, in the well-founded belief that the American reactions would be political, not military." [118]

c) But this second explanation that was given to these insiders, that Imre Nagy was not really different to the usual Communist leaders, is again, I suspect, not at all the truth. The more you look at the Cold War the more you are struck by how much both sides cooperated with each other in secret.[119] In particular it is now well known that Europe had been long ago divided into spheres of influence, which allowed the Soviet Union, by agreement with the West, to do whatever it wanted in Hungary. In fact there was talk in the air about these 'spheres of influence' before WWII had even started! [120] I would contend that it is more likely that this invasion was convenient at the time for both powers as they struggled to deepen their control over the countries allocated to them under these spheres of influence i.e. Eastern Europe given to Russia and Western Europe to the US and the UK. The sight of tanks in Budapest naturally concentrated the minds of the peoples in the East, while the US, at the exact same time, was able to introduce secret 'gladio' armies, attached to the NATO structure, which in time helped them to quietly control the peoples of Western Europe.[121] The spectacle of the Soviet invasion of Hungary was no doubt just the trick to persuade the Western European leaders to go along with these secret NATO arrangements. Its far more likely that this is no accident, I would suggest that the US knew all along what was going to happen in Hungary, and events transpired exactly as they intended.

The 1918 German Plot in Ireland.

> "Just before daybreak on the morning of Friday, April 12th, 1918, a German submarine surfaced near an island off the coast of Co.Clare. Out clambered my great-uncle, Joe Dowling, and proceeded to manouver his small rubber boat onto the beach of Crab Island.
> As dawn broke he realised that he was not on the mainland and while he was wondering what to do next he saw a fishing boat putting out from the mainland, some half a mile away. He waved at the crew and soon after they came and picked him up and took him back to the pier at Doolin Point." [122]

a) Such were the humble beginnings of the famous German Plot of 1918. The British government soon breathlessly announced that this Joe Dowling, who was said to have codes sewn into his handkerchief, was a secret agent sent to finalise military cooperation between Sinn Fein and the Irish Volunteers on the one hand and the German High Command on the other. Since this is just at the time of the crisis on the Western Front there was naturally enough an enormous outcry in the British media against what were seen to be treasonous communications with a mortal enemy. In response they therefore rounded up nearly all the main Volunteer and Sinn Fein figures and threw them in jail just as the East Cavan bye election was deciding the fate of the Irish Parliamentary Party. So we have version one of these events, which was pumped out relentlessly in the media at the time, and was extensively believed at least in the UK and maybe the US.

b) But not in Ireland. At the time Irish people had seen a lot of political dramas come and go and they tended to take a jaundiced view of whatever government line was being peddled in the mass media. Mostly they just didn't believe this explanation, and the thin evidence presented tended to reinforce this view. I think that Sceilg (a knowledgeable Kerry man who kept a beady eye on political goings on at that time) writing in his Catholic Bulletin articulates the view held by most Irish people then and since:

> "Another State Paper [meaning I think one of the big London newspapers] palliates the deportations [of the Sinn Fein leaders accused of the Plot] by blazoning the descent of a solitary invader upon a remote island on April 12th, heralded by mysterious warnings from the Admiralty to the Irish Command. No discussion is permitted of the tryst of this British soldier [he was one of the POWs recruited by Casement in Germany] with the local coastguard, of his speedy bent towards a police-barrack, and his subsequent confidences with the London authorities." ...[Sceilg goes on to quote the Manchester Guardian's account of Dowling's trial:]
> "The most surprising thing about the Dowling trial has been not what it disclosed, but what it did not disclose. Now not only was Dowling not charged with his connection with the plot, but not a word was said at the trial about it. On the contrary all the evidence showed that nobody in Ireland came to assist him or shelter him,

and that he wandered about, got drunk, and changed his suspicious money in the ordinary way. There was not a vestige of the plot. Nevertheless, Home Rule has been jettisoned and coercion reinstated on the strength of the plot story. There is something here that requires explanation."

[Sceilg commenting on that:] So there is. But, as the Manchester Guardian must know, it is quite in the order of things in Ireland. The whole 'plot' is quite in line with 'the perpetual Act of Repression, obtained by forgery, which graced Queen Victoria's Jubilee year.' " [123]

And that is how Irish historians have typically read it, some will of the wisp made up 'plot' used by Lloyd George to justify throwing the Sinn Fein leaders into jail, although one recent historian concedes that "an element of mystery remains." [124]

c) Indeed there does because I would suggest that actually there was such a plot! Richard Walsh was at that time both IRB centre for Mayo and on the Volunteer Executive in Dublin and later he wrote that he was quite certain that such a plot really existed. He is absolutely clear that Collins and possibly Dermot O'Hegarty had formalised elaborate arrangements with the German government at that time. He was also aware of much toing and froing between these two parties and German U-Boats anchored off the Mayo coastline in early 1918.[125]

So what exactly is going on I hear you ask :-) Well we have a certain Welsh wizard's movements to track here and I admit this does require a little speculation. The first point is that from the point of view of the British government what they always wanted to achieve I think was control over the leadership of each shade of public opinion in Ireland. In otherwords they wanted all groups to follow secretly compromised political leaders. That is the key, it doesn't matter at all what the different political leaders actually say, they can say whatever they like to keep their supporters happy, including criticising the British government, so long as the Irish people follow these false leaders not the real type. (After the war he can always plan to move around his secret pawns, the false leaders, to bring about whatever political outcome he wants, so long as he somehow gets control of these leaders first.) Now say for the sake of argument that the leadership of the two shades of opinion in Nationalist Ireland at this time - spring of 1918 - are NOT secretly under the control of the British government. These two groups are obviously the ageing dinosaur of the Irish Parliamentary Party (IPP) and the up and coming Sinn Fein party, and it might be useful to guess

what Lloyd George does to both in turn, using this German Plot:
- IPP. Maybe he simply assassinates this party by sabotaging their electoral chances during the all important East Cavan bye election. It has often being said that the German Plot arrests floored the IPP just as they
were getting their act together in the ongoing bye election war against
Sinn Fein at that time. John Dillon, the then leader of the IPP, is quite
clear on this point:

> "..we had Sinn Fein absolutely beaten. The tide had
> turned decisively against them and we would have won
> East Cavan by a decisive majority"

if it wasn't for the government's German Plot arrests.[126] (Which included the Sinn Fein candidate Arthur Griffith.) And believe it or not in
fact John Dillon himself did feel that the government was following a
policy of deliberately humiliating the IPP in order to support Sinn Fein
at that time, especially at strategic times during elections. His biography
calls it the "'conspiracy theory' to which Dillon was to become increasingly addicted as time went on." [127] He talked a lot about this in his
private letters at the time and even dropped some hints in a speech he
gave in Baillieboro during the election:

> "And so the game goes on (cheers). The reactionary
> government in England and their military advisers play
> the game of Sinn Fein an effective weapon to weaken
> and destroy the constitutional movement in Ireland -
> the only movement they are in the least afraid of - and
> having destroyed the constitutional movement, they
> think they can justify...breaking their pledges to the Ir-
> ish people...That is the position which the Sinn Feiners
> are helping to drive our people into. ...Sinn Fein plays
> into the hands of the British government through sheer
> political incapacity to understand the tactics of Lloyd
> George, who is undoubtedly one of the ablest and most
> audacious politicians now living in the world.
>
> ...As I said at the outset, the situation now created by
> the arrests of the Sinn Fein leaders is one of extraordin-
> ary difficulty. I have no hesitation in saying that if it
> had been part of the settled policy of the government to
> support and strengthen the candidature of Mr Griffith
> and do everything in their power to secure his return,
> they could not have taken more effective steps than by
> the arrests of last week, the publication of the alleged
> German Plot, and the character of the document which
> they have issued in support of these charges [which was

a very weak, vague document] (hear, hear)." [128]
From Lloyd George's perspective then that solves the problem of the IPP, using the Plot and some similar episodes he calculatingly destroys the IPP and with it the political careers of their leaders.

- Sinn Fein. Now what does he do with Sinn Fein? I suspect that he again does not control the actual leaders, or at least not all of them, of the party in 1918, but maybe he did have a clique in his pocket here including Michael Collins and his circle, people like Harry Boland, Dermot O'Hegarty, Mulcahy etc. (Yes I did just say that I thought Michael Collins was Lloyd George's agent :-) don't panic I elaborate on that in Chapter 3 and in this footnote!lol.[129]) Its interesting to note that in the months before the Plot arrests Sinn Fein and the Volunteers were making contingency plans for what they would do if their leaders were arrested as part of the Conscription crisis, and it turns out that they had selected this group, including Collins and Boland, as the future leaders if the main ones were to be arrested. Then as smooth as silk a few months later the old Sinn Fein leaders are arrested because of the Plot and deported out of Ireland and hey presto Collins and co. take over Sinn Fein and the Volunteers! Hence Lloyd George was able to use the Plot to switch over the leaders within Sinn Fein, installing his agents to control affairs from now on? That Collins "assumed a commanding position both in the Volunteers and Sinn Fein" as a direct result of the German Plot arrests is something that everybody agrees on I think, like Lawrence Nugent in that quote.[130] In fact the curious coincidence that it was the British government that handed Collins control over Sinn Fein like this seemed to raise some eyebrows at the time, and this slight suspicion might have also extended to wondering just why Collins himself had not being arrested along with the other leaders. One of the Sinn Fein leaders who was arrested, Darrell Figgis, describes here the control that Collins, and the IRB which was already run by him, now exercised over Sinn Fein and the selection of the candidates for the upcoming election:

> "The Brotherhood was therefore, in a strong position now to capture the control [over Sinn Fein] it had sought so long...And such was the curious chance by which the British government made the IRB masters of the scene. [Meaning the German Plot arrests.]
> In this manner then, came Michael Collins to the control for which he had striven, which he held so tenaciously, and which he maintained to the end. A man of ruthless purpose and furious energy, knowing clearly

what he wanted and prepared to trample down everybody to get it, he was the real master of the new executive.

...

In the second place a further purge had been made by
those who now controlled the IRB - and through the
IRB controlled Sinn Fein; by sending representatives to
be present at all Sinn Fein Conventions for the choice
of candidates, arranging identical dates for Conventions
in different constituencies, and giving each to believe
that the name or names desired by it were that day to be
chosen by some other; and by other adroit devices -
with the result that a substantial majority of the newly
created national parliament was ready to move to the
word of command.

...

[After observing the way that the IRB controlled Sinn
Fein he notes how] easy it is to manipulate political organisations so as to make them, with the appearance of
freedom and finality, the mere agents of skilful intrigue." [131]

Hence if Lloyd George controlled Collins then the German Plot arrests
neatly gave him complete control over the emerging Sinn Fein movement, so clever its almost beautiful!lol. I think too that LG planned for
the Plot to be a real plot for a number of reasons. He presumably would
have instructed Collins and co. to genuinely contact the Germans in order to have in his back pocket priceless blackmail information on these
agents. Obviously if they fell out with LG later he would spring genuine
telegrams etc that would prove the plot and a smooth path to the hang-
man's noose would await Collins! (Remember the legal system normally does not tolerate listening to wild 'conspiracy theories' by de-
fendants, which certainly would include Collins trying to blame LG at
any trial!) Secondly he needed to persuade the Irish executive and the
RIC of the real existence of such a plot in order to encourage them to
make those arrests, they would no doubt also be shown sight of genuine
intercepted telegrams to win them over. Therefore a 'real' plot was better than a completely faked one!

    The upshot then is that Lloyd George, after the 1918 elections, has
now got rid of those Irish Nationalist leaders that he didn't control and
swapped them for a collection of MPs that maybe he does control, all as
a result of the German Plot and the arrests that followed! That I think

anyway might be the real story of the whole episode.

I therefore respectfully submit that the political 'game', as John Dillon calls it, is often very complicated and if you don't believe in 'conspiracies' then you will never get to grips with what is really going on.

The pervasive influence of the modern mass media

But there is maybe an even deeper story here about the role of the modern mass media. The first thing to note is that stories in the modern media, about security issues particularly, are more controlled by the agencies of governments that at any time in the past. This is simply because crime scenes and places where 'terrorist' incidents have occurred are more systematically cordoned off from the public, by the police etc, than was probably the case in the past. What I mean is picture a reporter trying to report on the Tube bombings in London and ask yourself where he/she gets their information from. They turn up at the site and its been long ago cordoned off and huge numbers of security personnel are probably sealing off access to witnesses, stopping reporters getting into hospitals etc etc, and that this sealing off is probably more water tight now than ever before. Then all they can actually report on is whatever is released via the press offices of the various organs of the state. In fact in Ireland now there is a law against the Gardaí talking to reporters, except through the government press office, which led to an Evening Herald journalist being detained by the state, briefly, not long ago. So everything, and I would suggest absolutely everything, that you hear in the mass media about these incidents is entirely the story that the state wants you to hear. And of course, since time immemorial, the state lies from time to time about these things.

But what is happening is that the general public are not conscious that the story they hear in the mass media has this one, controllable, origin. The way they look at it there is a huge range of TV programmes packed with all kinds of knowledgeable reporters and experts giving their opinions, and a multiplicity of radio stations and glossy magazines and newspapers all rowing in with detailed coverage of a particular incident. So the reasonable enough conclusion that the public draw is that surely all these people couldn't be in on some vast conspiracy to hide the truth? They just don't realise that all these figures are only getting the story from one source, government agencies, and yes they often do, and often have a vested interest to, lie. And as pointed out in the un-likely event that information does come to the mass media from sources other than the government, they simply don't report it! After all it has to be 'confirmed' which in practice means asking the state is it true or not! As an example Morgan Stack has described how he packaged a lot of information together on 9/11 and personally tried to hand it out in RTE, only for them to throw him out and call the guards on him. It was made clear to him that they just don't report stuff like that, and they don't want to hear about it either. Morgan described how he previously had quite a lot of faith in the truthfulness of the Irish media and ended up so shocked by this that he was reduced to tears. Now he makes the point what else are they hiding from us? [132] Whether you agree or disagree about the 9/11 controversy the point is that the mass media in Ireland, and across most of the world, are definitely not going to tell you about information that is contrary to the government line, and therefore you might be thinking 'conspiracy theory' only because you weren't aware of the true facts that are out there.

Also it seems to this observer that the most controlled media in the West are those that are described as media 'of record', the most respec-ted highly thought of organs, like the New York Times [133] and the BBC.[134] In Ireland the Irish Times is often said to occupy the same space, but famously certain correspondence between the proprietor of the Irish Times, Major McDowell, and the UK government has now cast a long shadow over its independence from the powers that be. Here is just a bit from the correspondence of the UK ambassador in 1969:

> "But McDowell went on to say that he now felt that a
> certain degree of guidance, in respect of which lines
> were helpful and which unhelpful, might be acceptable
> to himself and one or two of his friends on the board;
> this was what he had had in mind in telephoning
> through to No.10." [135]

Surely the writing is on the wall then about the real role of the Irish Times for the last 40 years or so when you consider that the same Major McDowell "served as chief executive of The Irish Times between 1962 and 1997", retired as chairman of the Irish Times Trust in December 2001, and then made President for Life of the Irish Times Group. On top of that he is even said to have been a member of MI5! [136]

I respectfully submit that it is in fact possible that key organs in the modern media are being manipulated in a very systematic way by Intel-ligence agencies in London and Washington, with the former managing Dublin, just like what we now know about the role the British govern-ment traditionally held in secretly manipulating our media over centuries. Bearing in mind the pervasiveness of the modern media, and no doubt the subtle and advanced media manipulation that they use, I think you could almost speculate that the average modern Western citizen is probably now as brainwashed by his government as the former citizens of the Eastern block were by their regimes. And maybe then it is in fact this brainwashing which is now fashioning citizens to think 'conspiracy theory' any time a complicated story of government lies and manipulation comes to their ears? Hopefully not but I think anyway that this media role is the most important one in the increasing popularity of the phrase 'conspiracy theory' in modern times.

Footnotes

1. http://ireland.indymedia.org/article/83809.

2. Rodney Stich http://www.defraudingamerica.com/public_apathy.html .

3. Its not just in the Morris Tribunal that they are talking about this: "The routine lies that Guards peddle in the District Court to gain convictions are so common as to be barely worth remarking upon. Rarely acknowledged too are the regular beatings meted out to working class youths. The Department of Justice pays out over €1,000,000 annually in compensation for unlawful arrest, assault and harassment. And that figure represents the tiny minority who have bothered to make complaints that were successful. Many more are intimidated out of doing so; many never bother making a complaint at all." (Dec McCarthy http://www.indymedia.ie/newswire.php?story_id=66410)

4. This is true of the Special Criminal Court, which Barry describes here: http://www.indymedia.ie/article/82176 .

5. The MacManus quote is from Gerard MacManus, *Dark Corners* (Cork, 2008), p.144-146, 243, 246, 248, and 182; and the solicitor quote: http://www.rate-your-solicitor.com/forum/viewtopic.php?pid=937#p937 .

6. http://www.rate-your-solicitor.com/forum/viewtopic.php?id=115&action=new also referred to at http://www.indymedia.ie/article/82175 .

7. http://www.rate-your-solicitor.com/index.php?section=details&id=10364 .

8. 20 March 2007 Sunday Independent p.10.

9. "Shamrock Corporation, CIA Paymaster
Other CIA assets, including Gunther Russbacher, had described the role played by the CIA's Shamrock Corporation in Ireland, disbursing money for various CIA operations, including bribe money to federal judges and other covert agency assets. Crittenden described his relationship with Shamrock that focused on other areas of Shamrock's activities. He said that the Shamrock Corporation paid his airline for the flights flown, which he said totaled over $500 million for flights from 1976 to 1988." (Rodney Stich, *Drugging America: A Trojan Horse* (Alamo California, 2005), p.103.)

Also mentioned in another book by the same author:
"I was prompted to ask Russbacher about payoffs to federal judges after private investigator Stewart Webb heard of a bribe connection between U.S. District Judge Sherman Finesilver in Denver and a corporation in Ireland. After he passed the information along to me I questioned some of my CIA contacts to determine if they knew anything of it. In response to my questions, Russbacher explained the path of money for bribing federal judges, trustees, law firms, and

lawyers. Russbacher stated that the money for these payoffs came from a company located in Dublin and incorporated in Ireland, called Shamrock Overseas Disbursement Corporation. Its telephone is listed as Shamrock Overseas Courier Service. The function of this company was to place money at regular intervals into numbered bank accounts for the recipients to draw upon. Russbacher chuckled as he stated that the Chief Executive Officer at Shamrock Overseas Disbursement was the same person with whom he had worked at other CIA proprietaries: Donald Lutz.

Russbacher and Lutz were on the management staff of various CIA proprietaries, including Red Hill Savings and Loan and Hill Financial located at Red Hill, Pennsylvania, and at Silverado Bank Savings & Loan in Denver. Russbacher stated that the routing of the money funded by Shamrock was "From the Netherlands Antilles. And in turn came from Grand Cayman; that in turn came from the Southern Bank in Florida; that in turn came from Southern Savings and Loan in Illinois; which in turn came from National Brokerage Company."

"Where does the money originally come from? Is it from stolen Chapter 11 assets?" I asked. Russbacher replied, "That's part of it. It is a conglomeration of funds. It is what we call an all-purpose account. Arms shipments, the other stuff [drugs, weapons] that we were transporting back and forth. It is what we call the divisible surplus."

I asked if the federal judges he referred to, as recipients of these funds, were only Bankruptcy Court Judges, to which Russbacher replied, "No, that's not true. You have to include the DJs [U.S. District Judges] too."

"How is it determined the amount that each judge will get, and what judges are paid off?" I asked. Russbacher replied:

"It is predetermined. If you will remember from one of my earlier tapes, I told you that the judges receive their funds regardless of whether they have heard a case in six months or not."

"How do they determine which judges are recipients, what qualifies them to be on the payroll?" Russbacher replied, "The fact that they work hand-in- hand with the trustees, and they grant us full power to basically do what we [CIA] want in Chapter 11, 13, and 7 proceedings."

"Are there any other similar corporations in the United States like Shamrock?"

"No, Rodney, they are all funded from Shamrock. In other words, if you pull the plug on Shamrock, you have it all."

Russbacher explained how the recipients pick up the money. "They can get it overseas and pick it up, or they can go to Toronto and pick it up there, at the Royal Bank of Canada." Russbacher stated, "When they go in to make a withdrawal, they request to see the President or Chief Account officer." Russbacher explained that this scheme is part of Operation Woodsman, explained in earlier pages.

Russbacher explained that the recipient's available funds will be found on the bank's terminal screen and that "all they have to have is the account number. No ID is required. Just give them the account number and the four digit identification number." Russbacher stated that Royal Bank of Canada, Manufacturers Hanover Bank in New York, and Valley Bank in Arizona, cooperate in this scheme. Russbacher repeated what he had told me in the past: that funds would also be disbursed to the recipient judges, trustees, or law firms at gambling casinos, including MGM, Harrah's and Resort in Atlantic City, and Frontier, Stardust, and Horseshoe in Las Vegas. The CIA gave the money to the casino, which in turn gave gambling chips to the recipients when they arrived, after which the chips are cashed in for money. In some cases the casinos report the money as winnings and income tax withheld." (Rodney Stich, *Defrauding America* (Alamo California, 2005), Vol I p.132.)

10. http://www.thetruthseeker.co.uk/article.asp?ID=6042 .

11. The Bellamy quote is from Daily Express 5 Nov 2008 http://www.thetruthseeker.co.uk/article.asp?ID=9631 .
Some of this panic is described in a reference from politics.ie:
"Science magazine (Dec. 10, 1976) warned of "extensive Northern Hemisphere glaciation." Science Digest (February 1973) reported that "the world's climato-logists are agreed" that we must "prepare for the next ice age." The Christian Science Monitor ("Warning: Earth's Climate is Changing Faster Than Even Experts Expect," Aug. 27, 1974) reported that glaciers "have begun to advance," "growing seasons in England and Scandinavia are getting shorter" and "the North Atlantic is cooling down about as fast as an ocean can cool." Newsweek agreed ("The Cooling World," April 28, 1975) that meteorologists "are almost unanimous" that catastrophic famines might result from the global cooling that the New York Times (Sept. 14, 1975) said "may mark the return to another ice age." The Times (May 21, 1975) also said "a major cooling of the climate is widely considered inevitable" now that it is "well established" that the Northern Hemisphere's climate "has been getting cooler since about 1950."

"This cooling has already killed hundreds of thousands of people. If it contin-ues and no strong action is taken, it will cause world famine, world chaos and world war, and this could all come about before the year 2000."
-- Lowell Ponte "The Cooling", 1976

"If present trends continue, the world will be about four degrees colder for the global mean temperature in 1990, but eleven degrees colder by the year 2000...This is about twice what it would take to put us in an ice age."
-- Kenneth E.F. Watt on air pollution and global cooling, Earth Day (1970)

The continued rapid cooling of the earth since WWII is in accord with the in-crease in global air pollution associated with industrialization, mechanization, urbanization and exploding population.
-- Reid Bryson, "Global Ecology; Readings towards a rational strategy for Man", (1971)." (http://www.politics.ie/viewtopic.php?t=25189)
But if this is all a hoax then the question is why? My guess is that it is designed to give an intellectual backing for global, or supra national anyway, govern-mental institutions. Obviously the general public would welcome those type of

bodies to tackle this issue, because it would be important and because it clearly couldn't be tackled by national governments alone, so providing a very good raison d'etre for the existence of those institutions. I notice for example that the first pan EU fines are being proposed for environmental crimes.

12. Fr Denis Fahey, *The Rulers of Russia* (Dublin, 1938), p.100.

13. "FIANNA FÁIL has been compared by a well-known political insider as being like a McDonald's franchise but run with "a golden circle instead of golden arches".
The experienced commentator slated the Mount Street mandarins who pull Fianna Fáil's strings. "If you want to run for the party they'll roll out the hats, cups and straws. And if you succeed, well and good; but if you don't make it, then they don't want to know you."
Who's dishing the dirt on the Fianna Fáil leadership? None other than the former Mayor of Dublin, Royston Brady, Fianna Fáil's failed Euro candidate, who was routed by Sinn Féin's Mary Lou McDonald (absolutely no relation with the Big Mac empire).
Royston, now a morning chat-show host on Dublin radio station Newstalk 106, is telling anyone who'll listen that the Soldiers of Destiny have dragged his name through even more mud after his disastrous performance by not keeping their promise to pay his election debts. The deserted Soldier of Destiny has debts of between €50,000 and €100,000 a year after his glitzy, high profile campaign. Royston is also the baby brother of leader Bertie Ahern's right-hand man and chief fixer, Senator Cyprian Brady. Are they in Royston's "golden circle"?" (http://www.anphoblacht.com/news/detail/9115 . He revealed more information during a recent Late Late Show appearance.)

14. Just before the last election a FF Senator, Liam Fitzgerald, resigned over this: http://www.rte.ie/news/2007/0329/morningireland.html .

15. http://www.politics.ie/viewtopic.php?
t=24676&postdays=0&postorder=asc&start=24 .

16. Conor Cruise O'Brien, *Memoir My Life and Themes* (Dublin, 1998), p.175-176.

17. Michael Hopkinson ed., *The last days of Dublin Castle: The Diary of Mark Sturgis* (Dublin, 1999), p.43. The Roberts quote is from http://www.thetruthseeker.co.uk/article.asp?ID=9202 .

18. Ibid p.180.

19. Paul Larkin, *A very British Jihad* (Belfast, 2004), p.227.

20.

http://www.thirdworldtraveler.com/Pilger_John/Journalism_As_Propaganda.ht
ml .

21. As described at the 'Justice for the Forgotten' meeting in Dublin on the
27th June 2003.

22. Including Paul Foot and Duncan Campbell as you can read in his book:
Fred Holroyd and Nick Burbridge, *War Without Honour* (Hull, 1989), passim.

23. Paul Larkin, *A very British Jihad* (Belfast, 2004), p.227, p.283. The
reference to Holyroyd and Wallace is from Holroyd's book op.cit.

24. http://cedarlounge.wordpress.com/about-us/ .

25. http://www.politics.ie/viewtopic.php?t=23784 .

26. John Nalson, *An Impartial Collection of the Great Affairs of State* (London,
1683), Vol II p.809.

27. Chapter II of the *Sham Squire* from
http://www.chaptersofdublin.com/books/shamsquire/sham2.htm .

28. Dublin Evening Post No.1761 quoted in Chapter II of the *Sham Squire*
http://www.chaptersofdublin.com/books/shamsquire/sham2.htm .

29. Pearse St Library Gilbert Ms 218.

30. Pearse St Library Gilbert Ms 218 no.98.

31. Pearse St Library Gilbert Ms 218 No.102. For more on Walter Cox, who to
be fair suffered very severely at the hands of the govt., see http://www.chapter-
sofdublin.com/books/shamsquire/waltercox.htm which is an Appendix to the
Sham Squire book.

32. PRO CO 904/7 NLI M/F Pos 8165 p.482-507.

33. F.S.L.Lyons, *John Dillon* (London, 1968), p.460.

34. Daniel Sheehan, *Ireland since Parnell* (London, 1921), Chapter XIX
http://infomotions.com/etexts/gutenberg/dirs/1/3/9/6/13963/13963.htm .

35. See e.g. Lawrence Nugent WS 907 p.59 for references to the Independent-
Freeman feud.

36. Lawrence Nugent WS 907 p.180.

37. George Chester Duggan WS 1,076.

38. Michael Hopkinson ed., *The last days of Dublin Castle: The Diary of Mark Sturgis* (Dublin, 1999), p.61.

39. Kevin O'Shiel WS 1770 p.777. That's what O'Shiel says but oftentimes he has been described as the son of the proprietor.

40. Rev M.Curran WS 687 p.165.

41. Diarmuid Lynch, *The IRB and the 1916 Insurrection* (Cork, 1957), p.96 referring to c.1919/20.

42. P.J. Little WS 1769 p.38.

43. Diarmuid Lynch WS 4 in a section called 'Casement Pamphlet', this is c. post 1916.

44. *Irish World*, published in New York, 3rd March 1917 p.12.

45. Sean Farrelly WS 1734 p.22.

46. Ibid p.15. One Volunteer in Athboy seems to have been threatened by the Black and Tans in the guise of this gang, which shows its state connections (see Joseph Martin WS 1723 p.5).

47. Sean Boylan WS 1715 p.29. He was told that by Michael Hilliard TD, curiously enough.

48. Sean Hayes WS 172.

49. The media at one time printed a completely fictitious interview with Colonel Moore of the National Volunteers. (Lawrence Nugent WS 907 p.101).

50. Fr. Michael Browne WS 538.

51. Daniel Sheehan, *Ireland since Parnell* Chapter XVII
http://infomotions.com/etexts/gutenberg/dirs/1/3/9/6/13963/13963.htm .

52. P.J. Little WS 1769 p.39.

53. Interviewed on the *Conspiracy of Silence* video (available on youtube) which was made by Yorkshire Television in 1994 but was pulled before it could be broadcast.

54. Fred Holroyd and Nick Burbridge, *War Without Honour* (Hull, 1989), p.85.

The case is further described here: http://www.indymedia.ie/newswire.php?
story_id=68750#comment102800 .

55. Sean McPhilemy, *The Committee: Political Assassination in Northern
Ireland* (Boulder Colorado, 1999), p.303.

56. Johnston Brown, *Into the Dark* (Dublin, 2005).

57. Irish Independent 18 May 2007 p.10.

58. http://www.gavinsblog.com/?p=1984.

59. Brian Nugent, *Orwellian Ireland* (Co.Meath, 2008), Chapter 5, available at
http://oireland.tripod.com .

60. http://www.bilderberg.org/masons.htm#sweeney . The quote above it is
from the same source.

61. Liam Fay in the Sunday Times 1 Feb 2004
http://www.timesonline.co.uk/tol/newspapers/sunday_times/ireland/article1008
439.ece .

62. Eamonn Broy WS 1280 p.39.

63. Seamus Finn WS 857 p.2.

64. Eamonn Broy WS 1280.

65. Lawrence Nugent WS 907 p.163.

66. Lawrence Nugent WS 907 p.123.

67. T J McElligot, an RIC man who tried to set up an RIC union, WS 472 p.4
and 5. He says that the DMP "were highly organised at the time" to resist conscription, and that "I think John D. Nugent MP had a hand in it." The latter was
the Secretary of the AOH so you can be sure it was that organisation which had
infiltrated the DMP.

68. Colonel Winter's Correspondence PRO CO 904/177 p.392, available as
NLI M/F Pos 8480, containing a copy of the New Statesman 28 May 1921
p.205.

69. Sean Boylan WS 1715.

70. Joseph Martin WS 1723 p.5.

71. Sean Farrelly WS 1,734 p.13.

72. The quote is from Eugene Bratton WS 467 p.11 and the other references are from the same source. About Hodgett see also Michael Hilliard WS 1622 p.3.

73. Lawrence Nugent WS 907 p.194.

74. From Richard Walsh TD from Balla Co.Mayo who was on the Volunteer Executive WS 400. Yes I do think it means that the British government had some 'influence' in getting that order passed. Sin Scéal eile!lol

75. Sir Ormonde de Winter, *Winter's Tale: An Autobiography* (London, 1955), p.291.

76. TJ McElligot WS 472 p.5.

77. http://english.pravda.ru/science/tech/95965-0/ .
A Finnish victim describes here his opinion on the media:
"Why Does Nobody Speak Out?

Why doesn't anyone listen to, or grow concerned enough over these charges to investigate further?

A large part of the answer lies with how dependent we are on the major news media to shape our view of reality: if we see it on TV, hear it on the radio or read it in the newspaper it happened--if we don't, it didn't. Blacking out stories like mine--censoring them in fact--is the first line of defense the authorities take in defending or hiding their unethical and illegal activities.
...
Freedom of the press means the freedom not to print the news the powers don't want to be printed.

This blackout technique has a double effect: first, it allows the authorities to keep victims like myself isolated, out of contact with others who may have experienced the same things; second, if information does become public, like my using the posters and now this pamphlet for example, the person behind the publication is considered to be some kind of singular "kook" or "crazy", somebody beyond the fringe of "normal" society.

A second element playing a large part in cutting off investigation into claims like mine is the deliberately bizarre and frightening nature of it all. Telepathic terrorism with microwaves--none of us wants to believe it can happen.

When some people reacted to my posters and leaflets and called the RCMP to protest, the first tactic the police used was to sympathetically explain I was mentally ill. They advised the callers to just tear up my leaflet and forget about it.

...

Despite the evidences I had I was unable to get proper investigation from Finnish Police authorities. More obvious reason than simple stupidity is that Finnish authorities as authorities in many other countries, appreciate more good relations with another country than constitutional rights, health or even life of one Finnish citizen. If police don't investigate crimes of foreign intelligence services they won't find them."
(http://www.mindcontrolforums.com/v/mylife.htm)
There are 618 victims listed at that website here http://www.mindcontrolforums.com/victm-hm.htm and some 548 members in this forum saying much the same thing: http://groups.yahoo.com/group/mcforums/ . So like at some point people have to say that it is a greater 'conspiracy theory' that all these people have suddenly gone insane with these bizarre stories than it is just to believe them and admit that this type of thing is indeed going on?

78. http://www.countercurrents.org/us-paulinson161106.htm .

79. http://honoluluweekly.com/cover/2007/06/airborne/ .

80. Report prepared for the House of Commons page 3 http://www.ratical.org/radiation/DU/DUuse+hazard.pdf .

81. http://www.bilderberg.org/micwaves.htm .

82. Interviewed on the Investigative Journal 6 June 2007 http://arcticbeacon.com/audio/2007/2007-LRN/06-2007-LRN/ . There is a bit more about him here: http://www.campusactivism.org/phpBB2/viewtopic.php?p=3163&sid=ee9c3b79b17b34bf5649669e6f4fe50e .

83. http://en.wikipedia.org/wiki/Cessna_Citation_X .

84. http://en.wikipedia.org/wiki/Cessna_Citation_X .

85. http://en.wikipedia.org/wiki/SR-71_Blackbird .

86. http://news.bbc.co.uk/1/hi/programmes/newsnight/5079044.stm .

87. http://en.wikipedia.org/wiki/Aurora_aircraft .

88. A simple introduction to these technologies is given by Dr Allen Barker in his testimony to the National Bioethics Advisory Commission (set up by President Clinton to advise him on these issues) on 23rd Nov 1997: http://www.cs.virginia.edu/~alb/ugly/testimony.html . His website provides a lot more information: http://web.archive.org/web/20051218090804/www.datafilter.com/mc/ .

Also   see
http://web.archive.org/web/20060222234440/www.kimsoft.com/2000/nsa-
psy.htm . One interesting report on this was written by Gunther Russbacher, a
former CIA and ONI operative originally from Austria, showing the use of
mind   programming   in   those   organisations:
http://india.indymedia.org/en/2002/01/532.shtml . For some other links on
these strange technologies see Brian Nugent, Orwellian Ireland (Co.Meath,
2008), Chapter 3 footnote 117, available at http://oireland.tripod.com .
Note as well the description of one 'black' technology, possibly used by
Western intelligence agencies but not known to the general public, given in
detail at the end of Chapter 6 infra.

89. "Many leading members of the Masonic Order, were also commissioned
officers in the Volunteer movement, which perhaps explains the large Masonic
involvement amongst its membership. From the 1770s, when the Volunteer
companies were first raised there was encouragement from the leadership of
each new company to form their own Masonic lodge, and it was not unusual to
find the entire membership of a Volunteer company being in the same Masonic
Lodge." (Larry Conlon, *The influence of Freemasonry in East Cavan during
the rebellion of 1798*, Briefne VIII no.33 1997 p.791.)

90. "Evidence of clandestine or hedge Masonry being widespread amongst the
Defenders since their institution in 1782, are given in various historical accounts. There also exists evidence that their organisation was governed by a
'Grand Master' and operated a numerical lodge system similar to that of regular masonry."(ibid p.796.)

91. "The government spy, John Henry Smith, alias Bird, reporting from Belfast
to Dublin Castle, in 1796, wrote:
'there is scarcely a United Irishman who is not a Mason, nor a Mason who is
not both.'"(ibid p.805)

92. Larry Conlon, *The influence of Freemasonry in Meath and Westmeath in
the 18th century,* Riocht na Mídhe Vol IX no.3 1997 p.128.

93. WS 317 second part p.5.

94. A report of a speech by Sean Lemass in The Irish Independent 13 March
1929.

95. Daniel Sheehan, *Ireland Since Parnell* (London, 1921), Chapter XIX available at http://infomotions.com/etexts/gutenberg/dirs/1/3/9/6/13963/13963.htm .
That book goes into considerable detail describing the AOH. Another corroborating reference can be had from Kevin O'Shiel, the Tyrone barrister, who described it as "this secret, sectarian and political society" (Kevin O'Shiel
W.S.1770 p.139). As regards the whole atmosphere of the AOH dominated Ir-

ish Parliamentary Party for this period, I thought this letter from Archbishop Walsh of Dublin to Denis Gwynn of 25th May 1915 makes some pretty serious criticisms:

"I regret that, as one result of a radical change that has gradually been effected in Irish political affairs through the establishment of a working alliance between the "leaders" [his quotes] of the Irish Parliamentary Party and the late government, I have now, and for a considerable time, found it impossible to take any further interest in Irish politics. I am so saddened and, I must say, sickened by the change of front, the results of which I cannot but see in government appointment after government appointment, incontestably due to the active intervention of some of our leading politicians, that I have long since had to give up even the reading of articles or letters touching upon the political situation in Ireland. I never could have thought, 30 years ago when I came to Dublin as Archbishop, that I should live to see the great bulk of the nationalists of Ireland so hopelessly misled by the palpable misrepresentation of the obvious facts, as I see it today."(Rev M.Curran WS 687 p.15)

In the account written by Walsh's former secretary, Monsignor Curran, we are told that the Irish Party had abandoned "independent opposition as far back as 1906."(ibid p.302)

96. William O'Brien WS 1,766 p.75, and also see Donal Nevin, *James Connolly* (Dublin, 2005), p.624, which I think puts that question beyond any doubt.

97. The Labour leader, not to be mixed up with the other William O'Brien. (Diarmuid Lynch, *The IRB and the 1916 Insurrection* (Cork, 1957), p.101.)

98. Luke Kennedy WS 165 p.15.

99. Maud Gonne WS 317 p.13.

100. Valentine Jackson WS 409 p.4.

101. Tim Healy, *The Letters and Leaders of My Day*, Chapter III http://www.chaptersofdublin.com/books/THealy/healy3.htm .

102. Tim Pat Coogan, *Michael Collins: The Man Who Made Ireland* (New York, 2002), p.390 et seq. quoting Sean MacBride's interview in the Irish Press 16 and 18 October 1982.

103. Captain H.B.C. Pollard, *The Secret Societies of Ireland* (Kilkenny, 1998), p.62. The other references are from the same source except the Egan one which is from Tim Healy, *Letters and Leaders of my Day*, Chapter VI http://www.chaptersofdublin.com/books/THealy/healy6.htm.

104. Richard Walsh TD from Balla Co.Mayo WS 400 p.155.

105. Maud Gonne WS 317 p.13.

106. Richard Walsh WS 400 p.56.

107. Richard Walsh TD from Balla Co.Mayo WS 400 p.156.

108. Captain HBC Pollard, *The Secret Societies of Ireland* (Kilkenny, 1998), p.100.

109. Lawrence Nugent WS 907 p.89.

110. Michael Hopkinson, *Frank Henderson's Easter Rising: Recollections of a Dublin Volunteer* (Cork, 1998), p.2.

111. Irish Independent 9 Nov 1933 p.10.

112. Terence Brown, *Ireland: A Social and Cultural History, 1922 to the Present* (Cornell, 1985), p.119.

113. The Monnet quote is from Daily Telegraph 4 July 2007 p.21, and the MacDowell one: Vincent MacDowell, *Michael Collins and the Irish Republican Brotherhood* (Dublin, c.1997), p.x.

114. Although a well attended public meeting held in Dublin city centre this is the only media report of it made anywhere afaik: "An agreement was reached that all intelligence would be shared and that the 'Irish Government' would be vilified by the British (for the duration) for failing to deal with the IRA. This would create the impression that the Irish were soft and so would not be suspected of collaboration;" (Report in Saoirse on the Justice for the Forgotten meeting 27 June 2003 http://www.iol.ie/~saoirse/2003/jul03.htm .)

115. For which see Brian Nugent, *Orwellian Ireland* (Co.Meath, 2008), Chapter 4, available at http://oireland.tripod.com .

116. http://www.ashleymote.co.uk/topics.php?filter=2&sec=article&art_id=347 .

117. For which see Brian Nugent, *Orwellian Ireland* (Co.Meath, 2008), Chapter 4, available at http://oireland.tripod.com .

118. For this and the previous quote: Conor Cruise O'Brien, *Memoir My Life and Themes* (Dublin, 1998), p.176-180.

119. See http://www.indymedia.ie/article/81544 eg. at footnote 19.

120. http://users.cyberone.com.au/myers/red-symphony.html .

121. "In 1956, the arrangement was formalized in a written agreement, using the name "Gladio" for the first time. According to 1956 documents uncovered in Italy in 1990, Gladio was divided into independent cells coordinated from a CIA camp in Sardinia. These "special forces" included 40 main groups. Ten specialized in sabotage, six each in espionage, propaganda, evasion and escape tactics, and 12 in guerrilla activities. Another division handled the training of agents and commandos. These "special forces" had access to underground arms caches, which included hand guns, grenades, high-tech explosives, daggers, 60-millimeter mortars, 57-millimeter machine guns and precision rifles.
In 1956, Gen. Giovanni De Lorenzo was named to head SIFAR on the recommendation of U.S. Ambassador Claire Boothe Luce, the avidly anticommunist wife of the publisher of Time magazine. A key player in Gladio was now in place." (CAQ article on Gladio by Arthur E. Rowse http://www.mega.nu:8080/ampp/gladio.html .)

122. http://www.dowlingfamily.info/i1918su2.htm . Colonel Maurice Moore discussed the Joseph Dowling business in the Senate: http://historical-debates.oireachtas.ie/S/0001/S.0001.192307040010.html .

123. Catholic Bulletin July-December 1918 p.367-368.

124. Seán McConville, *Irish Political Prisoners, 1848-1922: Theatres of War* (2003), p.624.

125. Richard Walsh TD from Balla Co.Mayo WS 400 p.101.

126. Dillon to T P O'Connor 18 June 1918 quoted in F.S.L.Lyons, John Dillon (London, 1968), p.142.

127. The historian F.S.L.Lyons describes Dillon's analysis of government policy at the time:
"This is the first appearance of what one can only call the 'conspiracy theory' to which Dillon was to become increasingly addicted as time went on. The parliamentary party, he believed, had become a nuisance to Lloyd-George. On the one hand it stood in the way of a settlement based on the exclusion of Ulster. On the other hand, because it was a constitutional party, it could not be coerced. If, however, it became thoroughly rejected by the Irish people at the next election, then the way would be left clear to deal with the Ulster Unionists - presumably on the basis of six-county exclusion - and to impose, by force if need be, whatever settlement of the rest of Ireland seemed desirable to Britain. Because events were later to follow out this prediction with uncanny accuracy it is tempting to think Dillon's theory of conspiracy was well founded." [Although Lyons goes on to say that it wasn't a 'conspiracy', just blunder etc.]

(F.S.L.Lyons, *John Dillon* (London, 1968), p.426.) A few more references that show Dillon's opinions at that time: (I admit this number of references is overkill, but its fascinating to see his thinking with respect to these events.)

"In the three bye-elections fought since the beginning of the year - South Armagh, Waterford City, and East Tyrone - the parliamentary party had beaten off the challenge of Sinn Fein and more than held their own. But, as so often before, just at the very moment when the fortunes of Sinn Fein seemed on the wane, the Government had stepped in to revive them."(ibid p.434)

"There can be no doubt that L.G. has let loose Hell in Ireland and with our knowledge of his political instinct and intelligence it is very difficult to resist the conviction that his action during the last year has been all of a piece - a Machiavellian plot to escape from the necessity of granting Home Rule...[by discrediting the Irish Party in the US and:] make it safe for England to have a regular quarrel and stand up fight with Ireland." [The last point meaning that the UK wanted the situation militarised, because they would have been confident of crushing any Irish rebellion bearing in mind the huge size of the British army in 1918. It mightn't have worked out quite like that though!] (Dillon to T.P.O'Connor 23/24 April 1918 ibid p.435.)

"Considering the L.G.'s action in bringing forward his measure applying conscription to Ireland hot foot on our three successive victories over S.F. at the last three [bye] elections ...it is hard to escape from the conviction that he deliberately adopted the policy of destroying the constitutional party in Ireland and throwing the country into the hands of the Revolutionary Party. The purposes of such a policy are plainly apparent."(Dillon to C.P.Scott 24 April 1918 ibid, and from the same it is noted that most of Ireland apparently felt that somehow "the whole business has been an elaborate plot by LG.")

"L.G. is not a bit mad, but he is playing a very deep game, a game which necessitates the encouragement of S.F. up to a point sufficient to kill the Parliamentary Party and identify Irish nationalism with S.F. and pro-Germanism in the eyes of the world, and especially in the eyes of America. And he has played the game with immense skill and superb audacity. The S.F.'s, being utterly devoid of political sagacity, and overcharged with poetic fervour and wild unregulated enthusiasm, have played right into the hands of L.G. and Carson, who is now the practical dictator of Ireland."(Dillon to Shane Leslie 14 June 1918 ibid p.441.)

"I have a good deal of information going to show that the Castle authorities winked at and deliberately abstained from interfering with the outrageous intimidation of the S.F. bands on the polling day. And this combined with the well known fact that S.F. is riddled with spies and government agents will give you an idea of the devil's cauldron that L.G. has set going in Ireland."(Dillon to T.P.O'Connor 28/29 Dec 1918 ibid p.454.)

"L.G. will find that by betraying and killing the Irish Party he has not got rid of all his difficulties."(Dillon writing on Christmas Day 1918 ibid p.455.)

"This is a time when silence is golden. I will say, however, that I cannot understand the game the Government are playing. It seems to me that for a long while their policy has been directed to increasing and strengthening the revolutionary forces in Ireland." (John Dillon interviewed in The Times 25 May 1918.)

[Mentions the pursuit of a Republic which he says is pushing the country into catastrophe:] "believing as I do that there is a powerful and influential gang in the government of the country who are carrying on their present system of Government in Ireland with a view to producing such a catastrophe, and that this has been adopted as a deliberate policy, and as the safest method of killing the danger of Home Rule."(Dillon to Leslie 24 June 1919 Lyons op. cit. p.463.)

"But he [Lloyd-George] made one grave miscalculation - he utterly underestimated the forces he was letting loose in Ireland." [Which is an obvious reference to the surprising military capabilities and successes of the IRA during that winter.](Dillon to C.P.Scott 18 Jan 1921 ibid p.466.)

"But so far as I am able to judge, the military government which has been placed in complete control of Ireland by the policy of Sinn Fein, is determined, so far as power goes, to make any constitutional movement in Ireland impossible, and to goad the people to acts of violence and folly and to crime, in pursuance of a rule, and with a view to defeating any attempt to arrive at a rational and friendly settlement of the Irish question...[The policies of Sinn Fein] play into the hands of the military party, and all the bitterest enemies of the Irish people." (*The New Policy* a published letter by John Dillon of 30 December 1919.)

128. Speech given by John Dillon at Baillieboro Sunday 26 May 1918, printed in the Freeman's Journal. Btw I am not saying that the IPP, or maybe even Dillon, was free from corruption at this time because unfortunately it definitely wasn't. I think the British government needed to get rid of the IPP because it simply wouldn't have had any justification to deny it Home Rule after the War. The IPP had obviously lost a lot by backing the government in that war, not a few of whom fought in it, and they just couldn't be denied that promise of Home Rule which was supposed to take place after the War. With Sinn Fein they could use a whole pile of new excuses like not negotiating with 'terrorists' etc. For examples of that corruption, and their at times suspicious lack of real opposition towards the UK government, see Daniel Sheehan, *Ireland since Parnell* (London, 1921), available at http://www.gutenberg.org/files/13963/13963.txt , Colonel Maurice Moore,

History of the Irish Volunteers, serialised in the Irish Press in 1938 (e.g. 17 Feb that year), and the account by Diarmuid Coffey at WS 1248, which corroborates Moore's account.

129. I suspect Michael Collins, and this clique within the emerging new IRB, because of facts like the following which summarises what follows in Chapter 3:

a) He and his family were particularly friendly with the RIC in West Cork, not a crime of itself but somehow left out of most (?all) of his biographies.[i]

b) When in London in 1913 he became 'intimate' with Moya Llewelyn Davies, one of Lloyd George's personal secretaries. She and he are together then after that throughout 1919, 20, 21 and she described herself as a spy and a close adviser of Collins. Collins was also a good friend all this time with her husband Compton who "had been largely instrumental in getting Lloyd George into Parliament."[ii]

c) A fellow Cabinet Minister of Collins, Sceilg, pretty much accuses him of being a British agent. Sceilg, who's real name was John J. O'Kelly, was quite a learned intelligent figure as you can read in his biography by Brian P. Murphy, *The 'Catholic Bulletin' and Republican Ireland with Special Reference to J.J.O'Kelly (Sceilg)*(2005) passim.[iii]

d) We are told that he had many meetings and was well in with Alfred Cope from the date of Cope's arrival in Ireland, and specifically Richard Walsh says pre August 1920. Bear in mind that the war only really got going in the winter of that year (for example Tom Barry fires his first shot against the enemy on the 22nd Oct 1920) so Collins was closely involved with Lloyd George's main man in Ireland from the very beginning of the intensive phase of the conflict.[iv] Incidentally Collins is often said to have been very close to Eamonn Duggan, who preceded him as Director of Intelligence, and Duggan - believe it or not! - has been described as a close friend of Cope's throughout the conflict.[v]

e) Probably Collins' closest political adviser was Tim Healy, who was advising him at least since early 1918, during the time he was on the run, and at the Treaty negotiations etc. Healy was accused by Sean MacBride of being the Castle's biggest agent in Irish politics at that time.[vi]

f) A message was accidentally intercepted in August 1920 from a General in the 'Imperial Intelligence Service' writing to Collins.[vii]

g) Seamus Robinson TD, O/C of the 2nd Southern Division of the IRA and later a member of the Irish army's Bureau of Military History, felt that 'directions' were given whereby exaggerated and ultimately positive publicity was ordered to shine on Collins during the war. The most likely explanation for this would have to be that Collins himself was an agent.[viii]

h) Instead of it being the case that the British military were baying for Collins' blood at that time, and straining every sinew to lay hands on him, he even had a drink with a British captain at the time who well knew his identity.[ix]

i) Also his handling of IRA arms procurement,[x] unmasking of lesser spies,[xi] control of vital documents,[xii] and large operations like the French assassination attempt,[xiii] the Customs House and Stackumny railway attacks,[xiv] etc look a bit different in retrospect from the usual impression people have of Collins as "the man who won the war." So I'm a bit suspicious in any case!

Footnotes to the above.
(The WS numbers are witness statements in the National Archives in Dublin.)
i. Peter Folan WS 316.
ii. John J. O'Kelly (known as Sceilg) W.S. 384 p.66; Meda Ryan, *Michael Collins and the women who spied for Ireland* (Cork, 1996), p.21; Robert Barton WS 979 p.12; Pat Moylett WS 767 p.147; Peter Hart, *Mick: The Real Michael Collins* (Oxford, 2005), p.353.
iii. John J. O'Kelly W.S. 384 passim.
iv. Sceilg WS 384 p.60 et seq.; Richard Walsh WS 400 p.74; Lawrence Nugent WS 907 p.222-223.
v. James J O'Connor W.S. 1214 p.5 et seq. Even de Winter, the head of the British Secret Service in Dublin at the time, noted that "many of Cope's activities were centred in the person of E.J. Duggan, a solicitor whose office was situated close to the Castle gates." (Sir Ormonde de Winter, *Winter's Tale: An Autobiography* (London, 1955), p.341).
vi. Tim Pat Coogan, *Michael Collins: The Man Who Made Ireland* (New York, 2002), p.390 et seq. quoting Sean MacBride's interview in the Irish Press 16 and 18 October 1982; for the importance of Healy see e.g. Sean Moylan TD WS 505 p.2. and Richard Walsh TD WS 400 p.78.
vii. For a description of the message interception see Richard Walsh TD WS 400 p.74-76; and also Pat Moylett WS 767 p.51 who carried the message.
viii. Seamus Robinson TD, WS p.49.
ix. Sir William Darling, *So it looks to me* (London, 1952), p.212.
x. See e.g. the statement by Liam Mellows:
"He said he [Collins] was interfering with his job as Director of Purchases by buying arms across the water and paying more for them than he was. He was buying them, he said, not to use them but to prevent him (Liam) from getting them. This shocked me. .."(Peter Hart, *Mick: The Real Michael Collins* (Oxford, 2005), p.261 quoting Mrs Woods UCD P17a/150.) Richard Walsh, who was in England for a time trying to procure arms for the Mayo Brigade, said that:
"there seemed to be nothing being attempted by G.H.Q. agents, and it could not have been for want of money" (Richard Walsh TD from Balla Co.Mayo WS 400 p.131.)
xi. I think that the Quinlisk, Molloy and Jameson episodes are worth another

look in that respect for which see Richard Walsh WS 400 and Peter Hart, *Mick: The Real Michael Collins* (Oxford, 2005), p.237.

xii. De Winter describes in his memoirs the huge haul of documents that they recovered. His department compiled 'epitomes' of the most vital information in the documents and for the period Oct 1920-July 1921 they compiled 1,200 such epitomes, some over 200 pages long. He himself noted that "It was fortunate that the Irish had an irresistible habit of keeping documents." (Sir Ormonde de Winter, *Winter's Tale: An Autobiography* (London, 1955), p.303-304.)

xiii. This was described by Seamus Robinson who, along with some others based in Tipperary, used to assist in Dublin operations. He wasn't impressed with Collins' role at all:
"The first time I found Mick Collins to be a bit of an artful dodger, was when he arranged the first, the "phoney" attack on French."(Seamus Robinson TD WS p.47-50).

xiv. Both being large operations that went suspiciously wrong. For Stackumny see Matthew Barry WS 932 where Collins' military advise is found to be a bit perplexing in retrospect.

130. Lawrence Nugent WS 907 p.242.

131. Darrell Figgis, *Recollections of the Irish War* (London, 1927), p.218, 233, 245.

132. At a meeting in Dublin addressed by Webster Tarpley.
I think these comments on the media are by Noel O'Gara talking about the infomation that came his way with respect to the Yorshire Ripper case:
"Nobody wants to admit to being a fool. Nobody wants to admit to the extent to which we rely on the mass media for our perceptions of the world.
...
What does that imply for all the other things we consider to be facts because some other dirty little c--- walked out in front of a TV camera and recited some other pack of lies to us...? This changes everything. To face up to the Yorkshire Ripper cover up is a life changing experience. That is why people avoid it. It happened.
...
It reveals the degree to which we all have been such gullible fools in terms of what is presented to us in the mass media."
(http://www.indymedia.ie/article/76471)

133. From Carl Bernstein, using mainly revelations that came out during the Church Committee Hearings in the US:
"The Agency's relationship with the Times was by far its most valuable among newspapers, according to CIA officials. From 1950 to 1966, about ten CIA employees were provided Times cover under arrangements approved by the newspaper's late publisher, Arthur Hays Sulzberger. The cover arrangements were

part of a general Times policy—set by Sulzberger—to provide assistance to the CIA whenever possible.

Sulzberger was especially close to Allen Dulles. "At that level of contact it was the mighty talking to the mighty," said a high-level CIA official who was present at some of the discussions. "There was an agreement in principle that, yes indeed, we would help each other. The question of cover came up on several occasions. It was agreed that the actual arrangements would be handled by subordinates... The mighty didn't want to know the specifics; they wanted plausible deniability.

...

CIA officials cite two reasons why the Agency's working relationship with the Times was closer and more extensive than with any other paper: the fact that the Times maintained the largest foreign news operation in American daily journalism; and the close personal ties between the men who ran both institutions.

Sulzberger informed a number of reporters and editors of his general policy of cooperation with the Agency. "We were in touch with them—they'd talk to us and some cooperated," said a CIA official. The cooperation usually involved passing on information and "spotting" prospective agents among foreigners.

Arthur Hays Sulzberger signed a secrecy agreement with the CIA in the 1950s, according to CIA officials—a fact confirmed by his nephew, C.L. Sulzberger. However, there are varying interpretations of the purpose of the agreement: C.L. Sulzberger says it represented nothing more than a pledge not to disclose classified information made available to the publisher. That contention is supported by some Agency officials. Others in the Agency maintain that the agreement represented a pledge never to reveal any of the Times' dealings with the CIA, especially those involving cover. And there are those who note that, because all cover arrangements are classified, a secrecy agreement would automatically apply to them.

...

According to Wayne Phillips, a former Times reporter, the CIA invoked Arthur Hays Sulzberger's name when it tried to recruit him as an undercover operative in 1952 while he was studying at Columbia University's Russian Institute. Phillips said an Agency official told him that the CIA had "a working arrangement" with the publisher in which other reporters abroad had been placed on the Agency's payroll. Phillips, who remained at the Times until 1961, later obtained CIA documents under the Freedom of Information Act which show that the Agency intended to develop him as a clandestine "asset" for use abroad." (http://tmh.floonet.net/articles/cia_press.html)

The CIA is said to be able to intervene to censor all articles pre publication: http://digg.com/politics/New_York_Times_op_ed_article_censored_by_the_CIA_w_pic .

"In a Rome courtroom on November 10th, 1982, a close friend of Moro's testified that the former prime minister was threatened by ...[the former] U.S.

Secretary of State. The meteoric rise of the man the witness named as Kissinger will be dealt with later. It will be recalled that Prime Minister Moro was kidnaped by the Red Brigades in 1978 and subsequently brutally shot to death. It was at the trial of members of the Red Brigades that several of them testified to the fact that they knew of high-level U.S. involvement in the plot to kill Moro. ... The witness who delivered the bombshell in open court was a close associate of Moro's, Gorrado Guerzoni. His explosive testimony was broadcast over Italian television and radio on November 10th, 1982, and printed in several Italian newspapers yet this vital information was suppressed in the U.S. Those famous bastions of freedom with a compelling right to know, the Washington Post and the New York Times, did not think it important to even print a single line of Guerzoni's testimony.

Nor was the news carried by any of the wire services or television stations. The fact that Italy's Aldo Moro had been a leading politician for decades, and who was kidnaped in broad daylight in the spring of 1978, all of his bodyguards butchered in cold blood, was not deemed newsworthy, even though Kissinger stood accused as an accomplice to these crimes? Or was the silence BECAUSE of Kissinger's involvement?"
(Dr John Coleman, *Conspirator's Hierarchy* (1992), p.4-5)

There is also this reference from Paul Palango, former National Editor of the Globe and Mail newspaper, in Canada:
"We think we live in a safe, open society, but at the same time so many Canadians seem to believe that it is dangerous to ask questions or raise issues that might strike at the heart of something darker going on within the country.
....
In my career as a journalist and author, I've seen how power is wielded in the shadows.
....
In that investigation, I was among the first—if not the first—to uncover and recognize large-scale accounting fraud. I mistakenly believed that government, police, the banks, and the accounting industry would rush to the rescue, but I had not come to appreciate how much the world had changed in such a short period of time. The mainstream media, fed to the point of satiation on news releases and marketing by governments, business, and themselves, did not want to hear the story. In fact, they were more interested in attacking me.

I was made out to be the enemy, even though the company in question had hired private investigators to conduct surveillance on me and my family. Attempts were made to steal our trash. Someone tried to poison our dogs. My family lived in fear, and our circumstances were severely reduced, but we wouldn't give in. It took me a decade to fight that lawsuit off and win a favourable settlement.

The two books I had written during this period were not published because of

80

the outstanding litigation. The roaring tigers of the media and publishing world had been reduced to cowering kittens and stenographers.

...

Like a vast colony of J. Alfred Prufrocks, far too many of us are afraid of our shadows, of making a scene or getting peach juice on our clothing. We are caught up in our creature comforts, our ATVs, iPhones, and scripted reality television, willfully oblivious that everything we have can be taken away at a moment's notice, because no one really seems to believe in anything but the easy life.

'Dispersing the Fog' is more than the story of Maher Arar; it is an investigation and analysis of the past 30 years of Canadian politics. It conclusively shows, based upon hard and irrefutable evidence, that we have lost control of our own country. There is an appearance of democracy, but real democracy and accountability are an illusion.

...

I was booked to do a number of shows on national television—CTV's Canada AM, the CBC's Sunday Morning—and the CBC radio syndicate, among others. Each cancelled at the last minute. Why? We can't find out. My public-relations person, Pat Cairns, says she has never seen a media response like that. She's astonished. It's clear that not only my well-researched Arar story but everything else in the book—about the RCMP, Jean Chrétien, Brian Mulroney, Stephen Harper, and the state of Canada—is making too many people nervous.

Although the media is aware of what I have written, no one, to my knowledge, has bothered to confirm or refute what I report. To do so would only open a can of worms that no one—the government, political parties, or, especially, the mainstream media—wants to touch.

...

I have been tarred as a conspiracy theorist—the lowest of the low—which is the Canadian way of shooting the messenger. I've even heard reporters say that my Arar story is not credible because I do not have "official sources" confirming it, as if the government would admit to what it has done. Many of the facts I dug out were unknown to the original RCMP investigators in the Arar case, hidden from them by their own force. The great irony is that the Canadian media got sucked into the Arar story because it relied religiously only on official sources who manipulated it into a box. The facts speak for themselves—the   emperor   is   in   the   buff."
(http://www.thetruthseeker.co.uk/article.asp?ID=9835)

134. This is from ex BBC journalist Tony Gosling: "That the corporation was far too controlled, particularly in its news and documentary coverage, by the Foreign Office and by Downing Street. I know this because a friend worked as a temp for several months in the TV newsroom and explained to my horror that she was putting calls through regularly from top government officials and passing messages on to the editors about the best angle to take on sensitive

news stories."(http://www.bilderberg.org/milne.htm)

John Pilger: "While Alan Johnston was being held, I was asked by the BBC World Service if I would say a few words of support for him. I readily agreed, and suggested I also mention the thousands of Palestinians abducted and held hostage. The answer was a polite no; and all the other hostages remained in the memory hole. Or, as Harold Pinter wrote of such unmentionables: "It never happened. Nothing ever happened... It didn't matter. It was of no interest." "(http://www.thetruthseeker.co.uk/article.asp?ID=6919)

This view is from the former British ambassador to Uzbekistan, Craig Murray: "Ask yourself - when is the last time you saw an anti-war voice, as opposed to a pro-war "military" or "security" expert, asked by the BBC to comment on a Middle East development? Yet the majority of people in this country are against the war. If they want an ex-diplomat, they go for pro war cheerleaders Pauline Neville Jones or Christopher Meyer, even though eight out of ten ex British Ambassadors are against the war... No 10 have a policy of regularly putting pressure on news outlets, and the BBC in particular."
(http://www.craigmurray.co.uk/archives/2007/04/video_killed_th.html)

A letter written by Ashley Mote MEP to the BBC: "I referred in my original letter to the 40.4 million euros provided by the European Investment Bank [to the BBC] in 2002, and the 96.46 million provided by the same source the following year. These sums were in the form of loans, and are listed as such on the EIB website. In addition to these loans to BBC subsidiaries, another 240 million euros has been 'loaned' by the EIB to other broadcasting and production units in the UK since 1989.
Several questions arise: on what terms of repayment, over what period and at what rates of interest? Are these soft loans - meaning will they be written off quietly in a few years time because you know (and the rest of us can make an intelligent guess) that the BBC will never be in a position to repay such sums and is not expected to do so. Even the EIB's own website admits they were made under the "most favourable of terms...financing capital projects according to the objectives of the Union". It goes on to declare that one of its objectives is to "contribute towards the integration of member countries"!"
(http://www.ashleymote.co.uk/topics.php?filter=24&sec=article&art_id=319)

More from Ashley Mote MEP:
"Let me cite a few examples of the pro-EU bias which breaches the BBC's Royal Charter.

1. Listeners were invited to nominate the one piece of legislation they would most like to be repealed. The European Communities Act 1972, which took the UK in to what was then the European Community, was far ahead of all other nominations. The result of the poll was never broadcast.

2. The BBC's director general Mark Thompson admitted to the Daily Mail a lack of objective coverage and "serious flaws" in BBC coverage of EU matters. Nothing noticeable has since been done to improve the situation.

3. The BBC Trust tells me in writing it has nothing to do with the EU, later publishes an annual report entitled "Forging the Union" directly contradicting the fact, and has only last month been quoted on the BBC itself as "representing licence-payers"! Opaque, if not downright deceitful.

4. Within days of the first EIB loan the BBC's then Economics Editor broadcast a series of interviews and news items from around the EU about the prospects for the euro. Balanced and objective they were not. They were so embarrassingly deferential that any news editor worthy of the name would have binned them without a second thought.

5. During the signing of the Nice Treaty, within the hearing of many potential interviewees from the UK, the BBC producer on site instructed his crew not to record or report the significant demonstrations against the treaty going on all around them. Opposition was quite literally whitewashed from the screens of British viewers, whose money funds the EU and your bank in the first place.

6. Jonathon Chapman, described at the time as a senior BBC World News Reporter, told the Malta Press Club in March 2004 that "The BBC's job is to reflect the European perspective...and make the news less sceptical. That is why the BBC has such a large bureau in Brussels"."
(http://www.ashleymote.co.uk/?p=831)

135. British ambassador to Ireland writing to the Foreign Office 2 Oct 1969 http://www.indymedia.ie/article/64231. More on the correspondence here: http://www.spinwatch.org/content/view/182/8/ .

136. http://www.anphoblacht.com/news/detail/4342 .

CHAPTER 2

The 1641 Rebellion: A triple tiered Conspiracy?

The murky beginnings of the Irish rebellion of 1641 is possibly another good example of a complex conspiracy in action that mimics the pattern outlined in the previous chapter. Again I think that there are three stages in our understanding of this history, with some truth resting in each scenario:

1) The normal account of the time and since, which was that the Irish rebels were acting on their own iniative seeking to rid the wrongs of the Ulster Plantation.

2) That the King and the Royalist side of the upcoming English Civil War were somehow involved in the rebellion, which is now what a lot of Irish historians think.

3) I would contend that in fact the Parliamentarian side, and their national and international allies, were secretly involved in provoking and spreading this revolt.

Maybe it was like a triple tiered conspiracy with the second ring manipulating in a way the first, and the third manipulating both! I number each scenario below and have also included some references to the way the Irish people had great difficulty in setting the historical record straight. Anyway pull up a chair and see what you think...

1) On the evening of the 22nd Oct 1641 some of the dispossessed Irish of Ulster, led by Phelim O'Neill, rose up in rebellion against the government. This fatal step changed the whole political complexion of Ireland for centuries to come. In a few years time virtually all the Irish Catholic owned land in Ireland was taken from them as pay back for their supposed terrible deeds during this allegedly bloody rebellion. Of course it has been presented as a genuine uprising in the face of serious grievances, and genuine grievances they certainly had as even Dr George Leyburn notes, a friend of the Queen's who actually had a different view on the origin of the rebellion:

> "And all this, as things were disposed, was no hard matter to compass: For the Irish had not enjoyed such a pleasant bondage under the English, but that they had contracted ill-will enough against their masters, besides which, other things contributed."[1]

Particularly the British government had again betrayed the Irish by delaying implementing the 'Graces', religious toleration for the Catholic religion and other concessions, that the Irish had been promised long since. They had also confiscated Irish lands in Ulster, and given them to Scottish immigrants, and were proposing to do the same for Connaught. So yes a large part of truth I think is contained in the well known story of that rebellion, a simple enough tale of Irish people fighting back against their oppressors.

But imho this is by no means the whole story. The mysterious origins of this rebellion have been debated and argued about for centuries, starting with Sir John Temple's 1646 account of the 'conspirators':

> "This, as all such works of this nature, had its foundations laid in the dark, and sealed-up, no doubt, with many execrable oaths, the great engines of these times, bind-up the consciences, as well as the tongues, of men from discovery. Besides, they knew well enough, that the plot (being most abominable in itself, and to be carried-on with such detestable cruelty), would, even if it should take effect and be fully executed, (though success commonly gives to all other treasons applause and highest commendation), undoubtedly render the first authors, as well as the bloody actors of it, most odious and execrable to all posterity. Therefore it is not much to be wondered-at, that the first beginnings (which were so mysterious and obscurely laid,) should remain as yet concealed with so great obstinacy."[2]

2) I think that there is in fact wheels within wheels in the above quote. Temple is lingering on this subject of mysterious conspirators as part of the usual sly Parliamentarian tactic of hinting that the King himself was involved in the revolt. This was part of a pattern where they managed to slander the King, and particularly the Catholic Queen, with having some underhand role in this 'massacre' - as the Parliamentarians always described it - of the Irish Protestants.[3] Hence Charles I was supposedly the kind of person who couldn't protect English or Scottish Protestants, and their liberties, and so was unfit to be their King. It is usually felt that this sort of line, spread by a huge media pamphleting campaign, finally destroyed the position of the King, leading to the beginning of the English Civil War.

Most of the time historians have seen the vested interests the Puritans had in spreading this propaganda, and tended to discount any truth in these rumours. But in fact from the beginning it has been remarkable how much evidence there is that the King did secretly support the rebellion, although this didn't stop centuries of historians dismissing it as just another 'conspiracy theory'. Particularly when the Irish rebels came forward with a Commission from the King authorising the rebellion, and sealed with the great seal of Scotland, it rapidly became known as the 'forged commission' as part of this dismissive attitude some historians took to these murky allegations. Also when the Marquis of Antrim's statement of 1650 came to light, which details how Antrim was asked by the King to raise a rebellion in cooperation with others like Ormond, this again was dismissed as a convenient lie at the time when Antrim wanted to endear himself to Cromwell. They took this view even though it can be combined with numerous other accounts of the King's involvement.[4]

This historiographical viewpoint has survived until an article by Jane Ohlmeyer was published in 1992.[5] She wrote a biography of Antrim and came to the conclusion that he was telling the truth in 1650. This has now led Irish historians to look again at these conspiracies, like Tadhg ó hAnnracháin in his book on Rinuccini:

"[the 1641 plotting] in which members of the Old English community also participated and which may have enjoyed at least a tacit element of approval from the embattled monarch himself."[6]

The logic of this view basically is that the King was getting desperate in 1641 as his power was being slowly undermined by Parliament. (Including his power over Ireland because it was now ruled by two Lord Justices who were close to the Parliamentarians.) So if he could just get the Irish nobility, who were always very Royalist, to take back the country in his name, from these Parliamentarian figures, then he could have at least one place that he could rely on. This included getting control of the Irish army which had been raised by Strafford and was one of the only important standing armies now existing that the King could possibly call upon. That the King was really only manipulating the Irish Catholics you can see in this quote from the aforementioned account by Dr Leyburn:

"That, how the King's affections to Catholics stood, they did not know, but this was manifest, that if he could have compounded with his Parliament, he would have sacrificed them all."(p.23)

This viewpoint is then if you like a second stage in unravelling these conspiracies. Clearly the plain headline news accounts of the rebellion are now known to be false, there was some underhand plotting involved by the bigshots in the UK, not just in Ireland. Somehow at least the royalist side was mixed up in all this.

3) But maybe this is just stage two in this process, the real truth is even more conspiratorial in my opinion. Possibly the real key to understanding these events is to view the international context and on that score I will begin by quoting Dr John Nalson, a contemporary English historian and MP. Here he is writing about the way that the Parliament blamed the King, while he instead opts for another 'great person':

> "There were indeed some great persons I doubt not who gave the rebels all the countenance, encouragement and assistance they could possibly; but I am for setting the saddle upon the right horse. Cardinal Richelieu, I make no doubt, who was in his time the great incendiary of Europe, and who had a great share in the management of the Scottish rebellion, as before hath been observed, had also, a very great influence both upon the rebellion in Ireland, and that which followed it in England [i.e. the revolt of Parliament against the King], as in due time I shall endeavour to make it appear. ..[then presents a letter that Mr James Wishert communicated to Mr Pym showing Richelieu's support for the rebellion, which Pym showed no interest in exposing..]...there may be dangerous confederacies even between pretenders to reformation [meaning the Parliamentarians and the Scots], and the greatest papists though for different ends, the reformers to secure themselves from justice by embroiling the nation, and the popish ministers of foreign nations, to keep us busy at home, that so we might not be at leisure to keep the balance even [the Balance of Power in Europe], as the Kings of England have ever had the honour to do; but that our hands being behind us by domestic divisions."[7]

To explain this it is necessary to sketch the international situation I think. The rebellion actually occurs right in the middle of the 30 years war in Europe. This war in essence was between the Catholic powers of the Empire (mostly Germany) and Spain (which controlled Belgium and a large overseas empire) against the northern European Protestant powers in northern Germany, Holland, Denmark and Sweden. Cardinal Richelieu's France was the exception in that it fought on the Protestant side, ostensibly because it wanted to prevent being encircled by this German Empire-Spanish alliance. Of course this was an enormous conflict with all these countries fighting themselves to a standstill at this point. Men, military supplies and food were all in short supply as this all consuming war took its toll everywhere.

In a way then the position of the UK and Ireland is one of a kind of suspicious, to the combatants, neutrality. Both sides were constantly wondering what were the Stuarts going to do, will they intervene and if so on which side? I guess the atmosphere would be analogous to the USSR and the USA going to war in the 60s say and China remaining neutral. After the combatants have used up most of their supplies they would both be vulnerable to the power of China. You can imagine that if this ever happened that Beijing would be crawling with intelligence agents from both sides hoping to influence the government.

Such was the kind of atmosphere that existed then with respect to Charles I and the combatants in Europe. An added complication to this was the potential role of the UK navy. You see, as pointed out, Belgium was Spanish territory and was wedged between the allies France and Holland. As you can appreciate a lot of the battles in the Low Countries depended therefore on the capacity of the Spanish to communicate by sea to Belgium, and indeed on the ability of the French to link by sea to the Dutch. Any half glance at a map will instantly tell you that Britain's navy could quickly jeopardise either of these two groups from communicating with their allies through the English Channel, hence again the importance the combatants placed on the attitude of the British government.

My contention then, along with Dr Nalson's, is that at some early point in this saga, say 1636, Cardinal Richelieu took the view that if you are not with me you are against me. According to Francoise de Motteville, a friend of the Queen's at court, Richelieu:

"thought it absolutely necessary for the weal of France
that that prince [Charles] should have trouble in his
country."[8]

From that time on then he was constantly looking at ways to destabilise Charles I and his kingdoms.[9] Probably too he was allied to the Dutch in this destabilisation.[10] The reason is that at this time Charles had set upon creating an enormous navy, one that would dwarf any other navy in northern Europe. This was bound to have troubled the Dutch who had such a large overseas empire at this time. Hence I think it is reasonable to suppose that they might have been cheering on the Parliamentarians when they were agitating against the King, especially when they objected to the ship tax which was to pay for this navy.

My guess therefore is that rather than focusing on all the constitutional and religious aspects of Charles' woes, the chances are that it was these international intrigues which really lay behind his difficulties. So in short I would propose that there was throughout this time (1636-42) an alliance between Richelieu in France (an experienced plotter, the brains of the affair), the Dutch (crucial for transport for the allies across these islands, and possibly for money), the Parliamentarians in London and the Covenanting Scots in Edinburgh, and this alliance's goals were simply to destroy the stability of Charles and his throne. It's not difficult to see the stages through which this plot progressed. It starts with Richelieu funding Leslie, the Scottish general, c.1636, leading to Charles running out of funds trying to put down the Scottish revolt, and then having to recall Parliament to raise money, leading to the sorry state he was in in 1641.

Which brings us back to the atmosphere that existed before the Irish rebellion. During those months relations between Charles and the Parliament had deteriorated to the point where both sides probably felt that a Civil War was inevitable. As that spectre rose on the horizon the obvious question Charles had to ask was where was he going to get an army to fight for him? He spent a lot of time trying to persuade the Scots, who controlled a large army, to support him, he was involved in numerous intrigues and episodes involving the London militia, the royal strongholds of the Tower of London, and the arsenal at Hull, but was thwarted every time. His only hope now lay in Ireland. After all Ireland was Catholic, which meant that it was unlikely to support the extreme Protestant stand taken by the Puritans and the Scots. It also had this large standing army raised by Strafford and armed with a large stand of military supplies stored in Dublin Castle.

This though was also obvious to our plotters, the French - Dutch - Scots - and Puritans, who were all this time one step ahead of the King. Consequently their gaze must have fallen on Ireland as well, time to set off another of these revolts, to throw things into confusion before the King can secure that army and supplies? (There was quite a diplomatic dogfight going on with respect to that army, and the question of whether it might go abroad, alas too tedious to go into.) Bear in mind those Lord Justices, and the minority Protestant immigrant community, were the only blocks standing in the way of the King here. The Irish Parliament, and probably the army itself, was overwhelmingly Royalist.

As part then of this ongoing pattern of destabilising Charles I think these groups plotted to tear off this other chunk of his dominions, to follow on from their successful efforts in Scotland and indeed in London itself. There are also more specific reasons why each group might have wanted this revolt:

French - All throughout this long summer there were ongoing plans afoot to send this Irish army to fight with Spain on the continent. (The

Spanish were going to pay Charles handsomely for the privilege.) Then when the rebellion broke out it caught fire among the men of this army and those plans came to nought, which was obviously in the interests of France. Also Richelieu was careful to assist the Irish soldiers in the service of Spain to come to Ireland to join the rebellion and by these simple means he rid himself of some of the best soldiers in his opponents army. This was especially true of Owen Roe O'Neill, a general who even at that time had a high military reputation which ended up even higher after his exploits in Ireland.

Scots - The Covenanting Scots were at all times nervous about the potential threat from Strafford's army in Ireland. Strafford had anyway raised the army with a view to attacking the Scots, using possibly the short sea journey from Antrim, the soft under belly of the Scots military position. Again the rebellion put paid to any plans like that. Also the Scots had got quite a taste of Irish land already and some of their leaders probably wanted to get more of it using the excuse of confiscations resulting from the new rebellion.[11]

Puritans and the Dutch - My guess is that the Parliamentarians wanted Irish land to fund their side of the upcoming Civil War. Very shortly after the rebellion broke out, too short for it to be a new idea I think, the Parliament mortgaged the lands of the Irish Catholics to London bankers and used the money to fund their war effort. I wonder too if Holland, a natural ally of the Parliamentarians, might have instigated some of these banking arrangements, which seem to fit better with the advanced banking systems used in Amsterdam at that time. The rebellion was the trigger for these banking instruments to kick in, and they no doubt felt that in due course they could always send over a Puritan or Scottish army and destroy the Irish rebels without too much difficulty, and then reclaim their land, which is what eventually happened.[12]

Hence in 1641 as Charles in still wondering where he is going to get his army these conspirators are already way ahead of him in conspiring to destabilise Ireland, to deny him that army and for these other reasons. Richelieu then is busy working with the O'Neills, and others in France, trying to persuade them to rebel; the Parliamentarians are wining and dining the Irish MPs who had come over to London to give evidence against Strafford; and the Scots are writing letters across into Ulster to the Irish nobility promising all kinds of aid if they would rebel, all beavering away trying to 'invite and instigate' the Irish rebellion, as one contemporary Irish historian said of the Parliamentarians.[13]

But they have a problem, we may surmise, this is proving something of a hard sell. Richelieu is too far away to be persuaded of his overwhelming power, after all the Irish had been waiting decades for the mythical help from the Catholic powers of Europe, and it was usually a good bet that it wouldn't arrive! The problem with the Covenanting Scots and the Puritans was that they were clearly anti-Catholic, which naturally complicated an alliance with the Catholic Irish. Also the Scots immigrants had taken a lot of Irish land in Ulster, and both they and the new English settlers were swamping the natives a little bit, leading to some tensions no doubt. Here is one contemporary Irish poet complaining of their lot:

> "Where have the Gaels gone? What is the fate of the mirthful throngs? I catch no glimpse of them within sight of the green land of Gaoidheal...We have in their stead an arrogant impure crowd, of foreigner's blood, of the race of Monadh - there are Saxons there, and Scotch."[14]

This again didn't augur too well for the popularity of the Scots, and the immigrant English, at this time in Ireland.

They needed something else to really get this going and my guess is that the King provided it. The fact is that one of the most startling aspects of this period is the degree to which these enemies of the King were able to manipulate him to do their bidding for them. It seems many of the King's closest advisers were secretly working for his enemies, and were using their position to bend the King's will their direction - possibly the Earl of Holland, the big Scottish figures and maybe even Ormond. This is graphically illustrated by the King's signature on the death warrant on the Earl of Strafford, the King's closest ally and friend.

It must have been obvious to the conspirators that if they could somehow get the King's consent for such a rebellion then the Irish, almost entirely Royalist, would agree to it. It isn't difficult to imagine how they could have done this. Advisers, ostensibly looking after the King's interests, could talk about how easy it would be for a few key nobility to just organise a bit of a coup and get those arms in Dublin Castle and, they would claim, the King's position would be transformed for the better. In fact it might have been the case that they could combine this talk with vague plans to seize arms from the arsenals in Edinburgh and London simultaneously, so in one fell swoop hoping to turn the tables on the Parliamentarians. The Scots might particularly have been working on the King that way during his sojourn in Scotland that autumn. Maybe then this works, he agrees to send Antrim on that mission and in Scotland they land his signature on the famous commission. I appreciate that this account of the King's role is pure speculation but it seems to fit nicely with the available evidence, which does show, in my opinion, that the above conspirators were the real plotters of the rebellion,[15] but also shows this royal involvement.

With his fingerprints on the Irish rebellion they now had ensnared the King, who must have now found that he made a terrible mistake. These plotters let loose the dogs of the media, hyping up the rebellion and even darkly hinting that the King and Queen were 'soft' on the rebels. The conspirators who were actually responsible for the plot were the exact same people who flooded the media with gory details about it, accusing someone else of it.

Now the King is stuck. Although not of course involved in any massacre, which never actually took place I don't think, he nonetheless did have some connection to the 'plot', and so was vulnerable to being blackmailed about it by the Parliamentarians. The more hype circulated about the rebellion the more a bead of sweat must have been visible on the brow of the King! The aforementioned Dr Leyburn, who among other things was sent on a special mission to Ireland in 1647 to try and stop Dublin being handed over to the Parliament, is surely hinting here that the King was blackmailed this way, and ended up doing whatever the Parliament asked him to do with respect to Ireland:

"[The Puritans trying to stop the King from getting help from Ireland] had no so good way [to do this than] to affright the king from making use of that assistance, as by all means they could possible, to thrust the Irish into rebellion, and then to accuse the King, the Queen being a Catholic, as the author of it; from whence divers things would follow.

...Secondly, the King having this principle infused into him, that nothing was so necessary to his safety, as the clearing himself and the Queen from that Imputation, would be so far from seeking assistance that way, as he should not dare to refuse join with them [the Parliamentarians], in such Acts of Parliament as they should propose to him, for the better perfecting those designs; provided the pretence were the repressing or punishing of that rebellion, by which it would come to pass that they would levy what forces, or raised what monies they pleased, which afterwards they might convert to what uses they thought fit."[16]

So as the months go by you have a King actually paralysed in his Irish policy by this fear of being found out. This I think explains the anomaly of why he stuck with Ormond, and his other Irish officials, long after it became obvious that they were secretly working for the Parliamentarians.[17] Ormond himself no doubt had proof of the King's involvement in the rebellion, seeing as he himself was in the thick of it as shown by Antrim's account and other sources.[18] So all the King could do was somehow work around Ormond, by giving Commissions to people like Antrim and Glamorgan making them de facto Lord Deputies while never actually firing Ormond as the official Lord Deputy, because he was afraid of this potential blackmail. If true it was a crazy situation of course and I think goes a long way to explain his own downfall - which could have been prevented if he could have properly mobilised a united Catholic royalist Ireland - and the ruin of the first independent Irish parliament.

Conspiratorial Pattern of the Confederate Wars in Ireland.

I appreciate that much of that account involves speculation but I respectfully submit that it is at least one way of connecting the dots across the known facts, and maybe better than the current received wisdom which accepts the King's involvement but which doesn't seem to answer all the questions raised by the surviving evidence. Maybe this was then the real beginning of the Confederate wars in Ireland, secret conspiracies between Irish leaders and their supposed enemies, and this continued on giving the whole period the complexion of one long convoluted 'conspiracy' against the ordinary Catholic Irish. You can read a blow by blow account of this, where nearly every episode is in fact a secret conspiracy rather than a genuine battle, in a contemporary account called the Aphorismical Discovery written at that time. This book was written, I am certain, by a Dominican priest, and famous Gaelic poet, called Fr Patrick Hackett O.P.[19] It recounts the real goings on of those days, and the real role of the great Irish leader, and supposed royalist, the Marquis of Clanricard. Here he is trying to destroy his own army in Mayo in 1651:

> "We left Clanricard's army in the County of Mayo in Connaught, leading a miserable life, starving, though the county plentiful enough, and full of creaghts [small farmers], but durst not touch one cow without orders; no way was given to act any service on the enemy, going at random in loose companies in sight and upon ad-

vantage. When it pleased the Deputy-General [meaning the Lord Deputy Clanricard] (moved thereunto by the continual suit and earnest supplication of the distressed commanders) to grant his orders, in the behalf of the starving army's relief, to get some beefs from the said creaghts, to this effect issued his orders in the morning, picked out the matter of a 100 or sometimes 200 for the execution thereof; but commanding their stay in camp till about evening, commanding his dispatches in the interim unto the foresaid creaght[s] (whereunto the said party was to march), straightly charging and requiring them to stand in arms for proper defence, and rescue their cattle from such a party, notwithstanding his own orders to the contrary. [Meaning that he warned the creaghts to disregard any orders that the oncoming soldiers might show to them.] Whereupon inviting their neighbouring creaghts, intimating the Lord Deputy's intentions, who flocking together in great multitudes, point blank ready against the said party [the soldiers], who arriving to the place appointed without breath or courage (as coming 7 or 8 miles, for a long time before without meat, drink or rest), intending to put their said commands in due execution, which the creaght people observing, having more recent orders than the soldiers, did gather together in battle array (never regarding their orders, or that they were their confederates, or that they were in extreme necessity of relief, or that they were either Catholics or natives fighting, or at least exposing their proper lives in their behalf), ran with such furious and merciless behaviour on, putting them out of countenance by the over swaying number and better appointment of that multitude, killing, maiming, disarming, and stripping the poor innocent soldiers, such of them as could save themselves by the benefit of a good pair of heels, running with the best speed possible to the camp, as well to inform what happened unto the party, as also in hope to be a guide with a stronger party to the same place, to force satisfaction, and relieve the said party's misery, which notified in high measure of grievance unto Clanricard, would neither by himself repair the losses of both men and arms so miscarried, nor give to the respective officers and commanders interested to force satisfaction. This trick did the peer-deputy use several times, in so much that one moiety of the Leinster forces (in the behalf of whose destruction this plot was hatched) did not appear, as killed, stoned to death, or fled away from their colours, as not able to subsist under that merciless commander, and such as were extant, and did patiently bear all these miseries, were not useful as weak, naked and disarmed."[20]

It would be nice to be able to document in detail who in Ireland was most involved in these conspiracies but obviously that would be a huge undertaking. Suffice to say that in the above Aphorismical book, and in numerous other accounts like Commentarius Rinuccinianus, you can see clearly that the Earl of Ormond and the above described Earl of Clanricard were certainly heavily involved in these intrigues. Another, and possibly most interesting group, are the Jones family. These are the three sons of the Protestant Bishop of Killaloe: Dr Henry, Dean of Kilmore then Bishop of Clogher then of Meath (proffered to these sees on Ormond's recommendation); Michael, the main Parliamentarian figure in Dublin throughout this time; and Theophilius who succeeded Henry as scoutmaster general after the restoration.[21] Henry is I think the most important, and the most involved in these intrigues and intelligence work in general. He was a classic example of the kind of 'intriguers' or intelligence agents that were floating around at this time.

Deliberate Manipulation of the Historical Record.

It is a fascinating fact too that it was this intelligence agent who was most responsible for setting the predominant historiographical tone for the period - which basically amounted to blaming the Irish for the rebellion and supposed massacres. He was the "the master craftsman of the depositions", and it was his 'Remonstrance' book - which Temple just copied - which laid the foundations for the future historical inaccuracies.[22] He was even involved in the late 1680s in supplying information - probably fictitious - for Dr Borlase's history.[23]

Its no wonder then that such a false view of 1641 has been put abroad. Of course this false view relates mainly to these accusations that the Irish in Ulster in 1641 had massacred the recent Protestant immigrants who had come into Ulster since the Plantation of 1609. Speaking for myself I simply don't think that this is at all true. I think the government forces at the time, under people like Coote, were twice as bloodthirsty as any of the Irish. Even the famous Edmund Burke concluded that it was nothing more than "a pretended massacre". Burke had looked through the Depositions himself and discussed the subject with the historian Leland who agreed with him about this "but, when he began to write his history, he only thought of himself and the book-seller."[24]

Hence we see the same pattern of manipulated history while on the other side of the fence the Irish had great difficulties putting forward their version of what happened. For example the above account of Clanricard in Mayo survived in only one manuscript which was not published until the late 19th century, long after the enemies of the Irish had set the historical tone for that period. And this is no accident, the true history had a way of getting censored as this account by Fr Robert O'Connell O.F.M. (Cap.) of the troubles the writer had in getting his work published shows:

> "Hereafter on account of the Munstermen of the Irish Dominicans having been driven off from the former College of Louvain by the Provincial father, Fr Patrick O'Kearney, a man famous for his learning and virtue, and Fr Patrick Hackett, who adhered with great eagerness to the Nuncio and his supporters in Ireland...in this year [1652] writing in English to Fr Richard O'Ferrall, the Irish Capuchin, from Louvain to the City [Rome]:
> "I am compiling (he says) a tract of that damnedable defection of the anti Catholic faction from our confederation...[says that some of his 'friends' conspired to get his superiors to rule against his writing this work]...I compiled all the nefarious acts of the Parliamentarians, the edicts, declarations, proclamations and letters of the Council, and of the other prefects of the faction, as it is utterly forgotten..."
> The above I translated from the autograph which was written on the 29th of November 1652. But actually afterwards, after he had been dislodged from the Louvain convent of the Dominicans as I said, and after he had died a few years later in Louvain, the book (as the prefect [Dominican] Fr Patrick O'Kearney related to me), by now finished, he deposited the custody of it into the house of a certain friend, Irish by nationality, where, I fear, it might have perished by the tricks of the Ormondists and heretics, to the most grave prejudice of the Catholic cause."[25]

We are lucky to even have that reference, it is from the Commentarius Rinuccinianus which was not published until the 20th century. (Btw the manuscript it was based on was copied just before it was destroyed in an Allied bombing raid on Milan in WWII.) Even then this huge (five large volumes) and important account remains available only in the original Latin. Again the fact that this was not published at the time is no accident either as you can see in this letter from a spy of Ormond's writing to him from Florence in 1667 referring to this work:

"Here is at Florence an Irish Capuchin friar, a learned man formerly preacher at Sedan in France, called Fr Robert Farald [actually O'Connell, his former colleague was called O'Ferrall or O'Farrell], who to gratify the Gentleman Usher to the great Duchess; Cavagliere Rinuccini; whose brother was the Pope's nuncio in Ireland, hath finished a book begun by Fr Richard Farald, called the diary of the Nuncio in Ireland and intended for the press: but I fearing that partly to flatter the Nuncio's brother, he might report more magnificently of the Nuncio's proceedings than the truth would bear; and that partly out of zeal he might give too particular accounts, of the Actions, Endeavours, and Correspondences of the Nuncio and recall to mind what was much better lay in oblivion: And partly fearing that he might have wrote in Prejudice ['to our'?, word missing] Majesty of ever glorious memory, or the King my Gracious Sovereign and [word missing] or your Grace so great a Minister; I went to the friar and told him those annals relating to business of state so long and so bloodily d['one'?] he ought not to publish them without leave from his Majesty: or at least of his Privy Council. I asked him to see the book but he told me that [?without] license of his Superior he could not show it me. But he told me that Diary contained besides all the actions of the Nuncio, all the originals of Concernment written to, or from the Nuncio. I could heartily wish that [?'I was'] able to put papers of so high a nature into the Possession of your Grace. However I shall hinder the Printing in this state, and I hope po[?pressurise?] him to suppress them totally."[26]

Incidentally, as you can read in the earlier account of Hackett's troubles in the Dominican order, one of the major problems these historians had was trouble that was stirred up against them within the church. This again was no accident if this letter by the Irish Lord Deputy in

1673 is anything to go by:

> "I believe it to be one of the most important things I
> could do both for his Majesty's service and for the se-
> curity of his Protestant subjects here, either to keep
> those men [Catholic clergy] divided, or, if they were
> united, to break them [up] again. I made some of their
> friars, who always have their little wrangles with the
> secular clergy, to get up faction against their bishops."[27]

This is an important point because pretty much all the great Irish historians of this time, and I would say most other times, were Catholic clergy. One exception to this was Nicholas Plunkett of Dunsoghly who wrote an account of the later 17th century period which you can read at http://www.ucc.ie:8080/cocoon/celt/E703001-001. Its called "A light to the Blind" written in his old age after he had lost his son in the William-ite Wars. His experience of Irish politics makes his account also teem with 'conspiracies' rather than the plain history that people are used to. His instincts, and knowledge of events at the time, haven't being fol-lowed up much by later historians I don't think. Here is his thoughts on the Battle of the Boyne:

> "There are instances enough of this [deliberate treach-
> ery] in history, both old and modern. If the present war
> of Ireland can show any, I leave it to the judgement of
> the reader; yet in the interim I am informed (as I
> touched before) that the lord Coningsby, treasurer of
> Ireland for the prince of Orange, giving up his accounts
> at London, in the year 1692, from the summer of 1690,
> wherein the battle at the Boyne happened, he brought a
> bill of many a thousand pound laid out in Ireland on
> secret services performed there for facilitating the con-
> quest of that kingdom by several persons named that
> were on the king's side [meaning James II's]..." (p.85)

Its no wonder then that some people don't think that 'conspiracies' hap-pen, they often do not have access to real history, and especially Irish history, which I think shows that 'conspiracies' are the stuff of politics any day ever!

Glossary

Antrim - Randal MacDonnell, Earl of (later Marquis). He had extensive estates in Antrim and Scotland so was the natural person to transport an

Irish army to Britain to help Charles, and plans of that nature were in the works for a long time both before and after 1641. Eventually he managed to get some troops across in late 1643-44, and these helped Montrose a lot in his Royalist uprising in Scotland.

Carte - Thomas, he was the English Jacobite author of a very important and hugely researched 18th century biography of Ormond. He had access to so many sources in writing this work that Carte's book is often looked upon as a primary, rather than a secondary, source of information on the period.

Charles - Charles Stuart, officially "Charles, by the Grace of God, King of England [and his son was Prince of Wales], Scotland, France [a bit hopeful that!] and Ireland" at this time. He eventually fought a Civil War against the Parliamentarians, but lost, losing his head in the process!

Clanricard - Ulick Burke, Earl of (later Marquis). He was the Catholic head of the Burke family of Galway, a grandson of Sir Francis Walsingham, Queen Elizabeth's famous spy chief, and half brother of the Earl of Essex an important Parliamentarian general. He succeeded Ormond as Lord Deputy, technically Lord Lieutenant, but in the opinion of the Aphorismical Discovery kept up Ormond's duplicitous practices of destroying the Irish, and royalist, cause.

Covenanting Scots - The Scots had revolted from Charles seeking greater toleration for the Presbyterian religion, and had organised a Covenant pledging themselves to these aims. Hence during these years Scotland was pretty much an independent country, and mostly allied to the Parliamentarians.

The Depositions - A large collection of contemporary statements collected by the government shortly after the revolt broke out and purportedly proving the existence of a widespread massacre. Their true veracity has been hotly debated ever since, with Gilbert for example saying that they were taken under threat of torture or imprisonment. They are now housed in TCD.

Glamorgan - Edward Somerset, Earl of, sent by the King in 1645 to patch up his differences with the Irish parliament and then gather an Irish army together to help him in England. He was quite successful in this until Ormond threw him in jail accusing him of being a fraud and then the King disowned him.

Ormond - James Butler, Earl of (later Marquis, then Duke). He was the Protestant head of the Butler family of Kilkenny who started off as commander of the cavalry in Strafford's Irish army, then its leader, then a long time Lord Deputy of Ireland. As such he was supposed to be representing the King's interests in Ireland but many Irish commentators pointed to episodes like his surrender of Dublin to Parliamentarian forces as proof of his underhand cooperation with the King's enemies.

Owen Roe O'Neill - A nephew of the Great O'Neill he fought at Kinsale and was exiled during the Flight of the Earls only to come back decades later after the rebellion had broken out. He had previously distinguished himself fighting in Belgium for the Spanish against the French. His brilliant conduct of the siege of Arras, for example, was observed by Richelieu in person. During these wars he is often considered the greatest military commander and created a formidable Ulster Catholic army which went on to defeat the Scots at Benburb, despite the huge supply problems that he faced.

Parliamentarians - This was a group in England who pressed the King seeking the abolition of the Anglican episcopacy, and other Protestant religious aims, the scrapping of the hated ship tax, and hoping to compel Charles to summon, and answer to, regular Parliaments. By 1641 they had compelled Charles to answer to most of their demands and dominated the machinery of government. Many of these figures like Pym, and sometimes even Cromwell, are considered in English historiography to be heroes in the ongoing struggle for a democratic constitution in Westminister, but Irish historians have never been that fond of them, especially in the case of the latter! During the Civil War this group split up into an Independent group, lead by Cromwell, and a Presbyterian group, but they were united during the period of the Irish rebellion. They are sometimes described as Puritans, or Roundheads.

Irish Rebels of 1641 - There were quite a few figures in the know like Phelim O'Neill, Rory O'More, Lord Maguire, and some Irish Colonels then serving on the continent like Richard Plunkett,[28] as regards some of the more 'conspiratorial' :-) type figures involved in the Plot:
Philip MacHugh O'Reilly, before and after the Irish wars he was an officer in the Spanish army, who's mother was a close relative of Argyle's [29] and who might have been one of those Irish MPs who formed links to the English Parliamentarians, which possibly he kept up. He is the un-

popular Colonel mentioned in O'Donovan's letters for Cavan (p.56), and the Aphorismical Discovery (p.697-703) notes his expeditious exit from the second battle of Finea in early 1651. Could he be the Colonel Reilly, an Irish rebel, in receipt of moneys from England in 1646?; [30]

Fr.Iver (or Heber) McMahon, Catholic Bishop of Clogher, who was accused by Clarendon of being all along a Government spy.[31] Fr.John Lynch in his writings hints that he believes this,[32] and I notice he was Ormond's choice as leader of the Ulster army at the famous meeting at Belturbet [33];

Daniel O'Neill, Owen Roe's nephew, who was possibly in the know although jailed that summer, and who the Commentarius Rinuccinianus accuses of being behind a plot to kill his uncle [34];

and Rev Patrick Crelly - or Creely - the Cistercian abbot of Newry who seems to have been involved in the early stages of the rebellion in Ireland.[35] He was later a leading agent for Cromwell's spymaster Thomas Scot:

> "One of his best agents appears to be an Irish abbot
> called Father Creely. Creely also went under the name
> of Captain Holland. He was located in the Queen
> Mother's court in Paris but also worked in Flanders and
> had men in Vienna, as well as some intelligence in-
> terests in the Vatican amongst the cardinals."[36]

He was earlier an agent of Rinuccini's, then married, became a Protestant, and died in 1652. Fr Anthony Geoghegan had recommended him to become Bishop of Meath in a letter he sent to Propaganda dated 4th of Feb.1652.[37]

Richelieu - The Cardinal who was effectively the Prime Minister of France throughout this period. He was succeeded in this job by his friend Cardinal Mazarin. Widely considered to be very unscrupulous and vindicative - as you can see even in fiction in the 'Three Musketeers' - in his foreign policy he always favoured the Protestant position, and was followed in that by Mazarin. This begs the question, for me anyway, as to whether or not a little corruption in these matters was evident in the Vatican at this time. I'm definitely not accusing the Pope, or any of the Irish clergy, but the very fact that these two unscrupulous gents got those red hats, despite their constant support for the Protestant side in the 30 Years War, would surely make one a little suspicious of some of these Vatican officials. Say the Berberinis for example, who were close to the French. This raises an issue about Rinuccini, who lingered a long time talking to Mazarin before he came across to Ireland, and who seems to have been somewhat pro-French.[38] Could he have been acting deliberately when he caused so much chaos at the Confederation of Kilkenny, so banjaxing the Irish cause in the interests of Cromwell, Mazarin's ally?

Rinuccini - Rev Giovanni Battista, a Florentine Archbishop who came to Ireland as Papal Nuncio to the Confederation of Kilkenny. Second only to Ormond in his marvellous capacity to divide and confuse the Irish Catholics. Later a former ally of his in Ireland, Fr Richard O'Ferrall, and another Capuchin, Fr. Robert O'Connell, wrote a huge account of his time in Ireland called Commentarius Rinuccinianus.

Strafford - Thomas Wentworth, Earl of. Long time, and ruthless enough, Lord Deputy of Ireland before these events. He was a loyal adherent of Charles but was attainted by the English Parliament, sentenced to death, and executed on the 12th May 1641.

Footnotes

1. George Leyburn, *The Memoirs of George Leyburn* (Edinburgh, Clarendon Historical Society, 1886), p.13.

2. Sir John Temple, *The Irish Rebellion of 1641* (London, 1812), p.63 first published in London 1646.

3. For an example of the Parliamentarians accusing the King of involvement in the rebellion see *A Declaration of the Commons Assembled...concerning the rise and progress of the Grand Rebellion in Ireland* (London, 1643).

4. See particularly Antrim's deposition available at G. Hill, *An Historical Account of the MacDonnells of Antrim* (Belfast, 1873), p.448-451. Antrim says he was asked by the King in 1641 to help organise a kind of rebellion, in cooperation with the Earl of Ormond, to seize Dublin Castle etc - basically to mobilise Strafford's army in defence of the king.

One 75 year old correspondent of Dr Borlase's had no doubt but that the Commission was genuine and that Antrim "had done nothing but what he had orders and letters for" from the King. (Letter from Louis du Moulins to Dr Borlase (the historian and son of the former Lord Justice) 2 Sept 1679 Pearse St Gilbert Ms 190 p.126 copy of Sloane Ms 1008.)

After Antrim was acquitted of involvement in the rebellion, at his trial after the Restoration, one of the judges at his trial published a pamphlet reprinting King Charles II's letter of July 1663 which accepts that Antrim was all along acting under his father's instructions (Henry Bennett, *Murder Will Out* (London, 1689)). Antrim's instructions and letters are also discussed at length in Miciah Tougood, *An essay on Charles I* (London, 1748), c.p.41, where it is felt that letters in Antrim's custody proved the Queen's planning of the rebellion and the King's consent to it.

There are of course numerous references to the King's support for the rebellion in the Depositions and other sources e.g. in this deposition of Arthur Culme the owner and governor of Clogh-Oughter castle Co.Cavan:
"..was surprised by the sheriff who had knocked on his door, the sheriff [Myles the Slasher O'Reilly] (or his party) saying "they had a commission from his Majesty to disarm all the British", being by the deponent demanded the reason for it, they said the intention of his Majesty was by their means to bring into subjection the puritan faction of the Parliament of England, and that they would right the Queen's Majesty for aspersions laid on the royal [person] - too bold for them to speak or without modesty to be related." (Tomas Fitzpatrick, *The King's Commission*, U.J.A. Ser 2 Vol.XV Feb-May 1909 p.8.)

5. Ohlmeyer's defence of that version of events is in History Journal 35, 4 (1992) p.905-919.

6. Tadhg ó hAnnracháin, *Catholic Reformation in Ireland: The Mission of Rinuccini; 1645-1649* (Oxford, 2002), p.8.

7. John Nalson, *An Impartial Collection of the Great Affairs of State* (London, 1683) Vol II, p.897.

8. Quoted at http://www.uni-mannheim.de/mateo/camenaref/cmh/cmh410.html
.

9. A description of Richelieu's support for the Scots is given by Carte, quoting from sources like some French letters in 'Ambassades de M. d'Estrades' published in Amsterdam in 1718. He also points out that Neil O'Neill came over to Ireland in early summer 1641 with assurances of help for a rebellion from Richelieu. Carte also sees this overall link between Pym-the Scots-and Richelieu. At one point Carte relates that Pym deliberately refused to heed information that he had that Richelieu was plotting rebellion in Ireland "which shows it to be a tender point, and that the faction had measures to keep with that Cardinal." Carte says of Richelieu:
"who after enslaving his own country, made it his business to foment disturbances in all parts of Europe, who had contributed so much to the late rebellion in Scotland, and had too much influence upon that, which broke out soon in England."
Carte heads one of his paragraphs on the Scots rebellion: "Fomented by Cardinal Richelieu." He says that Richelieu began to work against Charles after the latter had opposed his taking Dunkirk in November 1637. Furthermore he says that Richelieu sent M. de Bellevre to stir up trouble in London around that time (for which he draws on Rushworth Vol II p.8). He also talks about correspondence between Richelieu and Alexander Leslie at that time. Leslie wanted 50,000 crowns to start a rebellion in Scotland and Richelieu replies giving him 100,000! Carte also says that the Scottish Covenant itself was largely drawn up by Richelieu in France. (Thomas Carte, *Life of Ormonde* (Oxford, 1851) Vol I, p.175-181 Vol II p.320, 369 and 18th cent edition book II p.183 and p.88-89.)

Some notes on this by a German historian:
"It cannot be doubted that alliances between the Scots and Cardinal Richelieu had already been formed [by 1639]; they were carried on through his almoner Charles...Belliévre considered that the old alliance between France and Scotland ought to be renewed, and the King of England hindered from ever embarking on hostilities against France without the fear arising in his mind that he would have the Scots against him."
Referring again to Richelieu's agent Bellievre: "For not only the Scots, but all those who even in England were in opposition to the court attached themselves to him."
Henry Rich, Earl of Holland..."had ever remained thoroughly French. Above

all he had held fast to Richelieu...and the closest ally of the Scots." Later he notes that "while the [French] ambassador was inciting the Scots against him [Charles], in order to keep him occupied within his own dominions and prevent him from opposing the undertakings of the French against Spain." (Leopald von Ranke, *A History of England principally in the 17th century* (Oxford, 1875) Vol II, p.156, 180; p.479, Incidentally he questions the authenticity of some of the Richelieu letters in the d'Estrades book mentioned above (p.456) but I don't think his arguments in that respect are particularly plausible.)

The Richelieu connection to the Irish Rebellion:
"In the mean time there landed one Neale O'Neale, sent by the Earl of Tyrone out of Spain, to speak with the gentry of his name and kindred, to let them know that he treated with Cardinal Richelieu for obtaining succour to come for Ireland, and that he prevailed with the Cardinal, so that to have arms, ammunition and money from him on demand to come for Ireland...[in reference to the same Colonel:] that the said Colonel was really with himself assured of the Cardinal's aid." (Examination of Conor Lord Maguire 21 March 1641/2 published in J. T. Gilbert, *Contemporary History of Affairs in Ireland, 1641-1652* Vol I, p.503 and 511, also on p.506-507 there are further references to the Richelieu connection.)

"..that the intended rebellion was made known unto the Cardinal Richelieu in France long before it was known in Ireland, and that the rebels did expect arms and ammunition everyday out of France when the wind should serve." (Examination of Colonel John Read taken on the rack Dublin 22 March 1641/2 published in John T. Gilbert, *History of the Irish Confederation and War in Ireland* (Dublin, 1882-91) Vol I, p.299.)

The Papal representative Rossetti, writing back to Berberini in Rome after interviewing Richelieu on 26 January 1642, says that Richelieu was supportive of the rebellion. But by the 15 February following he says that the rebels can expect no more material help from France. This is as one would expect of course from Richelieu, he wanted to start the rebellion but he actually wanted the Parliamentarians and the Scots to defeat the Irish so he closed the door behind them after the Irish had gone from the Continent to join the rebellion. In this well known correspondence Berberini stated that he had heard from the Papal Nuncio in Paris that France was friendly to the Parliamentarians and so he reckoned there would be no assistance from there for the Irish (from early 1642 on.) (*Catalogue of Irish material in the Berberini library in the Vatican.* Archivium Hibernicum Vol.XVIII (1955) p.132. This correspondence is described in detail in Gordon Albion, *Charles I and the Court of Rome* (London, 1935), p.376. Incidentally the Queen asked the Vatican for money to bribe the Parliamentarians like Pym (ibid p.363).)

The DNB under Thomas Preston also mentions Richelieu's support for the Irish rebellion.

The French ambassador had tipped off the five MPs that Charles wanted to arrest in the House of Commons, described by Belloc thus:
"As for the French ambassador's action it was but a part of all French policy had been doing since the beginning of the troubles, since Richelieu had secretly sent money to help the covenanting rebellion in Scotland." (Hilaire Belloc, *Charles I* (London, 1933), p.253-256.)

William Colville (brother of the Baron of 'Cleische') was one of the go betweens twixt Richelieu and the 'mécontents' of Great Britain, in 1639-early 1640. One of the letters from the Scots seeking help from Richelieu was signed by Leslie, Mar, Loudoun, Forester, Rothes, Montrose and Montgomery. (M Avenel edit., *Letters, Instructions, Diplomatics and Papers of State of Cardinal de Richelieu.* (Paris, 1867) VI 1638-1642, p.688 -689.)

10. Of course it was well known that Richelieu was allied to the Dutch at this point - and by the Dutch incidentally I am referring to the big merchants in Amsterdam who ran the Republic, rather than necessarily the House of Orange. The Dutch were also natural allies of the Parliamentarians and the Covenanting Scots, for religious reasons and as an example of a country that gained its independence from an over mighty Catholic ruler. (The Parliamentarians and the Scots tended to look upon Charles as a kind of half Catholic, not the full Protestant shilling!) Therefore it is probably unnecessary to show the links between the Dutch and these groups but here are two bits and pieces in any case:

Referring to the Parliamentarians the Papal representative, Charles Francis Invernizio, says this in a report to the Pope on events in Ireland, dated 1645:
"Just as the Hollanders, with whom if they did not strike secretly a treaty up to this point certainly they cherish the greatest friendship,.."
("quemadmodum Hollandi, cum quibus si foedus secreto non percusserunt, adhuc certe summam alunt amicitiam," Vatican Library: Barberini Lat. 2242 published in Archivium Hibernicum Vol VI 1917 p.125.)

"Most of these Grandee's [the big Parliamentarian figures] are reported to have for their retreat houses in the Low Countries, richly furnished with sequestered plate, linen, and stuff and great store of money in bank for their shelter, against such storms as their rapine, tyranny, and ignorance may happily raise here amongst us." (Clement Walker, *The History of Independency* (London, 1649) 2nd pt., p.11.)

11. For a description of these Scots- Irish issues see David Stevenson, *Scottish Covenanters and Irish Confederates* (Belfast, 1981), passim.

12. One correspondent outlines in this letter how the House of Commons decided on a Monday, after hearing the news of the rebellion the previous day,

to raise 50,000 pounds for the Irish war, while assuring the City that "they shall have an act for the repaying of it plus interest." (Letter of 6th November 1641 J.Dillingham to Lord Montagu HMC Montagu (1900) p.134-5.)

The main work on this question is by JR MacCormack who outlines that as early as November the 3rd deals were being struck involving "a judicious blend of London money and Scottish troops." Yet it wasn't until December that the Lord Justices are writing back to London talking about the possible defection to the rebels of the Pale gentry, the only people who had sufficient lands to justify these kind of loans - the Ulster rebels of course had almost no lands, they had already being confiscated under the Ulster plantation of 1609. So I am just adding to that by pointing out that on that tight time scale it must have been the case that those parties were planning this all along, before the rebellion broke out, which I think MacCormack himself hints at below (the 'brows' thing is from Clarendon):
"In the House of Commons, on November 1, the radicals, aware that Ireland formed a common focus of interest for the Scots, the London merchants and many of their supporters in the house, received the news of the rising with 'smooth brows'."
The article also describes how this money was actually used to fund a huge chunk of the Parliamentarian - and Scottish - war effort, not particularly in subjugating Ireland. (JR MacCormack, *The Irish Adventurers and the English civil war*, Irish Historical Studies, X (1956), p.21, 24.)

This is an account of the land sale by a Papal representative in 1645, showing I think that it was planned before it could possibly have been justified:
"Before this time a proclamation was published in London by the Parliamentarians, by which the goods of all the Irish Catholics are confiscated and bid for during a public auction, and [so that] the buyers, from wickedness, might not fail to profit from [this] stolen and illegal allotment, when gold might not be at hand, a certain imaginary distribution of land, and a sale, has been made...By which reckoning, and tyrannical invention indeed, a great body of money, arms and soldiers having been collected are sent into Ireland against the Confederate Catholics."
("Sub idem tempus Londini a Parlamentariis promulgatum fuit edictam, quo omnium Hybernorum Catholicorum bona fisco sunt addicta et licitantibus sub hasta venundata, et ne sceleri materies furtivae et illicitae designationi emptores deessent, cum non suppeteret argentum, imaginaria quaedam divisio terrarum, ac venditio facta est...Qua quidem ratione et tyrannico invento magna vis pecuniarum armorum, et militum collecta et in Hyberniam contra confoederatos catholicos missa est." by Charles Francis Invernizio reporting to the Pope Vatican Library: Barberini Lat. 2242 published in Archivium Hibernicum Vol VI 1917 p.102.)

13. Richard O'Ferrall OFM (Cap.) see the article at http://www.indymedia.ie/article/79358, written by the current writer, Appendix

D footnote 81. That both the Scots and the Parliamentarians must have been encouraging the Irish rebels at this time we can see from this account in Carte about the first explanation that the Irish rebels gave as regards their allies: "Thus they [the Irish rebels] gave out that one while, the Scotch were joined with them in covenant, not to leave a drop of English blood in England, as they (the Irish) would not in Ireland; and that they had a writing to that effect signed with the hands of the prime nobility of Scotland, and particularly depended on the Marquis of Argyle's assistance. Another while they maintained, that they had authority from the parliament of England for what they did, and should be supported by that body in the insurrection, which they had made against the crown and dignity of the King. But as these allegations were not so well adapted to gain the Roman Catholic nobility and gentry of English race in Ireland, who hated the Scots and dreaded the violence of the English parliament, they soon found it more for their purpose to pretend, that they were authorised by the King, and that Sir Phelim O'Neill had a commission from him to take up arms." (Thomas Carte, *Life of Ormonde* (Oxford, 1851) Vol I, p.360.)

14. "Cáit aꞃ ṡaḃaꞃan Ꞡaoiḋil?
cꞃéaꞃ ḋíol na noꞃoinꞡ ḃꞃoꞃḃꞃaoiliḋ?
ní ꞙoꞡḃuim a n-aṁoꞃc ꞃin
a ꞃaṫaꞃc ꞡoꞃmꞙuinn Ꞡaoiḋil.

Ní ꞙaicim an noꞃoinꞡ nꞩeaꞃcꞡlaiꞃ
um ḃꞃomċluiḃ ḋionn n-oiꞃeaċtaiꞃ,
a cconꞡáiꞃ ní claiꞃꞩeaꞃ leam
aꞡ caiꞃꞩeal oꞃláiꞃ Éiꞃeann.

...

Atá aꞡainn 'na n-ionaḋ
ḋíꞃim uaiḃꞃeaċ eiꞃioḋan
ḋ'ꞙuil Ꞡall, ꞩo ꞡaꞃꞃaiḋ Ṁonaiḋ,
Saxoin ann iꞃ Alꞇbonaiꞡ

...

Ní ꞙaic aoinneaċ ḋ'ꞙuil Ꞡaoiḋil
ní aꞃ bioċ lé mbí ꞃoꞃḃꞃaoiliḋ,
ní ċluin ꞡuċ aꞃ láinḃinn leiꞃ -
uch! a n-áiꞃṁim ꞩá n-aiċeiꞃ.

...

Ḋíbiꞃc Ꞡaoiḋeal ꞡuiꞃc Ḃanḃa,
ꞡé atá a ċlú aꞃ ċaċ n-alꞇlṁaꞃḋa,
ꞃeaꞃꞡ Ḋé ꞃé ccáċ ꞩá ccolꞡaḋ
iꞃ é iꞃ ꞙáċ ꞩá n-ionnaꞃbaḋ.

....

Ḋíoꞡalcaꞃ Ḋé aꞃ aḋḃaꞃ ann -
ꞃiꞃ Alꞇbon, óꞡbaiḋ lunnanꞩ
ꞩo anaꞩaꞃ 'na n-áic ꞃin -
cáit aꞃ ṡaḃaꞃan Ꞡaoiḋil?

Where have the Gaels gone? What is the fate of the mirthful throngs? I catch no glimpse of them within sight of the green land of Gaoidheal.

I do not see the dark-eyed throng around the heights of fortified assembly places; their tumult is not audible to me as I traverse Ireland's plains.
...
We have in their stead an arrogant impure crowd, of foreigner's blood, of the race of Monadh - there are Saxons there, and Scotch.
...
No-one of the blood of Gaoidheal sees anything at which to rejoice; he hears no voice he considers full-sweet - och the extent of their humiliation I (have to) relate.
...
The expulsion of the Gaels of the field of Banbha, although its vaunt is claimed for a foreign battalion, it is the wrath of God scourging them before all - that is the (real) cause of their expulsion.
...
The vengeance of God is the reason for it. The men of Scotland, the youths of London have settled in their place. Where have the Gaels gone?"
(William Gillies, *A Poem on the Downfall of the Gaoidhil*, Éigse Vol XIII pt III summer 1970, p.203.)

15. The references that link Richelieu, closely allied to the Dutch of course, to the Irish rebellion are listed in footnote 9 above. That just leaves the Scots and the Parliamentarians, taking first the Scots:
The opinion of Dr John Nalson, the contemporary historian and English MP:
"And the Confession of the Lord Maguire, which the reader shall presently see, does not obscurely hint, that the Earl of Argyle the head of the Covenanting Rebellious Scotch Presbyterians, was under-hand working the Irish into some conspiracy against the King, probably that his hands being full, they might procure better terms for themselves and divert the storm of the English arms, which then were impending upon them." (John Nalson, *An Impartial Collection of the Great Affairs of State* (London, 1683) Vol II, p.552-3).

Carte mentions "a Treaty formerly on foot between Tyrone and the Earl of Argyle, for an alliance and mutual assistance, and from some expressions of the latter, intimating that he had it in his power to set all Ireland in a flame." This Earl of Tyrone, who lived on the continent and was the recognised leader of the O'Neills (and succeeded in that by Owen Roe of course), died not long before the rebellion. Carte is saying that Argyle boasted of his ability to raise havoc in Ireland.
(Thomas Carte, *Life of Ormonde* (Oxford, 1851) Vol I, p.175-181, Vol II, p.329.)

Leslie in 1638 - the C in C of the Scottish army of course - is reported to have threatened that if the King attacked Scotland he would "find enough to do in both Kingdoms, especially in Ireland, o'er long." (David Stevenson, *Scottish Covenanters and Irish Confederates* (Belfast, 1981), p.26.)

In the famous King's Commission it was stated that the Irish are to seize all castles "except the places, persons, and estates of our loyal and loving subjects the Scots." (Edward Bowles, *The Mysterie of Iniquity* (London, 1643), p.36.)

George Ffercher of Toneheighe, parson of Cleenish Co Fermanagh, saw the King's Commission and the letter from the prime nobility of Scotland and something from the hand of the Earl of Argyle to that effect (Thomas Fitzpatrick, *The King's Commission* U.J.A.ser. 2 Vol XIII Aug-Nov 1907, p.136.). This is mentioned as well by Henry Jones in *A Remonstrance* (London, 1642), p.38 where he says "This Scots-Irish Covenant some in the hand of the Earl of Argyle seen by George Fercher of Tonchey Co.Fermanagh clerk.")

Nicholas Willoughby, from Cavan town, describes what he heard from Donnough McGuire:
"Expressing that the Scots were and had been always their friends, and that they had a Covenant to show whereby might appear the fair correspondence between them and the Scots in Scotland, which Covenant imparted that the Irish should never take part with the English against the Scots. And that the Scots should never take part with the English against the Irish, and that it was so Covenanted between many of the Lords of Scotland and many of the Lords and chief gentry of Ireland, and that Hugh McMaughon had the Covenant to show (which they would not show us.." (Thomas Fitzpatrick U.J.A. Ser. 2 Vol. VIII Oct 1902 p.170.)

Some more gossip from the Depositions:
Thomas Grant of Cavan saw the Covenant between the Irish and the Scots, and when he asked John Reilly why they did not meddle with the Scots: "he said the Scots did join with them." (Henry Jones, *A Remonstrance* (London, 1642), p.35, 37.)

Richard Bellings says that the conspirators in Ulster thought the Scots would join with them. (John Thomas Gilbert, *History of the Irish Confederation and the war in Ireland* (Dublin, 1882-91) Vol V, p.23.)

And the evidence linking the Parliamentarians to the Irish rebellion:
For a comprehensive list of the many contemporary accounts of their involvement in the Irish rebellion see http://www.indymedia.ie/article/79358 Appendix D towards the end (especially footnote 85). Here are a few more such references and some interesting opinions of later historians. (When you read references below to the Lord Justices note that most people accept that they were always acting at the behest of the Parliamentarians in London .e.g. the great historian Charles O'Conor noted simply that "The Lords Justices

leagued secretly with the Puritans in Westminister" (Charles O'Conor of Belnagare writing in the preface to Dr Curry, *Historical Memoirs of the Irish Rebellion in the year 1641* (Dublin, 1770), p.xvi.)):

"..two Lords Justices, named Sir John Borlase and Sir William Parsons. These were both ardent Puritans and partisans of Parliament. They were anxious to see the fall of the English monarch, for they were his bitterest enemies, and they thought that he would be embarrassed, in his fight with the Parliament in England, by a revolution in Ireland. And so the very men who were the guardians of the state lent themselves to promote the rebellion by every means in their power." (Fr Thomas N. Burke O.P., *Ireland's Vindication* (London, 1873), p.199.)

When the Irish Parliament proposed to raise an army to put down the rebellion: "This way of proceeding did not square with the Lords Justices designs, who were often heard to say, that the more there were in rebellion, the more land should be forfeited to them; and therefore, in the very height of the business they resolved upon a Prorogation;" (Dr Curry, *A brief account from the most authentic protestant writers..* (Dublin, 1752), p.141 quoting Castlehaven's memoirs p.34.)
Castlehaven also said, referring as well to the effect of the severity of the parliamentarians dealings with the Irish, that:
"..the Scotch, and their wicked brethren in the Parliament of England, [were] the main occasion of that horrid insurrection." (James Touchet Castlehaven, *The Earl of Castlehaven's Review* (London, 1684), p.20.)

Hugh Reilly, writing in 1693, says that when Charles I was "wheedled into such prodigious concessions" to the Presbyterian party, "then the fanatics of Ireland who all the while kept a strict correspondence with those of England" concluded that this was a good time for a rebellion. (Hugh Reilly, *Ireland's Case Briefly Stated* (first published 1695 this edition London, 1768), p.20.)

"Let him [an impartial person] bear in mind, that forged plots, supported by perjury and occasionally by the stupid and clumsy contrivance of letter-dropping, had been one of the steady and uniform machines in the government of Ireland, from the invasion to that period; and had produced the forfeiture of millions of acres...Clarendon, Carte, Warner, Leland and Gordon all agree that the grand object of the Lords Justices was, in the beginning, to extend the flames of civil war...for the purposes of producing extensive confiscations... [quoting Gordon Vol I p.403] "to involve as many as possible in the guilt of rebellion was part of the plan of the Lord Justices, whose great object was an extensive forfeiture of lands."...[referring to these land confiscations which, quoting Warner p.199] "unlocks the whole secret of their iniquitous practices...and for all their backwardness in putting an end to the rebellion." (M. Carey, *Vindiciae Hibernicae or Ireland Vindicated* (Philadelphia, 1819), p.344, 348, 349.)

"In fact the whole of the plan [the 1641 conspiracy] was made known to the Lords Justices from a very early period...But Parsons looked forward to a rebellion as his harvest. He had already gained a large fortune by trading in confiscations; and he trusted that a new insurrection would place at his disposal more estates than even Strafford had ventured to contemplate. In fact as Sir William Petty judiciously observes, there was now a great game to be played for the estates of the Irish proprietors." (W. C. Taylor, *History of the Civil Wars* (Edinburgh, 1831) Vol. I, p.262.)

"The only object of the Lord Justices was to multiply forfeitures by adding to the number of compulsory rebels...The inventors of that lie were themselves the rebels, and the insurrection which did really take place was a rising for the King against the English and Irish Regicides." (Notes by Gavan Duffy on the 1641 Rebellion NLI MS 4198A p.45, quoting a review of Rinucinni's Memoirs in Foreign Quarterly Review Oct 1844 and then a newspaper article which refers to that review.)

16. http://www.indymedia.ie/article/79358 Appendix D footnote 85. Another similar account can be seen in the memoirs of Nicholas Plunkett of Dunsoghly (he is described at that same website) who also states that the Parliamentarians were behind the rebellion, which they promoted to sate their:
"insatiable appetite of [for] wealth and arbitrary government thereby to compass and expedite the King's ruin, and asperse him too with this which was their own guilt, so as I defy history to match the Rebellion of those three nations from 1637 to 1660, and indeed the actions of those the Presbyterians and Rinuccians are so palpably known to be guilty of the whole deplorable mischief, as no insinuation of lies to veil over or varnish their execrable crimes is able to conceal the same from any judicious person but an ignoramus jury" (NLI Ms 346 p.844).

17. You can read this view of Ormond in the Aphorismical Discovery and countless other accounts written from an Irish perspective. Even Old English figures like Dr Nicholas French, the Bishop of Ferns, have no good things to say about Ormond in their later writings.

18. See http://www.indymedia.ie/article/79358 Appendix D footnote 83.

19. You can see he is the author of the Aphorismical Discovery when you consider these reasons:
a) Hackett was a poet in Latin and Irish,[i] and was, according to Commentarius Rinuccinianus, "an author elegantly skilled in Irish, English, Latin and (I believe) other languages.." [ii]. Gilbert meanwhile refers to the anonymous author of the Aph. Disc.:
"The whole supplies evidence of the author's familiarity with Latin, Spanish, Italian, French, and Gaelic." [iii] Yet notice how he, slightly unusually, writes in

English when writing to O'Ferrall in 1652, which may then show that English was the language that he preferred to use at that time - same as our author of course. (Btw the poetry that you see throughout the work, mostly in English but one in Latin, must have written by him.)

(b) The anonymous author and Hackett are fond of the word 'faction', used in the Irish introduction to some of his poems,[iv] and in the English letter that he sent to Fr O'Ferrall quoted in the text. (The full title of the book is the 'Aphorismical Discovery of Treasonable Faction', and throughout the work the author called the Ormondists the 'faction'.)

(c) Most people always knew of course that this anonymous author was probably an Irish cleric in one of the Regular orders but you can also see a particular bias in favour of the Dominicans e.g. the description of Owen Roe O'Neill dying in a Dominican habit, a mention of a miraculous intervention by St Dominic, and the long account of troubles in the Dominican convent in Cashel - where Hackett was based for a time.

(d) In the letter accompanying the work the anonymous author draws attention to the fact that he is of both Norman and Gaelic ancestry, and Hackett's father was Norman and his mother Gaelic Irish.[v]

(e) The first initial of the signature of the letter accompanying the book seems to be a signature device combining P and H.[vi]

(f) Obviously then, as you can read in the Commentarius quote in the main text, Hackett wrote a book exactly at the right time for this work and coming from the exact same political perspective. Gilbert reckons that the anonymous author wrote the Aph. Disc. between 1652 and 1660 which matches this timeframe exactly.

(g) Fr Nicholas French Bishop of Ferns writing to Fr Peter Walsh in Ireland 19 Sept 1665, hoping that Walsh will intercede on his behalf with Ormond and allow him to return to Ireland, mentions an account ('a Confession') that is surely the Discovery:
"I shall truly hold my fortune hard, having suffered so much, and so sharp afflictions and reproaches in Rome, Spain, and Flanders, upon the score of being taken for a great friend and servitor of his [Ormond], and (that I may use the language of those vexed me) a principal Leader in the Anti-catholick Ormonian Faction. Collige ex ungue leonim, by the Confession of Father Patrick Hacquet."[vii]

Footnotes to the above
i. For an example of Latin in his poetry see Éigse Vol XII pt IV 1968 p.295.
ii. "Author Ibernicam, Anglicam, Latinam, et (credo) alias linguas eleganter

callebat..." (Fr.Richard O'Ferrall and Fr.Robert O'Connell, *Commentarius Rinuccinianus* (Dublin, Irish Manuscripts Commission, 1932-49) Vol.V, p.75.)

iii. John T Gilbert, *A contemporary History of Affairs In Ireland* (Dublin, 1880) Vol I, p.ix.

iv. Mháire Ní Cheallacháin, *Filíocht Phadraigín Haicéad* (Dublin, 1962), p.38.

v. See Irish Genealogist Vol V No.2 Nov 1975 p.264 and A. Valkenburg, *Pádraigín Haicéad as Caiseal Mumhan*, Feasta 36 (1983) 15-19.

vi. John T Gilbert, *A contemporary History of Affairs In Ireland* (Dublin, 1880) Vol I, p.9.

vii. The letter was published in Peter Walsh, *The History of the Irish Remonstrance* (1674), and reprinted in

The Historical Works of Rgt Rev Nicholas French D.D. Letters p.136 available at http://ia310929.us.archive.org/2/items/historicalworkso01frenuoft/historicalwo rkso01frenuoft_djvu.txt .

20. John T Gilbert, *A Contemporary History of Affairs In Ireland* (Dublin, 1880) Vol II, p.193.

21. Thomas Carte, *Life of Ormonde* (Oxford, 1851) Vol II, p.350.

Personally I think that Henry Jones' presence in Cavan at the outbreak of the rebellion was the most important factor in rising that county out into revolt. My guess is that he encouraged the O'Reillys, especially the then sheriff of Cavan, to rebel, claiming that it was in the interests of the King. Then he writes an account of his time there putting all the blame on these O'Reillys and conveniently scrubbing out of history his own role there.[i] As I admit, about that episode I am only guessing because Jones' account of that time in Cavan is the only detailed history there is to go on. Then you have his diary as scoutmaster general, which has been preserved for 1649-50.[ii] Scoutmaster General made him a kind of "chief detective officer",[iii] although in practice I think it made him the most important agent provocateur. Incidentally after the Restoration, when he was succeeded by his brother Theophilius in that post,[iv] the latter got up to the usual government entrapment tricks in the Captain Blood plots of c.1663.[v]

Some of his services as a government agent include: taking Antrim's statement in 1650 and transmitted it to Cromwell [vi]; "gave timely information" to the government on the first siege of Drogheda [vii]; and capturing the Book of Kells and the Book of Durrow and giving them to TCD along with two oak staircases that adorn the Old Library.[viii] Some of the more underhand intel tricks he used came to light in the case of Redmond O'Hanlon the famous rapparee. He on the one hand put pressure on Redmond, by not opposing a proclamation going out against him, while simultaneously using many contacts to try to encourage him to take government money to give false evidence against St Oliver Plunkett. Eventually Ormond, his close ally, just commissioned two people to murder Redmond.[ix]

Again in the following case I think he probably deliberately put pressure, false allegations, on Fr Edmund Murphy in order to then pressurize the desperate Murphy to give evidence against Plunkett. This is Jones' own letter describing Murphy's difficulties:

"Edmund Murphy, a Popish priest, whose place of residence was in the Tory Quarters so as advantage was taken against him by one Baker and Smith living about Dundalk whereby to charge him with corresponding with Tories. His having before charged them in like manner their interests prevailing so as to cast the poor man into prison when he was to have been tried the last Assizes of Dundalk and had undoubtedly perished had he not seasonably escaped and put himself under the protection of Government as a prosecutor against the Popish Primate, Plunkett. That which is herein desired is that his condition be presented to the King for his pardon, in which I am concerned as being to me recommended lately by that honorable lord, and worthy patriot, the Earl of Shaftesbury."[x]

Footnotes to the above

i. Henry Jones, *A Relation of the beginnings and proceedings of the rebellion in the County of Cavan* (London, 1642), reprinted in John T Gilbert, *A Contemporary History of Affairs In Ireland* (Dublin, 1880) Vol I, p.478-497.

ii. JRSAI (1893) Ser 5 Vol III p.44 and UJA no.3 1907 p.153.

iii. Thomas Fitzpatrick, *Sir Phelim's Commission*, New Ireland Review (Aug 1904) Vol XXI p.333-48.

iv. John P. Prendergast, *The Tory War of Ulster ad 1660-1690* (Dublin, 1868), p.23-24.

v. Thomas Carte, *Life of Ormonde* (London, 1735-6), p.266.

vi. John P Prendergast, *The Cromwellian Settlement of Ireland* (Dublin, 1875), p.54. Of course it suited his then masters to blame the king at that time, which does not make the information inaccurate I don't think. It simply means that he is telling a story outlining only one side of the facts, the one that suited his purposes at the time.

vii. Letter of the Lord Justices to the English House of Commons 7 March 1641/2 HMC New Ser Vol II 1903 Ormond Mss p.92.

viii. IHS March 1958 Vol XI no.41p.5.

ix. John P. Prendergast, *The Tory War of Ulster AD 1660-1690* (Dublin, 1868), passim.

x. Dated 1 June 1680 quoted in Rev. William Burke, *The Irish Priests in the Penal Times* (Waterford, 1914), p.83.

22. Thomas Fitzpatrick, *The Bloody Bridge* (Dublin, 1903), p.233.

23. See Pearse St Gilbert Ms 190 p.126 which is a copy of Sloane Ms 1008.

24. Both quotes from NLI MS 4198A p.47 quoting a letter by Edmund Burke, writing to his son, published in "a late number of the Tablet".

25. "Porro ex Dominicanis Ibernis illo Collegio Lovaniensi a P. Provinciale deturbatis fuere Momonienses, P. Patricius O Kearneus, vir doctrina et virtute clarus, et P. Patricius Hacquettus, qui Nuncio atque ejus fautoribus, quanto studio in Ibernia adhaeserit, ...Hoc autem anno ad P. Richardum O Ferallum, Capucinum Ibernum, Lovanio in Urbem Anglice scribens:

"Compono (inquit) tractatum de illa damnabili anti-Catholicae factionis defectione a nostra confaederatione... .. ...Compilavi omnia nefaria Comitiorum acta, edicta, declarationes, proclamationes, et literas Concilii, aliorumque praefectorum factionis, donec prorsus evanuit..."

Haec ille, quae ex autographo 29 Novembris 1652 Lovanii scripto transtuli. Verum postea dicto Dominicanorum Ibernorum conventu Lovaniensi deturbatus, et post pauculos annos Lovanii mortuus, librum (ut mihi praefatus P. Patricius O Kearnaeus retulit) jam absolutum ita deposuit custodiendum apud quendam amicum, natione Ibernum, ut metuam ne Ormonistarum et haereticorum dolis interciderit in gravissimum causae Catholicae praejudicium." (Fr.Richard O'Ferrall and Fr.Robert O'Connell, *Commentarius Rinuccinianus* (Dublin, Irish Manuscripts Commission, 1932-49) Vol.V, p.75.)

26. John Finch to the Duke of Ormond writing in Florence 2/12 July 1667 Bodleian Library Carte Ms 35 fol 518.

Fr Robert O'Connell had written about the origins of the 1641 rebellion in his earlier work on the history of the Capuchin Order in Ireland:

"Therefore the former [the Catholics of Ireland] stood still, for a long while were very serene, away from the turbulence of earlier times. Yes certainly the ecclesiastical privileges were still desired by the Catholic public, they still desired its yet redolent splendour. Certainly the Catholic party observed the situation of the seculars, and saw the sight in front of them of a lasting peace being violated by great wars, caused by the corrupt and nearly servile politics of heterodox magistrates, the more violent of them cruelly violating lives and fortunes. Added to this, the recently started discord of the English and Scottish publics under Charles, the then King, supplied the last fuel to those Catholic Irish who were going to be attracted to the use of the sword. On the one hand one party feared that the heretic population were about to prevail about the King, which might cause the newest and most wicked of the Catholics to rise, with their superiors; on the other hand the other party, likewise on the Island of Saints, might claim liberty for not only the civil society but chiefly for the church itself. The chance [of rebellion] was thought to have arisen from heaven. From whence a flame, the shield of Phelim O'Neill, sprung from the blood of the Irish, kindled a tumult in Ulster. It crept on and step by step slowly captured the whole of the fatherland like a firm stirrup. So as in this year no tract of the island, no recess, did not shriek with the sound of the arms of the Catholics fighting against the heretics.

...

We spoke up to the year 1641 of Phelim O'Neill, armed with the regular soldiers of Ulster, having begun the war against the heretics, in which war all

Ireland itself was now implicated, seeing as how the Catholics in the year 1642 took an oath, with the sacrament, among themselves to guarantee the defence (like men) of faith, fatherland and king. At that time nearly all Scotland and the Anglicans of the Parliament, alongwith a majority of the multitude of the same people, having concluded likewise a league, had rebelled. Among whom - the zealots of the parties of the three parts of the kingdoms [sic], the heretics who both out of the British race, and those who were about to rise nearly alone [? but] with great strength near [? in] Ireland [the Scots?] - the superficial were wavering. Not indeed all were with the King, nor all with the opposite party, but they were likewise not standing firm, from the same cause [?]. The Catholic party alone stood firm for him [the King]. Because although the former [indecisive heretics] might waver between the two parties of heretics, yet always they might attack with united strength the Catholic soldier."

Although mistakes are always possible in translating from the Latin, nonetheless in the first paragraph he is definitely referring to 'new and wicked Catholics' among what has to be the Old English - or Ormond? - or the New Irish rather, as O'Connell normally refers to them. These two parties are clearly the Old English and the Gaelic Irish, with a remarkable bias in favour of the latter!

("Ita status ille anteriorum temporum turbine longe erat serenior. Verum beneficia Ecclesiastica publicum Catholicum splendorem redolentia adhuc desiderabantur. Quod vero ad saecularium conditionem spectat pene erat servilis Adeo politicis heterodoxorum magistratuum corruptelis justitiae speciem prae se ferentibus diuturna pax multis bellis suaviter violentior in ipsorum vitas ac fortunas crudeliter inviolabat. Accedebat populi Anglici et Scotici cum rege sub Carolo tunc recens inchoata discordia quae distringendo Catholicorum Hibernorum gladio ulteriorem fomitem subministrabat. Namque ab una parte timebatur ne si populus haereticus in Regem praevaleret, fierent novissima Catholicorum pejora prioribus; ab altera quoque parte quo Insula Sanctorum in utramque cum civilem tum maxime Ecclesiasticam libertatem se vindicaret, occasio coelitus natu putabatur. Unde flamma quam Felmidius O Nellus Aegis Hibernorum sanguine prognatus, in Ultonia tumultuario accendit, pedetentim [recte pedetemptim] serpit patriamque universam quasi stupam siccam occupat. Ut hoc anno nullus Insulae tractus, nullus angulus, Catholicorum armis adversus haereticos non strideat.

...

Diximus ad an 1641 Felmidium O Nellum gregariis Ultoniae militibus armatum adversus haereticos bellum inchoasse, cui tota deinde Hibernia se implicuit, ut Catholici an.1642 foedus jurisjurandi Sacramento munitum inter se percusserint de tuenda (pro virili) fide, patria, et Rege; in quem utique tunc Scotia pene tota et parlamentum Anglicanum cum majori ejusdem populi multitudine icto etiam foedere insurrexerunt. Inter quae trium Regnorum partium studia, haeretici qui ex utraque progenie Britannica, et prope sola oriundi magnis apud Hiberniam viribus poterant, desultorii variabant, nec enim omnes a Rege, nec omnes ab adversa parte, nec iidem [recte idem?] diu ab eadem stabant, hoc uno sibi constantes, quod licet inter duas haereticorum

117

partes alternarent, semper tamen unitis viribus Catholicum militem aggrederentur."
by Fr Robert O'Connell O.F.M. (Cap.), *Historia Missionis Hibernicae Capuccinorum*, (Charleville, 1654), p.494-495, 547, original Troyes Ms 706 this from the transcript in the Capuchin Archives Dublin, and many thanks again to Fr Pádraig O'Cúill OFM (Cap.) for all his kind help.)

27. Lord Lieutenant Earl of Essex in Dublin Castle writing to Ormond 17 Nov 1673 quoted in C.W. Russell and J.P. Prendergast, *The Carte Manuscripts in the Bodleian Library* (London, 1871), p.126.

28. His grandnephew Nicholas of Dunsoghly describes in NLI MS 346 how he took a lot of persuading before he believed that the King was not involved in the rebellion.

29. John T Gilbert, *A Contemporary History of Affairs in Ireland from 1641 - 1652* (Dublin, 1879-8) Vol I, p.531.

30. *Calendar of the Committee for Advance of Money - Cases. Domestic Series 1642 - 1656*, pt. 2 p.684.

31. Edward Earl of Clarendon, *The History of the Rebellion and Civil Wars in Ireland* (Dublin, 1719-20), p.133-37.

32. See Studies Vol XL (1951) no.159 p.327.

33. See the account of that meeting in Jane Ohlmeyer, *Civil war and restoration in the three Stuart Kingdoms: the career of Randal MacDonnell Marquis of Antrim, 1609-1683* (Dublin, 2001).

34. See Studies Vol XLI (1952) p.91.

35. The before mentioned Nicholas Plunkett in his NLI Ms 346 traces his exploits at that time, which he regards as highly suspicious.

36. Alan Marshall, *Intelligence and Espionage in the reign of Charles II 1660-85* (Cambridge, 1994), p.22.

37. John T Gilbert, *A Contemporary History of Affairs in Ireland from 1641 - 1652* (Dublin, 1879-8) Vol II, p.138-141, p.144 Vol III p.288 and Michael Hynes, *The Mission of Rinuccini* (London, 1932), p.302. (Those two references are via notes by Fr John Brady on Meath church history, I hope I have interpreted them correctly.)

38. For example in his letter of 29 June 1645 to the Grand Duke of Tuscany mentioned in Archivium Hibernicum XLVII 1993 p.82.

CHAPTER 3

Were most of the Irish leaders of the 1919-21 War really British agents? A different perspective...

Applying the former model to more recent history I would contend that you can divide this 'conspiracy' into three rings, with the second ring attempting to manipulate the first and the third manipulating both:
1) Sinn Fein and the IRA leaders striving for Irish independence.
2) The British intelligence and governmental apparatus attempting to manipulate the first ring in order to prevent Irish independence and crush Irish nationalism.
3) A higher clique in the UK, possibly senior figures in the Masonic Orders or the Fabian group, who all along wanted a type of fake Irish independence - a type where they would actually pull the strings in the background - and were using their influence over Lloyd George, and his agent Cope, and to a degree over the overall security apparatus, to aid this cause.

1) There is no need to dwell on this story because, like 1641, the facts are well known anyway. The Irish people were unquestionably being treated badly by an arrogant and deceitful government in London which led many brave and idealistic Irish men and women to take up arms against that government in defence of Irish independence and rights. This writer is definitely not trying to knock in any way the motivation or the actions of the vast majority of ordinary Irish people who fought in that War but nonetheless maybe there are issues to be explored here. Many of the old veterans of that time were badly let down by the high up leadership - on both sides of the Treaty I think - and might have been more open than you'd think to some more in depth look at the forces unleashed at that time. The late Vincent MacDowell is a person whose historical sense almost stretched across the whole of the 20th century considering that he had deep roots in the IRB and among Republicans in the Newry/Dundalk area, was interned as a Republican during the Second World War, and was a leading figure in the Green Party as late as the 90s. His view was that:
> "...it would seem in retrospect, that a hidden hand had been in operation in the upper ranks of the movement for several years; that in the discussions about the

Treaty, influences were brought to bear and decisions were made that were not in the interests of the Nation; that on many occasions when it would have been possible to heal the split and make peace, passions and tempers were deliberately inflamed...."

2) Of course this is a distinctly minority opinion on the politics and leaders of those days. Few historians have entertained the idea of widespread infiltration of their ranks, although there is also this reference to Paul Bew the well known Belfast historian:

"Covert operations took a more directly political form with Assistant Under-Secretary 'Andy' Cope's back-channel contacts with republican leaders and consequent extension to them of de facto immunity. Paul Bew has suggested that British Intelligence was so ascendant by the Spring of 1921 that it could manipulate these increasingly vulnerable men into an amenable negotiating position. Whether or not this proposition will be upheld by further research, it is clear that the government had a far better grasp of their opponents' positions and weaknesses during the Treaty negotiations than vice-versa." [1]

So, plunging in where only those few historians have gone before me !:-), this writer is suspicious enough of British Intelligence to wonder if in fact most of the leaders of the War of Independence were actually British agents, and hence were being all along manipulated by that Intelligence agency for its own ends. Believe it or not I would even include Collins, de Valera, Mulcahy, Childers, the big heavy hitters in the IRB: Dermot O'Hegarty, Bulmer Hobson, Dr Patrick MacCartan, Denis McCullough, Sean T O'Kelly, Harry Boland, even maybe Cathal Brugha, Liam Lynch, Ernie O'Malley; and almost all of the Treaty delegation: Gavan Duffy, Duggan, Barton and Chartres. I appreciate that few would agree with me on this point, and I cheerfully admit that I really have precious few explicit sources to back it up. This is just a theory, its not proven, its just this writers gut instinct about what was really happening? Hopefully everybody gains by looking at this history from a different perspective and some facts might be surprising enough to those only acquainted with the usual history. And its important too because if we don't find out the truth here then we are condemned to repeat it!

I can only really point to one contemporary political figure, Sceilg,[2] who seems to suggest that both Collins and Dev were working for the

British. His real name was John J. O'Kelly, from Valentia island in Kerry, and is mainly famous for his efforts in the Irish language movement, second only to Douglas Hyde in Gaelic League circles. He chaired the First Dail debates and even some Cabinet meetings in 1920, while also being successively Minister for the National Language and then Minister for Education. He was furthermore a serious historian, a prolific and learned author, and the long time editor of the Catholic Bulletin which was a highly respected journal of the time.

Apart from his hints there are maybe a few facts about the then leaders which raise a few eyebrows in retrospect. Erskine Childers for example is a key figure at that time. He transported the guns from Germany that landed at Howth in 1914, he was probably the most important adviser to de Valera and controlled access to him when he came back from America [3] - obviously de Valera was President of the Republic at the time -, he played some role in Collins' intelligence apparatus,[4] Director of Publicity for the Dáil - the only non TD chosen to head a government department - and continued in that role for the anti-Treaty side, was secretary to the Treaty delegation,[5] joint author of de Valera's Document No.2, and at least some of the IRB/Dail money that was transferred from the US went through his bank accounts in London [6] etc etc. It comes as a bit of surprise when you read then in the foreword to the Penguin edition of his book that "in 1916 he was posted to Intelligence at the Admiralty." Later "he was appointed by Lloyd George to the secretariat of the Irish Convention of 1917."[7] This was obviously in the middle of his time as an Irish Republican but we are assured by one recent biographer that as a gentleman and all that there is no question of the Admiralty taking any interest in these activities! This biographer has nonetheless admitted that Admiralty Intelligence even sent a telegram to the Irish Volunteers looking for Childers when WWI broke out![8] Incidentally the Admiralty don't seem to have looked upon him as a traitor or anything because after his death they named a new Destroyer after him. Only Griffith seemed to find all this suspicious, in the Dáil on the 27th April 1922 he said:

> "In this present week there is a paper Poblacht na
> hÉireann, edited by an Englishman who has spent his
> life in the Military Secret Service of England - I will
> give Childers' record if necessary." [9]

There are a few other advisers appointed by de Valera after his return from America that caused at least one contemporary commentator to baulk. This was Pat Moylett, a Mayo businessman and long term political activist who conducted negotiations on behalf of Griffith with the British Cabinet in 1920, who described how Dev had set up a kind of kitchen cabinet including Childers, who was also a Major in the British army, as Director of Publicity, Major Robinson, his cousin "just retired from the British army", as secretary of the White Cross and:

> "We had a new star arise over the Republican horizon in the shape of John Chartres, a man who had been sent to Ireland by Lloyd George on a secret service mission in reference to munitions. We also had Mr.Smith-Gordon, an Englishman, who was appointed M.D. of the National Land Bank, and one or two other visitors of the same ilk. These were put up as an inner cabinet or advisory board by Mr. de Valera."[10]

It'd make you wonder!

It might be important as well to place these leaders in the context of the time. I would point to the period 1900-1914 as possibly the most important era in the shaping of the future Sinn Fein leadership. During that period Ireland is industrialising somewhat, and growing a commercially minded middle class, its the famous time when W.B. Yeats talks about the people being concerned only with adding the 1/2 pence to the pence. In that kind of era, unfortunately, frequently the Irish general public tend to despise those hardy few who would be more concerned with the welfare of the nation than their personal wealth. You can see some of that antipathy experienced by the old Fenians for example who, as pointed out by Sean Moylan T.D., were despised because

> "they were all poor men...It is a difficult matter for a rich man to appreciate the courage and selflessness of a seemingly ineffectual effort by poor men, and so the Fenians were misunderstood by the well-intentioned but thoughtless, and despised in the homes of those whose only standard of success is material advancement."[11]

This makes life very difficult for those Irish idealists, and correspondingly very vulnerable to some largesse from the powers that be, which by restoring their wealth enhances their standing in the eyes of the people. This is also a time when the police were hugely popular - not always justifiably so! - and respected, which again might have smoothed the path to the Castle door for at least some of these future leaders.[12] Also at that time there is high morale and ample funding among the various police and intelligence agencies all across the Empire and in America, and no doubt they were heavily focused on infiltrating the nascent Irish nationalist movement, the GAA, Gaelic League, IRB etc. Of course this changes dramatically later, especially post 1916, but most of the leaders were involved in the earlier period, and the post 1916 influx of activists tended to look up to and follow the direction of the earlier pioneers. In short I would say that the lifestyle of those leaders pre-1914 is captured in works like Joseph Conrad's *Secret Agent*, leading lives that were very vulnerable and very infiltrated by the police and intelligence agencies. So you would expect to find a lot of agents in this period and the absence to any reference to them makes this writer suspicious that maybe they rose to such prominence that they were able to snuff out any awkward questions about their past. And unfortunately the comparative silence on this subject makes me suspicious that a lot of the key leaders were agents, in other words a large group rather than one or two, because otherwise you would expect those that weren't to have exposed the others.

Again I know I am only speculating but I think also that you can see some of the more crafty intelligence agency techniques at work during those years. One trick that is frequently used by governments, intelligence agencies, (or even Secret Societies?) that control a country's media is to allow some apparently negative publicity to shine on a figure that they will use later as a political leader. As an example of what I mean take a government that controls the media and is using that control to kind of brainwash the citizens into thinking that the economic climate in the country is prosperous and booming. An example of that could be East Germany whose government frequently hyped its supposed economic success through a controlled media. But say the govt. knows perfectly well that this is not true, and knows that a generation of people are coming forward who are anything but prosperous. So the trick is that you will give some, apparently negative, publicity to some champion of the poor and oppressed knowing that he will become the future leader of that generation. And of course since the govt. controls the media, it can direct that publicity on one of their own agents. So anyway one commentator of the time has noted that de Valera got a lot of curiously favourable publicity at the time he was avoiding the death penalty at the end of the Rising in 1916.[13] Also there is some evidence that the media hyped up Collins' activities during the War of Independence, in a way that greatly enhanced his status later. Here is a comment on that by Seamus Robinson TD who was the O/C of the 2nd Southern Division of the IRA in 1921:

> "Towards the end of 1920 and the beginning of 1921 the British press had been changing its description of Collins from a "thoug" and "murderer" to "a daredevil"; romanticising him with damnation that praised him in the sight of the Irish people. He was

"seen" all over the country leading the columns from Dublin to West Cork where he had been "seen" riding on a white charger like King William at the Boyne. But it was Tom Barry who rode the horse because of a strained foot and King William rode a brown horse! This sort of journalism is not history but it is blatant propaganda. In the case of Mick Collins it put him on a pedestal where he did not properly belong. It enhanced his undoubted influence beyond all bounds. "What's good enough for Mick Collins is good enough for me." It is clear that the British press had got its directions and the anti-national press in Ireland simply quoted the British press without comment...knowing the reports were false. They could see the aim behind this personal propaganda."[14]

Maybe then that 'good enough' phrase could turn out to be the classic example of media brainwashing of the Irish people!

The other point I would make about intelligence agency tactics is the way that the Collins-de Valera split dominates the post Treaty atmosphere to the exclusion of other figures and a more conciliatory outcome. It would be classic intel practice to polarise the political situation around two or more political figures that they control. Once they control those leaders, and the extremes of the political spectrum, then they just leave it up to the ordinary people to decide who they want to follow. They don't care how it ends up, or who wins elections say, so long as they control the key figures in all shades of opinion. I know that sounds very speculative and convoluted, its just interesting how many insiders, like Sceilg and Tom Barry, noted the close friendship and link between Dev and Collins who then emerge later as supposedly great enemies dominating their respective camps.[15]

Anyway I don't really think that there is enough uncensored material out there to figure out what was really going on, so my aim is just to get this thesis across two huge hurdles. There are I think two enormous blocks to any such theory that the Irish Independence leaders were dominated by British intelligence agents. The first obvious one is that Dublin Castle is well known to have leaked a lot of information in the 1919-21 period, when the police were under huge pressure and badly run down, so how could they keep these agents secret? And secondly how could there have been a successful War of Independence at all if all these leaders were working for the enemy? Taking each of these in turn:

A) This first problem is I think quite obvious. The RIC Special Branch, DMP Political Department, and maybe Army Intelligence after 1916, were heavily infiltrated by the Irish Volunteer Intelligence Department, certainly not all of whom were British agents, and yet somehow we are to believe that Dublin Castle still housed some super secret all powerful intelligence agency that ran all these Irish rebel leaders as secret agents unknown to everybody?

The first thing I would say, in reply to that, is that the history of the high up duel between the IRA intelligence department and the Castle remains to be written, because at the end of the day Irish historians are only working on censored documents that the Irish and British governments have eventually released. For me anyway, sources like the DMP/RIC personality files are clearly not complete in the form they come down to us. Even some of the Bureau of Military History witness statements are heavily censored e.g. Austin Stack's memoirs as passed on by his widow.[16] Also of course it didn't suit anybody to admit later that he/she was a British agent while the Irish government for many years was dominated by people like de Valera, who might have had a vested interest in covering things up, and the UK government would of course like to continue running these agents in later Irish politics and so obviously also had no interest in revealing the real truth. So how do we really know what was happening? If for example Eamonn Broy, later head of Irish intelligence, was actually running Collins as a police agent, rather than Collins running him, whose interest would it be to reveal that? [17] Nobody's, so we can only keep guessing. Its no good taking the word of observers a little outside the loop here because how could they really tell? They obviously knew that Broy met Collins very frequently, to exchange intelligence, but how would they know which direction the intelligence really flowed? Certainly it has to be admitted that Collins, and the whole GHQ staff, seemed to live a charmed life in Dublin those years as even Tom Barry remarked:

> "..they seemed to have no fear of arrest or, if they had, they did not show it...Their lack of precautions was amazing and even made one angry...Mick then became serious and before long convinced me that their only hope of survival was to act as they were doing. That he was right is proved by the fact that during all the Anglo-Irish war not a single senior G.H.Q. officer was captured, recognised and detained."[18]

For all that I readily concede that there was a huge lower level IRA intelligence apparatus, involving a large number of people collecting valuable intelligence on Dublin Castle, who couldn't all have been under the control of the enemy. RIC codes, telegraph, mail, and telephone communications were routinely intercepted, and the country was full of Irish people, from all walks of life, passing on pieces of intelligence to the local volunteers. Hence it would be very difficult for the Castle to run these agents without arousing the suspicion of this large and alert Volunteer intelligence network. So any attempt to run these highly placed Sinn Fein leaders must have involved very few intermediaries, or entities not so well infiltrated. I would propose three possible modes of running these agents which could have been feasible in the face of the local dominance of IRA intelligence circles:

(i) My first guess is the Americans. Obviously the US and UK Secret Services had cooperated very extensively during the war, just ended in 1918, and presumably it is reasonable to suppose that they continued to cooperate closely against the IRA. Don't forget that a very large percentage of the leaders had been for a time in the US and their funding as well came almost exclusively from there. If some of those Irish American leaders, like McGarrity, were quietly working with US Intelligence, along with the British Embassy in Washington and US Consul in Dublin, then you can obviously see how they could have run a number of agents using entities that were not particularly vulnerable to the local IRA intelligence effort. For example I don't think that the US consulate in Dublin was infiltrated by them, and yet that office seemed to work very closely with senior Castle figures. The US Consul, Mr Dumont, admitted that he was in close touch with the Castle when talking to Pat Moylett before the Truce in 1921, and explained that: "I might tell you that I am more than a Consul here. I am a political agent."[19] This is Sceilg's opinion on the subject, I suspect referring to money that McGarrity might be corrupting the Irish leaders with:

> "McGarrity came over on a visit about the time of the Treaty debates. He turned up after a Party meeting at which I had just presided: that was the first time I had met him, and we never became cordial friends - because I would not be exploited. All the Envoys - MacCartan, Boland, de Valera - were a bit immature for the responsible roles they had to fill, and very easily exploited. Of course, it would be an insult to suggest it then; but they were so, in fact.
>
> ...
>
> Yes it struck me as very singular that de Valera should declare for the Platt amendment - the Cuban plan: it struck us all as somewhat inexplicable. How that was

126

put into his ears, I don't know. Somebody must have got after him. I am afraid it came from the Cope side - from the British Minister in Washington perhaps. When the suggestion came to the Dail, there was no disagreement, but certainly no ardour for it."[20]

(ii) My next guess is that the pattern of running these agents could have been the same as during the 1798 rebellion. Historians found out later that the most important and extensive British spy ring in Dublin at that time was run not by the Police or Army, but by the editor of the Freeman's Journal who reported back directly to the Castle. In other words you don't have to look for some trained intelligence figure to run such a ring, it could be a political figure who reported back only to high up government circles in Dublin or London. My favourite candidate for such a person would be Tim Healy who turns up everywhere at this time. He was in close contact with important IRB figures since at least 1915,[21] in fact it is said that he was a member of the IRB,[22] he interviewed the prisoners in Frongoch and was instrumental in getting them released, a close adviser of Collins during the war - and in receipt of IRA intelligence despatches [23] - and present at the Treaty negotiations,[24] and simultaneously is best buddies with the movers and shakers in London like Lord Beaverbrook the biggest media baron in the UK at the time.[25] Tim Healy is obviously a barrister that was central to the downfall of Parnell, a self confessed expert in political splits! He was not without some disillusioned clients,[26] and the Parnellites openly accused him of accepting money from the Castle to banjax his client's cases.[27] Sean MacBride later explained in an Irish Press interview that Healy had been originally blackmailed by the Castle, and was all along their tool during his long career in law and politics.[28] This casts a long shadow when you even hear of him giving money to Michael Collins.[29] Veterans of that time relate many rumours of Tim Healy's secret influential role in events, which presumably could only be true if he had some 'influence' on many of the key leaders. For example this is what Albert E.Wood, one of the leaders of the Irish Bar, said to Sean Moylan TD who led one of the Cork flying columns:

> "Don't go to see Tim Healy! You have ideals, for which you fought, and Healy is involved in the centre of an intrigue which, if successful, will dash the hopes held by you and your comrades."[30]

(iii) In any case Ireland is a small country and you don't really have to look hard to see some close links between the Sinn Fein leaders and the

Castle in those years. James MacMahon for example, the Irish Undersecretary which makes him no.3 in the Irish administration at the time, just happened to be a good friend of de Valera's, from Blackrock days.[31] Dublin is also at this time quite a small cosy kind of place which you can see if you stand on Dame St. today and look across at Eamonn Duggan's old office as IRA Director of Intelligence, no.66, and then look at the short distance from it to the entrance to the Castle. We are in fact told from one source that those neighbours Andy Cope, the "mainspring of Castle rule" in David Neligan's phrase,[32] and Duggan just happened to be best friends during the War. As pointed out Duggan was IRA Director of Intelligence in 1919 and at least for a time in 1920.[33] Of course as gentlemen we are assured that there is no question of them discussing politics! [34] The same account revealed that Cope's pockets were constantly full of Secret Service money. In fact Cope personally met with most of the important Irish leaders before and after the Truce. He exchanged written and verbal messages with de Valera,[35] and then met him "in town" not long before the Truce,[36] he is said to have been well in with Boland, and personally met with those leaders imprisoned in Mountjoy also while the War was continuing.[37]

But most interesting of all are the numerous accounts of his frequently meeting Michael Collins from the summer of 1920 on. Remember again that Cope is pretty much the British government's man on the spot at this time, he said himself that "he had superceded both the Lord Lieutenant and the Chief Secretary" in these political matters [38] and he also addressed full Cabinet meetings in London.[39] Hence it is not surprising that this ongoing Cope-Collins relationship, which was reported to continue at the height of the war, attracted some suspicion from veterans like Richard Walsh TD who was on the Volunteer Executive and also was IRB Centre for Co.Mayo. He is very definite that the two met about the summer of 1920 in the house of a legal friend of Tim Healy's in Dublin: "I heard at the time that more than one meeting was held at this man's house."[40] The house was owned by the lawyer called Kelly from Tuam and he also heard that Lord Beaverbrook was one of the prime movers in these machinations. Lawrence Nugent in his account says that he knew of separate meetings that Cope and Collins were holding together, this time in Dundrum in the house of Martin Fitzgerald's. (The owner of the Independent and Freeman's Journal, he appointed Collins a Publicity agent for the Freeman's Journal). Again Nugent found the thing a bit fishy:

> "It was strange that Mick carried on these meetings on his own as both Dev and Cathal Brugha were available."[41]

Walsh in his account clearly entertains some serious suspicions about Collins' role in events during this whole time, just stopping short of accusing him of being a British government agent. He knew Collins very well from his dealings with him in the Volunteers and IRB and he doesn't join in with the universal praise of his abilities. He says that Collins was vain and egotistical with "none of the qualities of statesmanship and foresight." His main skill

> "was his keenness in grasping what the key position [in the various nationalist groups] was and then getting control of it."

He also relates a story that at one of the Volunteer Executive meetings Cathal Brugha accused Collins of

> "making contacts with some people working in Dublin Castle and accused Collins and some others of acting with those Castle contacts without any authority."

Walsh discussed this with Rory O'Connor later and they figured that Collins wanted and got the position of Director of Intelligence of the Volunteers (previously he was Adjutant General) in order to quell any more of that kind of criticism. Now he had

> "an opportunity of establishing any contacts he liked...and could always use the excuse that he was seeing an individual ...for the purposes of getting information."[42]

So you can appreciate what his attitude to these Cope-Collins meetings was. This suspicion was not helped when he accidentally found out, in August 1920, that Collins was receiving messages, or one anyway, from a "General Cocker or Cockerbourne" of the "Imperial Intelligence Service".[43] So the bottom line is that the important Irish leaders were in close personal communication with at least one key Castle/ British government figure for a long period both before and then after the Truce. One historian notes simply that

> "Cope...Lloyd George's confidential agent...had long consorted with leading Republicans at Vaughan's Hotel and elsewhere."[44]

Consequently you don't have to worry about looking for any other intermediaries or police or intelligence personnel who could have run these agents. They were themselves in close contact with Lloyd George's agent most of the time it seems.

Maybe then at some high level in London these various strands come together, the US - Healy - Cope agents, and only there do they get to see the whole canvas, which I suspect, unfortunately, might not be a pretty picture from the Irish point of view!

B) Then you come to the second pretty massive hurdle that blocks this particular thesis. Clearly if all these leaders were working for the other side then how did the War of Independence take off at all? Surely with the amount of documentation that flowed across Collins' desk for one, is it not the case that the rebellion couldn't have succeeded for a week if he was a British agent? Which is as I say a good point and requires a bit of going into. Again this is mostly guesswork but I will put forward an explanation looking at it from the point of view of a British Intelligence apparatus hoping to keep the Empire together, dividing it into a number of seperate time periods as I try to guess the thinking of British Intelligence during each of these phases in turn:

1912-1919
OK picture the scene, Ireland c.1912. Ignore for a minute the later impression that the Irish Parliamentary Party (IPP) was corrupt or pusillanimous in the face of the old enemy - and I am certainly not excusing Woodenbridge. Look at the unity and serried ranks of Irish Nationalism united for once since the split had been healed in 1899. The IPP backed up by the flourishing branches of the United Irish League, and the more secret AOH circles, was firing on all cylinders in the House of Commons. For once they had stuck together and genuinely had the UK Liberal government over a barrel. They had even compelled that government to abolish centuries of parliamentary practice and crush the House of Lords veto and so had finally got the Home Rule Bill passed. And that Bill, backed by the determined Nationalist mood in Ireland, must have felt threatening to those in Britain who feared that it meant the end of an Empire. Because obviously if Ireland could wrangle out of them her independence then what about India or South Africa etc? And remember this is an Empire with huge resources of money and experience in dealing with similar situations. There is also plenty of evidence that the most devious minds the Empire could put together were on the case, like the unscrupulous Alfred Milner, that political general Sir Henry Wilson,[45] and maybe even King George himself.

So how were they going to do it? How do you crush the Irish Parliamentary Party? Maybe you simply hype up, fund, and arm her enemies. Unleash the extremes of the political spectrum and crush the IPP in the middle. Specifically you hype up the whole Ulster-Unionist-Protestant question, arm them and use them to try and block Home Rule, and simultaneously you do the same for the extreme Nationalist enemies of the IPP, arm them and let them loose in the political sphere to discredit and campaign against the IPP. The beauty of it is that both wings can feed off one another. The more forthright, and anti-IPP, Nationalists can get a great shot in the arm as the public gets alarmed at the rampant, and government sponsored, activities of the Unionists. The Unionists in turn will become ever more militant claiming that every Nationalist is now an unreasonable Sinn Feiner. The two extremes, by 1913 say, begin to crowd over, dominate the debate, and ultimately crush the IPP.

In a way all they are trying to do is destroy the unity of the Irish political leaders. Now instead of a united unstoppable mass of IPP MPs bringing their great weight to bear on the government, the seats in Ireland are now contested among the competing Irish Nationalist groups, and her unity vis a vis the UK government is lost. So until 1919-20, when the IPP had obviously been crushed, the British government might have been happy to back the later Sinn Fein/IRA leaders as a counterweight to attack the IPP. Then at that point they gradually turn their sights on Sinn Fein which now became the united force of Irish Nationalism, starting with the media maybe. Lawrence Nugent, who was a platform speaker for Plunkett during the Roscommon bye election, shows in his account how the 'Irish Independent' backed Sinn Fein after that election until about 1919/20. Then:

> "'The Irish Independent' having attained its ambition in smashing the Irish Parliamentary Party now started to work on the IRA operation and published a serious attack on Republicans."[46]

1919-early 1920.
But before they start to really try and crush Sinn Fein I think they complacently, and deliberately, allowed the rebellion to start in the 1919-mid 1920 period, confident that they could crush it in due course. After all from their point of view they probably thought that they could always pull the rug out from under the movement later because they controlled the leaders. Secondly as a serious military threat to their position they probably felt that the IRA position was hopeless simply because they didn't have the proper arms and their agents among the leaders were going to make sure that they never got any.[47] For arms read rifles specifically, no other armaments really mattered to the IRA, even in the built up areas of Belfast revolvers, shotguns and homemade grenades were pretty useless when set against the all important rifle.[48] And rifles, up to about mid 1920, they simply didn't have in any serious quantity. The Mayo IRA for example only had 2 rifles during much of

this period,[49] Cavan only ever had 5.[50] So maybe from the sober perspective of the professional soldier the IRA just didn't have a prayer when you consider that there were as much as 30,000 British troops travelling through Co.Mayo alone,[51] and big numbers of British forces in all parts of Ireland. So for the period 1919 to late 1920 the British government maybe felt that they could, if they wanted to, tolerate a kind of hopeless rebellion, which could be crushed later with ease and with it maybe any hope of Irish independence. But why would they want to? Why not just destroy the Sinn Fein independence movement straight away in 1919, now that the IPP is hardly much of a threat? Easily done seeing as how they control the leaders? I will give two answers to that.

Firstly I think they were maybe deliberately letting the rebellion develop in order to militarise the situation, which then allowed them a free hand to use their military to crush all hope of Irish Nationalism. What I mean is that their military couldn't justify using harsh warlike methods until the situation was seen to have become an out and out military conflict, in which environment they might have felt that they would always win.[52] So if they wait and let the war develop then when they move in and destroy Sinn Fein the aftermath could be like the end of the 1798 rebellion with Home Rule, Irish Independence, and all the rest of it crushed once and for all.

The other related point is that maybe they hoped that the IRA campaign would descend into a lawless mob like orgy of violence, like unfortunately many revolutions, which the army could then crush and gain many kudos as kind of law abiding white knights saving the island from some kind of sectarian or class massacre, again just like 1798. (And maybe not unlike some more recent British army propaganda!) They might have hoped specifically that the Sinn Fein courts, which they at first made no attempt to suppress, would descend into this kind of arbitrary revenge and sectarian stuff which could then discredit the whole concept of Irish independence. As part of this they might have planned the Ulster anti-Catholic pogrom that broke out in Belfast in mid 1920, as an attempt to add fuel to the sectarian flame. Seamus Dobbyn worked as an Intelligence Officer attached to the Belfast Brigade of the IRA and he said that that pogrom was planned long in advance, having "being prepared by the Masonic pro-British junta."[53] That phrase 'junta' would make you think that whoever was planning all this was not necessarily the real government but seemingly some short of powerful and shadowy Masonic cartel, but anyway his account clearly shows that this pogrom was no arbitrary act and presumably they must have thought that the IRA and the whole Catholic community would take this bait and reply in kind to the Protestant and Unionist establishment.

These then are my guesses as to what was going on during 1919 and early 1920, which if true shows again why the government was not as antagonistic to the Sinn Fein movement, yet, as some might presume.

Late 1920-1921.

But this just didn't work. What stands out loud and clear from the available evidence is that the Volunteers were not, unlike in many revolutions, blood thirsty or undisciplined or prejudiced against any group in society, only dedicated to seeing Ireland free. They never took that sectarian bait, they responded by organising a Belfast boycott and later housed the Catholic refugees in Masonic buildings in Dublin, well knowing who was behind the pogrom! [54] The Sinn Fein courts did not develop into the sordid kangaroo courts of class or religious prejudices that the British might have assumed would happen. The exact opposite is true, they were very fair to all parties, classes and faiths, proved very popular and brought great credit to the Sinn Fein cause. Sean Moylan highlighted two decisions in the courts in Cork which illustrate this. One was where the English wife of a serving British soldier took a case in the Sinn Fein courts against her local Irish landlord who wanted to evict her in order to get a higher rent. She won the case after pleading her poverty trying to raise a family on her husband's wages. The other case he mentioned was that of two sets of poachers who fished on, I think, the Blackwater. Of course the fishing rights were held by the usual Protestant establishment figures and the poachers seemingly had no hesitation in taking their case in the Sinn Fein courts, arguing about a net. The court confiscated the net and fined them for poaching.[55] So as you can see the IRA at the time, and everybody involved in these courts, were distinguished in their respect for private property and the lives of those they might have disagreed with. Bear in mind we are talking about ordinary everyday Irish people here who were enforcing court decisions and sitting as judges, lawyers were initially not present at all and "no difficulty was created by their absence"! [56]

So why anyway were they so respectful of life and property? (I admit that you could argue that this was not as true post Truce, where you could talk about the many executions - official and unofficial - of the Free State army and the large number of pretty indiscriminate burnings of stately homes by the anti-Treaty side in the Civil War.) I think that their fondness for religion, particularly the Catholic religion, was central to this. This point really comes across from the accounts of the time where no operation was planned without elaborate preparations being made to ensure that all the Volunteers had received confession for example. And I think simply that they were sincere in trying to follow the dictates of that religion in respecting life and property etc. This included the lives and property of Protestants, contrary to what some might say where a sincere Catholic is assumed to be anti-Protestant. Maybe this is what the British didn't bank on! The Irish Volunteers were basically decent people who just wouldn't resort to the sort of steps common in other revolutions, maybe partly because they took their religion seriously and also heeded the views of the clergy. I know some might disagree with me but this is definitely a feature of the accounts of the time, with some, like Seamus Robinson's, going into great detail about their theological views.[57] So therefore, unusually among revolutionaries, they had if you like an outside standard of morality which was not dependent solely on the orders or mores of the movement and government that they were following. What I mean is that if you look at the French or Russian revolutionaries they generally follow pretty blindly what their philosophy or leaders tell them to do, like 'death to the aristocrats' or whatever, whereas the Irish rebels were following a conscience that was maybe rooted in an older set of standards, and taught to them by people mostly outside the Revolution. This might have proved very helpful if those leaders were actually working to some other agenda! Anyway if you read the accounts of the time this point will strike you, and is so different to the experience of other countries.

Effectively then my guess is that the government might have been complacent until you get to late 1920 say. Then a different atmosphere develops. The Volunteers proved to be unbelievably resourceful and courageous in my opinion. They continued in the same way that they had won the Roscommon bye election, where they had got around censorship by writing election manifestos in the snow! [58] Where they couldn't get any arms from their GHQ by hook or by crook they wrestled them off the RIC and British army. Also some of the individual Brigades set up their own quiet smuggling operations in the UK, in the teeth of resistance from IRA GHQ, and transported them across the country via personal connections among the very nationalistic and brave railwaymen.[59] The fact was that the people, now united again after 1919, were unstoppable, the British had underestimated what they let themselves in for. Untrained and unpaid blacksmiths and small farmers proved to be military experts and were giving the British a torrid time irrespective of the arms and other difficulties. With great courage, organisation, and locally great leadership, the Irish were simply winning hands down against the British army and state in this period. Whatever complacency existed before, now it must have been obvious that the Irish were going to get their independence unless the British could swiftly crush the rebellion.

So now what can the government do? Obviously the trick here is to somehow use their control of the leaders to destroy the IRA campaign. I'm sure they teach this in some obscure British military academy somewhere! How to destroy an army that you are the general of! It has its risks and the obvious need of a certain discretion!:-) So say in the intelligence sphere they got Collins et al to resort to the usual tricks to ensnare those Volunteers not already working for them, such as:

- Maybe putting forward new people that they know are government agents and encouraging those IRA leaders not already working for the British to get close to them and possibly be betrayed by them. Betrayed in the sense of being charged later with IRA offences using those new agents as witnesses, they couldn't use their more senior figures for this. Dick Walsh for example says that Quinlisk, the famous agent shot in Cork, was helped a lot by Collins and that Collins specifically asked him to be friendly towards him.[60] Liam Tobin was very suspicious of one new agent called Fergus Molloy who nearly trapped him after Collins forcefully compelled Tobin to deal with him despite Tobin's misgivings.[61] Another new agent that emerges at this time was called Jameson and in reference to this case we are told that: "One thing is certain: it wasn't Collins who found him out - Collins had to be convinced to see sense, and didn't until it was almost too late."[62]

- By deliberately encouraging, and compelling, the individual Brigades to send detailed information, including the names and address of the Volunteers, back to GHQ and then deliberately losing those documents to the enemy in repeated raids. Seamus Robinson noted "GHQ's insatiably maw for written reports" and complains that 12 houses of Volunteers were burned down after Ernie O'Malley had sent down these addresses in his reports to Dublin.[63] In fact some of the more successful units like in West Cork,[64] Longford,[65] and indeed Tipperary (that's why O'Malley was in Tipperary, he was sent down by GHQ with a typist to report back from there because they were unhappy with the previous state of reporting in that area) seem to be those that were reluctant to supply that kind of paper work. Eamonn Duggan,[66] Collins,[67] and especially Richard Mulcahy,[68] attracted some contemporary criticism, if not suspicion, for the way that they didn't destroy and then lost in raids these very important documents.

- Possibly also in some areas they encouraged important IRA people to take charge of kidnapped enemy personnel, with a view to the eventual release of those prisoners and the later bringing of charges against the IRA people who had held them.

- Finally as you get into 1921 they might have reverted to more desperate measures. De Valera, just back from the US, thought it a great idea that the IRA should gather together in strength and attack some targets in numbers of 100 or so. These could have been deliberately designed as death or capture traps for large numbers of Volunteers. As part of this tactic the Dublin Brigade organised an attack on the Customs House and a huge number of the attackers were picked up because "due to an early warning" the Auxiliaries had advance knowledge of the operation.[69] Around the same time in Meath Collins decided to send in 100 members of the Meath and Fingal IRA to attack a troop train crossing the flat country of North Kildare with 700 British soldiers on board. When they got there they were surprised by a number of lorry loads of military and by a spotter plane although they managed to fight their way out safely.[70] Some bright spark decided to send the cream of the Belfast Active Service Unit to Cavan, where they were surprised and captured in circumstances that are thought to point to an informer.[71]

- It should be pointed out too that at the same time it was decided to order Sean McKeon to Dublin, and on his return the local police and military were out in force with full descriptions of McKeon and his travelling companion, and then famously shot and captured him. Collins had confiscated his revolvers before he left, apparently to avoid being discovered with them.[72] Tom Barry was similarly invited to Dublin and at the end of his journey home to West Cork he ran into a huge contingent of Essex military under the direct command of Major Percival. Luckily they didn't identify him and he got away.[73]

Nonetheless the IRA were still very much in the field and so the next logical step was to cobble together a sweetheart deal with those leaders which possibly garnered the British a better Treaty than their real military situation warranted. Its just my opinion but I think that the military situation in 1921 was much more favourable to the IRA than is commonly written, the British were very much beaten and simply wanted to leave the country in my view. Sean McKeon even said that in London in 1923, he assured the British that if they had any doubts on that score they could declare war again in the morning and he and the rest of the IRA would beat them all over again![74] So in fact the British were lucky to get away with Partition at that time, and maybe their skills in intelligence - including control of the Treaty delegation - had something to do with it!

Hence one way of looking at how it panned out was that the British were using the Sinn Fein movement to crush the Irish Parliamentary Party in 1913-1919 (including manipulating the German Plot episode of 1918, as described in the first chapter), then in 1919-20 they were happy and complacent about the nascent rebellion which they expected to crush in due course quite easily, then ended up being beaten despite pulling out all the stops in trying to destroy the IRA using their control of the leadership in the late 1920-21 period. This therefore would explain how the rebellion succeeded despite their control of the leadership, because they only tried to use them to crush the rebellion in that late phase, and failed to do so.

3) Returning to an episode described earlier, the above mentioned General in the 'Imperial Intelligence Services' who was communicating with Collins in the summer of 1920 was Brigadier General Sir George Cockerill, MP for Reigate, close friend of Lloyd George, and 'Director of Special Intelligence at the War Office' and he throws up an interesting clue that maybe points to a different story behind the whole conflict. He seems to use the kind of language that the Fabians and Masonic Orders use in these well chosen words about Michael Collins and the emerging Ireland:

> "These indeed are Michael Collins' own words and he
> shows statesmanship and vision of a high order when,
> exhibiting a rare comprehension of the forces which are
> reshaping the modern world, he declared that "in the
> creation of the Irish Free State we have laid a
> foundation on which may be built a new world order."

That and Dobbyn's reference to the 'Masonic Junta' throw up the possibility that maybe there is another, corrupt, group here which actually wanted a kind of Irish independence for their own purposes.

This tallies in with a recurring problem in this account of British Intelligence agencies manipulating the Sinn Fein and IRA leaders. The problem is that there is some evidence that people like Cope were really very active in assisting the Irish independence movement, at all times, as if they really did want Irish independence.[75] Why? Well maybe they are nice guys and are fond of the ideal of Irish freedom, but frankly I think not! Maybe quite simply they wanted to install a kind of fake independence in Ireland, by giving her nominal freedom while secretly controlling her political establishment? They were granting independence to a clique that they in turn controlled? And maybe they didn't control the IPP as much as they later controlled the Sinn Fein leaders and so needed to swap over the two sets of leaders before conceding Irish independence?

Who 'they' are is a vexed question. Taking up the use of code words by Cockerill I would guess the people to watch would be the Fabian circle in London. These would include Bertrand Russell, a friend of Crompton Llewelyn Davies, Moya Davies' husband, H G Wells, a good friend of Lloyd George's that Pat Moylett was sent to see when he was negotiating on behalf of Griffith in London, possibly Lord Longford, a friend (and biographer) of de Valera's and Childers' and obviously high up in government circles in the UK on occasion, maybe even W. B. Yeats and G. B. Shaw as well as the obvious Cope and Lloyd George. Who was in the British Intelligence loop but outside this circle is hard to say except its definitely the case that de Winter, the head of the British Secret Service in Ireland, was not in this inner circle. He in fact was clearly suspicious about what was going on and had Cope under surveillance. He had also tried to persuade the Cabinet to keep de Valera in prison when he was arrested after coming back from America but he failed and I think overall felt that his, and the security apparatus in Dublin, efforts were being undermined by somebody in his own government, which neatly matches this theory.

What's interesting in that context too is the role of the Secret Societies. In practice Ireland at this time is clearly dominated by those societies, the Freemasons and Orange Order on the Protestant side, the Ancient Order of Hibernians (AOH) backing the IPP and the moderate wing of Irish nationalism, while the Irish Republican Brotherhood (IRB) controlled everything that moved in the sphere of the more forward Irish nationalism. It is said of the Freemasons in 1918 that:

> "The Exclusion of Catholics is secured through the
> machinery of the Masonic Lodges and that machinery
> is of course dominated by his Grace the Duke of
> Abercorn...And yet Ireland has been bled and starved to
> the point of death, while the compass and square
> dominate the Castle, the Judicial Bench, the Bar, the
> Constabulary, the Magistracy..."[76]

To counteract this many Catholics were secretly organised into AOH branches and they dominated whatever was going for Catholics in the professions, trades and government appointments in the period 1900-16 as you can see in this quote from one observer who knew them well:

> "The AOH up to this period [c.1916] and for a number
> of years afterwards was the most insidious organisation

ever established in Ireland as those of us who had to work with them and against them knew only too well. They controlled every form of business and profession in the country. Various types of business had each an AOH branch of their own. Contracts were arranged with institutions for good members...I was offered one of those contracts if I would join. The same applied to the professions: doctors had their own branch and appointments were made accordingly. The same applied to the law, education, and every other walk of life in the country...They even tried to get control of the GAA."[77]

Then throughout this time, in the words of Dorothy Macardle, "the IRB was establishing everywhere its secret but effective control" over the emerging organisations like the Gaelic League, Irish Volunteers, Sinn Fein and the GAA.[78] As you can see some of these organisations like the GAA, and in 1914 the Irish Volunteers, were subject to fierce internal wars between the two Secret Societies with the IRB usually winning out though post 1916. The IRB were secretly pulling the strings in the background throughout this time, especially in the case of the Irish Volunteers as Seamus Robinson relates:

"IRB members were told "We must make sure that no one will be elected an officer of the Volunteers who is not a member of the 'Organisation.' " - as if that was something new or something that we would be allowed to forget, and without adverting to the fact that that sort of thing would undermine the authority and the efficiency of the whole Volunteer movement. Without waiting for the meeting to start officially I walked out in disgust thinking of Tammany Hall. I never again bothered about the IRB...After the oath of allegiance to the Dail the IRB became a sinister cabal."[79]

Of course the vast majority of Irish people at the time had no idea that their country was sewn up like this by the Secret Societies. They even controlled the electoral system by a clandestine hold on the nomination of candidates by the big political parties. Kevin O'Shiel tells us that in Tyrone the AOH undermined Murnaghan as the local IPP MP simply because he was not AOH, his convention "was rigged by the powerful secret society." O'Shiel is clear that the AOH

"was unquestionably engaged in carrying out a policy of weeding out every non-Hibernian Member of Parliament in the [Irish Parliamentary] Party."[80]

Meanwhile the IRB controlled the candidates on the Republican side. Dick Walsh talks a lot in his account about "the IRB...interference in the selection of candidates" in the emerging Sinn Fein party. He says that

"the IRB did take an active part in the selection of republican parliamentary candidates in the General Election of 1918, and the previous by-elections."

In the bye elections "as far as I know all the candidates were IRB men" except maybe Plunkett and White. Later in the 1918 election "the IRB members were being put forward as Sinn Fein candidates."[81] Dorothy Macardle also says that some of these Sinn Fein TDs complained in retrospect "that no one who accepted responsibility as an elected representative ought to be subject to secret control."[82] So as you can see any outside commentator who ignores the role of the Secret Societies is going to be badly mistaken if he feels he understands Irish politics at that time.

In fact the political power in Ireland rests then with these Secret Societies, who unknown to the general public really controlled all that happened on the island. And so the question of who in turn controlled them might yield some answers in trying to figure out what was going on in the power play from 1910-24. Obviously the Freemasons are linked back to the head of their organisation in London while the IRB were controlled by Clan-na-Gael in the US. The AOH (Board of Erin) on the other hand refused to make a secret deal with Clan-na-Gael in 1909 and so remained independent.[83] So if I may be permitted to speculate - and I admit I am doing that a lot !lol - I wonder if perchance it was the case that Clan-na-Gael was secretly allied to or controlled by the Lloyd George group in London, and with the Freemasons, then the whole island would be nicely controlled by this clique with the sole exception of the AOH. Hence they, and their Irish Parliamentary Party, just had to be crushed? This might then be the link between the Lloyd George group in London and the IRB controlled IRA in Ireland?

You might think that I am being overly speculative here talking about this secret society question and placing it in the centre of the real political undercurrents of the period, but in my defence I will point out that many commentators at that time knew well how important those societies were. One book in particular was written on this subject in 1922 by a British army captain, H.B.C. Pollard, serving in the office of the Chief of Police in Dublin Castle.[84] For him this whole question of the Secret Societies, including the clandestine war between the AOH and the IRB, is the real political story of Ireland from 1910-21, and he drew on confidential Castle documents to prove his case.[85] He traces the story of these societies back into the 19th century outlining the curious links between these societies and important figures in the UK. For example he draws a connection from the Irish rebels to the Carbonaries in Italy and then notes that they were quietly assisted by Lord Palmerston, when British Prime Minister, because he was also a leading Freemason. Fr George Dillon also drew attention to this Fenian-Palmerston link, writing not long after the Fenian uprising:

> "..yet strange to say the leaders of the disastrous movement [the Fenians], the Irish, and the American organisers, were permitted by the English Government, at least so long as Lord Palmerston lived, to act as they pleased in Ireland."[86]

So Pollard, and Fr Dillon, link Irish revolutionaries, and international anarchists/revolutionaries, to the Freemasons which obviously included a lot of important UK (and US) political and security figures over the years. Pollard also says that the head of the Invincibles, the famous No.1, was P.J. Tynan and that he was "closely in touch with government circles in England and a frequent caller at the Irish Office."[87] He even says that the head of the IRB James

> "Stephens had received some £25,000 from the British government ... and in later years it was a matter of common knowledge that Stephens, besides being Head Centre, had also an agreement with the British government, which threw a peculiar light on his immunity from arrest and his later escape from prison and leisurely retreat to France."[88]

He draws on works by Barruel, Robinson, Clifford and the Alta Vendita to explain these links between the Freemasons and these Irish and other revolutionaries, and why the Masons favored revolutions. He even refers to the controversial Protocols of Zion, but he - and this writer - ignores, and hopefully disbelieves, any anti-Jewish sentiments in it, but seems to draw on the curious insight that the writer of those Protocols appears to possess about the thinking of the senior ranks of the Masonic Orders.[89] Rather than the Jews he actually links those groups, that Robinson et al mention, back to the Jesuits.[90] So effectively I think that Pollard's basic theory is the same as in those Protocols, that sometimes these secret revolutionary groups are allied to the Masons and control countries between them.

Amazingly he even goes further and takes a keen interest in the rituals that societies like Clan-na-Gael practice. He seems to say that these groups are really linked to the occult and those, what might be called, esoteric religions that he is quietly knowledgeable about.[91] In reference to these occult circles he claims that "such societies still exist and are by no means inactive."[92] Incidentally the old name for the IRB is 'The Phoenix Society',[93] which some say is an important occultic symbol,[94] and the clandestine name for Clan-na-Gael was the Universal Brotherhood,[95] which certainly sounds Masonic.

Hence, following on the pattern of the Fenian period, you have here another potential explanation for what transpired in Ireland from 1910-22. The theory is that these Masonic Secret Societies were asserting their control over the country, Masonic leaders in the UK being quietly linked to IRB figures in Ireland and between them destroying the more independently Irish, and Catholic, IPP and AOH. Btw I am only referring here to some of the leadership, I am sure that the vast majority of groups like the IRB were perfectly decent people not involved in any such intrigue.

Whatever the truth of what was going on I venture to suggest that it is a lot more complicated than the history that is normally taught in Ireland! Nonetheless I agree with Richard Walsh who concluded that:
"It was, as I said, a heroic age, and whatever mistakes or blunders were made at the end, it is well that we keep in mind that this generation that lived in Ireland were a great generation...and can without fear face the verdict of history."[96]

Footnotes

The WS numbers listed are Witness Statements taken by the Irish army's Bureau of Military History in the 40s and 50s. There are 1,770 of them, some as much as 300 or even 800 pages long representing an enormous fount of new information on the period. I say new because they were kept secret for about half a century, only released to historians in the last few years. They are available in the National Archives in Dublin, whom I'd like to thank. Btw I should point out that many of these writers including Richard Walsh and Seamus Robinson - but not Sceilg I don't think - do include complimentary phrases about people like Michael Collins, which I have discounted, because I think they were just been charitable about an old dead comrade.

1. The quote from Vincent MacDowell is from Vincent MacDowell, *Michael Collins and the Irish Republican Brotherhood* (Dublin, c.1997), p.155 which draws heavily on Michael O'Cuinneagáin, *On the Arm of Time* (Taratallon, Donegal Town, 1992). The Bew reference is from Peter Hart ed., *British Intelligence in Ireland, 1920-21: The Final Reports* (Cork, 2002), p.15. Hart footnotes this to Bew, *Moderate Nationalism and the Irish Revolution.* pp.741-6. Paul Bew's thinking on these lines can also be seen here: "This, after all, is historically how Britain achieves peace in Ireland. In 1920-21, the police and army regularly made raids on leading Sinn Féin figures, only to discover that they were under the protection of other parts of the British state. Those arrested were rapidly released even when incriminating material was found; in one famous case, that of Erskine Childers in 1921, a senior British official [Cope] carried his bags out of jail" (Paul Bew Yorkshire Post December 22 http://www.cpgb.org.uk/worker/606/sinn%20fein.htm).

2. John J. O'Kelly [known as Sceilg] W.S. 384, he was also later the President of Sinn Fein c1926 after De Valera split off to form Fianna Fail:
"Long afterwards, I laughed when I found that Harry [Boland], like Michael Collins, was in close touch with Cope."(p.60)
...
"While de Valera was in America, he and Collins came to be a good deal in touch with each other, though de Valera did not seem a man who would let anybody get very close to him before going out. For a time, Collins, indeed, seemed almost in charge of the correspondence, and some of us began to suspect that the Lloyd George machine was operating here. I am not likely ever to investigate the thing now.

The line to go on would be to try and trace Cope's first meeting with Collins, and follow it down. Cope was sent here specially for that work. It was very freely said - and I believe it to be true - that Lloyd George was fully aware that de Valera was returning to Ireland at the Christmas of 1920, and that, of course, would have been arranged by Cope and Collins. The details would have been kept probably from Cathal Brugha's knowledge...[Sceilg liked Brugha, and wrote an Irish biography of him. He goes on to say that Collins was annoyed at the peace feelers of Fr. O'Flanagan and the Galway County Council resolution...] The reason being that it was breaking into his own negotiations with Lloyd George. You may take it that Collins was in close negotiations with Lloyd George, through Lloyd George's agents at that time.

Another thing that occurs to me is that Archbishop Clune did not come over until the day after Collins accepted the appointment as Substitute-President. When Griffith was arrested - this was well before de Valera came back - it devolved on me to preside at meetings of the Cabinet until a substitute was appointed. Griffith sent out a letter from Mountjoy by Noyk, the solicitor, suggesting Cathal Brugha as his substitute. If Brugha refused, Stack was to take it on; failing him, Michael Collins was to act. I was in the chair when the letter was read by Diarmuid O'Hegarty. Brugha or Stack would not act, but Collins consented; and Dorothy McArdle has a most misleading account of it. He was hardly twenty-four hours in harness when the New York Gaelic-American had a full page photograph of Ireland's new fighting chief. Had I time, I could easily trace all those all those developments. But then I have no heart for that kind of thing. I am quite sure you will look upon it as I do. If you investigated it, and found something unworthy of the period, you would rather not have found it.

The selection of Archbishop Clune and the sending of him here looked very fishy to me also. It was not accidental: it was being hatched for a good while. The mere fact that they would send Dr. Clune to Mountjoy prison to see Griffith is suspicious. Cope had been visiting Griffith, and he would, no doubt, exonerate his employers and the Imperial Government by throwing all the blame on the Castle, and Griffith would get an opportunity of sending that information out to Collins, and to others, especially the gullible. The investigation of all that would be very sickening. I got plenty of revolting echoes of it even in Mountjoy." (p.63 et seq.)
...
"I knew all about Mrs Llewelyn Davies from London friends...Earlier, Mrs Davies lived in Donegal a good deal. We knew well she was very intimate with many people - among them Michael Collins. I don't think I ever introduced her name into anything I wrote. We did not care about her. She was a daughter of James O'Conner M.P., who was pretty well known to me, and they lived in Bray. One Sunday, they ate shellfish, and it poisoned the whole family except this girl, who happened to be away, so far as I can recollect. She went over to London, and became a clerk in Lloyd George's office. In time, she went up very much in his estimation. There was then a man to whom the Wizard felt very much indebted, Llewelyn Davies, who was a solicitor, and had been largely instrumental in getting Lloyd George into Parliament. In gratitude, let us presume, Lloyd George arranged that the Davies marry Miss O'Connor. Some years after her marriage, she came over and, with two children I think, lived a good deal in Donegal. Her husband, who was solicitor to the Post Office, I think, used to come over to see her in the beginning. In time, she had rooms at the Gresham. The whole story is something one would rather

forget."(p.66)

...

"Looking back casually on the whole thing, I feel I would much rather forget it all. I was much surprised the other day at a statement by William O'Brien of Galway, who said he thought Arthur Griffith was one of the greatest men our race produced. Griffith had some ability, and he had a mighty respect for his own views; but, in all the time that he was in the Dail and I presiding, I can't remember one suggestion from him that would be worth preserving. You know with what reluctance I say that. He did not distinguish himself in any way whatever, except by his opposition to the Republic to which he had sworn allegiance. He would make casual references to Davis and to Irish industry, and anybody who did not accept his view was dense! He had become a very terse writer and would have been an excellent journalist, if he had the broad outlook of Rooney. To meet him at his fireside as I used to when he returned from South Africa was a pleasure not easily forgotten, and it is in that role that I prefer to remember him.
...[Also says that "I think it was very easy for any man of substance to get Griffith's ear." Including Martin Fitzgerald the wine merchant.(ibid p.20) As outstanding intelligent personalities of the time he mentions particularly Joseph MacDonagh, the brother of the executed Thomas.] I have no hesitation in saying that Joe MacDonagh was the man who impressed me most. Both Collins and Griffith used seem vexed with him or envious of his facility in discussing a wide range of pretty vital subjects, but they were not in the same plane as he...
De Valera was not on the same plane as MacDonagh either. He was recognised as leader, because described as the only surviving Commandant after the Rising. ...As far as my recollection goes, de Valera never said anything of real moment. He was always well received, and would talk a great deal, but I don't know of any subject relating to any of the departments towards which he contributed a really helpful suggestion. I say that without prejudice. He once clashed with Count Plunkett and appeared in a very sorry light; and he certainly had lost the confidence of the majority of his Sinn Fein colleagues before the Sinn Fein split came in 1926."(p.67)

...

"Diarmuid O'Hegarty was Secretary to the First Meeting of the Dail, and then Secretary to the Cabinet. I feel that Diarmuid was one of the mysteries of our political life. I am saying nothing against his soldiery qualities or anything like that. He was arrested in 1916 and deported to England. I don't know whether he was sentenced. When the train got to Chester or some such station, a porter walking up and down shouted: "'Egarty, 'Egarty! Anybody by the name of 'Egarty?" Of course he attracted the attention of everybody. At last, somebody said to Diarmuid: "I wonder could this be you?" Diarmuid got right back to Dublin on the plea that T.P. Gill could not get on without him. So we were told, and we accepted the statement at its face value. There was a wonderful feeling of trust then. Diarmuid got into touch with the Prisoner's Dependent's Fund, and moved about in the old circles. When the amalgamation took place in

145

August, 1916, O'Hegarty and Belton were put on the composite committee. O'Hegarty and Collins were very close friends. O'Hegarty and I were fairly intimate too, because we rehearsed plays together in the Keating Branch.

...

[Michael Collins was appointed to a post with the National Aid Committee] largely through O'Hegarty and Belton. Thus links were established with all the prisoners coming out of jail. Diarmuid had no special qualifications or claims that I could see; yet he became Secretary to the first meeting of the Dail, then Secretary to the Cabinet. Later, he abandoned the Republic, and became Secretary to the Cosgrave Government. In time, he was put into the Board of Works, and is now in charge of it. But what is he worth from the point of view of national service and national character, or national culture or the national language? He is alert where his own interest is concerned; and I hope he has some better traits than those I have discerned.

I have already said that I feel Michael Collins was in touch with Cope from the date of his arrival here, and I am convinced that de Valera came entirely under Collins' influence in this respect when he came back from America, if not earlier."(p.70-71)

...

"She [Dorothy Macardle] wrote that book under de Valera's direction and tutelage, and, so far as I can recollect it - except in so far as it embodies official documents acceptable to de Valera - I do not hesitate to brand it as altogether the most misleading volume that has been written on the Republic.

...

I have little doubt that there was great influence brought to bear on him after he [de Valera] came over [from the US], and none whatever that he came over on invitation to continue the negotiations in which Michael Collins had long been engaged.

...

As regards the military situation at the time, its alleged weaknesses must have been put forward as a reason for inaugurating negotiations. Yet I don't doubt that Collins and his group had a supply of arms within reach."(p.74)

...

[At the meeting when the delegates first returned from London Collins said practically nothing:] "It was not the attitude or statement of a candid man. If you were present or witnessed it, that is what you would think too."(p.76)

He refers to Moya Davies in response I think to a query from the Military History Bureau researcher who asked was it she who tried to entrap Austin Stack. Sceilg says no it was Mrs. Maud Walsh, a sister of the judge Sir James O'Connor: "a sinister figure. He wrote a History of Ireland afterwards, which was just terrible." This spying was on behalf of Cope.

Michael Collins knew Mrs Moya Davies since 1913. Her husband Crompton "at that time was Lloyd George's solicitor and Solicitor General at the Post Office." (Meda Ryan, *Michael Collins and the women who spied for Ireland*

(Cork, 1996), p.21.) When a Sinn Fein delegation went to see President Wilson in London in January 1919 they stayed with the Davies' in London, apparently because Mrs Davies was "a close friend of George Gavan Duffy and Michael Collins."(Robert Barton WS 979 p.12) He also used to stay with Mrs Davies in Portmarnock in 1920 and 21.(Pat Moylett WS 767 p.147) Of course she is the person who is said to have borne two children by Michael Collins, and rumour has it that he was afraid to have his private life exposed by the powers that be, in case he might go the way of Parnell! She herself claimed later that she was a spy and a close adviser to Collins. (Peter Hart, *Mick: The Real Michael Collins* (Oxford, 2005), p.353.)

I appreciate that Sceilg is really only talking about a few of the leaders, and I start speculating about a longer list, but I just think that it is unlikely that those really in the know would not have seen what Sceilg seems to have, and their silence is what I am going by. This includes people like Cathal Brugha that are very close to the centre of the action, although Sceilg likes him and defended him from charges that he went unhindered to his work everyday during the height of the war. He did attend his business during the troubles, Sceilg concedes, "it is true, but not regularly while the crisis was on." (JJ O'Kelly WS 384 p.58) But even Sean McKeon was interviewed by Brugha at his business premises in Dublin (Sean McKeon WS 1716 p.159), showing that he conducted IRA business openly where everybody knew he worked? It is said btw that Cathal Brugha had important Castle contacts since at least early 1918, Walsh reckons it might have been Broy which seems likely because of their shared interest in athletics. (Richard Walsh TD from Balla Co.Mayo WS 400 p.151.)

As I say I am only guessing about these leaders, some facts just jar with the usual interpretation of events e.g. Robert Barton, a Captain in the British army, is reported to have been placed in charge of prisoners effects in Dublin Castle after the rebellion in 1916. That could of course be just a cover story for identifying the prisoners on behalf of British intelligence, who would certainly have wanted him there to do that at that time (Robert Barton WS 979 p.43).

3. "I tried to see Mr. de Valera through various channels, but on each occasion I was sent back to Erskine Childers as I was informed he was the only man that could make an appointment for me with Dev." (Patrick Moylett WS 767 p.81.)

4. James Maguire of Glenidan Co.Westmeath WS 1439.

5. He "was the brains behind this, as he was behind many of the Irish documents" prepared by the Irish plenipotentiaries in London (Peter Hart, *Mick: The Real Michael Collins* (Oxford, 2005), p.298).

6. This is discussed in the coded part of a letter from Michael Collins and Cathal Brugha to Diarmuid Lynch in America (Diarmuid Lynch, *The IRB and the 1916 Insurrection* (Cork, 1957), p.224).

7. The Foreword by Geoffrey Household in the Penguin edition of Erskine Childers, *The Riddle of the Sands: a Record of Secret Service* (London,1978), p.16-17.

8. Leonard Piper, *Dangerous Waters* (London, 2003), p.137.

9. Barton admits that they called a "new British Destroyer" after him. (Robert Barton WS 979 p.28.) The Griffith quote can be read at http://historical-debates.oireachtas.ie/D/DT/D.S.192204270003.html .

10. Patrick Moylett WS 767 p.82. The John Chartres mentioned, known as "the Mystery man of the Treaty", prepared one of the documents used by Collins during the negotiations on the subject of the Commonwealth. It proposed changing the structure of the latter so that it could embrace maybe all nations, including the United States, become an alternative to the League of Nations, leading to a "new world order" in which "war would become impossible." (Peter Hart, *Mick: The Real Michael Collins* (Oxford, 2005), p.304-5.)

11. Sean Moylan WS 838 near the beginning. Lawrence Nugent describes the difficult economic pressure that was exerted on these pioneers in the c1914 period. (WS 907 near the beginning.)

12. "When I left my home for the Depot in the Phoenix Park [to join the RIC in 1907] I carried with me the regards and good wishes of all and sundry. It never occurred to anyone that I was doing anything unpatriotic - not even the old Fenians and Land Leaguers who still survived, amongst them my father - a veteran of both organisations." (JJ McConnell WS 509 p.1.)

13. Lawrence Nugent WS 907 p.48.

14. Seamus Robinson TD, WS p.49. "One member was specially selected by the Press and the people to put him into a position which he never held; he was made a romantic figure, a mystical character such as this person certainly is not; the gentleman I refer to is Mr. Michael Collins." (From a speech by Cathal Brugha during the Treaty debates.)
When Martin Fitzgerald bought the Freeman's Journal Piaras Beaslai became the leader writer for it and at that point "a good deal of publicity was given to Mick Collins" in the paper. (Lawrence Nugent WS 907 p.180) From the same source we are told that deliberately to court personal publicity he dressed up in military uniform for the Sinn Fein ard fheis and "gained some of the popularity which he was looking for." (ibid p.161.)
Seamus Robinson had more things to say about Collins, not all of it complimentary!:
"The first time I found Mick Collins to be a bit of an artful dodger, was when he arranged the first, the "phoney" attack on French." French was actually never expected in Dublin at that time which was the occasion of a big

Volunteer gathering in Dublin, giving him an opportunity to show off to the gathered delegates:

"However, Mick was able to give the impression to the Volunteer officers, from all over the country that he not only organised the attacks on spies that had begun in Dublin but that he also led them, taking part in them!...And that was the nearest I ever saw Mick Collins to a fight...This dummy attack on French was followed by several other apparently serious attempts but they all failed because of inaccurate information."

He then refers to his question during the Dail debates, which he stands over and adds: "One looks in vain to find either the question or the answer in the new editions (27/2/'25) of the Dail debates." (Seamus Robinson TD, from Belfast and Glasgow originally, then O/C of the Tipperary Brigade during the War and later (c.Sept 1921) of the 2nd Southern Division WS p.47-50.)

This is the question:

"There are many thousand people enthusiastic supporters of the Treaty simply because Michael Collins is its mother—possibly Arthur Griffith would be called its father. Now, it is only natural and right that many people should follow almost blindly a great and good man. But suppose you know that such a man was not really such a great man; and that his reputation and great deeds of daring were in existence only on paper and in the imagination of people who read stories about him. If Michael Collins is the great man he is supposed to be, he has a right to influence people and people ought to be influenced by him. Now Dr. MacCartan said that he could understand many people saying: "What is good enough for Michael Collins is good enough for me." Arthur Griffith has called Collins "the man who won the war." The Press has called him the Commander-in-Chief of the I.R.A. He has been called "a great exponent of guerilla warfare" and the "elusive Mike" and we have all read the story of the White Horse. There are stories going round Dublin of fights he had all over the city—the Custom House in particular. If Michael Collins was all that he has been called then I will admire him and respect his opinions, if my little mind cannot comprehend his present attitude towards the Republic and this Treaty. Now, from my knowledge of character and psychology, which I'm conceited enough to think is not too bad, I'm forced to think that the reported Michael Collins could not possibly be the same Michael Collins who was so weak as to compromise the Republic. The weak man who signed certainly exists and just as certainly therefore, I believe the reported Michael Collins did not ever exist. If Michael Collins who signed the Treaty ever did the wonderful things reported of him then I'm another fool. But before I finally admit myself a fool I want some authoritative statement. I want, and I think it all important that the Dáil, the country, aye, and the world, got authoritative answers to the following questions: (a) What positions exactly did Michael Collins hold in the army? (b) Did he ever take part in any armed conflict in which he fought by shooting; the number of such battles or fights; in fact, is there any authoritative record of his having ever fired a shot for Ireland at an enemy of Ireland?" (Seamus Robinson TD during the Treaty debates http://historical-debates.oireachtas.ie/D/DT/D.T.192201060002.html .)

149

Robinson had plenty of experience of mythologising because he feuded with Dan Breen as to the latter's real role during the War of Independence in Tipperary. He ended up calling it "The Great Tipperary hoax."! (Seamus Robinson WS 1721 Appendix IV.) Breen it seems sometimes called himself the O/C of the Tipperary brigade that actually Robinson was in charge of, and apparently Mrs Seamus O'Doherty wrote *My Fight for Irish Freedom* (ibid Appendix II). He tried to write to the newspapers, the Press group, about this in the 40s and 50s but they never published his letters.

I wonder if the British army's dealings with General Smuts form a kind of model for what they hoped would happen with Collins. Could Smuts too have been a kind of double agent? This is from PJ Little who was for a time the Dail's representative in South Africa:
"A word about General Smuts may be important...Smuts was really a follower of Cecil Rhodes originally, and, being an ambitious and clever lawyer, he was very much, at that time, in touch with the British, but, just before the Boer War, Kruger, who was President of the Transvaal, made him Attorney General in the Transvaal...His colleagues told me that he was not a military genius himself..."(WS 1769 p.80. He also says that the British had poisoned the food that they gave to people in the concentration camps in order to kill off more of them.)
When Smuts became Att General he also took over and became the dynamic head of their Secret Service.(http://rapidttp.com/milhist/vol032gb.html) A few bits from the wikipedia article on Smuts:
"Through 1896, Smuts' politics were turned on their head. He was transformed from being Rhodes' most ardent supporter to being the most fervent opponent of British expansion. ...After the Jameson Raid, relations between the British and the Afrikaners had deteriorated steadily. By 1898, war seemed imminent. Orange Free State President Martinus Steyn called for a peace conference at Bloemfontein to settle each side's grievances. With an intimate knowledge of the British, Smuts took control of the Transvaal delegation. Sir Alfred Milner, head of the British delegation, took exception to his dominance, and conflict between the two led to the collapse of the conference, consigning South Africa to war." Of course it was well known that Milner wanted that war all along and therefore was looking for those negotiations to collapse. You can read Smut's role in the negotiations that ended the war here: http://www.ourcivilisation.com/smartboard/shop/armstrng/index.htm . Its fascinating, if you read those chapters, how much it is similar to Ireland in 1921. Then after that of course he once more became a close ally of the British and fought with them during WWI and II.

15. "..those two leaders...seemed to be close friends." (Tom Barry, *Guerilla Days in Ireland* (Tralee, post 1955), p.158.)

16. Mrs Austin Stack WS 418.

17. Broy in his witness statement includes an account of Stephens' jail break that he claims he has from old DMP files. (Eamonn Broy WS 1284 p.12) I notice that that contrasts with Captain Pollard's statement that it was well known that Stephens was working for the Castle (see below in the main text) so maybe Broy is covering up the degree of police infiltration of the Fenians? I wonder then if he was really persona non grata with his superiors in the DMP as he claimed? He is very well read, an expert French speaker, as you can read in his statements. He and Collins used to share a love of Russian nihilists. He also goes on and on about how the RIC were despised in the country when he was growing up but this again is clearly exaggerated and, I would say, blatantly untrue. Even lots of his Sinn Fein Colleagues had old connections to the RIC: Michael Staines was from an RIC family, Eamonn Duggan was the son of an RIC constable based in Longwood Co.Meath, and Michael Collins' family were always very friendly with the local RIC in Clonakilty (Peter Folan WS 316).

18. Tom Barry, *Guerilla Days in Ireland* (Tralee, post 1955), p.148-9.

19. Pat Moylett WS 767 p.85. Pat Moylett later bumped into the consul in the toilets of the Gresham talking to General Brind who was a high up Intelligence Officer for the British!

20. JJ O'Kelly W.S.384 p.62. There is quite a bit of evidence of close and secret US involvement in Ireland at the time:
Richard Walsh thought that the US government had a lot of leverage because the UK government was so heavily indebted to the US after WWI. (Richard Walsh TD from Balla Co.Mayo WS 400 p.79.)
From an article on the 'secret' US role of the time:
"'The United States was both the rose and the thorn of the Irish problem.' These words -- which adapt one of Hegel's most famous formulations - flowed from the pen of Carl Ackerman, an American journalist, in the Atlantic Monthly in the summer of 1922. Ackerman's three lengthy articles had one theme; he wished to stress the 'secret' role played by American diplomats, politicians and journalists in the resolution of the 'Anglo-Irish war' by the 'Treaty settlement' of 1921.
...
The 'American education of Michael Collins' consisted of informing Collins that the decisive American injection of support for his cause [money and possibly arms]-- which he had been promised by his comrades in arms Eamon De Valera and Harry Boland - would never materialise. A key figure here was the Dublin US Consul, Frederick Dumont, who had been lucky not to lose his life on Bloody Sunday in November 1920 - he had been playing cards with some British intelligence officers just before Collins's death squad struck at them."
(Spectator 31 May 1997 available at

This American journalist Carl Ackerman, who interviewed Collins twice, was also a British spy reporting back to Basil Thomson in London. (Peter Hart, *Mick: The Real Michael Collins* (Oxford, 2005), p.293.)
The implication then is that the US government had some influence over this money arriving from America, that it had strings attached which the US government could pull.
The Treaty delegation were all collectively treated to dinner in London by an important US banker during the negotiations. (Robert Barton WS 979 p.39.)

21. "From the first then [c.1915], the "Sinn Feiners", as they were then called, regarded T[imothy].M.H[ealy] as a man whom they instinctively turned to in their needs... " (Mrs T.M. Sullivan, Timothy Healy's daughter, WS 653 p.1.)

22. See footnote 28 below.

23. He also had a secret printing press in his home (Patrick Meehan WS 478). I think these despatches might be from T J McElligot who was in close touch with Collins and leaked some secret RIC documents (TJ McElligot WS 472). Healy c.Nov 1918 is reported "receiving Michael Collins and Harry Boland at his Chapelizod home, Glenaulin, and discussing the wisdom (or otherwise) of their plan of campaign. He was often visited by Collins while the latter was 'on the run.' "(Mrs T.M. Sullivan, Timothy Healy's daughter, WS 653 p.2.)

24. "Mr Healy was I understood brought over to London [during the negotiations] but not as a lawyer. He was asked to do some political work which was the wrong thing altogether for he had always been quite candid about his attachment to the crown." (Austin Stack via his widow WS 418.)

25. He used to write to him describing the latest happenings among the "Shinns" (NLI Ms 23,266 et seq).

26. Hannah Sheehy Skeffington, the widow of Francis that was murdered during the 1916 rising, had employed Healy to act for her during the inquest. Later she had some harsh words to say about her barrister as Healy himself complained that she had "published appalling lies about me in the Irish World to the effect that I had offered her a bribe from Asquith and threatened to deprive her of her own son if she did not consent." (Frank Callanan, *T.M. Healy* (Cork, 1996), p.732.)
Healy acted for PJ Little in defending a libel case against his New Ireland newspaper: "I had to settle, as my counsel, T M Healy and A M Sullivan, were against me, as I soon found out." (P J Little, later a Fianna Fail chief whip, WS 1769 p.19.)

27. It was reported in the Freeman that he had "sold his clients for blood-

money to Dublin Castle".
(http://www.eiretek.org/chapters/books/THealy/healy26.htm)

28. "MacBride argued that there was considerable alarm at what he [Collins] might yet do to 'Thorpe', the pseudonym given to the Castle's longest serving and probably most important informer. The Burke and Cavendish murders in the Phoenix Park of 1882 which outraged England and dashed Home Rule from Parnell's grasp were carried out by a Fenian splinter group, the Invincibles, who were thought to have been sent to the gallows by an informer called Carey who was himself subsequently murdered. But then rumours began to circulate that the real informer was 'Thorpe'. ...MacBride's theory was that Collins had learned that 'Thorpe' was in fact Tim Healy, a trusted adviser of his, an uncle of Kevin O'Higgins, and destined after Collins' death to be the first Governor General of the Irish Free State. If Healy was a spy he changed Irish history, being the most active of Parnell's opponents in the disastrous split of 1890...MacBride's theory however was that Healy, then a member of the IRB, with a Clan na Gael emissary, returned to the Clan man's hotel unexpectedly one evening to find the proprietor, Captain Jury, a British agent, going through the Clan man's luggage. Somehow they managed to poison Jury. The Clan man got back safely to America but the Castle made Healy an offer he could not refuse. Either he went to work for them, or he faced a murder charge. Accordingly to MacBride, Healy then became an agent and remained one throughout his long career in law and politics." (Tim Pat Coogan, *Michael Collins: The Man Who Made Ireland* (New York, 2002), p.390 et seq. quoting Sean MacBride's interview in the Irish Press 16 and 18 October 1982.)

29. "We did not know what was going on behind the scenes, nor indeed did we much care. In the first place, Collins became very intimate with Tim Healy. Fanny Sullivan told me afterwards that, one night out at Glenaulin, Tim Healy put £25 into Mick's pocket! - to meet the out-of-pocket expenses Mick must incur every day. And when Mick had left, Tim said: "Sure he is only an overgrown baby, a big baby." Collins and Tim Healy became intimate, Tim Healy and Gavan Duffy had family ties, and Mrs Duffy began to refer, in Rome, to "her cousin Michael Collins." Great times! And the results became pretty obvious." (JJ O'Kelly WS 384 p.80.)

30. Sean Moylan TD WS 505 p.2. Another example is Richard Walsh who said that Healy was "supposed to play a large part in the business" of the Cope-Collins links (Richard Walsh TD from Balla Co.Mayo WS 400 p.78).
St. John's Ambulance Brigade secretly transported British officers around Dublin during the 1916 Rising, and also transported Tim Healy! (Lawrence Nugent WS 907 p.38.)

31. Michael Hopkinson ed., *The last days of Dublin Castle: The Diary of Mark Sturgis* (Dublin, 1999), p.157.

32. David Neligan WS 380 p.18.

33. Ormonde de Winter described him as Director of Intelligence at least for a time in 1920. (see under Duggan in Peter Hart ed., *British Intelligence in Ireland, 1920-21: The Final Reports* (Cork, 2002).)

34. Incidentally Eamonn Duggan never signed the Treaty, his signature was pasted on from an old card that the delegation had access to (Robert Barton WS 979 p.34).
This is from James J O'Connor who was a Solicitor in Dublin and nephew of Judge James O'Connor a leading, and controversial, figure in the peace negotiations of the time:
"The British government sent over to Ireland one Alfred Cope as a special representative of the British Cabinet in Ireland to act as an Assistant Under-Secretary, the Under-Secretary then being Mr. James McMahon. While here Mr.Cope became very friendly with Mr. Eamonn Duggan, a solicitor, who was later one of the signatories of the Treaty and was a very active man in the Republican Movement.

Cope, of course, knew this but when he met Duggan in the Dolphin Hotel or other places socially he never asked him any questions. One night Mr. Eamonn Duggan arrived home about 12 o'clock and just as he was going to bed the telephone rang. At the other end of the telephone at a place about 9 miles outside Dublin was a man who was high up in the Republican Army, who told Duggan that he and two others were on a very important mission into Dublin and that their car had broken down at this place, asking Duggan if he could do anything to get them into the city which was at that time surrounded by sentries, curfew being imposed. Duggan asked him for his telephone number and said he would ring back in a few minutes. He rang Mr. Cope and said, "My dear Cope, there are three friends of mine stranded at a village about nine miles outside Dublin. Their car has broken down. Could you do anything to get them into the city?" "Where are you?" said Cope. "I am at home". "I will be with you" said Cope " in about twenty minutes". Mr.Cope rang up one of the British military barracks, ordered out a staff car which, of course, in view of his position was always at his disposal. The staff car driven by a British Staff Officer arrived at Cope's house, collected him and drove to Mr.Duggan's house, collected Mr.Duggan and drove out through the sentries to the village about nine miles outside Dublin. Here they met the other three men in a licensed premises. They had a drink, as men do on these occasions, drove back into the city, again passing the sentries on the outskirts.

When the car got to College Green Duggan said to Cope, "Now my dear fellow, you have done all I asked you to do, stop the car here and let these three men out. They can walk the rest of the way home and you and I will go down to the Dolphin and have a drink, which they did.

The next day Cope went into his office in Dublin Castle. He went into James McMahon, the Under-Secretary, who told me the story. He related to him the events of the night before and said "I am very worried. I know, as you do, all about Duggan's activities. I know most of the officers who drive these staff cars but I don't know the Captain who drove me last night. I don't know the three men whom he met or who they may be. They may be all right, but they may be associates of Duggan's and the other men who are in this movement. If this Captain goes to Macready who is the G.O.C. of the Forces I may have some difficulty in explaining my conduct."

McMahon thought a bit and said, "I will tell you what you will do. Get out another staff car as quickly as you can. Go up to French (who was then Lord Lieutenant in the Vice-Regal Lodge), tell him that you are associating with Duggan for the purposes of getting information from him." "But, of course, that's not true" said Cope, "I never ask Duggan any questions". "It doesn't matter" said McMahon. "Tell French also that you use some of the Secret Service money which you always carry in your pocket to give Duggan drink and that you used more of it last night to give the three men, whom you met out in this village, drink and that you got some useful information from them."

After some hesitation Cope rang up the military barracks, got out another staff car, drove up to the Vice-Regal Lodge and asked to see the Lord Lieutenant, whom he saw. He told him all about the incidents of the night before and about the information he was supposed to be getting from Duggan and about the information he had got the night before. He also told the Lord Lieutenant that he was sending a report over to the Prime Minister which was so secret that he could not even show it to His Excellency. He went away and that forenoon General Sir Neville Macready arrived at the Vice-Regal Lodge to see the Lord Lieutenant. He told him that the Captain who had driven Duggan and Cope the night before had reported to him (Macready) the events of the evening and that he was going to have Cope arrested as a traitor and that, were it not for his important position, he would have had him arrested but did not like to take any steps without the approval of the Lord Lieutenant.

"You will do no such thing" said French. "Mr Cope has already been here this morning and has made to me a full report about the incidents of last night and in my opinion he risked his life to get some important information to His Majesty's Government. I have just dictated a letter to my Secretary addressed to the Prime Minister recommending that some suitable honour be conferred on Mr.Cope by His Majesty the King in the next Honours List."" (James J O'Connor W.S. 1214 p.5.)

35. Through Mrs Nugent in fact (Lawrence Nugent WS 907 p.223).

36. David Neligan, *The Spy in the Castle* (Dublin, 1999, 1st pub. 1968), p.147.

37. See footnote 2 above.

38. Pat Moylett WS 767 p.88. Even Austin Stack talks about Cope:
"I mention this incident [where Cope tried to contact him] here as I believe Mr Cope was England's chief instrument in bringing about the signing of the "Treaty". I know he frequently met some of our Ministers and others who subscribed to and supported the document." (Mrs Austin Stack enclosing her late husband's memoirs. WS 418.)

39. Michael T. Foy, *Michael Collins' Intelligence War* (Gloucestershire, 2006), p.229. Mark Sturgis said that "not only does he do all the work in the Castle but the plotting laurels fall to him too." (Michael Hopkinson ed., *The last days of Dublin Castle: The Diary of Mark Sturgis* (Dublin, 1999), p.158.)

40. Richard Walsh WS 400 p.74. At one of these pre Truce Collins-Cope meetings Collins even gave his correct name and had a drink with a British officer.(Sir William Darling, *So it looks to me* (London, 1952), p.212.)

41. Lawrence Nugent WS 907 p.222-223.

42. Richard Walsh TD WS 400 p.69, 71 and 73.

43. Ibid p.74-79. This is Brigadier General Sir George Cockerill, MP for Reigate, close friend of Lloyd George, 'Director of Special Intelligence at the War Office' (Nicholas Pronay and Keith M. Wilson, *The Political Re-Education of Germany and Her Allies After World War II* (1985), p.54), and author of *What fools we were* (London, 1944) and *Scribblers and Statesmen* (Melbourne, 1943). This is from Pat Moylett's account, it was he that was delivering the message: WS 767 p.51. Cockerill had taken an interest in Irish intelligence for a long time before this, see for example CO/904 Personality file on Thomas Ashe 2 Dec. 1917. Dermot O'Hegarty was furious when he realised that Walsh had found out about this message.

44. David Fitzpatrick, *Harry Boland's Irish Revolution* (Cork, 2003), p.398 referring to c.September 1921. The truce had only been signed in mid July.

45. Kevin O'Shiel names Bonar Law, Wilson, and Milner as the big names trying to stop Home Rule (WS 1770 p.329).

46. Lawrence Nugent WS 907 p.180.

47. Liam Mellows, appointed Director of Purchases for GHQ in Nov 1920, complained to Mary Woods:
"He said he [Collins] was interfering with his job as Director of Purchases by buying arms across the water and paying more for them than he was. He was buying them, he said, not to use them but to prevent him (Liam) from getting

them. This shocked me. .."(Peter Hart, *Mick: The Real Michael Collins* (Oxford, 2005), p.261 quoting Mrs Woods UCD P17a/150.)

In the procuring of arms Richard Walsh TD said that "there seemed to be nothing being attempted by G.H.Q. agents, and it could not have been for want of money" (Richard Walsh TD from Balla Co.Mayo WS 400 p.131). Walsh was himself in England procuring arms so he knew the true situation.

The Cavan IRA come just short of accusing Collins of embezzlement of the funds they sent down to procure arms, so frustrated were they of their treatment on that score (Bernard Brady WS 1626 and Sean Sheridan WS 1613).

The Meath IRA were in fact not permitted to use the rifles captured at Trim, they were put in a Divisional dump which was not used until the train ambush at Stackumney late in the war (David Hall WS 1539).

Sceilg relates what happened in Kerry: "My wife got a substantial sum of money from Denis Daly of Caherciveen to get guns, and Collins or his associates would not give them." (JJ O'Kelly WS 384 p.75.)

In West Cork Tom Barry had no better luck: "Sean McMahon was Quartermaster General. I had little contact with him except on two occasions when I had failed to beg, borrow or steal .303 or .450 ammunition from him. ...To one of the officers from a particularly inefficient unit who asked for arms, Mick [Collins], with a scowl on his face, his hands deep in his pockets, his right foot pawing the ground, shot back, "What the hell does a lot of lousers like you want arms for? ...Get to hell out of this and do not come back until ye have done some fighting." (Tom Barry, *Guerilla Days in Ireland* (Tralee, first published 1949), p.150-152.) His account seems to detail almost every rifle they had, I don't believe any came from GHQ.

Sean Moylan in North Cork didn't get on any better: "My own experience of GHQ was not a too happy one." (Sean Moylan WS 838 p.101.) So much so that when Ernie O'Malley came down and asked some questions on behalf of GHQ (that seems to be O'Malley's job most of time, feeding info back to GHQ) the fed up Moylan "answered all the questions with perfect inaccuracy"! (Ibid p.102). He had tried to purchase arms from GHQ using an inheritance that he had got but came back feeling ripped off with little to show for it, a few bits and pieces and only one rifle and bombs that only exploded by immersion in a turf fire!lol (Ibid p.95.)

Lawrence Nugent's impression, he was an IRA Quarter Master in Dublin, was that the US Irish leaders did not wish to supply weapons in any quantity into Ireland before the Truce. (Lawrence Nugent WS 907 p.27) Then during the truce period he discovered that a typed agreement existed between Michael

Collins and the British where Collins agreed not to import arms (Lawrence Nugent WS 907 p.287).

Notice the curious financial situation here. The IRA received a lot of money from the Dail, who raised it using a loan, to purchase arms yet the IRA volunteers had to try and buy arms from IRA GHQ. Where did the money go is a question asked by many of these writers like Sceilg, Lawrence Nugent and Dick Walsh (e.g. Dick Walsh WS 400 p.172).

48. Roger McCorley's WS 389.

49. Dick Walsh WS 400.

50. Bernard Brady WS 1626, Sean Sheridan WS 1613 and Peadar MacMahon WS 1730.

51. Dick Walsh WS 400.

52. Eamonn Broy says that the British military were always looking for an excuse to take control in Ireland, like in the aftermath of the 1916 rebellion: "It was felt by the police, and by a great many others, that the net result of the insurrection had been to put the British military in complete control, a thing the military had always desired." (Eamonn Broy WS 1280 p.67.) See also some of the comments by John Dillon in chapter 1 footnote 127 infra.
Arthur Griffith thought this way too:
"There was a fear that the British might deliberately provoke an insurrection in order to undermine a serious Sinn Fein passive-resistance movement. Griffith had long warned about this and linked it to the violence in Ireland from 1919 onwards."
(Brian Maye, *Arthur Griffith* (Dublin, 1997), p.131.)

53. Seamus Dobbyn WS 279 p.15. It was planned a long time in advance and timed to go off after some IRA operation so that they could say that it was in response to nationalist provocation.

54. Lawrence Nugent WS 907 towards the end.

55. Sean Moylan WS 838 p.30-31.

56. Sean Moylan WS 838 p.26.

57. Seamus Robinson WS 1721 near the beginning.

58. Lawrence Nugent WS 907 p.72.

59. Dick Walsh WS 400.

60. Ibid.

61. Ibid p.97.

62. Peter Hart, *Mick: The Real Michael Collins* (Oxford, 2005), p.237.

63. Seamus Robinson WS 1721 p.37.

64. Quoting Tom Barry: "No orders or anything else were written at that time —in our brigade anyway" (http://www.indymedia.ie/article/80362). It is definitely the case that those written documents were very common elsewhere, Lawrence Nugent describes these kind of documents which he tripped across when he was clearing out one of his arms dumps in Dublin. They were very detailed and specific apparently, naming all the names of the IRA people without demur (WS 907 near the end).

65. Sean McKeon WS 1716. Collins was fed up with his lack of reports so he sent down a GHQ man to check things over but he only lasted a few days.

66. Eamonn Duggan writing to Collins after his offices were raided explained that the British have seized "a lot of intelligence stuff, which I had hidden away in clients bundles." (Peter Hart ed., *British Intelligence in Ireland, 1920-21: The Final Reports* (Cork, 2002), p.88.)

67. Documents seized on a raid of Collins' safe house unnecessarily yielded the Castle valuable info when they "ought to have been destroyed long previous" (Eamonn Broy WS 1,280). GHQ eventually issued a directive asking that at least those Departments that have been raided should inform the others that are likely to become known about from the captured documents. De Winter notes that "Mulcahy the Chief of Staff, and Collins the Minister for Finance, must have been fully occupied sending out the necessary communications" (Hart op.cit.). British Secret Service got another valuable haul of papers from Collins at the time of the Customs House fire (Michael Hopkinson ed., *The last days of Dublin Castle: The Diary of Mark Sturgis* (Dublin, 1999), p.182).

68. Richard Walsh notes, pointedly, that "on two or three occasions very important documents in his [Mulcahy's] custody were captured by the British." (Richard Walsh TD from Balla Co.Mayo WS 400 p.66)

69. David Neligan, *The Spy in the Castle* (Dublin, 1999, 1st pub. 1968), p.147.

70. Matthew Barry WS 932.

71. Seamus McKenna WS 1,016 p.30.

72. Sean McKeon WS 1,716 before p.186.

73. Tom Barry, *Guerrilla Days in Ireland* (Tralee, post 1955), p.164.

74. Sean McKeon WS 1228. Richard Walsh said that "A moderate estimate" of IRA strength in 1921 would be about 50-60,000 troops albeit partly unarmed. (Richard Walsh TD from Balla Co.Mayo WS 400 p.166), and Sceilg had an even higher figure. This is in great contrast to the figures that Collins is usually quoted as mentioning.

75. Lord Muskerry stated in the House of Lords in 1924 that Cope:
"attended meetings held by heads of Department to consider the best means of putting down outrages and restoring law and order, and then conveyed the information to the leaders of the Sinn Fein organisation, with the result that the plans came to nought, and in many cases her Majesty's officers and men lost their lives." Muskerry went on to say later that:
"Since the debate he had received a number of letters from officers and ex-officers of the RIC and others, and they all made damning statements. Some of these letters were signed and bore the addresses of the writers, but they were marked "private and confidential" and he could not give up their names" (The Times 20 March 1924 p.8).
The British Secret Service were watching Cope at least from September 1920, (Michael Hopkinson ed., *The last days of Dublin Castle: The Diary of Mark Sturgis* (Dublin, 1999), p.46.) and in turn Cope was going through de Winter's files in the days before Bloody Sunday (ibid p.76). Could this be what Muskerry was referring to?

76. The Cockerill quote is from Sir George Cockerill, *What fools we were* (London, 1944), p.97. Pat Moylett meeting H G Wells, who was just back from observing the revolution in Russia, can be read in WS 767 p.56. For Moya, and Crompton, Davies see footnote 2 above, and for the latter's friendship with Bertrand Russell see Bertrand Russell, *The Selected Letters of Bertrand Russell: The Private Years, 1884-1914* (2002), p.315 et seq.
Winter's views are from Sir Ormonde de Winter, *Winter's Tale: An Autobiography* (London, 1955), passim. He complains, in italics!, for example that it was only "*after three days*" that the government eventually gave him permission to search a hospital where an IRA suspect had escaped into (p.316). It wasn't just de Valera that he was frustrated to see released out of custody, the same happened with Childers. de Winter had interviewed him personally and among his captured papers was aghast to see an invitation to Buckingham Palace where his wife was to receive an MBE! (p.328). It is from his book p.335 that I get the reference to Lord Longford being a friend of Childers and de Valera. Btw the Lord Longford who wrote *Peace by Ordeal* was of course too young to play a leading part in any of these events but he may nonetheless have known about the machinations of that time.
The quote describing the influence of the Masonic Order is from John D.

Nugent, *The AOH and its critics* (Dublin, 1911), p.22-23. Curiously 1921 was the best year in the history of Irish Freemasonry with flourishing membership and branches (The Times 27 Feb 1922 p.12). A few other references to Masonic influence in Ireland at the time:

"All officers of the Post Office who held senior positions were Freemasons - the Secretary, the Controller, the Senior Floor Superintendent, various Assistant Superintendents and overseers." (Diarmuid O'Sullivan WS 375 p.6.)

Lawrence Nugent, who served on a Dublin jury, explained how, when it wanted to, Dublin Castle could pack a jury with Freemasons (Lawrence Nugent WS 907 p.179).

It is worthy of note I think that at a meeting in the Viceregal Lodge when it was decided to bring over the Black and Tans "all the members of the Kildare St Club were invited." (Peter Folan WS 316 p.12)

77. This is by Lawrence Nugent, originally from Roscommon, he later resided in Dundrum, then he lived in Mount Street and had a high class drapers shop at 22 Baggot St in Dublin (WS 907 p.7). The reference to the GAA was an attempt to use the AOH dominated C.J. Kickham club in Dublin to control the GAA in early 1917 (ibid p.86). The GAA was otherwise a totally IRB show.

In the account written by Archbishop Walsh's former secretary, Monsignor Curran, we are told that "their job-hunting was notorious since the Liberals came to power and was openly and unashamedly practiced by Joe Devlin and the AOH (Board of Erin) since the Insurance Act of 1911...the all powerful AOH became a replica of Tammany Hall as painted by its enemies" (Rev M.Curran WS 687 p.302).

When the treaty was signed the AOH burst back into life and recommended acceptance of the Treaty (Lawrence Nugent WS 907 p.273), a strange echo of the IRB's position! Incidentally the two Belfast leaders of these organisations, Denis McCullough President of the Supreme Council of the IRB and Joe Devlin President of the AOH (Board of Erin), didn't get along as badly as you might think because at one point McCullough was able to get some machine guns from Devlin, these had been imported by the National Volunteers (Denis McCullough WS 915 p.8).

78. Dorothy Macardle, *The Irish Republic* (Dublin, 2005, first published 1937), p.23.

In Diarmuid Lynch, *The IRB and the 1916 Insurrection* (Cork, 1957), p.34 you can read how the IRB controlled secretly the Oct 1917 Sinn Fein Convention, following the pattern they had used at the Gaelic League Ard Fheis of 1915. He points out that: "When the Provisional Committee of the Volunteers was formed in Oct-Nov 1913: The majority of the Committee were members of the IRB, a fact unknown to the minority (which included the Chairman) - the IRB being a secret body, the continued existence of which was unknown to the public." (ibid p.44)

Captain Pollard stated that the IRB controlled so many organisations that "it was its influence and corruption which achieved those mysterious appointments to position of persons singularly devoid of all merit, which were, and are, a marked feature of Irish life." (Captain H.B.C. Pollard, *The Secret Societies of Ireland* (Kilkenny, 1998), p.75.)

A few notes by Sceilg on the IRB:

"As to what some of these people say, groups of them had ulterior motives all the time."(JJ O'Kelly WS 384 p.48)..."Thus, Collins had a secret organisation within the Army and even within the Dail.".."His [Collins] position in the IRB gave him and his followers influence because unknown and unsuspected."..."Without it [the IRB], I don't think the split would ever have reached the dimensions to which it grew. To my mind its secret nature was its most sinister aspect." ..."Still the secret organisation was operating behind the scenes, and the effects and extent of this were subsequently seen only too vividly."(ibid p.51)

"I don't like to harp back now, and follow the intrigue that was carried on by the IRB in the Dail. ...No doubt about it there was intrigue." Goes on to describe how they maneuvered him out of his position as Minister for the National Language and instead "got some unripe fruit at the expense of the Republic." (ibid p.53)

79. Seamus Robinson WS 1721 p.18. No doubt the IRB is referred to in this reference from Sceilg:

"How Mr Collins - up to then practically unknown in Ireland - was being pushed into prominence by a hidden force, some of us first detected on the occasion of the Ashe funeral." (Peter Hart, *Mick: The Real Michael Collins* (Oxford, 2005), p.152 quoting Sceilg in the Catholic Bulletin Oct 1922 Vol XII p.629.) And a few other corroborating references:

"I understood at the time that the main function of the IRB was to control both the leadership and the activities of the Volunteer movement from within" (Seamus McKenna WS 1,016 p.1 of Addendum).

"For years past the IRB (a secret organisation) was in existence and controlled and directed the Irish Volunteers" (Sean Farrelly WS 1,734 p.8).

80. Kevin O'Shiel W.S.1770 p.139.

81. Richard Walsh TD from Balla Co.Mayo WS 400 p.46-47.

82. Dorothy Macardle op.cit. p.23.

83. Owen McGee, *The IRB* (Dublin, 2005), p.322-4. The Clan-na-Gael emissary was wined and dined by Eoin McNeill oddly enough. Is he closer to all this intrigue than is usually said?

84. Captain H.B.C. Pollard, *The Secret Societies of Ireland* (Kilkenny, 1998 first published 1922).

85. Diarmuid Lynch says that Pollard has one error in that he describes a 1914

IRB constitution when it was actually a 1917 one seized in a government raid. (WS 4 p.10)

86. Pollard op.cit.p.38 and Msgr. George Dillon, *Grand Orient Freemasonry Unmasked* (London, 1952), p.110. Consider also this quote that was highlighted by Fr Denis Fahey:
"The ritual and form of initiation [into the Clan-na-Gael] were framed entirely on Masonic precedent; and to the vast majority of the members (of the Clan-na-Gael), the statement will come no doubt as a great surprise that the much vaunted secret forms of the Masonic order need be secret to them no longer, inasmuch as that, when being admitted to a Clan-na-Gael club, they were going through the same forms and ceremonies as attached themselves to that great source of mystery and wonderment in the eyes of the non-elect, the Masonic-Brotherhood. I have often laughed to myself at the surprise shown by some Masons on the occasion of their initiation to Clan-na-Gael - for there are Masons in the Clan - at being brought once more into contact with the familiar procedure." (Rev Denis Fahey, *The Mystical Body of Christ in the Modern World* (Dublin, 1952, 1st published March 1935), p.105, quoting Henri Le Caron [also known as Thomas Beach], *Twenty-Five Years in the Secret Service*, p.111-112.)

87. Ibid p.62. Sceilg knew Tynan in New York: "Some say he [Tynan] was not No.1 at all, but I feel convinced he was" (JJ O'Kelly WS 384 p.85). Actually Pollard says that Tynan was involved in the Maamtrasna murders.

88. Ibid p.45.

89. To clarify he only refers to the Protocols at one point and then glosses it with the statement that the Times had discovered them to be forgeries. But I don't think he would have referred to them at all if he thought they were just useless forgeries.

90. Ibid p.12. By the way if you wanted to speculate about that it is interesting that Clan-na-Gael was centered on Notre Dame University, which is a major Jesuit university in the US (Owen McGee, *The IRB* (Dublin, 2005), p.322-4).

91. The book was reviewed in 'The Occult Review' in December 1922. It is even said that he possessed Jack the Ripper's knives! (Robin Odell, *Ripperology: A Study of the World's First Serial Killer And a Literary Phenomenon* (Kent State University, 2006), p.121.)
Later Major Hugh B C Pollard he was a firearms expert who traveled through Mexico c1910, served in WWI, edited the sporting life before WWII during which he served in the SOE. He was at one time MI6 station chief in Madrid. It should be pointed out that he isn't very sympathetic to Irish nationalism and is somewhat condescending with regard to Irish claims for self determination.

92. Pollard op.cit. p.196.

93. The "Phoenix Society...thenceforward...should be known as the IRB." (Eamonn Broy WS 1284.)

94. http://www.illuminaticonfessions.webfriend.it/newarticles_61_70.htm .

95. Pollard op.cit.p.53.

96. Richard Walsh TD from Balla Co.Mayo WS 400 p.181.

CHAPTER 4

Secret Societies in Ireland

Building on the references in the last chapter I just hope to show that Secret Societies or groups sometimes exercise great power in Western countries and that Ireland has not escaped this phenomenon.

Possibly the best insight into the power that a secret grouping could amass in Ireland is given in the book called *The Committee* which details the great power wielded by some mysterious secret Loyalist coalition which was active at least c1990. A Derry television producer, Sean McPhilemy, aided by Martin O'Hagan and a researcher Ben Hamilton found out that the Loyalist paramilitary campaign was not some anarchic disparate collection of groups and events but was actually formally, and very secretly, coordinated by a group that included representatives from all the various members of the Unionist community. Known as 'The Committee' it had representatives from a large secret group in the RUC called the Inner Force which was in turn controlled by a smaller RUC group called the Inner Circle and both these groups were on hand to assist the Loyalist paramilitaries who were working for the Committee:

> "The Inner Force themselves say there's a third actually [of the RUC] who are members of the Inner Force. There's a third, but there's also the two thirds who are not members but would be sympathetic to the aims of the Inner Force...[And] the Inner Circle controls the Inner Force. They have manoeuvred through various ways, they have manoeuvred men with sympathies towards the Inner Circle in to prominent positions ...at local police station level, and therefore at division level."
>
> ...
>
> "He [Jim Sands, Philemy's source which he found via Martin O'Hagan] had witnessed the formation of a unique coalition of Loyalist forces, covering virtually every significant sector of Loyalist Ulster - The Ulster Workers' Council "which had been revamped and reorganised...and is organised in factories such as Shorts, Harland and Wolff shipyard, the power stations;" the various Loyalist paramilitary groups;

middle class professionals and business people; and, most importantly, the RUC and UDR. A coalition encapsulated in Abernathy's [a leading Ulster banker and chairman of the Committee] question: "Makes you wonder who runs this place, doesn't it?"

So the Committee's fifty to sixty conspirators who met regularly to plan murder knew, as they did so, that those present represented all significant groups within the Ulster Loyalist family; no grouping of any importance had been excluded and, as a result, none of those present felt they had anything to fear from outsiders. That is why the Committee had been able to mobilise and operate the Loyalist death squads in the province throughout 1989, 1990 and 1991.
...

And there is a further reason [the main reason being the protection offered by the senior police members of the Committee] why the fifty to sixty Committee members felt themselves to be invulnerable. They had taken the trouble to ensure that the political elite within the Loyalist family, the leading Unionist politicians, would be on hand to do their "duty," if a crisis were ever to erupt as a result of the scandal becoming publicly known. One prominent Ulster Unionist MP, as we shall see, was to prove particularly helpful to the conspirators..."[1]

The book is not shy about naming that person as David Trimble and goes into great detail to show links between him and members of the Committee. McPhilemy won a massive libel trial in London related to these allegations despite heavy weights like Trimble himself appearing as a witness against him.[2]

The Freemasons are I guess the most famous secret society worldwide and are often stated, for example, to have great power in the English judicial/police system as pointed out in the Seanad in 4/3/2004:

"The masons are also a secret society, no matter what they say. There is a large number of masons in Ireland — there are approximately 50,000 in the North and 20,000 in the South. If anyone reads a book called The Brotherhood they will see the effect the masons have on the police and Judiciary in England, where nearly all police officers and most judges are masons."[3]

166

This reference from the Seanad (12/10/1993) clearly indicates that the Freemasons were very powerful in Ireland in 1920:

"Much has also been made of the suggestion that the Catholic Church plays too big a role in Irish current affairs and there are many people who would agree with that. However, we must also take into account section 65 of the Government of Ireland Act, 1920, which states:

'It is hereby declared that existing enactments relative to unlawful oaths or unlawful assemblies in Ireland do not apply to the meetings or proceedings of the Grand Lodge of Free and Accepted Masons of Ireland, or of any lodge or society recognised by that Grand Lodge.'

That means that the Grand Lodge of the Order of Freemasons can have unlawful meetings and if the Grand Lodge recognises another society it, also, is outside the legalities to which everybody else must adhere. Section 65 also states:

'Neither the Parliament of Southern Ireland, nor the Parliament of Northern Ireland shall have power to abrogate or affect prejudicially any privilege or exemption of the Grand Lodge of Freemasons in Ireland, or any lodge or society recognised by that Grand Lodge which is enjoyed either by law or custom at the time of passing of this Act, and any law made in contravention of this provision shall, so far as it is in contravention of this provision, be void.'

The British Government can declare that the privileges of the Grand Lodge of Freemasons' can be withdrawn but under section 65 they cannot be withdrawn. There are anomalies which must be taken into account by both sides. If Articles 2 and 3 are, as is suggested, inhibiting factors, so also are sections 65 and 75 of the Government of Ireland Act, 1920. There are those in Britain who would say that the Anglo-Irish Agreement removes these sections of the Government of Ireland Act but that is not true because that Act has never been repealed."

Some commentators like Pat Culhane allege that the Masons still have considerable power in Ireland.[4]

Moving to the other side of the great divide there are then the famous nationalist and Catholic Secret Societies like the Irish Republican Brotherhood which, as pointed out in Chapter 1, contained not only shadowy revolutionaries but even well known politicians and writers like Joseph Biggar and the novelist Charles Kickham.[5] Later it of course secretly acted to control the Irish Volunteers and Sinn Fein during the period 1913-24. Another semi secret society that was very active politically at that time was the Ancient Order of Hibernians and if this account from Paddy Harte is correct then it retained some political influence for longer than most people think:

> "Until I arrived on the scene, all Fine Gael TDs in County Donegal were members of the Ancient Order of Hibernians (a Catholic organisation). James Dillon, leader of Fine Gael, was president of the Ancient Order and many active Fine Gael supporters at branch level were also members. When I was discussing my possible candidature with Dr McGinley it did not occur to me that I might have to join the Order. But when I approached my senior officers of the County Board, it was soon made clear that if I wanted the Fine Gael nomination I would have to join the AOH. I asked why I should be forced to join an organisation about which I knew little and in which I had little interest, and was told, 'that's the way things are done around here.'..
>
> The pressure put on me was not something I couldn't handle; nonetheless I availed of the earliest opportunity to discuss the matter with the leader of the party at a national council meeting of Fine Gael...Mr.Dillon advised me that the choice was mine."[6]

Then there are the various lay Catholic societies which are a popular topic of the rumour mill in nationalist Ireland. One such organisation is the very low profile Knights of Malta headed in Ireland by Justice Smithwick [7] and claimed to be close to the CIA.[8] Another lay Catholic society is called the Knights of Columbanus which is whispered to have a big influence over the Irish legal scene, with some also claiming too that they have influence over the media,[9] and some Gardaí.[10] The hope is that they have not been involved in any of the well known activities that have tarnished the church is recent times although that is exactly what has happened to at least one branch of the Knights of Columbus (a sister group to the Columbanus Knights) in Canada.[11] As you can see there has been a lot of talk about these Knights over the years in Ireland:

Tom Garvin:
[The Knights] "became a considerable political force after independence... At one stage many officials in the Revenue were in the organization."[12]

Dail 10 June 1953 Dr Noel Browne:
[Elections to Hospital Boards:] "On the Catholic side it is done through the Knights of Columbanus and on the Protestant side it is done through the Freemasons. It is completely undemocratic."

Dail 1 July 1953 Dr Noel Browne:
"What we should like to know is, in the event of a Multi-Party government being formed, which party would be the real government? Would it be a Fine Gael government? Would it be a Labour government? Would it be a Labour Party policy - or would it be a Knight of Columbanus policy?"

Seanad 28 Nov 1956 Professor Stanford:
"One of the things that is doing most damage to our nation at the moment is the existence of these conflicting Secret Societies [interpreted as meaning the Freemasons and the Knights] and I hope the Minister and the other Minister will do all in their power to prevent their gaining any control of the national economy, or the politics of the country."

Dail Dr Noel Browne 16 July 1969
"In regard to the whole business of appointments [to the Universities], I do not think there is much to choose between the two of them—the Knights of Columbanus predominantly in University College and the Freemasons in Trinity College— and the two of them going on together presumably sharing out the different jobs to suit themselves."

Paddy Devlin relates some political manouverings by the Knights (and it is often said the Catholic hierarchy) at the beginning of the troubles:
"What I learned from a friendly Catholic lawyer was that Hume had been at a meeting in Donegal designed to form a Catholic national party. .. What surprised me was that none of our group [the group which later became the SDLP] were invited to come to the meeting or were even involved with it, which we had heard later, had been attended by middle class Catholics, mainly from Derry. I could smell that the

Knights of Columbanus were involved."[13]

Dail Dr Noel Browne 18 Oct 1977:
"There are still diehards of my generation within the profession but the new intake is not only extremely highly qualified but is better qualified because you cannot get into a consultant situation and then into a position as a consultant in a hospital unless you are extremely well qualified now because of the appointments system. It is no longer confined, as it was in the old days, to the Knights of Columbanus on the Catholic side and the Freemason Order on the other side."

Dail 15 May 1985 Mr. Haughey [referring to some pretty famous international groups that he (and now many others) look upon as powerful Secret Societies. Liam Lawlor, who figured prominently during the next FF government, was a member of the Trilateral Commission, as is Mary Robinson.[14] According to an interview with Mike Peters of Leeds Metropolitan University "members of Bilderberg helped to conceive, establish and create all of the major European institutions." This is based on his research into sources like the Gaitskell papers.[15]]:
"The Taoiseach also used his visit to America to attend this secret Bilderberg Conference, a group about which many people have grave doubts. It does not matter how the Taoiseach comes in here to shout, bluster and use personal abuse, because we have grave doubts about this organisation and its conferences. I have always had the impression that the Taoiseach had strong views about Secret Societies; yet he belongs or has belonged to a number of very powerful international bodies and groups whose aims and objectives, methods of operation and meetings are definitely secret and none more than this Bilderberg group. How can the Taoiseach justify attending a Bilderberg meeting? If it is wrong for a Taoiseach, and I believe it is, or a Minister to be a member of the Free Masonic Order, the Knights of Columbanus or Opus Dei, why is it all right for him to be a member of an arguably far more powerful secular secret society like the Bilderberg Conference?
...
If Deputies opposite would consider this thing calmly and objectively they would agree with me that it is not appropriate for the Taoiseach to continue to attend secret meetings which have a heavy NATO presence and with NATO subjects figuring in a major way on the agenda. How can the Taoiseach credibly object to NATO matters being discussed for instance in the European Council when he voluntarily attends this type of meeting.

Another aspect is the entitlement of this House to know precisely what took place and to have all the important relevant documents laid on the table of this House. By that I intend to judge the Taoiseach. If the Taoiseach does that and we have an opportunity to consider the documentation, all of us, in fairness, will have to review our accusation of secrecy about the Bilderberg conference. If those documents are not placed on the table of the House and if we are not given this vital information we will have to form our own opinions and confirm ourselves in our worst suspicions.

Apart from the NATO aspects the purpose of bodies like the Bilderberg group and the Tri-lateral commission is to foster an international élite and to promote the interests of huge multi-national corporations. I am absolutely certain that at that gathering with all those bankers and heads of huge multi-national corporations and others of that ilk, the position of the unemployed in my constituency of Coolock did not rate as a very high priority. It would have been far more appropriate if our Taoiseach were devoting himself in any international forum to this type of problem rather than these very dangerous subjects and discussions which take place at things like the Bilderberg Conference. I suspect that the Taoiseach remains a member of that organisation for some personal political reason. I understand that that type of organisation is prepared to support particular politicians in their objectives in their own countries. Will the Taoiseach say if anything like that was involved at this conference?

...

Can the Taoiseach expect some assistance in his own political career from these multinational friends, these international bankers?

..

Proinsias De Rossa: The Taoiseach is treating this as if the only question involved was one of neutrality and whether this State would be a member of a military bloc, but there are greater implications in that the Bilderberg group as I understand it is involved with influencing the foreign policies of the countries which are represented on it.

...[quoting the Irish Press:] "The object is not to 'draw the attention' of the greater population to Bilderberg activity. Bilderberg's existence is often denied, even by foreign ministry officials. Apart from planted newspaper articles, no Bilderberg publications are available to the public. The extent of media blackout is remarkable; insight into how this is achieved comes from a confidential memo of the steering group meeting in preparation of the 1984 conference at Williamsburg."

171

Fintan O'Toole and Kieran Rose:
"A leading right-wing activist wrote in 1988 that members of the Knights of Columbanus occupy positions of influence in many walks of life and at the highest level. They are asked to be confidentially politically active:
'We also need to keep our eyes on hospital boards; ethics committees; school boards; parent's groups...trying to keep the right government in power, or at least the one which is the lesser evil... such a network (of activists) if well motivated and highly confidential could do wonders quietly without coming out openly as Knights. An organisation or a group is never more powerful than when it influences events without being itself regarded as the initiator.'"[16]

Dail 14 Nov 1991 Pat Rabbitte:
[Hoping that soon will be dispelled:] "the suspected shadow of the Knights of Columbanus from the Customs House."

Dail Mr Bree 27 Sept 1995:
".. the Knights of Columbanus, a patriarchal, sectarian, secretive and fundamentalist network of influential men who have exerted power and influence in all sectors of society. While some people might be under the impression that the Knights of Columbanus is a type of charitable organisation, this is not the case. ... Despite the fact that they wish to remain in the background where they can manipulate and influence the agenda in a subtle and simple manner..."

Lord Laird reported in the Belfast Telegraph 11 May 2006:
"Allegations that a cross-border body is being run by a Catholic organisation have been levelled by an Ulster Unionist politician. The claims about Waterways Ireland, which has its headquarters in Enniskillen, were raised in parliament by Lord Laird.
He said members of staff within the public body believed it was "now being run" by the Knights of Columbanus, an Irish Catholic lay organisation."[17]
..from the Irish News 12 May 2006:
"Lord Laird last night (Wednesday) explained why he made the allegations about the Catholic groups, saying that when he was making private enquiries about Waterways Ireland he kept being told: "It's to do with the knights."
"I thought at first they meant something that happened on a Thursday night but I soon learnt it was the Knights of Columbanus, although I

know nothing about them or Opus Dei," he said."[18]

What follows are just a few international examples that show how it is feasible for a secret society to exercise a remarkable level of power even in a democracy:

Wales
"Roger Everest says he was told 30 years ago that he would never get on in the legal profession after turning down an invitation to join the Dinas Llandaff lodge of the Freemasons in Cardiff...Earlier this year Mr Everest, who practises from chambers at Pontyclun near Cardiff, had a claim that his career had been blighted by his non-membership of the freemasons rejected by the European Court of Human Rights.
Yesterday he said, "The judiciary in South Wales is a closed shop which I believe excludes ethnic minorities, women and men who are not part of a masonic network.
...He added, "It is my firm belief that there is a masonic connection with the miscarriages of justice that have occurred in South Wales."[19]

France
"The scandal-ridden French resort of Nice has been rocked by fresh corruption claims. The city's chief public prosecutor says a network of freemasons is perverting the local justice system...Dossiers that have been "buried", according to Mr de Montgolfier, include paedophilia allegations against a number of Nice's magistrates and cases involving large-scale fraud. ...According to insiders, he presented her [the Minister of Justice] with evidence that the National Grand Lodge of France was behind the "infiltration" of various levels of the magistrature."[20]

Philippines
This is from Wayne Madsen, an important source for intelligence gossip in Washington, who says that Opus Dei is sometimes manipulated by US intelligence agencies particularly in the Philippines and Venezuela:
"The documents were passed by Aquino to Philippine opposition figures linked closely to a powerful Opus Dei movement in the country. That movement was reportedly participating in a planned coup against Macapagal-Arroyo. (The April 2002 U.S.-supported abortive coup against Venezuelan President Hugo Chavez was also supported by Opus Dei elements in Venezuela). The Philippine Department of Justice has asked for an arrest warrant to be issued against Aquino and his one time police assistant Cesar Mancao for the murder of Philippine publicist

Salvador "Buddy" Dacer and his driver Emmanuel Corbito in November 2000. The Aragoncilla-Aquino ring is being linked to a wider Opus Dei espionage and political black bag operation that reached into the highest levels of the FBI."[21]

From the same in relation to East Timor:

"The Bush administration is using Opus Dei in destabilization efforts in Venezuela, Mexico, Peru, Ecuador, and Brazil. The Iberian roots of the organization and the adherence of many Spanish and Portuguese Catholics to the sect make it an ideal vehicle for stirring up problems in Spanish and Portuguese-speaking nations. East Timor is a former Portuguese colony. Opus Dei is very strong in the Liberal Party of Australia, one of the two conservative parties that make up John Howard's coalition."[22]

Ukraine

"leader of Ukraine's Social Party Alexander Moroz says, about 300 high-ranking officials in Ukraine are members of a Masonic lodge which representative office is located somewhere abroad. These are Ukraine's prosecutor general, chief of the Ukrainian security service, the minister of defence, the first president of Ukraine and parliament deputies...

The matter concerns the Order of Saint Stanislav into which representatives of Ukrainian elite and high-ranking officials are actively dubbed."[23]

Italy

"Between 1965 and 1981, it [P-2 Masonic Lodge] tried to condition the Italian political process through the penetration of persons of confidence to the inside of the magistracy, the Parliament, the army and the press..."Banker of God" Roberto Calvi's connections with the Worshipful Master Licio Gelli became a particular focus of press and police attention, and caused the lodge (then secret) to be discovered. A list of adherents was found by the police in Gelli's house in Arezzo in March 1981, containing over 900 names, among which were very important state officers, some important politicians (4 ministers or former ministers, and 44 deputies), and a number of military officers, many of them enrolled in the Italian secret services."[24]

The wiki article also notes the links between P-2 and the CIA. As another of the wiki articles points out the Lodge was heavily involved in the promotion of terrorism in Italy:

"The strategy of tension (Italian: strategia della tensione) is a way to control and manipulate public opinion using fear, propaganda, disinformation, psychological warfare, agents provocateurs and false flag terrorism actions.

The term was coined in Italy during the trials that followed the 1970s and 1980s terror attacks and murders committed by neofascist terrorists (such as Ordine Nuovo, Avanguardia Nazionale or Fronte Nazionale). The terrorists were backed by intelligence agencies, P2 masonic lodge and Gladio, a NATO secret "stay-behind" army set up to perform guerilla and resistance activities should Italy be successfully invaded by the Soviet bloc ...

The suspected aim of these crimes was to make the public believe that the bombings were committed by a communist insurgency, to promote the formation of an authoritarian government, and to prevent the growing Italian Communist Party (PCI) from joining the ruling Democrazia Cristiana (DC) in a government of national reconciliation ("historical compromise")."[25]

South Africa

"The Afrikanerbond or, as it has been known throughout most of its history, the Afrikaner Broederbond (or simply Die Broederbond), is a fraternal organization dedicated to the promotion of the interests of Afrikaners. The society was active during the rise to power of the Afrikaner nationalists and during the apartheid years most government ministers and many influential Afrikaner churchmen, academics, professionals, military officers and policemen were members of this very successful and tightly-knit secret society). It was often alleged and always denied that the important decisions of the South African State in those years were mandated by the then very secretive Broederbond. The organization has in modern times opened itself to public scrutiny and little resembles the omnipotent "hidden hand" of the middle years of the 20th Century. In its heyday, the Broederbond was one of the most watertight and successful Secret Societies in history. Infiltration by outsiders was insignificant.

...

Every prime minister and state president in South Africa from 1948 to the end of apartheid in 1994 was a member of the Afrikaner Broederbond. Indeed, nearly every prominent Afrikaner in any field was a member of the Broederbond."[26]

Note too that the Western intelligence agencies and the apartheid government had a surprisingly close relationship on occasion, like over the death of Dag Hammarskjold.[27]

Wikipedia on the Muslim Brotherhood:

"The Brotherhood is one of the most influential political and religious forces in the Islamic world, and especially so in the Arab world. The first Muslim Brotherhood was founded in Egypt in 1928, and Egypt is still considered the centre of the movement; it is generally weaker in the Maghreb, or North Africa, than in the Arab Levant. Brotherhood branches form the main opposition to the governments in several countries in the Arab world, such as Egypt, Syria and Jordan, and are politically active to some extent in nearly every Muslim country. There are also diaspora branches in several Western nations, composed by immigrants previously active in the Brotherhood in their home countries."

Palestine
"The Islamic Resistance Movement, or Hamas, founded in 1987 in Gaza, is a wing of the Brotherhood, formed out of Brotherhood-affiliated charities that had gained a strong foothold among the local population. These had been permitted by Israeli occupation authorities to operate in the Palestinian Territories to counter the influence of the secular Palestinian resistance movements.."

Jordan
"The Jordanian branch of the Muslim Brotherhood was formed in 1942, and is a strong factor in Jordanian politics. While most political parties and movements were banned for a long time in Jordan, the Brotherhood was exempted and allowed to operate by the Jordanian monarchy. The Jordanian Brotherhood has formed its own political party, the Islamic Action Front, which has the largest number of seats of any party in the Jordanian parliament."

Egypt
"By 1936, it had 800 members, then this number increased greatly to up to 200 000 by 1938. By 1948, the Brotherhood had about half a million members. ...
The Brotherhood has been an illegal organization, tolerated to varying degrees, since 1954 when it attempted to assassinate Gamal Abdel Nasser, head of the Egyptian government; it is still periodically subjected to mass arrests. It remains Egypt's most popular opposition group, advocating Islamic reform, democratic system and maintaining a vast network of support through Islamic charities working among poor Egyptians."[28]
You can read here how the brotherhood has also close links to British and US Intelligence:

http://www.redmoonrising.com/Ikhwan/BritIslam.htm .

Footnotes

1. Sean McPhilemy, *The Committee* (Boulder, Colorado, 1999), p.342-3.

2. http://www.blythe.org/Intelligence/readme/115sum . The chairman of the Committee is named by the BBC here:
http://news.bbc.co.uk/1/hi/northern_ireland/622765.stm see also:
http://www.geocities.com/CapitolHill/Lobby/8151/committee.html .

3. http://debates.oireachtas.ie/DDebate.aspx?F=SEN20040304.xml&Node=397

4. Brian Nugent, *Orwellian Ireland* (Co.Meath, 2008) Chapter 5 footnote 60, available at http://www.indymedia.ie/article/72186 .

5. http://www.geocities.com/athlonelaura/irb.html .

6. Paddy Harte, *Young Tigers and Mongrel Foxes* (Dublin, 2005), p.33.

7. http://www.orderofmalta.ie/irish_assocation/welcome.htm .

8. http://www.motherjones.com/news/feature/1983/07/willbedone.html .

9. soc.culture.irish 20 Aug 2001 article 'Irish Times' by David Noone.

10. alt.religion.christian.roman-catholic 16 Oct 2005 article "Another MA RCC Priest Pleads guilty to abuse" comment by bernard_con@yahoo.co.uk .

11.
http://web.archive.org/web/20050301223411/projecttruth2.com/timeline+and+the+story.htm ,
http://web.archive.org/web/20050224211113/projecttruth2.com/Ron+Leroux+Affidavit.htm , html http://www.ritualabusetorture.org/inthenameofgod.pdf p.100 and http://www.laxat.com/More-Knights-of-Columbus-in-Corruption-Pedophilism-Sexual-813281.html .

12. Writing in McCormack, *Blackwell Companion to Modern Irish Culture.* (2001), p.524. Points out also how President Sean T O'Kelly was a Knight much to the displeasure of DeValera.

13. From his autobiography *Straight Left* p.137-140 quoted in a comment by Brendan Heading to the article "All them killings" at soc.culture.europe 28 Jan 1998.

14. *The Evaluation of Gay and Lesbian Politics in Ireland* (Cork, 1994), p.29.

15. http://en.wikipedia.org/wiki/Trilateral_Commission .

16. http://www.propagandamatrix.com/bbc_radio_4_bilderberg.mp3 .

17.
http://www.blather.net/zeitgeist/archives/2006/05/opus_dei_knights_of_colum
banus.html .

18.
http://www.nuzhound.com/articles/irish_news/arts2006/may11_Lairds_theory_
bordered_fanciful.php .

19. Western Mail 20 Aug 2003
http://www.prisonplanet.com/freemason_closed_shop_blocked_me_says_barri
ster.html .

20. The Telegraph 17 October 1999
http://www.freemasonrywatch.org/france.html .

21. 14 Oct 2005 http://www.waynemadsenreport.com/intelwhispers/intel.htm .

22. 4 June 2006 http://www.waynemadsenreport.com/index.php .

23. From Pravda
http://www.propagandamatrix.com/ukrainian_opposition_unveiled_masonic_c
onspiracy.htm .

24. http://en.wikipedia.org/wiki/Propaganda_Due .

25. http://en.wikipedia.org/wiki/Strategy_of_tension .

26. http://en.wikipedia.org/wiki/Broederbond .

27. http://www.globalpolicy.org/secgen/pastsg/murder.htm .

28. http://en.wikipedia.org/wiki/Muslim_Brotherhood .

CHAPTER 5

Is Satanic Ritual Abuse for real? The Case of Sarah Bland

As pointed out at the end of Chapter 3, mixing in the general milieu of these Secret Societies are occult groups and esoteric religions which might not be well known to many but are nonetheless the subject of some serious allegations. The question of satanic and pagan cults, and their political power in history, is possibly worth exploring because imho it is a little known but serious issue facing the world today. I list two historical examples of satanic cults, to explain what they are, then I look at the modern allegations surrounding satanic activity and finally I relate the experiences of Sarah Bland at the hands of such a cult in Laois and her mother's shocking allegations about the Irish legal system's response to her family's plight.

The first detailed account of such a cult in the modern age comes to us from the France of Louis XIV and in particular from an investigation that the King ordered in response to a scandalous court case in the year 1676. The King, trying to stem the tide of scandalous rumour and gossip which linked the Court to the story of poisoning and immorality thrown up by the trial of the Marquise de Brinvilliers, ordered his Chief of Police, the famous Gabriel Nicolas de la Reynie, to conduct a widespread investigation into these poisonings. This has resulted in 4 large volumes of the 'Archives de la Bastille' full of the most incredible insights into the French elite of that time, as explained here by Joseph McCabe who quotes many of these documents in his *Testament of Christian Civilization*:

> "There is no need to quote passages on the morals of Louis XIV...and his appalling Court, but the Satanism that was mixed up with the epidemic of murder and adultery is now much misrepresented...The idea that we depend on Parisian gossip purveyed by scandal-writers of the time is quite wrong. The verbatim official records of the examinations and trials were - except for the parts exposing the highest persons of his court, which Louis burned - published (*Archives de la Bastille*, 17 vols.) in 1873 by F. Ravaisson, and though some of the witnesses were grossly ignorant and coarse women who made absurd statements occasionally, the general picture afforded by several years of trials - it is

false that the evidence was got by torture - is appalling. Every class, lower, middle, and noble, is involved, a dozen of the highest ladies of the Court employing priests to say Black Masses...
(On July 18, 1680 Lesage testified):-

"Guibourge said mass on the belly of many women, one an actress (to get influence with the King), all naked...on the belly of a lady of quality (Mme. de Montespan, then the greatest lady in France)...and on after-births, from which La Voisin afterwards distilled a liquid...He said other masses in a cellar in the presence of women and children who chanted invocations to the devil...The priest Rebours also said mass on the belly of a woman. She would not employ (the priest) Davot because he was a drunkard...Mme. de Vivonne told me that Filastre gave one of her own children as a sacrifice to the devil for the success of her affairs, and this was done by her parish priest and Mme. de Vivonne was present...The priest Tournet also said masses on the bellies of naked women. He ordered one woman to offer her daughter, a fine girl of 14 or 15, to the devil...He said three masses on her and raped her during one of them."

Guibourg's mistress, as foul and ugly as he, was examined on August 9:-

"She said that she had had seven children by Guibourg, and he had taken charge of each after birth (and, she hints, killed them)...one was born under a hedge in the country..."
...
On October 9 she (Voisin's daughter) testified:-

"She saw her mother burn three or four infants (sacrificially killed by Guibourg, who was always careful to baptize them) in her baking furnace (the police found this). At the mass of Mme. de Montespan (the King's famous mistress) a prematurely born child was put in a basin, and Guibourg cut its throat and poured blood in the chalice and consecrated it...and her mother took away its entrails to be distilled (for drugs) and the blood and host in a glass vessel that Mme. de Montespan had brought...she spoke of the fouling of the chalice by Guibourg, Des Oeillets (chief maid of Mme. de Montespan) and an English Lord."

...

I must be content to say that four large volumes of the Archives, covering a dozen years of life in Paris under Louis XIV, are full of this sort of thing. It is an academic scandal that some historians still speak of the "glory" of the age of that gluttonous reprobate."[1]

So that is the type of activity that is alleged to occur among satanic cults, activities ranging from burning circles and chants and robes etc all the way to human sacrifices. The latter, it is claimed, involves the murder of children - in modern times it is said unregistered - deliberately conceived for such purpose among members of the cult and less commonly the killing of strangers. Serious allegations I know but that is obviously what happened in France and that is what some say happens now.

In any case there is a slightly less lurid example of a satanic cult which comes to us from history, this time from England in the 18th century. It is related here by Gyeorgos Ceres Hatonn in an admittedly polemic manner but most people I think accept that this group did include a remarkable who's who of Georgian England, and did involve some degree of satanic ritual:

"As we have noted, a number of Satanic cults grew to such a degree and achieved such tremendous wealth and power that in time they began to wield mighty political influence in Europe. Such was the case with a Satanic organization, created in 1748 in England, which in later years virtually ran the British Empire.

Founded under the name, "The Friars of St. Francis of Wycombe", in honour of its creator and leader Sir Francis Dashwood, a wealthy member of parliament, it became known as "The Hell-Fire Club" because of its similarity to a "defunct" Satanist group which had operated in London some years earlier. According to Daniel P. Mannix's history of that organization, *The Hell-fire Club* (Ballantine Books, New York, 1959), it was "an association dedicated to Black Magic, sexual orgies, and political conspiracies..." ...

The members of the Hell-fire Club were nearly all closely connected with the government and included such influential persons as Sir Francis Dashwood, the Chancellor of the Exchequer; The Earl of Sandwich, First Lord of the Admiralty (one of the most important men of the time, whose control of the English Navy and friendship with the King "exerted a profound influence on the destiny of the British Empire"); the Earl of Bute, the Prime Minister of England (he played a large part in training the boy who became King George III); Thomas Potter, son of the Archbishop of Canterbury ("an ardent Satanist [who] wrote psalms for the Black Mass ceremonies"); and, Paul Whitehead, the "Atheist Chaplain" and Secretary of the Club who acted as a sexton during the Black Masses (a composer of blasphemous "hymns," he was its brains and backbone")...

Other Hell-Fire Club members included the Lord Mayor of London, the Prince of Wales, several of England's greatest artists (Hogarth) and poets...

At its headquarters on Dashwood's estate at West Wycombe, some thirty-three miles northwest of London, the members of the Hell-Fire Club engaged in depraved sexual rites carried out over a span of more than twenty years. Having outfitted a network of underground grottos for the purpose, Dashwood often presided over Black Masses where the body of a naked woman was used as an altar and the unholy congregation "drank the sacrificial wine from her navel." During these ceremonies, "The crucifix was inverted and black candles were burned [while]...lamps of lewd design were used." To summon up the forces of evil, herbs were burned in braziers: "belladonna, hemlock, henbane, verbena, and mandrake - all powerful narcotics."

Upon the death of King George II in 1760, and after the 21-year-old son of Prince Fritz had ascended the throne as George III, members of the Hell-Fire Club became all-powerful in Britain...

In 1781, after an incredible life of wanton debauchery and Satanist perversion, Sir Francis Dashwood died at the age of seventy-three. The immoral activities and conspiracies of Dashwood and the Hell-Fire Club had polluted an empire."[2]

There are two remarkable aspects to this group I think. First while it was involved in 'political conspiracies' its membership included politicians from a wide political spectrum who in fact in public life were nominally opposed to one another. So for example the greatest popular radical of the day, John Wilkes, was known for his vicious attacks on the Earl of Bute and later the Earl of Sandwich who were at the same time both secretly his colleagues in this cult. This political controversy, which culminated in Sandwich reading a lewd poem of Wilkes' into the record of the House of Lords, dominated the political discourse of the day and now some historians who have looked at the Club's activities in detail feel it was all along some kind of sham operation.[3] Presumably they felt that by opposing each other in this way, as the extreme ends of an artificially polarised political climate, they could dominate the political life of the country and drown out their real critics.

The other thing to note about this cult is that the members seemed to control the intelligence apparatus of the UK at this time. Two key government positions in the intelligence system at this time were probably First Lord of the Admiralty - in the UK and later the US the origins of the modern intelligence system are usually traced to groups under the control of the navy - and Postmaster General - because of its role in the interception of mail - and both sinecures were held by members of the Club for most of these years.[4]

That they were interested in the espionage game we can see from this quote from a history of cryptology:

> "The next cryptologist of note (not to say downright notoriety) was Sir Francis Dashwood (1708-1781; from 1763, Lord le Despencer), a larger than life character, who managed to combine his spying and cryptology with diversions such as gambling, devil worship, and debauchery...As to the cryptology, Dashwood has been reported as both Crown and Jacobite agent in the 1740s, but was in truth probably a double agent for the Crown (Deacon, 1980). Certainly, by catering to the lusts of powerful people he made powerful friends,

serving as Chancellor of the Exchequer for a few months in 1762, and as Postmaster General - de facto controller of the British black chambers [an intelligence term], remember - from 1766 to 1781, and it was in this latter role that he was visited in 1773 by the American Deputy Postmaster General, Benjamin Franklin (1706-1790).

...

"Four members of [Dashwood's Hell-Fire Club] were undoubtedly mixed up in espionage and gained much of their intelligence through belonging to it. Almost certainly several of the other members were at one time or another working for British Intelligence. The four were John Wilkes, the Chevalier D'Eon de Beaumont, a French diplomat, Sir Francis Dashwood himself, and, surprisingly enough, Benjamin Franklin, the statesman and philosopher." (Deacon, 1980, p.100.)"[5]

Enough of this 18th century smoke and mirrors we now come to the question of satanic cults in modern times. In 1980 the publication of a book called 'Michelle Remembers' for some heralds the dawn of public recognition of satanic activity in recent times, and for others is the beginning of the satanic 'panic' of the 80s. This book, which became a best seller and recounts the life of one person in such a cult in Canada, kick started a whole wave of accusations of satanic abuse activity in Canada, the US, UK, Australia and New Zealand.[6] The authorities set up special satanic abuse task forces in places like L.A.[7] and in the UK huge numbers of arrests were made in major investigations across the country. To give you some idea of the sort of statements made at this time I will quote two speeches made by Conservative MPs in the House of Commons, firstly Mr. David Wilshire (Spelthorne) MP speaking in the House of Commons in 1988:

"My second example is satanism. All too often, its mention produces giggles and images of witches on broomsticks, but satanism is not the same thing as witchcraft. It is about the ritual mutilation and torture of people, particularly children, human and animal sacrifice and cannibalism. I shall quote from an article in Style magazine, published in January of this year, which states:

"Sam Hoyer's nightmare began at birth. Sam spent the

185

first 16 years of her life in an orphanage in New England ... When Sam was 9 years old, cult leaders designated her and a handful of other children as candidates for the role of high priestess. Testing the children's powers, the religious impostors strapped six of the candidates' to crosses and burned them. Sam alone survived. As part of her grooming, Sam was required to watch other children being sacrificed; then she was forced to witness and participate in cannibalism."

In case any of my colleagues are tempted to dismiss that report as the exaggerated ramblings of American journalists, I must tell hon. Members that I have a list of 30 recent satanic murderers who have been brought before United States courts. If any of my colleagues are tempted to believe that those things do not happen here, I must tell them that only 10 days ago one of my local newspapers, the Egham and Staines News, carried a headline stating:

"Baby in satanic killing. Throat cut by coven members."

I hope that I have said enough to prove that cults do not consist of eccentric people who wear black robes and funny pointed hats. All too often they involve the deliberate abuse of children and young people. We cannot afford to laugh cults off. The time has now come to take them much more seriously than we have in the past. We must warn the public about them and the real dangers that they represent. We must act against the organisers of such depravity and cruelty."[8]

His comments were echoed by a fellow Conservative MP Geoffrey Dickens (Littleborough and Saddleworth) on 19 Dec 1988:

"I have resisted the temptation to dwell on the growth of the occult and groups practising black witchcraft, devil worship, black magic and satanism, but work to deal with this growth is going on behind the scenes, and it is proceeding very well. Children are being delivered from the hands of such groups. It is evil, it is spreading, but many of us are fighting. I will not mar my speech by moving down that road today, but I shall return to that subject because it is worse than any hon. Member would dream.[9]...[and from the same 10 May 1990:]

"Will my right hon. and learned Friend consider arranging a debate on the spread of satanism and devil worship in the United Kingdom and the involvement of children? [Interruption.] I well remember the reaction in the House 10 years ago, when I warned of the spread of child abuse. I was greeted with disbelief, but we now know differently. Two years ago, I warned of the spread of devil worship, satanism and black witchcraft...We now know that that is true because of the NSPCC report. Such a debate would help me to identify others in this House who are willing to stand up to those people."[10]

This wave of media interest and police activity surrounding satanic abuse faltered somewhat though in the early 90s as some scepticism began to emerge about these cases. It was felt that some of the allegations were just too much of a 'conspiracy theory' because in many cases they involved allegations against very powerful but highly respected public figures (like in the case of 'Jane' from Leeds in 1989 [11] and Derry Mainwaring Knight in 1986 [12]) and also because some of the claims were made against what was considered to be an implausibly large number of people in places like Rochdale near Manchester, Nottingham and Orkney. Hence new thinking began to appear which attributed a lot of the allegations to over zealous social workers asking leading questions of the victims ('false memories') and also to a kind of mass psychosis where people make allegations as a kind of peer pressure in response to the widely publicised satanic 'panic'. This backlash, so to speak, culminated in two reports, one a handbook for the FBI prepared in 1992 by Kenneth V. Lanning,[13] and the other a report for the UK Dept. of Health by the LSE professor Jean La Fontaine [14] which have often been said to have ended any official recognition of the instance of satanic abuse in the US and the UK respectively.

But this state of affairs now seems to have changed and there appears currently to be a quiet recognition in official circles in places like Italy, the UK and Ireland that Satanic Abuse is a very real and serious problem. In Italy for example the local police are now investigating the possibility that a number of horrific murders initially attributed to one 'Monster of Florence' might in fact be the work of a satanic cult, as reported in the Sunday Times:

"In one search warrant, prosecutors wrote that "a group

of people who celebrated black masses and magical rites put the weapon in their hands." A lawyer an entrepreneur, an artist and a former university medical professor were all suspects for a time.

...Michele Giutari, the former head of the Florence flying squad, who has investigated the case for more than 10 years, has argued that the mastermind behind the Monster were "respectable citizens above suspicion" who formed "a satanic sect"."[15]

The changed climate in the UK can be seen I think in the fact that the Dept. of Health commissioned a new report on Satanic Abuse in 2000 which found that the problem does exist, as detailed here in an article in the 'Independent on Sunday' entitled 'Satanic Abuse no Myth say Experts':

"A specially commissioned government report will this week conclude that satanic abuse does take place in Britain. It will say that its victims have suffered actual abuse and are not suffering from "false memory syndrome".

The report, ordered by the Department of Health, focuses on the experiences of 50 "survivors". Compiled by Dr John Hale [sic], director of the Portman Clinic in London, and psychotherapist Valerie Sinason, it will reopen the debate which started a decade ago with testimonies from children in Nottingham, Rochdale and Orkney.

Its findings contradict the claims of a report ordered by the Conservative government in 1994, which concluded that satanic abuse was a "myth". It follows the growing concern of child protection agencies, and the Government, over organised child abuse.

...

The latest report was welcomed by Dr Joan Coleman, a Surrey psychiatrist who has spent 14 years treating victims. "A lot of children are born into satanic families who indulge in this ritual abuse," she said. "It's only now that child sexual abuse is being exposed that people are beginning to believe ritual abuse exists.""[16]

One of the authors of that report, Valerie Sinason, formerly a consultant child psychologist at the Tavistock Clinic in London and now the

Director of the Clinic for Dissociative Studies in Harley Street [17] and consultant at St George's Hospital Medical School in London, is probably the leading academic working in this area (you can read her impressive list of academic publications here http://www.valeriesinason.com/PublicationsVSinason.htm). She has been interviewed by the BBC on this question where she tells of the horrific experiences related to her by her patients and passed onto her by the over "40 psychiatrists, psychologists and mental health experts" that she liaises with.[18] You can see the seriousness of what she has uncovered from this report in the Express 2/10/00:

> "…..Psychotherapist Valerie Sinason, who has been paid by the Department of Health to study adult survivors of alleged organised ritual abuse, said yesterday she was "completely convinced" Satanic abuse does occur. She claimed to have evidence about children whose births were not officially registered being reared for abuse and sacrifice. The scientist, who edited a clinical textbook on Satanist abuse after the controversies in Rochdale, the Orkneys and Nottingham in the early 1990s, has claimed previously to have evidence of at least 100 murders. Her study of cases from nearly 40 psychiatrists, psychologists and mental health experts will claim that she has seen evidence of physical injuries in adult survivors, who tell of seeing people drugged and killed. She said that out of 76 patients she has seen at her London clinic, 46 claimed that they had witnessed the murder of children or adults."[19]

Scotland Yard launched a major investigation based on these reports, in close liaison with Ms Sinason, which in 2006 was reported to have swelled to investigating the claims of over 200 victims.[20] Just to clarify btw, we are definitely talking about satanic rituals among Caucasians native to the US, UK etc. not involving the African or Haitian communities as some people spin it.

In Ireland meanwhile the quiet official acceptance of the reality of this abuse is illustrated by the special satanic abuse helplines that have been set up by the Rape Crisis Centre. Fiona Neary, the national coordinator of the Rape Crisis centres, has explained that she took this step because they were already dealing with such abuse cases, with 5 cases been handled by one of their centres for example.[21] The full details of what those victims are saying are I guess unknown but she has hinted that:

"We could be talking about high levels of organised abuse which could almost be beyond the belief of many of the agencies tasked with dealing with this problem."[22]

She explained this in an article in the Irish Mirror of the 24 Oct 1999 which included an amazing story by 'Kate' of this abuse in the outskirts of Dublin. Another victim quoted in the article was:

"Sarah Bland from County Laois has battled for years to make the authorities investigate her claims that she was subjected to ritual satanic abuse by an Irish paedophile ring.

She believes her alleged abusers are still on the loose.

The 22-year-old student says she can recall being repeatedly gang-raped from the age of four.

"It went on for two years before my mother took me to Canada. But I had nightmares throughout my childhood.

"I remember lying naked on a dining table surrounded by candles. They would smear blood and then the men would rape me. There was usually about six of them and they were all dressed in suits.

"I remember a younger one very well and I think I could recognise him if I came face-to-face with him now.""

Sarah Bland, with the exception of this article, has faced the familiar blackout of her case in the Irish media and been ignored as well by the Irish political and justice system. So much so that in desperation her mother has tried to get Northern Irish politicians to raise the case in order to break this wall of silence, as Ian Paisley junr related in the Northern Ireland Assembly 10/9/01:

"Mr Paisley Jnr:

I beg to move

That this Assembly notes with concern the failure of the Irish justice system to resolve the rape/incest case of the daughter of British citizen Sarah Bland.

I bring the motion before the House because I believe that the rights of a British woman and her daughter, who lived in Dublin, were trampled underfoot in a most appalling manner by the authorities there.

The matter should have been debated in Dáil Éireann; it should have been processed by an Irish court. It is on today's Order Paper because of the failure of successive Dublin Governments and the Dublin courts to face up to their responsibilities. The case is a political message to all those in the political establishment of the South and, as long as the gross injustice, known as the Bland case, remains unresolved, anything that the Irish authorities may say about rights, equality, justice, honour and truth should be treated with contempt. If the Bland case is a lesson in how the Dublin authorities would treat one of its own, the political significance of that should never be lost on Unionists in the House and outside.

The case concerns a young Roman Catholic woman, Sarah Bland, living in the midlands of the Republic from 1980 to 1982 and the 20-year fight by her resilient mother, Patricia Bland, to right the crimes visited on that family. The case continues to this day, but I want the Assembly to note it because of the rape, incest and abuse that occurred during the early 1980s when Sarah Bland was a child.

The case is the only example that I can find in which a child suffered rape and incest as a result of being placed, by a High Court order, into the hands of the abuser. Instead of rescuing and protecting the child from abuse by a court order, the courts in the Irish Republic lent themselves to that abuse. We must publicly ask the Irish courts and the political establishment why a four-year-old girl was sent back to her abusing father by a court order after he had admitted in open court to being an abuser, a wife beater and an alcoholic. The child was subjected to incest, torture, drugging and rape by a number of men in a stately home, which, by Christmas 1980, was run down, filthy and chaotic. Had common sense prevailed in the Irish Republic's legal establishment, Sarah Bland would never have been placed in the care of her father.

For two years, Sarah Bland exhibited signs of extreme trauma. She endured hundreds of hypnotic comas and revealed to her mother the extent of the hedonistic torture and debauchery to which she had been subjected. However, no solicitor would act to defend the rights of this child or her mother. When the mother tried to get help, she was also made a victim. Sneering allegations and threats were made against her. In this case, a child was raped and a family was robbed of its rights and, later, of its finances.

The case has been brought to the attention of five former Taoiseachs and the serving Taoiseach. It has also been brought to the attention of several TDs, including the current Minister of Foreign Affairs in the South of Ireland, Mr Brian Cowen. They have done absolutely nothing to investigate this terrible case of abuse. Why did the Dublin Government do nothing? The authorities know that to deal with the case in an open and transparent way would be to expose the hideous cover-up by the court system in the Republic of Ireland, where justice appears to be possible only when it will not damage a certain Dublin elite.

Mr and Mrs Bland lived in Rath House from 1971 until 1980. The family was given legal advice by a firm of solicitors called Gerrard, Scallan and O'Brien. Mrs Bland approached the family solicitor to get help for her husband, who was already suicidal, in a state of depression and involved in domestic violence. She sought to have him made a ward of court for his own and his family's protection until his suicide attempts had ceased and he had received psychiatric help. Because of this action, increasing domestic violence was visited on Patricia Bland by her husband, and she had to flee the family home. She was amazed that the same company of solicitors — Gerrard, Scallan and O'Brien — then began action on behalf of her husband. They did so in the knowledge that he was unable to manage his own financial affairs and that, if their legal action were successful, the children would be placed back into the care of the abusive father. Despite the conflict of interest, the company chased Mrs Bland and her children and had them brought to Dublin for that very purpose.

In an attempt to protect her children, Mrs Bland fled to England on the advice of another solicitor, Mr Guy French of Fred Sutton and Company. He gave her bad advice, but his intentions appeared to be good. However, despite a hearing in England at which her husband admitted in open court to wife-beating, alcoholism, catatonic collapse and psychiatric problems, Gerrard, Scallan and O'Brien fought to have Mrs Bland returned to Dublin with her children. That duly happened, and her flight to England to seek justice in a British court was used continually against her in Irish courts to prevent her from having full custody of her children.

Once she was back in Dublin, Mrs Bland paid £1,600 to McCann, Fitzgerald, Roach and Dudley to fight her case. However, that company came to a private deal with the first company, Gerrard, Scallon and O'Brien, to ditch this "troublesome British woman". The agreed action resulted in a court order to place her children in the care of their father, even though they both knew of the evidence that he had committed rape and incest against his children. I hope that the case would have had a different outcome if that evidence had been brought to the attention of the Dublin courts. Not only is the fact that the evidence was never allowed to be brought to their attention alarming, but it shows that impropriety, greed and cover-up ruled the day.

Patricia Bland then turned to Dublin's leading family law expert, Mr Alan Shatter, who is known as "Mr Family Law" because of the many books that he has published and written on the subject. She paid him £2,000 and hoped that he could rescue her children from degrading torture. Mr Shatter had just commenced his political career in Fine Gael. In order for him to act in the interests of his new client, young Sarah Bland, he would have had to sue the previous solicitor, Mr

Michael O'Mahoney, for negligence. Mr O'Mahoney just happened to be the legal adviser to Fine Gael, the political party of which Alan Shatter was a member. That aspiring TD, "Mr Family Law," did nothing. Later, he became the shadow Justice Minister in the South of Ireland. He still did nothing. It was only later when Patricia Bland recovered her legal files from his office that she discovered that her calls had been treated with contempt and that "Mr Family Law" had suppressed the evidence of seven witnesses, including a leading psychiatrist and a senior social worker.

The handling of this case by the legal and political elite of Dublin makes Charles Haughey look squeaky clean. Every legal and ethical code has been trampled, tattered and debased. Every attempt that the mother made to protect and get justice for her children in the courts — or with the help of politicians — and regain her good name were met with indifference, obstruction and malice.

Her child was finally rescued when Judge McWilliam reversed a court order and sent the mother and children to Canada in 1983. They lived there in hiding, under police protection. However, after the rape came the robbery. Her estate was sold, and legal expenses of over £432,000 were claimed by and paid from that estate to Gerrard, Scallan and O'Brien, the original solicitors who should have declared their conflict of interest and refused to act.

In the following 15 years, Patricia Bland contacted five Taoiseachs, numerous TDs and MEPs — the list reads like a 'Who's Who' of Irish politics — all of whom did nothing. Only in the North was her case considered, first, by the Northern Ireland Forum for Political Dialogue and today by the Assembly. It is an indictment of the Irish Republic and its establishment that it did not at least consider this case and the matters raised by it. I hope that this debate will prompt someone with integrity in the South to come forward and say that enough is enough and seek an inquiry or tribunal into a sorry nightmare that could have been avoided if appropriate action had been taken in the first place. The evidence for the allegations is well-documented, and the documentation, tape recordings and video cassette can be made available to any Member who wishes to see them.

Sarah Bland is now 24 years of age. She is in the Building today. She has had a difficult life and has experienced fear and post-traumatic stress. From an early age, she has known little but abuse, exile and poverty, but at long last she can see her case put forward. Today's vindication does not come from a Southern courtroom or the Irish state or any of its statutory bodies. Sarah Bland is willing to meet MLAs and tell them about her plight. She is also willing to be an advocate for victims of child sex abuse. I hope that the House can lend its full support to the motion and show that we want to see justice and honour in the case.

...I hope that no flimsy excuse will be used by any Member to avoid taking a decision that others have been too frightened to take because of fear of the elite — legal or political — whom they wish to protect."[23]

In case anybody remains unconvinced of the reality of Satanic Ritual Abuse I will conclude with a few more examples of documented cases of this type of abuse from around the world:

South Africa
The police there have set up a special Occult-Related Crime Unit to deal with these kind of cases in South Africa. This is from 'Servamus' which 'is the official policing magazine for the South African Police Services':

"In South Africa more than 60 statutory Acts concerning the occult, have been and are still being violated. These crimes include murder, attempted murder, rape, attempted rape, sodomy, bestiality, drug abuse, weapon smuggling, kidnapping people (to cruelly torture and sacrifice them to Satan, for example street children, the homeless and prostitutes), abortion (of unwanted babies usually fathered by other Satanists, who are then sacrificed to Satan), cruelty to animals (to torture them and sacrifice them to Satan), desecration of graves, etc."[24]

Bear in mind that they are referring here to Satanism as basically a problem among the white population in South Africa which in turn takes it inspiration from European sources, although the native 'muti' practices are also a problem for the police.[25]

Italy

Here they are said to be about to set up a similar police unit in the wake of some well publicised satanic murders.[26]

Kenya

The Kenyan government instituted a Presidential Commission of Inquiry into the question of devil worship in that country. Chaired by a Catholic Archbishop its report was published in 1999 (partially released a few years earlier) and called for the setting up of a special police force to tackle the problem. It said that

> "the allegations of devil worship ["very true and very serious,"] should be taken seriously because they emanated from a cross-section of the society including pastors, senior administration and education officials, senior politicians, civic leaders, heads of institutions and students."

It "found devil worship at every level of society but mostly among the elite", that the cultists were often "rich, educated and powerful people," and that recruitment was frequently through Masonic lodges, golf clubs and groups like that which clearly show that they aren't by any means referring to native African animist beliefs. The shocking range of allegations was noted by the President of Kenya, Daniel arap Moi, who issued a statement noting some of the evidence given to the commission:

> "According to the testimonies, satanic cult include the following in their rituals: human sacrifice, drinking of human blood, eating of human flesh, black Mass, wine, nudity of the participants in the ritual, incantation in unintelligible language, sexual abuse and rape, especially of children and minors, black magic, narcotic drugs, presence of snakes."

It also warned of 'abetting or getting involved in devil worship which is in its formative stages in our country.' From that last comment you can see that they are referring to Satanism that is coming into the country - it was felt mainly in the guise of some of the new age or 'born again' religious groups which the commission found often act as "doorways" to Satanism.[27]

Poland
According to the BBC "there have been a series of high profile violent crimes associated with Satanism in Poland over the past couple of years."[28] This story is particularly about two murders in a military bunker.

Spain
ABC, the second largest daily newspaper in Spain, examined the issue in 1998 and came to some disturbing conclusions:

"The Spanish bishops' conference offered a higher estimate: 250,000 people engaged in devil-worship, associated with 40 major cult groups. Father Manuel Guerra Gomez, a theologian and specialist in cult activities, said that there was substantial evidence to support the belief that some of these cults had engaged in human sacrifice; he mentioned an incident in Barcelona, in which a young gypsy girl was apparently killed at a black mass. The ABC article also cited statistics from the international law-enforcement consortium, Interpol, suggesting that the number of such ritual sacrifices is on the rise across Europe. Interpol reported that there were at least 100 human sacrifices in Europe in the years 1989 and 1990."[29]

Mexico
There is obviously the well known Constanzo group in Mexico unearthed in 1988 and investigated, and accepted as a case of satanic human sacrifices, by both the Mexican and Texan police. Quite a number of important people were associated with the cult including Florentino Ventura, the head of Interpol in Mexico, and Salvador Garcia, the head of Narcotics investigations for the Mexican Federal Judicial Police.[30]

Australia
An incredible speech by Senator Bill Heffernan in the Federal Senate in Australia has unmasked some of these problems although "apart from a brief mention on a radio station, it has not been reported in the media."[31] Here is some of it:

"Recently I made a speech in which I highlighted the

code of silence which protects worldwide child sex networks, in particular, Australian paedophile networks. These networks include people in the judiciary, parliament, clergy and the Public Service. Many of these people live in an abhorrent culture in which is included, as a spoils of office, the right to have sex with children."[32]

In the few cases where these kind of allegations get publicity its often twisted in the media by powerful government spin doctoring, as you can see in this resignation speech of Peter Lewis as Speaker of the South Australian Parliament on the 4th April 2005:

"That information coming into my office from a few of the very many people claiming knowledge about the activities of paedophiles in general was of concern to me because, of the few people who spoke about parliament's problem, more than half had been killed. ...

I never had any intention of allowing the same [paedophile rings to operate, like what happened to the church] to occur on my watch here in parliament and was quietly, and as quickly as possible, bringing some of the people who had made the allegations to the point where they might pluck up enough courage and confidence and swear the truth of those allegations, enabling them to be more carefully investigated.

But they were being 'bumped off'—that is, murdered and viciously assaulted—quicker than I or the people who were helping me could get them to write down their allegations and then swear that what they were saying was true. Of course, I told Nigel Hunt that they should be protected from murderous acts. At no time have I ever said that they were being murdered or violently bashed into serious long-term mental dysfunction at the hands or the instigation of any MP. That was an improper speculation made by government ministers and their specialist spin doctors to the press across the length and breadth of the state to try to show me in a bad light. In retrospect, I believe it was another deliberate red herring contrived by them, just like the one about homosexuals and their haunts, to discredit me.

...

The most outrageous thing of all, which disturbs me most about the information which has come in to my office is not the matter of paedophiles in South Australia's parliament but what appears to be the related and organised activities of those paedophiles in high public office—that is, the judiciary, the senior ranks of human services portfolios, some police, and MPs, across the nation, especially within the ranks of the Labor Party. Yet you only have to recall in recent years the investigations, charges and successful convictions against such people as Darcy, Liddy, Wright, Wells, a former senator, and other current and past MPs in Queensland, New South Wales and Victoria to understand my concern. They have not acted alone or in isolation, it seems to me.

...

It is not surprising that we find them [Paedophiles] in the jobs and roles of leadership...The victims are the least powerful of all victims of crime in our society."[33]

One website links this paedophile ring to the activities of a satanic cult and which includes all the other gory and shocking allegations that surround those cults.[34] This includes particularly the account of Dr. Reina Michaelson who found out about these cults when she started to enquire into child abuse in the school system in Australia.[35]

Footnotes

1. Joseph McCabe, *Testament of Christian Civilization* (1946), p.237.

2. Gyeorgos Ceres Hatonn, *Heave-Up: Phase One* (1994), p.150-153. Mannix's account, which Hatonn is quoting, is admittedly not footnoted but for contemporary accounts of satanic rituals involving this group see Lady Theresa Lewis ed., *Extracts from the Journals and Correspondence of Miss Berry* (1865); *Town and Country* March 1769 p.122 and May 1773 p.245; and by the Limerick born Charles Johnstone in *Chrysal or the adventures of a Guinea* (first two volumes published in 1760 two later volumes 1765, and first complete edition in 1767, all said to be published in London but the latter edition possibly Dublin) Vol III. See also Montague Summers, *Witchcraft and Black Magic* (New York, 2000 originally published 1946), p.220.

3. For a discussion of how hypocritical the debate between Sandwich and Wilkes was see Marvin Olasky, *Fighting for Liberty and Virtue* (1995) Chapter 4 page 36 footnote 67: "Jones [Louis C. Jones, *The Clubs of the Georgian Rakes* (New York:. Columbia University Press, 1942),] (p.136) writes that Wilkes had read the poem to Sandwich and Dashwood who enjoyed it and encouraged Wilkes to have a copy printed for each Medmenham member. This would make Sandwich's action an even more hypocritical set-up, but there is insufficient evidence on this point."
(http://www.olasky.com/Archives/liberty/14.pdf).
You can see that Wilkes didn't really believe what he was writing against Bute from his reply to Bute's daughter in later years denying that he ever hated Bute: "Hate him?" he said. "No such thing. I had no dislike to him as a man, and I thought him a good Minister. But 'twas my game to abuse him."
Mind you these arguments were not without their humour as when the Earl of Sandwich told Wilkes that he "will die either on the gallows, or of the pox," Wilkes replied, "That must depend on whether I embrace your lordship's principles or your mistress." (Both references from http://www.williamsburgwoodlands.com/Foundation/journal/summer03/wilkes .cfm .)

4. Dashwood was Postmaster General 1766-81, and the Earl of Sandwich was First Lord of the Admiralty 1748-51 and 1771-82, while later he was joint Postmaster in 1768. Their friend Benjamin Franklin also worked in the Post office at this time and was Postmaster General in the American Colonies 1775-6.

5. Derek J. Smith, *Codes and Ciphers in History, Part 1 - To 1852*. As regards Benjamin Franklin the article goes on to point out:
"Franklin was a regular visitor at Dashwood's home, West Wycombe House, where he stayed in the summers of 1773 and 1774. In the papers of one John Norris, of Hughendon Manor, Buckinghamshire, there is the enigmatic comment: '3 June 1778. Did this day heliograph intelligence from Dr Franklin

in Paris to Wycombe'. Norris had built a 100-ft tower on a hill at Camberley, Surrey, from the top of which he used to signal and place bets by heliograph with Lord le Descencer at West Wycombe. // Franklin refers to a sixteen-day visit at Dashwood's home, West Wycombe House, in July 1772 which is significant in that it was in the months of June and July that the Chapters of the Brotherhood were held." (Deacon, 1980, pp112-113.)"
(http://www.smithsrisca.demon.co.uk/crypto-ancient.html).

6. The UK Independent on Sunday outlines some of this story, in an article by Rosie Waterhouse 12/8/90 (http://www.skepticfiles.org/rumor/is120890.htm) . You can see some of the allegations here:
http://www.skepticfiles.org/rumor/index.htm ; and some of the convictions achieved:http://www.healingroads.org/ra_cases.html ; Wikipedia covers it maybe from the sceptical perspective?:
http://en.wikipedia.org/wiki/Satanic_ritual_abuse . This is a rebuttal of the allegations from a sceptical
perspective:http://www.saff.ukhq.co.uk/truthtal.htm. The Guardian writer Bea Campbell is one of those who feel that SRA abuse should be taken seriously: http://www.mail-archive.com/leftlink , here is an article that believes that SRA is real and covered up:
http://web.archive.org/web/20041023235022/http://www.econcrisis.homestead. com/MajorCoverupsSatanism.html , from the same viewpoint in the US:http://www.skepticfiles.org/rumor/res_stna.htm . Audrey Harper published a book which detailed her experiences in the occult in Surrey as mentioned in the Birmingham Evening Mail 5 Oct 1990:
http://www.skepticfiles.org/rumor/audrey.htm , and more on her case here: http://www.paganlibrary.com/witch_hunting/beyond_reason.php. Some gossip on the Mainwaring Knight allegations:
http://groups.google.com/group/uk.politics.misc/msg/2553eaffedd873ab? .

7. http://www.skepticfiles.org/rumor/bugspray.htm .

8.   http://www.publications.parliament.uk/pa/cm198889/cmhansrd/1988-12-19/Debate-4.html .

9.   http://www.publications.parliament.uk/pa/cm198889/cmhansrd/1988-12-19/Debate-3.html .

10.   http://www.publications.parliament.uk/pa/cm198990/cmhansrd/1990-05-10/Debate-2.html .

11. http://www.offmsg.connectfree.co.uk/OffBEAT/britton.htm .

12. http://www.skepticfiles.org/rumor/dmknight.htm .

13. http://www.religioustolerance.org/ra_rep03.htm .

14. http://www.rickross.com/reference/satanism/satanism4.html .

15. Sunday Times June 4 2006 p.20.

16. Independent on Sunday 30 April 2000
(http://www.offmsg.connectfree.co.uk/broxtowe/hsrep.htm#Independent).

17. Which was founded with the aid of Tavistock and Portman NHS Trust as an independent provider to the NHS.

18. http://news.bbc.co.uk/1/hi/uk/636302.stm. For information on her see the Independent and Express articles mentioned and her website at http://www.valeriesinason.com . There is a long interview by her at http://www.valeriesinason.com/VS%20talks%20to%20GG.htm .

19. http://www.freerepublic.com/forum/a3962cb2c7e2f.htm .

20. http://www.valeriesinason.com/newss.htm , where she replies to a recent article in Private Eye. That magazine had written:
"Sinason, author of a book Treating Survivors of Satanist Abuse, previously conducted research on "sadistic ritual abuse", funded by the Department of Health, in which she claimed to have interviewed 76 children and adults who made allegations involving sexual abuse and murder. In 2000 the Metropolitan police investigated her allegations but found no evidence." And she replied:
"This is incorrect. 51 children and adults were part of the original study funded by the DOH. 76 children and adults formed part of later clinical material, and now it is sadly over 200. Due to the difficulties found in investigating these cases the Clinic was privileged to be given a Scotland Yard link."

21. Sunday Times 11 July 1999 page 13 article by Phelim McAleer entitled "Irish rape crisis centres defend satanic abuse helpline." See also http://www.menz.org.nz/Casualties/1999%20newsletters/conth.htm .

22. Irish Mirror 24 Oct 1999
(http://www.hiddenmysteries.org/news/europe/ireland/022800a.html).
Incidentally Fred Holroyd mentions a Patrick Duffy from Portadown who was said to have been murdered in this kind of 'ritualistic' way in 1974 - the case also involved rape etc. He said that Wilfie Cummings (presumably the author of The Dark Corner (2001)) and a Mr Clarke were wrongly convicted of the murder in 1975 and served 14 years in jail. (Fred Holroyd with Nick Burbridge, War Without Honour (Hull, 1989), p.82.)
A little bit of gossip from a discussion of this subject at politics.ie:
"In ref to "Recovered Memory syndrome". It is common for people abused to bury, or be brainwashed into denying
an event [described in Chapter 6 infra]. It can take years of good counselling to

'safely' dig this out. It is common for people who endure this abuse,
to commit suicide ether because of repressing, or in the early stages of disclosure.

Sometimes abused are drawn into joining the abuser in to gaining new victims. I know a case of this in Belfast. I have met the girl in her teens, who worked for loyalist groups
to gain new victims for their ring. When she was pursuaded to go to the Police and Social services,
they ignored her, even when she could give names of perpetrators, victims , times dates etc."
(sparxz1000 at http://www.politics.ie/viewtopic.php?f=88&t=40145&start=48)

23. http://www.niassembly.gov.uk/record/reports/010910.htm . For the Bland case see also http://www.missingpersons-ireland.freepress-freespeech.com/archive-sarahbland.htm .

24. http://www.servamus.co.za/serv_bundel/bund_myst.htm .

25. http://www.pfsa.org.za/expression.html .

26. http://newsvote.bbc.co.uk/2/hi/europe/6168827.stm .

27.
http://www.findarticles.com/p/articles/mi_m1058/is_32_116/ai_57893312/pg_
1 , http://www.rickross.com/reference/satanism/satanism58.html ,
http://www.skepticfiles.org/american/aane1163.htm ,
http://www.nationaudio.com/News/DailyNation/130899/Comment/Comment3.
html .

28.
http://news.bbc.co.uk/hi/english/static/audio_video/programmes/correspondent
/transcripts/772870.txt .

29. http://www.cwnews.com/news/viewstory.cfm?recnum=9064 .

30.
http://news.bbc.co.uk/hi/english/static/audio_video/programmes/correspondent
/transcripts/772870.txt .

31. http://www.gaiaguys.net/vic.qldopp29.7.03.htm .

32. 29 May 1998 http://www.aph.gov.au/hansard/senate/dailys/ds290598.pdf .

33.
http://www.parliament.sa.gov.au/catalog/hansard/2005/ha/wh040405.ha.htm .

34. http://www.gaiaguys.net/aus.childabuse2005.htm .

35. http://www.gaiaguys.net/victoria.htm .

CHAPTER 6

Did Wayne O'Donoghue really kill Robert Holohan?

All this talk of paedophile rings at very high levels of the state establishment might unfortunately find an echo in events in Ireland. Specifically there are quite a few strange anomalies in the Robert Holohan case which are difficult to explain away if one accepts the standard interpretation of these events. I hope to solve this particular 'conspiracy theory' by reference to some strange hypnosis and memory technologies that are in use by the big Western Intelligence Agencies, and which I explain in depth at the end of this chapter.

The bare facts are well known in Ireland by everybody I'm sure but just to recap. On 4th Jan 2005 11 year old Robert Holohan went missing from his home at Ballyedmond, a rural area near Middleton Co.Cork, giving rise to huge local and even nationwide interest in his disappearance. Inevitably in the days to follow there was much speculation about paedophile rings in the area, which even gave rise to questions in the Dail,[1] until Robert's next door neighbour, Wayne O'Donoghue, was arrested and charged with his murder. O'Donoghue was acquitted of murder but convicted of manslaughter and has recently been released after serving a comparatively short time in jail. His conviction effectively rested on his statements to the Gardaí admitting the crime of killing Robert Holohan by strangling him accidentally during 'horseplay'.

The perplexing thing about this case (as has been pointed out by a number of people e.g. by Stephen Rae, the Evening Herald editor, on Questions and Answers on the occasion of O'Donoghue's release) is that Wayne O'Donoghue's statement does not seem to tally properly with the facts outlined in court and in the media, in fact the version of events in his statement seems to be physically impossible based on the forensic and other evidence. The anomalies of the case, and how it conflicts with O'Donoghue's statement, go something like this:

1) He said that Robert had thrown stones at his car which began an argument between them but Det Garda Thomas Carey gave detailed forensic evidence to the court ruling out the possibility of the car being recently hit by stones like that.[2]

2) Robert Holohan is said to have made a 999 call either on the day he

205

died, or late the previous night (which it is depends on the timing of Robert's phone, a subject in high dispute). Obviously this is completely contrary to O'Donoghue's account and the official explanation of this is apparently that Robert was seen once messing with his phone and accidentally rang 999 and that maybe the same thing happened this time. Mighty coincidental though isn't it? [3]

3) Images were deliberately deleted from Robert's mobile phone when it was found and examined, again contrary to O'Donoghue's statement.[4]

4) The whole question of the semen. For those who haven't been following this the official explanation is that semen was found on Robert's hand, was sent off by the prosecution to the lab of Dr Jonathan Whitaker in England and he reported back, with a certainty of 1 in 70 million, that the semen was Wayne O'Donoghue's. Then the Gardaí sent over for testing semen from the family's bathroom mat and in response Whitaker changes his report to say that he is no longer certain it was Wayne's. The defence get these reports, do their own testing, and conclude it definitely wasn't Wayne's and so the whole story of the semen is not put before the jury at the trial. Then Robert's mother dramatically raises the issue in her victim impact statement, when the trial is effectively over, in a way that incidentally kick starts a huge tabloid frenzy that, for a time anyway, badly demonised O'Donoghue.

Maybe the curious thing here is the strange way that Whitaker's statement changes so markedly after only a few months. Effectively we are being asked to believe that a geneticist would change his story so dramatically when confronted by the evidence that people living in the same house as Wayne O'Donoghue had similar DNA and hence could have been the source of the semen. But of course geneticists know that relatives have similar DNA - that's pretty much the whole point of genetic science! - and presumably virtually every crime scene has the potential for this kind of crossover, because relatives with similar DNA normally live with one another, e.g. parents with their children etc. Therefore how could Whitaker go from being so confident to so unsure in such a space of time? Btw this same scientist was a leading figure in the Omagh prosecution case in Belfast which collapsed recently, along with the reputations of many of those government figures connected with it. That trial has become notorious for its "forensically altered" evidence and the judge himself was not at all happy with Dr Whitaker.[5] The suspicion is that if the powers that be wanted to stitch up somebody, using dodgy DNA goings on, then Whitaker was the man to contact and was that why he was brought into the Holohan case?

5) The prosecution initially claimed that Robert had taken a photograph on his phone in Wayne's bedroom at 7.30 am one morning, apparently therefore showing a more sinister side to the friendship between these two people. But the defence was able to show that the phone was not even purchased by Robert at that time, and therefore that this was impossible. There is also apparently a statement made by a third party, Heather Harte, which corroborates Wayne's statement that the picture was taken in the afternoon or late in the evening. How is this discrepancy to be explained, except that maybe somebody had deliberately tampered with the phone settings on Robert's phone to discredit O'Donoghue, or maybe to disguise the real timing of the 999 call? [6]

6) The forensic examination of the body was not consistent with Wayne's account, according to the State pathologist at the trial. In particular there were marks on Robert's buttocks, mouth and back that remain unexplained. Also there is evidence that somebody tried to burn Robert's body, or at least that some fire was involved in his death, but Wayne is adamant that that is not the case. He admitted only to a small feeble effort to burn the plastic bags not to touch the body at all:

> "Yet the forensic expert Det Garda Thomas Carey told how he found charred twigs under Robert's buttocks some 10 feet from the burnt plastic, while there were burn marks on the hem of his T-shirt and the waist of his pants."[7]

7) Other forensic evidence is seemingly incompatible with Wayne's statement eg. there is no mention there of Wayne wearing gloves but when Robert's bicycle was found, which Wayne had planted, a number of sets of finger prints were found but not Wayne's. As regards the two black plastic bags which he said he used to transport the body no prints were found on them either, only on a separate small white plastic bag found near the body. Also at the trial Det Garda Carey explained that he found mud stains on Robert's clothing which matched neither where he was found nor where he was killed. Furthermore, according to Barry Roche in the Irish Times, "perhaps the most puzzling aspects of O'Donoghue's version of events relate to" the time it took to go back to the scene and relocate Robert's body at Inch. Apparently its impossible to do that in the short space of time between 7.55pm, when he was seen on CCTV in Foley's garage in Middleton, and 8.30, when he was watching TV with his girlfriend. Also Ivan O'Flynn, a

telecommunications expert, at the trial contradicted his statements on the route he took to Inch, apparently O'Donohue's mobile phone shows that he went a different route from the one in his statement.[8] Btw when he was transporting the body in the trunk of his car, in a blind panic we are told, he called into Foley's garage and bought a lucozade.

8) Finally, and intriguingly, we have the whole bizarre story of Robert's phone being tracked to Inch and exposing the body's location many days after he went missing. We are told that by some complete magic the phone company was able to boost the phone's signal, charging its battery via the phone masts, and locating it long after most had assumed the battery had gone dead (because why else could they not have tracked it earlier?) Afaik this is a completely new, and you'd have to wonder, utterly made up capability for mobile phones and hence maybe casts doubt on the Garda explanation as to how it targeted that location to retrieve the body.[9]

But if his statement is so incorrect then what exactly happened? Wayne O'Donoghue is of course totally adamant that he did kill Robert Holohan, as well as his statement given to Gardaí, including a video statement shown during the court case, he basically confirmed this in his speech to the press when he got out of jail some time ago. Furthermore, if you think about it, it doesn't seem that O'Donoghue has any good reason to lie about these matters. Once he admitted to the killing then the chances were he was going to go to jail for quite a while, it really would be, and was, unexpected that he would get such a light sentence. I suspect in a lot of these cases if people are going to admit their guilt, because their conscience dictated they should, then the chances are they will just outline the true version of events. To sort of come clean with only half the story would strike you as unlikely and not really in O'Donoghue's interests. Another thing that would strike you about the case is the character of Wayne O'Donoghue. He comes across a very nice guy, running errands all the time on behalf of his brother, his girlfriend and even Robert Holohan. Press accounts frequently refer to this with his teachers for example prepared to go character witness on his behalf, and his own statement to the media seemed to be a modest account of how sorry he was to have caused trouble for everybody etc. No doubt this also impressed the judge which is why he gave that lenient sentence. But if you look at the official version of the case, not to mention the controversial parts like burning the body, it is hardly the actions of somebody like that? Also a lot of the anomalies in the case could hardly be placed at Wayne O'Donoghue's door, like the mobile phone mast thing or the whole semen imbroglio which happened while he was in jail.

At this point I cheerfully admit I now enter the realms of speculation, and no doubt, in the eyes of some, into conspiracy theorising, not to mention science fiction! This is just this writers opinion for what its worth, one attempt to connect the dots across what seems a completely contradictory landscape. My guess is that what happened is similar to the explanation given by the late Joe Vialls into the Soham murders in England. In a number of articles this famous Australian researcher claimed that the evidence showed that Huntley was incarcerated in a mental hospital in the run up to his trial and there, using a combination of hypnosis and drugs, a false memory was implanted into him that he had killed the two girls when actually he was innocent.[10] That the powers that be have the capacity to implant false memories into people is I think beyond doubt as you can see in some quotes from a Guardian article:

> "Alan Alda had nothing against hard-boiled eggs until last spring. Then the actor, better known as Hawkeye from M*A*S*H, paid a visit to the University of California, Irvine. In his new guise as host of a science series on American TV, he was exploring the subject of memory. The researchers showed him round, and afterwards took him for a picnic in the park. By the time he came to leave, he had developed a dislike of hard-boiled eggs based on a memory of having made himself sick on them as a child - something that never happened.
>
> ... "If the formation of false memories depends on beta-adrenergic activation, then it would seem very possible that propranolol [a drug that 'interferes with the neurochemical pathway' in the brain] administration could affect them," says the UCI neuro- biologist Larry Cahill, who has also investigated the effects of the drug in PTSD patients. But Ray Dolan of UCL, a co-author with Bryan Strange of the study on memory for emotional words, points out that not all false memories have a common basis. If they are interpolations into gaps in memory, such as the gap that opened up before the presentation of an emotionally arousing word, or possibly the gap into which Alan Alda inserted a memory of having over-indulged in eggs, then it is conceivable the drug would work. But, says Dolan,

"Other classes of false memory, for example, where the memories are fantasies or out-and-out fabrications, would be immune to propranolol."

The idea of doctors having the power to wipe the memory clean sends shivers down many people's spines. False memories could safely be erased, perhaps, assuming there was a reliable way of differentiating them from true ones. Although brain-imaging techniques highlight some differences in patterns of brain activation when a person recalls a true as opposed to a false memory, these are statistical differences only. "We are so far away from being able to use these techniques to reliably classify a single memory as being real or not real," says Loftus, "Yet that is what the courts have to do."[11]

For more details on that researcher, Dr Elizabeth Loftus who is a leading expert in this area, we have this from the Orange City Register:

"She says it's super easy to get people to remember things that never happened."[12]

And from the New Scientist:

"I've spent three decades learning how to alter people's memories. I've even gone so far as planting entirely false memories into the minds of ordinary people - memories such as being lost in a shopping mall, cutting your hand on broken glass or even witnessing demonic possession as a child, all planted through the power of suggestion.

Psychological scientists have learned so much about planting false memories that some say we almost have recipes for doing so. But we haven't seen anything yet. Over the next 50 years we will further master the ability to create false memories. We will learn more about who is most susceptible and what works with what kind of people. The most potent recipes may involve pharmaceuticals that we are on the brink of discovering."[13]

And that is what I think happened to Wayne O'Donoghue, that he didn't do it at all but that somehow somebody has implanted into him a false memory of having killed Robert Holohan. I know I know of all the daft explanations you ever heard about...lol...the point is that the above accounts do make it clear that this is possible and should be considered

210

no matter how outrageous it sounds. But of course it is a dangerous road to go down, clearly if you are going to start explaining away testimony that way you could neatly cast doubt on virtually every court case imaginable, I mean without any evidence for this surely it should just remain as idle and highly unlikely speculation?

There is just one itsy bitsy little clue that I am clinging onto that might point this way. To go back to the Soham murders in England one clue was picked up by Vialls that pointed to the fact that Huntley had been hypnotised into saying what he said. Its a well known feature of hypnosis that it is very difficult to get people to do something, or give people a false memory of having done something, which is contrary to their inbuilt morality. If for example stealing money from a church collection was something you would never ever do then in hypnosis it would be very difficult to get you to believe that you had done that. If you bear that in mind you could wonder at the explanation that Ian Huntley gave as to how the two girls died in Soham. Initially he denied of course that he did anything wrong (and in video evidence given to the police shortly afterwards he and his girlfriend can be seen completely relaxed giving this innocent version of events) then he later admitted that the girls had died because of some bizarre nose bleed that one of them had in his bathroom. In other words he never admitted to any really bad motivation on his part, only a kind of an accident but it was enough to convict him in most people's eyes because it was in total contrast to his earlier denials. Just like O'Donoghue's account, this lie on Huntley's part (as Vialls, and others, stated the evidence shows it couldn't have happened that way) seems to have no logical motivation, he couldn't have expected to be treated leniently once he admitted they died in his presence. Obviously this kind of innocentish explanation, which both people have emerged with and which convicted both, seems to tally with somebody using hypnosis on them, these bizarre explanations might have emerged because the moral code of both Huntley and O'Donoghue might have meant that it was impossible to get them to admit to the full horrible murders.

In any case thats this writers tuppence worth on why O'Donoghue's statement and the surrounding facts seem to be so much in conflict. It seems in retrospect too that O'Donoghue might have known details about the real circumstances of the case which could have made him dangerous to the real perpetrators and which memory might also have become erased, and anyway as the last person to see Robert Holohan alive he, just like Huntley, becomes the obvious target if anybody is to be stitched up for it. It is known that in the few days before he admitted the killing to his father he had been in close contact with the Gardaí, apparently giving a number of statements including one that seemed to implicate Robert's family although very little is in the public domain about what he was saying in those statements.[14] Anyway if he was hypnotised it could have been done then, the point being that he was in touch with the powers that be before he made an admission to his father. Other than that we are told that he has been on anti-depressants but we get no other facts on whether or not he was in touch with psychiatric personnel or institutions (where a lot of this mind manipulation is done apparently.)

Thinking outside the box I admit but still it's an explanation that does explain why his statement and the surrounding facts are so much in conflict?

Hypnosis and Trauma, Mind Manipulation Technology

In fact there is a lot of evidence out there that the Western Intelligence Agencies have developed very advanced mind and memory manipulation techniques which it may be worthwhile explaining in depth.

Hypnosis
Might as well start with this quote from Dr George H Estabrooks, writing in the *Science Digest* Easter 1971, describing some of his hypnosis work for the US military during both world wars:

> "One of the most fascinating but dangerous applications of hypnosis is its use in military intelligence. This is a field with which I am familiar though formulating guide lines for the techniques used by the United States in two world wars. Communication in war is always a headache. Codes can be broken. A professional spy may or may not stay bought. Your own man may have unquestionable loyalty, but his judgment is always open to question.
>
> The "hypnotic courier," on the other hand, provides a unique solution. I was involved in preparing many subjects for this work during World War II. One successful case involved an Army Service Corps Captain whom we'll call George Smith...
>
> Then I put him under deep hypnosis, and gave him --

orally -- a vital message to be delivered directly on his arrival in Japan to a certain colonel -- let's say his name was Brown -- of military intelligence. Outside of myself, Colonel Brown was the only person who could hypnotize Captain Smith. This is "locking." I performed it by saying to the hypnotised Captain: "Until further orders from me, only Colonel Brown and I can hypnotize you. We will use a signal phrase 'the moon is clear.' Whenever you hear this phrase from Brown or myself you will pass instantly into deep hypnosis." When Captain Smith re-awakened, he had no conscious memory or what happened in trance. All that he was aware of was that he must head for Tokyo to pick up a division report.

On arrival there, Smith reported to Brown, who hypnotised him with the signal phrase. Under hypnosis, Smith delivered my message and received one to bring back. Awakened, he was given the division report and returned home by jet. There I hypnotised him once more with the signal phrase, and he spieled off Brown's answer that had been dutifully tucked away in his unconscious mind.

The system is virtually foolproof. As exemplified by this case, the information was "locked" in Smith's unconscious for retrieval by the only two people who knew the combination. The subject had no conscious memory of what happened, so could not spill the beans. No one else could hypnotize him even if they might know the signal phrase."[15]

Trauma induced hidden memories

No doubt these intelligence agencies have long seen the value in the use of hypnosis to hide memories, and hence create perfect couriers etc, but unfortunately it is alleged that these agencies have also copied practices that have been used in the past by certain cults which involve the use of trauma as a better way to hide memories in people. Apparently what these cults discovered is that extreme trauma (both physical and psychological e.g. rape) can be the best way to hide memories in people. It works a bit like the shell shocked soldiers of WWI. What happened in that case was that some of those soldiers were so traumatised by what they witnessed (on the battlefields, when they were literally 'scared out of their wits', incidentally one such traumatised soldier is portrayed in the film *Ryan's Daughter*)[16] that they were unable to remember what actually happened to them, until, sometimes years later, they got 'flashbacks' of those traumatic episodes. Their minds/brains had deliberately shut down the memory, making it unavailable to the conscious person, in order to save the person's sanity because it was just too traumatic, but had stored the memory in the brain behind a kind of 'amnesiac wall'. This wall then often breaks down as the years go by giving rise to 'flashbacks' or maybe a realistic dream of the memory. Also this 'flashback' [17] could be 'triggered' sometimes by seeing something that reminded them of the memory or maybe by a sound that was like the sound of the artillery during the war.

It is claimed that it is this kind of effect that has been harnessed by these intelligence agencies for their own purposes. (Actually its even claimed that an institute set up in London to study those WWI patients - the Tavistock Institute - was one of the places used by the intelligence agencies to master this technology.) To take a simplistic example: an agent might be allowed to view secret plans in the interval between being traumatised (incidentally they have a wide range of ways of inducing the trauma e.g. electro shocks [18]). That memory is then stored nicely behind these internal mind walls so that the person himself cannot recall the memory and so cannot be interrogated about the plans etc. This person could then be used to transport the plans to somebody else, the receiving person is told what triggers are needed to call up the memory from the messenger (remember the 'trigger' is just something that causes the person to recall the memory, the same way that an ordinary memory can be recalled e.g. by a sound or smell or sight or form of words similar to that contained in the memory) who then recalls the memory, passes on the plans, and then is further traumatised so that the original agent cannot recall passing on the message. For the intelligence agencies they have the perfect courier, hence their great interest in these horrific technologies.

Another aspect to this is that they found that when they manipulate the mind like this in their unfortunate subjects they could tap into some of the hidden resources of the human mind and how it affects the body. Again, to explain this using a simple example, consider what happens when a goalkeeper makes a 'reflex save' in football. This is obviously where the ball is going so fast that the goalkeeper is not really conscious of saving the ball, he just shoots his hand out instinctively to catch the ball without his conscious mind directing his arm. Somehow its his unconscious mind that does it for him. If you think about it this is a fascinating concept. This 'instinct' is not ingrained in a person from birth (like the reflex of moving your leg when somebody hits your knee etc) somehow your conscious world, the world that demands the ball be saved, has impressed onto your unconscious or instinctive self that the ball should be saved. Another example might be instinctively putting on the brakes or clutch when driving a car. It wasn't that you did those things without thinking about them at first, at first you had to learn them and were very conscious of what you were doing then afterwards it became 'instinctive', meaning that somehow the skill went from your conscious mind to your unconscious one who handled it from thereon. The point here is that your unconscious mind often has greater physical capacity than your conscious one, its usually quicker. After all think about that goalkeeper again, the 'reflex save' is the most difficult one, the one where the ball - and hence the arm - is going fastest, it is tapping into this 'instinctive' ability that allows the best goalkeepers to do what they do. This is what these 'mind manipulators' are doing, they are bypassing the normal conscious mind and therefore can tap into the awesome capabilities of the 'unconscious' mind. Specifically when they are manipulating minds using this trauma technique they can call on e.g. a photographic memory - taking advantage of the faster reading ability of the unconscious mind - , or extreme tolerance for cold and lack of oxygen - useful to develop a great swimmer - because they are playing around with this powerful unconscious mind.

A further trick that these controllers try was actually used by the British Army in the North at one point. This is sensory deprivation. It was found that if the body cannot feel any of the normal human sensations (say hearing sound, seeing light, feeling touch etc) then your mind can start to wander and enter into this 'dissociative' type of state just like under trauma. In that state you can again receive messages etc much like under hypnosis or under trauma. Apparently these intelligence agencies have developed large water tanks where they submerge these patients using body suits and breathing apparatus, where they would be in total darkness, complete silence, and with a feeling of weightlessness as they float in the water, and in this state they can receive the messages and instructions like under trauma.

Deliberate Creation of Agents with Multiple Personalities
But the intelligence agencies have gone way beyond even that in manipulating the mind, they have also developed multiple personalities in their agents, as the aforementioned Dr Estabrooks also describes:
> "Not all applications of hypnotism to military intelligence are as tidy as that. Perhaps you have read

'The Three Faces of Eve'. The book was based on a case reported in 1905 by Dr. Morton Prince of Massachusetts general Hospital and Harvard. He startled everyone in the field by announcing that he had cured a woman named Beauchamp of a split personality problem. Using post-hypnotic suggestion to submerge an incompatible, childlike facet of the patient, he'd been able to make two other sides of Mrs. Beauchamp compatible, and lump them together in a single cohesive personality. Clinical hypnotists throughout the world jumped on the multiple personality bandwagon as a fascinating frontier. By the 1920's, not only had they learned to apply post-hypnotic suggestion to deal with this weird problem, but also had learned how to split certain complex individuals into multiple personalities like Jeckyl-Hydes.

The potential for military intelligence has been nightmarish. During World War II, I worked this technique with a vulnerable Marine lieutenant I'll call Jones. Under the watchful eye of Marine Intelligence I spilt his personality into Jones A and Jones B. Jones A, once a "normal" working Marine, became entirely different. He talked communist doctrine and meant it. He was welcomed enthusiastically by communist cells, was deliberately given a dishonorable discharge by the Corps (which was in on the plot) and became a card carrying party member.

The joker was Jones B, the second personality, formerly apparent in the conscious Marine. Under hypnosis, this Jones had been carefully coached by suggestion. Jones B was the deeper personality, knew all the thoughts of Jones A, was a loyal American, and was "imprinted" to say nothing during conscious phases.

All I had to do was hypnotize the whole man, get in touch with Jones B, the loyal American, and I had a pipeline straight into the Communist camp. It worked beautifully for months with this subject, but the technique backfired. While there was no way for an enemy to expose Jones' dual personality, they suspected it and played the same trick on us later."[19]

What Dr Estabrooks doesn't say, but what was well known even then, is that Multiple Personalities are usually created as a result of traumatic episodes, which begs the question about how he really created the personalities that he describes. Apparently what the cults had found out earlier - the intelligence agencies are said to be copying practices known about first in those occult cults described in Chapter 5 - was that if you try these trauma-creating-hidden-memory techniques with very young children you can get them to develop different personalities which correspond to the different memories. A young child is obviously developing their personality every day, copying adults and developing likes and dislikes etc in response to what happens to them in the wider world. If then the child is in this trauma state for a long period - the same type of state that the WWI soldiers were in -, and experiencing these locked in memories, they might develop a different personality that goes along with the memory.[20] For example if during one of these states their controllers teach them sexual tricks and coach them into using a personality that goes along with these tricks (believe me these accounts are very disturbing, apparently this is exactly the type of thing that goes on even to young children) then when the memory is called up later (using the 'trigger') the child might exhibit the personality of a sex addict, as they were trained to do at the time they got that memory. Then as time goes on and as the trainer repeatedly calls up that memory, to give more and more sexual instruction, the child might develop a whole new personality with different mannerisms and even a different name to their usual name. It is this type of practice that has apparently created a lot of people with Multiple Personality Disorder, hence this condition is now known as Dissociative Identity Disorder (DID) because its realised that the separate personalities are created in this type of 'Dissociative' state.[21] These 'MPD' victims are then very useful to the intelligence agencies, they can use the sex addict personalities for entrapment operations etc.

Apparently in training in these different personalities into a person the trainers sometimes use their own techniques but also some standardised 'scripts'. What they seem to be aiming for when they are doing this, and hence what they need from the scripts, are something like this:
1) They want the child's imagination to take off when they are in this trauma or 'dissociative' state, because that way they will develop good

'personalities' easier. Obviously some children can have good imagination, and even imaginary friends etc, and if they can use that imagination when they are being trained with the new personalities then the personalities will take on a life of their own within the child, which is the effect they are looking for.

2) When they use the different triggers to access the different personalities (believe it or not some people end up with hundreds of these different personalities) they need a simple system that the child - and the trainer in fact - can remember. So for example they might get the child to imagine a rubrics cube and then access the different personalities via grid numbers, or they might get the child to imagine a kind of virtual world - like in the videogame Quake perhaps - so that they could later get to the personalities by walking through this 3d imaginary world.[22]

3) They want to make it difficult for the person to reconstruct their memories if in later life the amnesiac walls break down. So for example if they had developed this kind of virtual world, as described above, they might include traps so that if a person walked the wrong way, or broke through the wrong wall or mirror etc, they would trigger suicide programming or extreme trauma memories that would scare the person into not delving further into their own mind.

One curious aspect of these 'scripts' that they use is that they are usually well known fairy tales (it helps, as Shane Dunphy - the Child Protection worker and Irish Independent writer - explains in one of his books, that some fairy tales can have surprisingly horrific twists and endings [23]), or popular children's books or films. I guess the reason why they use sources like that would include the following:
1) It allows them to hide things in plain sight, as intelligence agencies always like to do. For example picture the scene where one of these contrived trauma sessions goes wrong. Imagine some mind expert is doing this to their own child and accidentally drowns him/her in the bath during a trauma episode. (These practices usually happen in military bases apparently, but are backed up as well by practising trauma, and then entering dissociative states, at home.) Then the Gardaí come and survey the scene. Obviously if they find some book entitled 'Pentagon Manual for Creating Dissociative States', or some such, on the side of the person's bed then they have a big clue into what was going on, whereas if they find a copy of the Wizard of Oz or a DVD of Disney Movies then there is no such problem. All they need is some

script that will catch the child's imagination, as pointed above, so saying she is Dorothy and only has to click her shoes to change her environment (meaning change personalities) works as well as any other manual.[24]

2) It helps if a person is reminded of these scripts later, it reinforces the original trauma and hypnotic conditioning. Since these are normal films and books, that are out there in everyday life, the chances are that a child will trip across references to them in the normal media and when that happens it will reinforce their 'programming'. (They refer to this process of creating personalities etc as 'programming' the mind.)

Manipulating the memories to discredit the victims
In order to preserve the secrecy behind all this the perpetrators also use tricks like scrambling memories. For example, they sometimes get their victims to watch films during an episode. To explain this imagine a victim is sent to deliver a message, in the way described above about passing on secret plans, in this case maybe to a person in Wall Street. Then when the person gets there to deliver the message, in this artificial traumatic state of mind, they are instructed to watch the film Wall Street. Imagine the scene in later years when the person is trying to piece together those memories. Imagine him/her relating it to a therapist say - or in court - he/she would try and remember a name and the only name that comes to them is 'Gecko' and when described he looks like Michael Douglas! Then of course the victim loses all credibility and is left unsure whether they really did experience the episode they remember or whether they just had dreams about a film they saw. This is described in some detail by Kathleen Sullivan:

> "In Washington DC, I was allegedly taken several times to a movie theater named Janus that is allegedly owned by the CIA. A middle aged male handler sat to my right and quickly put me in a hypnotic trance. As I watched the large movie screen, he told me that the movie was real and that I was one of the characters in it. I believed him, and the movie became another screen memory. This was usually done after an covert op. The people who allegedly ran me for the CIA chose movies that had at least one item or event in them that parallelled the real op I had just been a part of. And again, if I remembered later, the movie would come up first as reality to me, blocking the memory of the op. I've since learned to scan the room in my memory, using my

219

peripheral vision. Seeing the handler sitting beside me in a seat, I know I'm dealing with another screen memory.

Later in my adult years, my handlers used a newer technique. I was put in rooms that had full, wall-sized movie screens on both sides and in front of me. I was usually drugged or put in a trance, or both. My handlers made me sit in a stripped-down car that didn't go anywhere, although I could turn the steering wheel and press the pedals. The movies on the screens would change simultaneously, which made me feel as if I were actually driving somewhere. This was probably done to confuse me about where I went during my stateside road trips.

Another screen memory device was used on a regular basis in a library. It was a large black goggle permanently attached to a machine in which I could watch a video of my choice. These videos worked especially well if my handlers pulled out child parts that couldn't distinguish movies from reality.

On one occasion, I was put in a fake room atop hydraulic lifts. The fake "windows" inside the room were actually movie screens. The room looked just like the inside of a UFO. Powerful sound equipment was used. Between the equipment moving, the sound of blasting off, and the movies working in sequence in the fake windows, I was supposed to believe I was leaving earth and going into space. Fortunately, I've been able to remember seeing the outside of the fake UFO, and the hydraulic equipment that supported the bottom of it.

On another occasion, a career politician I knew for a long time took me into a large warehouse that was decorated to look like the inside of a huge UFO. He didn't try to trick me with it; he let me look around as if he was trying to impress me with his genius. I saw tall people dressed in alien costumes; their appearance did scare me a little, but I could tell they were human.

This space travel theme was used on me again, allegedly at the Lockheed plant in Marietta, Georgia. A large gutted plane sat on the parking area outside a warehouse. I and other people inside it were made to wear costumes that remind me of Star Trek. The other adults acted out their preplanned roles, drawing me into the story. I was made to believe I was a crew member. Again this was done to a part of me that didn't know better, so when I first remembered the experience I believed the whole thing was real." [25]

Hence this is why so many of these accounts are packed solid with implausible tales of aliens, and time tunnels etc etc, these are just hoaxes that were deliberately created at the same time as the trauma, to discredit the unfortunate victims as they come forward to tell their story. Its easy to see how this happens, after going through all the horrors of bringing back these previously hidden memories the victims are sure that they now have real memories of aliens etc, but what they don't realize is that they have real memories of hoaxed incidents, which it was easy for the programmers to arrange because their victims were so run down by lack of sleep, drugged out etc. (They seem to put a huge amount of effort into these hoaxes, and seem to want to spread them around in the wider population, why it is hard to say but I wonder if these hoaxes are played out in a more dramatic way in future years that there might not be some benefits to the globalist agenda, eg.:
- If they could stage an 'Independence Day' type alien scenario it might serve to unite world populations against what would be perceived to be their common foe, in the same way that the Greek states used to unite only when the external threat from Persia arose, an excuse then for a world government?
- If they could claim that advanced technology developed at CERN allowed them to Time Travel then they could control the past, by claiming x or y happened in the past even when it didn't, and as they say he who controls the past controls the future because a distorted picture of the past can impact on how people act going forward.
Anyway in the meantime these hoaxes do great work discrediting 'conspiracy theorists'!)
In any case this is very much a feature of eye witness accounts of this type of practice, totally implausible hoaxed information. (Which is not to discount the possibility that in rare cases there is real advanced technology in evidence.) For example Shane Dunphy, in his book *Hush Little Baby*, describes a traumatised character called Clive Plummer

trying to defend himself against a Satanic sect in Ireland.[26] He was locked up in a psychiatric ward because all he talked about were 'monsters' who were trying to kill him. Either the preparators wore some kind of masks or makeup to discredit his memories, or they used memory scrambling as described here by Kathleen Sullivan:

> "Memory scrambles aren't the same as screen memories. Scrambles are created by handlers to confuse or disorient the victim, either at the time or when the victim remembers the experience later on. If just one detail of the experience doesn't make sense, the handlers hope that their victim will then discount the entire memory. Or better yet, the victim will talk about the still-scrambled memory to others and will discredit his or her self. I'll give you a couple of examples from my own life.
>
> Because one of my handlers knew that I adored Robert Redford, he decided to hypnotize me and convince me that he was Redford. Every time I looked at the handler, both at that time and later in memory, I saw Redford's face instead of his. But one time the trance broke and I saw the handler's real face. Redford looks a lot better."
> [27]

One final point, that I know sounds weird but has to be said, is that sometimes when this is practised by the occult - or satanic - cults (in the eyewitness accounts you come across intelligence agencies - in the US, UK, Germany and Russia particularly -, the mafia, and then these occult type cults, all kind of intermixing [28]) they are reported to try and input demons into their victims - via strange and horrific rituals -, and use them to reinforce the programming. Curiously this sort of demon raising ritual is described in detail in an episode of *Dalziel and Pascoe*, which also included a victim with a Multiple Personality and the use of stun guns, which I guess is only fiction but is remarkably like some of these cult eyewitness accounts.[29]

So thats it, I know it all sounds seriously bizarre but I think if you read the various accounts you can see a great consensus as to how this is done, and actually most of it isn't science fiction, these techniques are possible and I think the psychiatric profession accepts that MPD victims could be formed that way. I guess it all depends on how much faith you have in those agencies and governments, they wouldn't do those kind of things would they? Or would they...lol

Footnotes

1. http://archives.tcm.ie/irishexaminer/2005/01/31/story957039821.asp .

2. Irish Times article by Barry Roche Jan 28 2006.

3. Sunday Tribune 30 April 2006 p.13.

4. Ibid.

5. See for example http://www.phoblacht.net/MG011206g.html and
http://www.anphoblacht.com/news/detail/23712 . Some comments from the
judgement itself:
"What I do find extraordinary is that, knowing that these items had not been collected or preserved using methods designed to ensure the high degree of integrity needed not merely for DNA examination but for the more exacting requirements of LCN DNA, examinations were performed at Birmingham with a view to using them for evidential rather than solely intelligence gathering purposes. The findings of those examinations were put forward and stoutly defended by Mr Whitaker of the Birmingham FSS laboratory as evidence that the Court might safely rely upon as tending to establish the guilt of the accused. This despite the fact that one police and SOCO witness after another and also Dr Griffin had candidly made clear that possible examination for DNA was not in their minds at all as they were collecting, storing, transmitting and dealing with these items in 1998. Why therefore would they then have had present to their minds and been complying with the exacting integrity requirements which reliable DNA examination and most especially that in its LCN form demands? All this NIFS must have known very well when it co-operated in searching for and collecting items for LCN examination in Birmingham and again later when the idea of using the results of those examinations as evidence in this trial must have been under discussion. By that stage the problems inherent in the need to prove integrity had plainly come to be appreciated by one or more police officers concerned in this investigation as was shown by the mendacious attempts to retrospectively alter the Altmore Forest evidence so as to falsely make it appear that appropriate DNA protective precautions had been taken at that scene.

...

In the present case an experiment had been done at Birmingham [the DNA laboratory] in which three tests had in fact been run with the result that the consensus produced by the first two tests was removed by the differing results then thrown up by the third. Thus the normal approach used in the United Kingdom had unintentionally been demonstrated by its own proponents to be potentially (and in that particular instance actually) misleading.

I was concerned about the manner and content of the response of Dr Whitaker to these criticisms. He was most unwilling to accept that the continuing absence of international agreement on validation of LCN (unlike SGM+)or the

variations in the way in which it was being implemented in different countries should be any impediment to the ready acceptance by any court of the Birmingham approach. I found him inappropriately combative as an expert witness and his unwillingness to debate constructively the various matters put to him was unhelpful in the extreme."
(http://business.timesonline.co.uk/tol/business/law/article3083217.ece)

6. Irish Times 28 Jan 2006 Weekender p.1. and Sunday Independent 28 Jan 2006 p.21.

7. Ibid.

8. Ibid.

9. The official explanation:
"Officers had worked with the mobile phone company O2 to boost the signal from Robert's Nokia mobile phone, which went dead shortly after he disappeared. This allowed them to narrow down the search to the area around Inch Strand. An enormous mobile phone mast overlooked the site where Robert's body was eventually discovered. "
(http://archives.tcm.ie/breakingnews/2005/01/15/story184880.asp)
and:
"Although mobile operators will not discuss the capabilities of their systems it is believed that, even after the main battery runs out, a mobile phone sends out some sort of signal to the nearest mast." (http://www.emigrant.ie/article.asp?iCategoryID=177&iArticleID=39518).

One blogger tried to have a stab at explaining this but received quite a few negative comments!: http://blog.teamgearedup.com/2006/01/how-to-triangulate-a-mobile-phone-location.html , and a commentator at politics.ie is also mystified at the explanations given: http://www.politics.ie/viewtopic.php?t=30520 .

10. The 3 articles by Joe Vialls:
http://web.archive.org/web/20041108024944/http://www.bigwig.net/softwaredesign/hollyjessica/who_really_murdered_holly_wells_.htm
http://web.archive.org/web/20041108084408/homepage.ntlworld.com/steveseymour/hollyjessica/who_really_murdered_holly_wells_2.htm
http://web.archive.org/web/20041022011220/www.joevialls.co.uk/transpositions/pedophile1.html .

11. Guardian 4 Dec 2003
http://www.guardian.co.uk/science/2003/dec/04/science.research1 .

12. http://williamcalvin.com/2002/OrangeCtyRegister.htm .

13. New Scientist Magazine 18th Nov 2006
http://www.newscientist.com/channel/opinion/science-
forecasts/mg19225780.112 .
For a list of drugs that are used to manipulate memory see:
http://web.archive.org/web/20070427032610/http://www.whale.to/b/sp/spring
meier.html#CHAPTER%203 .
and for a list of electronic ways of doing the same thing see:
http://web.archive.org/web/20070427032610/http://www.whale.to/b/sp/spring
meier.html#CHAPTER_6:_SCIENCE_NO._6-
THE_USE_OF_ELECTRONICS_&_ELECTRICITY_
These are chapters of a pretty incredible book by Fritz Springmeier and
obviously this writer is not in a position to vouch for most of what he says (a
lot of what he says is happening today would be dismissed as implausible in a
science fiction movie!). The point is that those two chapters are the only places
afaik where any attempt is made to describe in detail the drugs and the
electronic methods of affecting the brain's memories.

14. Sunday Independent 28 Jan 2006 p.20.

15.   http://web.archive.org/web/20051218013001/www.mindspring.com/
%7Etxporter/scidig.htm .

16. Another film worth looking at in this context is *A Clockwork Orange*. As
you can see in this review of the book, by Anthony Burgesss that the film is
based on, in the London Independent, it was somehow based on real life:
http://www.independent.co.uk/arts-entertainment/film-and-tv/news/cia-
mindcontrol-trials-revealed-as-secret-inspiration-behind-a-clockwork-orange-
613885.html .

17. "A flashback is a dissociated memory that returns to consciousness. It can
be a smell, a taste, a sound, an image, an emotion, or all these things together.
It can last a moment or linger on for weeks.

People describe smelling alcohol or perfume when none is present, hearing a
phrase over and over again in their heads, feeling panic or dread for no logical
reason, or seeing images, like snapshots or movies behind their eyes. All these
are fragmented memories rising up into consciousness. They can be extremely
vivid and can appear to be happening in the present. The more fragments come
together at the same time, the more intense the flashback.

Flashbacks are terrifying if you don't know what they are and if you don't
realize they will eventually stop. Experiencing flashbacks doesn't mean you
are going crazy - it means that you are at a point in your life when you are able
to deal with things that you couldn't cope with earlier. They tend to lose their
intensity when you have assembled the fragments into a coherent memory,
talked about it, cried about it, and absorbed the memory into your life."

(http://www.ra-info.org/faqs/ra_faq.shtml)

18. Actually the electric shocks, either from dedicated machines attached to genitals etc or portable stun guns and cattle prod devices, can create marks that can identify victims, as described here by one survivor:
"Now I'll talk about stun guns. I've had many memories that suddenly end just as a handler finishes doing something with me, or I switch and get out of control. I've had other memories that suddenly begin when I find myself inside a building, not knowing how I got there or where I was. These are not blackouts where parts are missing that hold the rest of the information. The memory is completely gone.

I have many small, circular marks on my arms and other parts of my body that are lacking in pigmentation - they are whiter than the rest of my skin and they shine in the sunlight. Whenever I looked at them I sensed they were from stun gun assaults. I finally got up the nerve to talk to a former police officer who's now a private detective. Without saying what I thought the marks were from, I held out my right arm and showed him the marks. He told me they were from stun guns. I asked him how he knew. He said they were identical to marks created on prisoners' arms after he and other officers used stun guns on them. I still have difficulty looking at my forearms. Every time I do, I feel such pain and anger about what was done to me.

I don't have another verification for this yet, but one programmer claimed that when a stun gun is held against a muscled area for a certain number of seconds, it can create about ten minutes of memory loss before the application and another ten minutes after. If this is true, then handlers might use stun guns not only to torture and control their victims, but also to wipe out memory of short-term events, like getting out of a car and going inside a building.

I've collected several different stun guns, to desensitize myself to being around them. A handout came with one of them. It states that an application of over three seconds will "cause loss of balance and muscle control, mental confusion and disorientation." Another manufacturer's website states that if a stun gun is applied for five seconds, the person will feel as if he fell from a second story building onto a concrete sidewalk. I've read where stun guns can make a victim confused and dazed for up to 30 minutes. If all of this is true, then the victim's brain is definitely affected by the electricity. And if the brain is affected, it only makes sense that stun gun applications can affect or even erase memory."
(http://web.archive.org/web/20030104000255/members.aol.com/smartnews/ks 01.htm)

19.   http://web.archive.org/web/20051218013001/www.mindspring.com/ %7Etxporter/scidig.htm . Some people have found interesting references to research into this area among archived CIA documents, like this from

MKULTRA Subproject 136 Proposal, 30 May 1961, *Experimental Analysis of Extrasensory Perception*, approved by the Chief, Technical Services Division/Research Branch, Central Intelligence Agency, 23 August 1961:
"In working with individual subjects, special attention will be given to dissociative states, which tend to accompany spontaneous ESP experiences. Such states can be induced or controlled to some extent with hypnosis and drugs... The experimenters will be particularly interested in disassociative states, from the abaissment de niveau mental [a state of mind characterised by: "the damage of the logical connection of thoughts; loss of the control of whole regions of mental contents with the production of split fragments of the personality; the invasion of the consciousness on the part of contents usually inhibited conscious functioning and, in consequence, caused inadequate or inappropriate emotional reactions"] to multiple personality in so-called mediums, and an attempt will be made to induce a number of states of this kind, using hypnosis."
(http://web.archive.org/web/20051125173603/www.datafilter.com/mc/mkultra HypnosisManchurian.html)

20. A survivor called TygerWolf explains here the basic mechanism:
"A child will use dissociation when they are being emotionally or physically harmed, may fear death will result if the situation continues, and are unable to physically escape the situation. Dissociation is a process in which the person mentally leaves the situation (such as imagining they are elsewhere), loses awareness of the environment or their body (such as no longer being aware of the sensations of pain), or believes that the abuse is happening to someone else (such as seeing the event happening to them as if they were a bystander).

When the stressful situation is severe, repeated, or perpetrated by someone the child must maintain contact with, the dissociation becomes stronger. The child may try to forget the event and contain the memories in a mental lock-box, in order to keep relating to the perpetrator as needed (such as to act normal around the parent in order to continue getting love, food, shelter, and other basic needs).

For some children the abuse is very intense, often repeated, may involve more than one perpetrator, and may result in the creation of Multiple Personality Disorder. Some researchers believe that a high level of intelligence and creativity increase the chances that MPD will form. The brain of a very young child is also forming neural pathways, setting up long-standing habits and personality traits, and mapping a great deal of information for life-long use. These combined factors (stress, abilities, age) allow some people to create alternate personalities: other people who share the same body but can have different emotions, thoughts, skills, interests, etc. For these children it becomes life-saving to have another part of their brain become a different person, who can experience the abuse, contain the memories, have strained or severed relationships with the perpetrator, and hold the distress while the other child

227

continues the needed relationship with the perpetrator. As the child grows they may continue to make alters to deal with abuse, stressful situations, life challenges, isolation/loneliness, fear, and other obstacles in their life.

Based on the different life stressors, the child may form alternate personalities (usually called alters) who are needed frequently. These alters start to have their own identity, history, skills, interests, and other identifying features. Sometimes a fragment personality is created to deal with one specific event and will not develop many identifying features seen with alters because they have very little interaction with the external and internal world."
(http://www.2multiples.com/twcrew/47_page.html)

21. This is further described here:
"What is Multiplicity?
In some children, the mental fragments are organized or arranged into "personalities" which seem to have a history and a life of their own. Often the personalities are so separated that they are not aware of each other's existence. This is called an amnesic barrier.

Imagine a child with a mother who is loving one moment and cruel and sadistic the next. The child will obviously react differently, depending on the mother's mood. The child will learn different ways of responding to the "good" mother and the "bad" mother. All children do this to some extent because no adult is perfectly consistent.

Now imagine that the child is so stressed out that memories of interactions with the "bad" mother are dissociated. When the "good" mother is around, the child has no knowledge of the "bad" mother, or of the "bad" child. But as soon as the mother turns nasty, the child switches, and knows exactly how to react. That's multiplicity.

What is an Alter?
An alter is one personality of a person with multiplicity. The personality who is "out" most of the time is often called the host personality, and personalities seen less frequently are called alternative personalities, or alters. Some people have only one or two alters, others have hundreds or even thousands.

Some people with multiplicity experience each alter as a separate person. Others experience them as different from their usual self, but not as different people. Multiplicity is not exactly the same from person to person and each person's experience of their inner reality is unique.

Often alters have names, have a distinct age, and have specific jobs to do. One may be in charge of feeling anger, another of going to school or work, another may be the one who decides which alter gets to be in control of the body at any given time. Alters may have a different gender from the body or a different sexual orientation from the host. There may even be alters who are animals, objects, or abstract ideas. Sometimes people have alters who are experienced as being dead or immortal.

The formation of alters is a natural psychological process, given extreme early childhood stress. Abusive adults who are aware of the process can manipulate and train the emerging personalities to their own ends. Some survivors of ritual abuse have alters trained by their abusers to do certain tasks and to behave in ways desired by the abusers. And some survivors have alters organized in elaborate patterns designed by the perpetrators, with strict rules about how the alters communicate with each other."
(http://www.ra-info.org/faqs/ra_faq.shtml)

Another reference that describes this:
"Our instinctive reactions to an assault are fight or flight. However, neither works when children are abused by sadistic adults. The only option left is to freeze, and take flight through the mind. A common initial coping mechanism is to escape the body. It is the beginning of clinical (amnestic) dissociation, which allows a shutting out of an unbearable reality. It is held unassimilated---in effect, frozen in time...In some cases the dissociated aspects of self, immediately or over time, form their own and separate sense of self.

A dissociated identity, like a dissociated experience, can hold the entire event or parts of it. ...One hundred abusive/traumatic incidents may be held by one identity or by one hundred or more identities. It may be helpful to think of each identity as holding an abusive experience. In this context, taken together, the identities hold a person's overwhelming traumas and express a survivor's entire life story.

When the abuse is over, the original self "returns" and resumes "normal" life, having no/little awareness of what has just transpired. If severely abused children were forced to experience the trauma they just lived through, they would probably NOT survive.

Some children maintain a complete split between their everyday life and the abusive episodes. They may be seen smiling when posing for family photographs. Perpetrators often use such photographs to prove there is nothing bad going on.

As abused children grow, their problems typically begin to mount. The load on their unconscious becomes increasingly great, and they feel overwhelmed. As some identities stay out more and more, they may begin to take over and operate in the child's day-to-day world. If the abuse continues or increases, the original self may stay out less and less and, in time, stop coming out at all. The survivor is then functioning through identities who "switch" to cope with day-to-day life.

...

Each identity within the same person may have unique neurological and physiological responses. For example, some identities may require glasses, while others have perfect vision: some identities are allergic to smoke, while others may be chain smokers: some identities are almost deaf, while others have exceptionally good hearing: different alters within one person will register unique electroencephalogram, electrocardiograph, blood pressure, and pulse readings. Alters may have different allergies and different ailments and unique responses to medications. One identity may be diagnosed with an ailment, but a different identity may be "out" when the medication is taken. In this case, the original alter isn't helped, and the receiving alter may have unfavorable side effects. Prescribing medication to survivors who are multiple should be done with special care and extra monitoring."
(http://www.hiddenhurt.co.uk/Articles/dissociation.htm)

On the mechanics of personality switching:
"The therapist needs to become acquainted with detecting alter switches. This involves eye shape changes, eye color changes, eye movement changes, blinks, body posture changes, voice pitch changes, word usage changes, perception and value changes, mood changes, etc. Upon detection of this, the therapist may gently ask, "Do you ever feel that there is another part of yourself that comes out and does things that you would not do?" "Do you ever feel that when you are alone, someone else or some other part of you is watching you?" Any answer except a definite "no" is a red flag, that reconfirms the switching clues, and other clues that the therapist has assembled. Not all victims of mind-control have extensive alter systems. In our previous books, we have covered situations when this does not occur. Another way that therapists can determine mind-control would be to interview people close to the victim, and to visit the victim's work place and home. Some victims of mind-control surround themselves with objects that pertain to their programming. For instance, the therapist may find a man who has a passion for Mickey Mouse objects, or a woman who loves white rabbit figurines or star trek objects."
(Cisco Wheeler at http://www.angelfire.com/d20/01/deeper2.txt)

22. Described here by a programmer:
"...trainers will try to create internal structures within the person's personality systems. Why? They believe this creates better stability. It also gives the alters and fragments a place to "hang on to" inside, and creates a convenient way to call them up.

...

These are some common programming structures. Again, there are many, many other types of internal structures used and the number and type are only limited by the trainer's and survivor's creative abilities. The way that these structures are placed within the person are fairly similar. Under drugs, hypnosis and electroshock, the person is traumatized into a deep trance state. In the deep trance they will be told to open their eyes and look at: either a projected image

of the structure, a 3D model of it, or a holographic image using a virtual reality headset. The image will be ground in, using shock and bringing the image closer and closer to the person's visual field. It may be rotated, if graphics are available, or a 3D is used. They may be told that they are entering inside it, if it is a temple or pyramid, under deep hypnosis, that they (the alter being programmed) will now "live inside" the structure/box/card, etc. This will also be used to reinforce amnesia and isolation programming internally, since the structure will be used to reinforce walls between the alter/ fragment and other alters and fragments internally."
(Chapter   10   at http://web.archive.org/web/20050729113558/http://www.geocities.com/lord_vi sionary/svali_index.htm)

Ron Patton describes further some of these virtual worlds:
"One of the main internal structures, (of which their are many) within the system is shaped like a double-helix, consisting of seven levels. Each system has an internal programmer which oversees the "gatekeeper" (demons?) who grant or deny entry into the different rooms. A few of the internal images predominately seen by victims/survivors are trees, the Cabalistic "Tree of Life," with adjoining root systems, infinity loops, ancient symbols and letters, spider webs, mirrors or glass shattering, masks, castles, mazes, demons/monsters/aliens, sea shells, butterflies, snakes, ribbons, bows, flowers, hour glasses, clocks, robots, chain-of-command diagrams and/or schematics of computer circuitry boards."
(http://www.whale.to/b/patton.html)

23. "These folk-tales are also extremely dark.
...
But psychologists and child protection experts have long seen the value of the older, more sinister fables. As I sat in the cramped library, under the slanted eave of the roof, I leafed through a book by the great, though disgraced, psychologist Bruno Bettelheim.
...
However, I must admit to a lasting affection (and yes, a certain amount of pity) for Bruno Bettelheim, or Dr B as he came to be called by his posthumous biographers. It seems that he saw the horror of the war as an opportunity to reinvent himself, to rebuild a shattered life, to rise phoenix-like from the ashes of a charred Europe. Isn't that a wonderful symbol for what social-care is really all about: glorious rebirth?

"The Uses of Enchantment" is Bettelheim's book on storytelling as a therapeutic tool. I read it when I was a student and I remember being struck by the concept that things as seemingly innocuous as stories could be used to heal children of deep emotional wounds. According to the book, fairy-tales contain subconcious symbols, archetypal images that we all respond to without even knowing it."

(Shane Dunphy, *Last Ditch House* (Dublin, 2007), p.113-115.)

24. The way that the film's plot is woven to enhance the programming is described by Cathy O'Brien here:
"Much of The Wizard Of Oz lends itself to themes commonly used by perpetrators. For example, nearly all MPD/DIDs have suffered the loss of pets during ritualized torture. And all of Baum's primary character Dorothy's nightmarish experiences "over the rainbow in Oz" stemmed from her desire to risk her own life to protect her threatened pet. Abusers use this lesson to condition the victim to drop all resistance and cooperate or "I'll get you, my pretty, and your little dog (or child) too."
The "over the rainbow" scramble of dreams vs. reality provides abusers a theme by which to manipulate an MPD's subconscious perception of switching personalities. Oftentimes this theme is transdimensional as is Oz, or that which was just experienced was "just a bad dream" like Dorothy was told upon her awakening in her own bed back in Kansas."
(Cathy O'Brien and Mark Philips, *Transformation of America* (1995), Chapter 6 at: http://earthsfinaldays.com/mind_control1.htm)

Another description of this process:
"Next, the people in the child's life who are guiding the programming will tell the child programming stories, such as the Wizard of Oz stories and Alice In Wonderland. In the 50's and 60's, the Tall Book of Make Believe was popular. For instance the character Mr. Moon became a foundational part of the programming. Over the years the Wizard of Oz, Alice In Wonderland, and Mother Goose seem to have been overall favorites. The child will most often be in a trance state when these story lines are told. The children will have the stories repeated and they are expected to memorize these scripts. Because the programmers will build upon the child's awareness of these stories, the stories are modified to better fit the future programming. For instance, if a programming team is going to use the Goldilocks and the 3 Bears story, they might modify the story like this: The 3 bears and Goldilocks went for a walk. Goldilocks was somewhere she shouldn't have been, so she was eaten up by the bears. Bears will eat you up. Policemen are like bears. A Policeman found her? Do you know what happened to her? Goldilocks got locked up and put in a cage. Or maybe they might say, Goldilocks was sitting where she wasn't supposed to.-- At that moment the chair is pulled out from underneath the child and the child is probed with a stun gun."
(Fritz Springmeier and Cisco Wheeler, *Deeper Insights* ... (1997), p.261: http://educate-yourself.org/mc/deeperinsightsbook.shtml)

25.
http://web.archive.org/web/20030104000255/members.aol.com/smartnews/ks0 1.htm . More from this source: "Dad especially liked using what he called acted-out scenarios to develop screen memories in victims. Acted-out scenarios were created by people who pretended to be someone or somewhere they were

not. Sometimes real Hollywood actors and actresses were paid to participate. This was done to trick and confuse the minds of victims, who were often drugged or hypnotized or both. Dad favored acted-out scenarios as opposed to using movies and videos to create screen memories. I heard him argue more than once that the more senses the handlers and programmers could engage in the victim, the harder it would be for the victim to believe that the screen memory wasn't a real event."

26. Shane Dunphy, the Irish Independent writer and child protection worker, *Hush, Little Baby* (Dublin, 2008), p.251, a character called Clive Plummer. Although it is fiction he makes it quite clear in his books that he is drawing on real cases that he came across while working in child protection in Ireland.

27.
http://web.archive.org/web/20030104000255/members.aol.com/smartnews/ks0
1.htm .

28. You can read the various eyewitness accounts at these links:
Brice Taylor, *Thanks for the Memories* (1999): http://www.illuminati-news.com/e-books/BriceTaylor-ThanksForTheMemories.pdf ,
Cathy O'Brien and Mark Philips, *Transformation of America* (1995): http://earthsfinaldays.com/mind_control1.htm ,
James   Casbolt,   *Agent   Buried   Alive*:
http://jamescasbolt.com/book/chapter1.html ,
Carol Rutz, *A Nation betrayed* : http://www.raven1.net/nabetray.htm ,
Laura Landsberg Hanning, *Study of Evil*:
http://web.archive.org/web/20030402054435/www.angelfire.com/journal2/Stu
dyOfEvil/ ,
Svali:
http://web.archive.org/web/20050729113558/http://www.geocities.com/lord_vi
sionary/svali_index.htm ,
GaryP: http://members.tripod.com/garyp99/index.html ,
Mrs James Card: http://jdcard.com/mpdfrnd1.htm ,
Robert   Duncan   O'Finioan:
http://www.wintersteel.com/RobertDuncanOFinioan.html ,
David Marr: http://www.danofisrael.com/id33.html ,
TygerWolf: http://www.2multiples.com/twcrew/47_page.html ,
Donna: http://www.angelfire.com/poetry/firekat/ ,
Kathleen   Sullivan:
http://web.archive.org/web/20030104000255/members.aol.com/smartnews/ks0
1.htm ,
Ron Patton: http://www.whale.to/b/patton.html ,
See also a lecture by Dr. Corydon Hammond of the University of Utah at a Conference on Abuse and Multiple Personality Disorder (MPD), Thursday June 25, 1992:
http://www.whale.to/b/greenbaum.html ,

Fritz Springmeier and Cisco Wheeler, *Formula Used to Create Undetectable Total Mind-Controlled Slave* (1996): http://educate-yourself.org/mc/IlluminatiFormulaindex.shtml ,

Fritz Springmeier and Cisco Wheeler, *Deeper Insights* .. (1997): http://educateyourself.org/mc/deeperinsightsbook.shtml ,

(The two Springmeier books are hugely more complicated than the others, but well worth reading if you can follow them. Btw I am obviously not in a position to vouch for all that is written in these books, there are of course details that I don't believe or don't agree with, but nearly all of them describe the basic model of how MPD can be deliberately created.)

29. Dalziel and Pascoe, Season 12, Episodes 1 and 2, *Demons on our Shoulder*, starring Richard E. Grant, first aired 6th and 13th of May 2007.

CHAPTER 7

Russia in the crosshairs: NATO's next target?

While the last chapter - if you were convinced by my thesis! - might have shocked you about the state of the justice system in Ireland, and about the kind of advanced and horrific technology used by intelligence agencies, it is unfortunately nothing in comparison to the era in world politics that we currently live in. For the globe is in a state of foreboding, 'a state of chasis' as Sean O'Casey would say. Since the advent of George Bush to the White House every other year seems to bring forth a war or talk of war. Few commentators believe that this will stop at Iraq. Last July even Newt Gingrich was quoted as saying that "we are in the early stages of what I would describe as the third world war..."[1] Many people are now openly speculating about who is next. Syria? North Korea? Saudi Arabia? And especially Iran are the subject of fevered speculation even in the established media. This writer would just like to opt for Russia as the next ultimate target.

Of course the obvious thing to do in this analysis of US/NATO intentions is to look at the real reasons why the US went into Iraq and then use that and apply it to Russia to see if they might wish to invade it. I am guided here by the revelations of Karen Kwiatkovski, a Lieutenant Colonel who served in the Pentagon during the run up to the last Iraq war. She describes some three or four issues that dominated the thinking of the Pentagon prior to the invasion.

1) Firstly she refers to the question of US bases:

> "One reason has to do with enhancing our military-basing posture in the region. We had been very dissatisfied with our relations with Saudi Arabia, particularly the restrictions on our basing. There was dissatisfaction from the people of Saudi Arabia, and thus the troubled monarchy. So we were looking for alternate strategic locations beyond Kuwait, beyond Qatar, to secure something we had been searching for since the days of Carter — to secure the energy lines of communication in the region. Bases in Iraq, then, were very important — that is, if you hold that is America's role in the world. Saddam Hussein was not about to invite us in."[2]

Apparently then they wanted to establish themselves more centrally in the Middle East region, and right on top of the oil reserves. Iraq gave them that, it gives them extensive borders with nearly all the Middle East countries. The value of this is that in their future negotiations with say Syria and Iran they can threaten those countries with invasions from all sides. This threat can then hang over those countries and they can be more amenable to US pressure as a result.

If you look at Russia then it is a hugely strategic country in that way. If you could locate bases in Russia it gives you strategic access all the way from Central Europe, Kalingrad, to China and Japan, dominating all the oil and gas fields in between. Russia looks more and more isolated in that sense because they definitely do not permit NATO bases on their soil. Almost all of Europe, and much of the rest of the world, seems to have succumbed to US/NATO influence and permit bases within their borders. These bases could be in a way a sign of a country's sovereignty, if you have them then you aren't an independent country. Only India and China look like important countries that remain sovereign and outside US/NATO influence but these are obviously compact countries with huge militaries and anyway few natural resources that aren't absorbed by their own populations. Russia is spread out across 12 time zones making it more vulnerable to attack, its military hardware was, until recently anyway, rusting away, and they are sitting on huge untapped natural resources like oil, gas, wood, diamonds etc. They are also outside some of these supranational organisations like the EU which often seems to work in close concert with the US.

Some prominent Russians are looking at the ever tightening ring of US bases that surround them and are wondering what this bodes for the near future. This is from Aleksander Solzhenitsyn speaking in April last year:

> '"Though it is clear that present-day Russia poses no threat to it, NATO is methodically and persistently building up its military machine - into the east of Europe and surrounding Russia from the south," Solzhenitsyn was quoted as saying.
>
> "This involves open material and ideological support for 'colour revolutions' and the paradoxical forcing of North Atlantic interests on Central Asia," he reportedly said, adding that there was "little substantial difference" between the actions of the US and NATO.
>
> "All this leaves no doubt that they are preparing to completely encircle Russia and deprive it of its

sovereignty," Solzhenitsyn was quoted as saying.[3]

2) Lieut. Col. Kwiatkovski also worked on some of the "information manipulation" that went on prior to the war:

> "What the [Douglas] Feith group and the Office of Special Plans was doing was information manipulation, not the production of what we legitimately call "intelligence.".... Unlike intelligence, this effort was designed not to inform decision makers, but to shape a national conversation such that decisions already made by the administration (to topple Saddam and get bases in Iraq) could be pursued without political backlash."

In the Pentagon they were cooking up this brew of "propaganda and falsehoods" and feeding it into the big US media organisations like the New York Times etc, with a view to preparing the US public for a war they had already decided on waging.[4] This widespread, and quite long term, media manipulation by the US and UK intelligence agencies prior to the Iraq war has been confirmed by countless other sources too like the Downing St. memo. The effect, and intention, was to brainwash the public in those countries into believing all kinds of total nonsense about Iraq to smooth the path for the army to go in.

It just seems to this observer anyway that the Western media are now doing that with respect to Russia. Personally I think that both Politskaya and Litvinenko were genuine Russian heroes, and deserved to be honoured as such, but the hype that surrounded their deaths appears unusually critical of Russia.[5] Look at Ireland and the fate of Martin O'Hagan as a comparison. His death received nothing like the media publicity that even the Irish media bestowed on the two Russians. Maybe then the media drift points to war against Russia? Or at least some action in the short term like sanctions?

3) She gives another slightly less well known reason why they went into Iraq:

> "Another reason is a uniquely American rationale, and it relates to our currency, and our debt situation. Saddam Hussein decided in November 2000 to sell his Food for Oil program oil sales in euros. The oil sales permitted in that program aren't very much. But when the sanctions would be lifted, the sales from the country with the second largest oil reserves on the planet would have been moving from the dollar to the euro.

> The U.S. dollar is in a sensitive period because we are a
> bigtime debtor nation now. Our currency is still
> popular, but it's not backed up like it used to be. If oil, a
> very solid commodity, is traded on the euro, that could
> cause massive shifts in confidence in trading on the
> dollar...
> In any case, the first executive order regarding Iraq that
> Bush signed in May [2003] switched trading on Iraq's
> oil back to the dollar."[6]

I'm sure this seems somewhat complicated, or unimportant, to some but it is often mentioned by others as a key factor in modern politics today. This is my tuppence worth as to how it works:

The US dollar is a fiat currency which means that you hold no collateral when you own a US dollar. It is just paper, its a confidence thing, you are confident that somebody will take it from you and give you value for it so you don't care that it is not backed up by gold or anything like that. If it is just paper then why doesn't the US govt. just print off a whole load of dollars and pay all its public wage bill like that, for example? Some countries have actually done that, like Mobutu in Zaire, but the problem is that this new money just sloshes around putting up prices, then you have to increase that wage bill so govt. employees can continue to afford the essentials, and so set off a disastrous inflationary cycle which in time would destroy all native businesses. But the beauty of it for the US govt. right now is that other countries are buying these dollars, which they are just printing off for free, so there is no native inflationary cycle. They can do this because it is an international reserve currency. Foreign governments need to hold dollars specifically because they need them to buy oil. Hence the fact that oil sales are nearly always denominated in dollars is central to US economic well being. Of course its all more complicated than that but this I think is the basic setup. The US govt. is running up huge debts using this kind of funny money dollar, which are in turn purchased by foreign governments who need them to buy oil, and then this money is used to build up the unbeatable huge US military apparatus. Or something like that, this is a quote from Paul Roberts explaining the current situation, as pointed out in Chapter 1 he was Treasury Undersecretary under Ronald Reagan and a former associate editor of the Wall Street Journal:

> "The Bush Regime's ability to wage war is dependent
> upon foreign financing. The Regime's wars are
> financed with red ink, which means the hundreds of
> billions of dollars must be borrowed. As American

consumers are spending more than they earn on consumption, the money cannot be borrowed from Americans.

The US is totally dependent upon foreigners to finance its budget and trade deficits. By financing these deficits, foreign governments are complicit in the Bush Regime's military aggressions and war crimes. The Bush Regime's two largest lenders are China and Japan. It is ironic that Japan, the only nation to experience nuclear attack by the US, is banker to the Bush Regime as it prepares a possible nuclear attack on Iran.

If the rest of the world would simply stop purchasing US Treasuries, and instead dump their surplus dollars into the foreign exchange market, the Bush Regime would be overwhelmed with economic crisis and unable to wage war. The arrogant hubris associated with the "sole superpower" myth would burst like the bubble it is.

The collapse of the dollar would also end the US government's ability to subvert other countries by purchasing their leaders to do America's will.

The demise of the US dollar is only a question of time. It would save the world from war and devastation if the dollar is brought to its demise before the Bush Regime launches its planned attack on Iran."[7]

Iran certainly is thinking of changing over its oil sales from dollars to the euro, which is maybe why it is talked about so much as a possible target, but also Russia is quietly thinking of 'reforming' its oil trades away from the use of the dollar.[8] Such speculation may be going down badly in Washington.

A related point is that the Western powers might be anxious to restrict the supply of oil onto the world markets because this then puts up the price which in turn provides better support for the dollar. (Obviously if Japan say purchases x amount of dollars to buy oil at $20 dollars a barrel, it will now have to buy three times the amount of dollars to pay for the same amount of oil at $60 a barrel, so providing a nice parachute for the dollar.) As well as that from the point of view of

239

the Western oil companies a higher oil price simply allows them to charge a higher price at the pumps, which pads out their profits very nicely. Don't be under any illusions, these oil companies are not buying that wholesale oil at the current $140 world market price, they simply sell at that price! They have their own long term reserves that they are drawing on. So it is not surprising to hear that in 2004 British Petroleum's "rule of thumb" was that a dollar increase in the Brent price of crude oil added $570 million dollars to their pre-tax profits in a full year.[9] This would be the extra profit for every dollar increase from c. $20 a barrel. As you can see at current oil prices we are talking astronomical profits!

These oil companies are quite influential in all Western countries - some would even include Shell in Ireland in that category - and might in fact be involved in artificially inflating the oil price right now, by restricting the supply and no doubt other means. Clearly the world economy has been there and done that in the 70s and here are a few interesting comments on that period from the famous Saudi oil minister Sheikh Yamani:

> "His voice quickens further when he reminisces about the era of great oil diplomacy in the Seventies and his contemporary, former US Secretary of State Henry Kissinger.
>
> At this point he makes an extraordinary claim: 'I am 100 per cent sure that the Americans were behind the increase in the price of oil. The oil companies were in real trouble at that time, they had borrowed a lot of money and they needed a high oil price to save them.'
>
> He says he was convinced of this by the attitude of the Shah of Iran, who in one crucial day in 1974 moved from the Saudi view, that a hike would be dangerous to Opec because it would alienate the US, to advocating higher prices.
>
> 'King Faisal sent me to the Shah of Iran, who said: "Why are you against the increase in the price of oil? That is what they want? Ask Henry Kissinger - he is the one who wants a higher price".'
>
> Yamani contends that proof of his long-held belief has recently emerged in the minutes of a secret meeting on

a Swedish island, where UK and US officials determined to orchestrate a 400 per cent increase in the oil price."[10]

That was in an interview in the Observer. It makes interesting reading doesn't it? The point is that if something like that is happening now Russia would have to play a huge part in it because she is now I think the world's largest oil exporter. Basically then if the Western powers want to continue to manipulate the oil price then they need to have control over Russia because otherwise she could undercut them in the marketplace. This might again be another reason to put Russia in the crosshairs.

4) I would add in another point about the invasion of Iraq that Kwiatkovski doesn't mention. While it might seem a strange reason I think that those Western leaders that dealt with Saddam Hussein over the years, like famously Donald Rumsfeld, might have been anxious to get into Baghdad simply to control the flow of information from there. They might have liked to seize their archives and imprison their leading intelligence and diplomatic figures in order to cover up the close relationship between the neocons and Saddam Hussein in the 80s. It might strike some as an unusual reason to give but I think if you were in Rumsfeld's shoes, and George Bush Sr's, then it might be a quietly good reason to get into Baghdad in a hurry.

This kind of reason would make even more sense if you compare it to Russia today. Many members of the elite in Eastern Europe, who are now in the EU and NATO, rose to prominence during communist times and might not be uninterested in what is locked away in Russian archives and in the memories of old KGB agents.[11] This might even include prominent clerical figures like famously members of the Polish hierarchy.[12] Some of these intelligence leaks that are now coming out of Moscow are also hitting closer to home among the elites in Western Europe. One English MEP announced in the EU parliament that Litvinenko before his death had fingered Romano Prodi as a leading old KGB agent. This MEP, Gerard Batten, clearly now thinks that that was the reason for his assassination.[13] Obviously Romano Prodi has recently served as EU President which makes you wonder under what kind of influence the EU is now under. Another interesting leak has come from Vladimir Bukovsky who is a prominent Russian veteran of the gulags. He managed to get access to some of the Soviet Union archives in 1991 at a time when Boris Yeltsin wanted his help in fighting a major constitutional court case in Moscow. He says that some of these Russian documents show that the EU was designed as a Western clone of the

Soviet Union, particularly from the mid 80s on. This was as part of a secret alliance between some of the European parties and Gorbachov. Apparently this alliance began when Valery Giscaird d'Estaing visited Moscow representing the Trilateral Group, and pressed for Soviet help in deepening and expanding the EU. According then to this important Russian dissident it is 'no accident' that EU institutions work exactly like Soviet ones:

> "The Soviets came to a conclusion and to an agreement with the left-wing parties that if they worked together they could hijack the whole European project and turn it upside down. Instead of an open market they would turn it into a federal state.

> According to the [secret Soviet] documents, 1985-86 is the turning point. I have published most of these documents. You might even find them on the internet. But the conversations they had are really eye opening. For the first time you understand that there is a conspiracy – quite understandable for them, as they were trying to save their political hides. In the East the Soviets needed a change of relations with Europe because they were entering a protracted and very deep structural crisis; in the West the left-wing parties were afraid of being wiped out and losing their influence and prestige. So it was a conspiracy, quite openly made by them, agreed upon, and worked out.

> ...

> It is no accident that the European Parliament, for example, reminds me of the Supreme Soviet. It looks like the Supreme Soviet because it was designed like it. Similarly, when you look at the European Commission it looks like the Politburo. I mean it does so exactly, except for the fact that the Commission now has 25 members and the Politburo usually had 13 or 15 members. Apart from that they are exactly the same, unaccountable to anyone, not directly elected by anyone at all."

It is not just Bukovsky who is saying this, at a recent meeting in Waterford Kathy Sinnott MEP was asked what model the EU is now following, and replied:

> "Do you know what the Polish say? And the Czech, and the Lithuanians? And the Latvians?...I have heard

MEPs [from those four countries] say, that after they
have been there for a while, they begin to get this
feeling that the closest model is Soviet. And you know
one time when a Polish MEP said this, a woman who
was born and raised under Communism, she was
screamed at by the Finnish MEP Alexander Stubb, who
is one of the stars of the Lisbon Treaty, that she must
never say that again...I was sitting next to her and she
just turned to me and said that's what the Soviets used
to say."[14]

In any case you can easily see then why the Western political
establishment might like to cut off once and for all this intelligence flow
from Moscow. Any more leaks from people like Bukovsky and it will
shake the complacency of the Europeans about the EU project!

I might mention one potential flaw in the above reasoning. Why would
the very right wing neocon group want to go to war against Russia to
protect the good names of these socialist figures in Europe? Aren't they
their enemies, opposite sides of the ideological coin? Frankly you'd
wonder how much those differences really matter at the high level of
the political establishment while they seem to occupy all the time of the
lower ranks. Think about some of these extreme left figures in Ireland at
the time, the Workers Party say, who might - and I'm not making any
accusations - be uncommonly interested in those archives. They seem to
get on quite well now in the upper reaches of the Irish state and
commerce, in the media, judiciary, the Labour party, in some famous
cases arguing an extreme right wing philosophy as aggressively as they
did a left wing one before. Don't get me wrong there is nothing wrong
at all with changing your opinions, or holding them and receiving high
office at the same time, but the list of senior figures that seem to
oscillate freely between the extremes of this spectrum makes this writer
feel that those ideological differences are not taken seriously among the
powers that be.[15] Half the time I think they are just bamboozling the
general public, hiding the real political drifts behind endless talk about
where this or that policy or person stands in the right/left political
spectrum.

This is Karen Kwiatkovski's impression of neocon ideology which she
must have known quite well:

"Neoconservative ideology does not embrace free trade
in the sense that libertarians or Adam Smith embrace it,
but instead prefers significant state involvement and
leans towards a social democratic model of domestic

governing."[16]

So its all kind of mixed up! Looking at things from a left/right perspective only clouds what is really going on? This is Ashley Mote's impression of the big political power plays in the EU parliament that he is a member of:

> "Such as it is, the EU's parliament has a built-in majority in favour of the social market. It is the repository of an unspoken agreement between the left and the multinationals. This 'understanding' appears to have the backing of the bureaucratic elite..."[17]

Presumable the neocons and multinationals favour heavy native government control over a country's economy because they usually exercise more influence over the government than the ordinary people, and so as the government's power increases so does theirs. Look at Rossport for example. Shell had no trouble getting land from Coillte, and every other facility from government bodies, and was only upset in its plans by the fact that some of the land was privately owned. Even stranger alliances are possible behind the scenes, consider this quote from an OSS report on Giovanni Montini's secret diplomacy in 1944:

> "... the discussion between Msgr. Montini and Togliatti was the first direct contact between a high prelate of the Vatican and a leader of Communism. After having examined the situation, they acknowledged the potential possibility of a contingent alliance between Catholics and Communists in Italy which would give the three parties -- Christian Democrats, Socialists and Communists -- an absolute majority, thereby enabling them to dominate any political situation. A tentative plan was drafted to forge the basis on which the agreement between the three parties could be made."[18]

This is a very important report because of the personalities involved, Montini was arguably the most influential Vatican diplomat for some 30 years before his death as Pope Paul VI in 1978, and the OSS officer who dealt with this was probably James Angleton who served later as CIA chief of Counter Intelligence. These people don't mess around with idle fancies, this was possibly a serious reflection of things to come. But how could these parties come together like this, what about all those ideological differences? The more you read of the Cold War the more you think that all these ideological differences are only to amuse and divide the plebs while the big shots run off with the loot! [19]

I might as well leave you with one final comforting thought :-). It might not have escaped your attention that Russia is bristling with long

244

range nuclear weapons, the only part of their arsenal that never rusted, and they have every intention of using them against the civilian population of an invading country. The aforementioned Dr Paul Roberts raises this chilling spectre:

> "It is obvious that American foreign policy, with is goal of ringing Russia with US military bases, is leading directly to nuclear war. Every American needs to realize this fact. The US government's insane hegemonic foreign policy is a direct threat to life on the planet." [20]

'Interesting times' and all that!

Footnotes

1. http://www.newsmax.com/archives/ic/2006/7/16/155736.shtml

2. http://www.lewrockwell.com/kwiatkowski/kwiatkowski128.html .

3. http://www.hinduonnet.com/holnus/003200604280921.htm .

4. "What the Feith group and the Office of Special Plans was doing was information manipulation, not the production of what we legitimately call "intelligence." Intelligence is vetted, contextualized, and conservative. What Feith's OSP wanted, needed and produced was inflammatory bits of data, cherry-picked statements, and isolated observations by often shady characters, presented as if they were vetted, contextualized and conservative intelligence. Unlike intelligence, this effort was designed not to inform decision makers, but to shape a national conversation such that decisions already made by the administration (to topple Saddam and get bases in Iraq) could be pursued without political backlash. That's what Doug Feith and his folks did for Bush and Cheney in the Pentagon." After it was compiled "the offices fed information directly and indirectly to sympathetic media outlets, including the Rupert Murdoch-owned 'Weekly Standard' and FoxNews Network, as well as the editorial pages of the 'Wall Street Journal' and syndicated columnists, such as   Charles Krauthammer."(http://www.scoop.co.nz/stories/HL0703/S00070.htm   and http://www.commondreams.org/headlines03/0807-02.htm). A bit more from her from this interview:
"It seems clear that many in the Congress were fed OSP derived and developed information and talking points from the Pentagon -- and that this information was believed by those Congressmen to be "intelligence" instead of propaganda and falsehoods. Frankly, I believe that many in Congress wanted this invasion of Iraq, and didn't care if what they were seeing from Feith, Wolfowitz and Rumsfeld was true or not. This is why "politicized" intelligence – the focus of the so-called Part II investigation was so critical, and so successfully opposed and blocked by many Senators and Congressmen.
It seems even more certain that the New York Times and other major papers were fed the same type of material by Pentagon and Office of the Vice President as if it were verified intelligence, and that they believed that it was. Doug Feith today denies he did anything wrong at all. Feith and many of the neoconservatives are fundamentally ethically challenged when it comes to American national security. Given everything we know, it is unlikely any of these war advocates told the truth to Congress about the story they were helping to "sell" to Congress and the rest of the country back in 2002 and early 2003."

5. They were mentioned on indymedia at
http://www.indymedia.ie/article/70223 .

6. http://www.lewrockwell.com/kwiatkowski/kwiatkowski128.html .

7. www.informationclearinghouse.info/article17035.htm . Who knows maybe they will also attack Iran but I still think that Russia is the ultimate prize. This is from an article in the Observer:
"The majority of countries that require oil imports require dollars to pay for their fuel. Oil exporters similarly hold, as their currency reserve, billions in the currency in which they are paid. Investing these petrodollars straight back into the US economy is possible at zero currency risk.

So the US can carry on printing money - effectively IOUs - to fund tax cuts, increased military spending, and consumer spending on imports without fear of inflation or that these loans will be called in. As keeper of the global currency there is always the last-ditch resort to devaluation, which forces other countries' exporters to pay for US economic distress. It's probably the nearest thing to a 'free lunch' in global economics."
...[Then it goes on to talk about the euro and whether that might take over from the dollar, and shows that the Saudi government, at least, knows well the importance to the US of pricing oil in dollars :]
" 'The Saudis are holding the line on oil prices in Opec and should they, for example, go along with the rest of the Opec people in demanding that oil be priced in euros, that would deal a very heavy blow to the American economy,' Youssef Ibrahim, of the influential US Council on Foreign Relations, told CNN.

Last year the former US Ambassador to Saudi Arabia told a committee of the US Congress: 'One of the major things the Saudis have historically done, in part out of friendship with the United States, is to insist that oil continues to be priced in dollars. Therefore, the US Treasury can print money and buy oil, which is an advantage no other country has. With the emergence of other currencies and with strains in the relationship, I wonder whether there will not again be, as there have been in the past, people in Saudi Arabia who raise the question of why they should be so kind to the United States.' "
(http://observer.guardian.co.uk/business/story/0,6903,900867,00.html)

From a recent article by the Council on Foreign Relations:
"The dollar is ultimately just another money supported only by faith that others will willingly accept it in the future in return for the same sort of valuable things it bought in the past...
Four decades ago, the renowned French economist Jacques Rueff, writing just a few years before the collapse of the Bretton Woods dollar-based gold-exchange standard, argued that the system "attains such a degree of absurdity that no human brain having the power to reason can defend it." The precariousness of the dollar's position today is similar. The United States can run a chronic balance-of-payments deficit and never feel the effects. Dollars sent abroad immediately come home in the form of loans, as dollars are of no

use abroad. "If I had an agreement with my tailor that whatever money I pay him he returns to me the very same day as a loan," Rueff explained by way of analogy, "I would have no objection at all to ordering more suits from him."

With the U.S. current account deficit running at an enormous 6.6 percent of GDP (about $2 billion a day must be imported to sustain it), the United States is in the fortunate position of the suit buyer with a Chinese tailor who instantaneously returns his payments in the form of loans — generally, in the U.S. case, as purchases of U.S. Treasury bonds. The current account deficit is partially fuelled by the budget deficit (a dollar more of the latter yields about 20-50 cents more of the former), which will soar in the next decade in the absence of reforms to curtail federal "entitlement" spending on medical care and retirement benefits for a longer-living population. The United States — and, indeed, its Chinese tailor — must therefore be concerned with the sustainability of what Rueff called an "absurdity." In the absence of long-term fiscal prudence, the United States risks undermining the faith foreigners have placed in its management of the dollar — that is, their belief that the U.S. government can continue to sustain low inflation without having to resort to growth-crushing interest-rate hikes as a means of ensuring continued high capital inflows."(http://cryptogon.com/?p=706).

8. For talk of Russia, and Iran, changing from the dollar trade in oil see .e.g. http://en.rian.ru/analysis/20060627/50549408.html .

9. The Times 5 Oct. 2004 p.46. I think this was their source: http://www.bp.com/liveassets/bp_internet/globalbp/STAGING/global_assets/d ownloads/S/strategy_2004_supplementary_information.pdf . Here is a quote from that report showing these sort of figures:
"For the purposes of cash returns analysis, BP adjusts for a blend of oil and natural gas prices. As a simplifying assumption, a blended marker price is calculated using a 60% / 40% Brent [crude oil price] / Henry Hub [Natural Gas price] weighting. A pre-tax adjustment of $800 million is then applied to the Group's RCP BIT [Replacement Cost Profit Before Interest and Tax] for every $1 change in this blended marker price while a post-tax adjustment of $475 million for every $1 change in blended marker price is applied to the Group's RCP. Although this is merely an estimation, statistical analysis has shown that over the 2000-2003 period changes in this blended Brent / Henry Hub price are correlated to changes in the Group's RCP BIT / RCP, with $800 million and $475m per $1 change representing the magnitude of this relationship."

10. The Observer 14 Jan 2001
http://observer.guardian.co.uk/business/story/0,6903,421888,00.html . For an example of how powerful oil companies can be see: http://www.thetruthseeker.co.uk/article.asp?ID=6561 .

11. This story has blown up again with the drama in Poland involving the Archbishop of Warsaw, you can follow some of the political earthquakes that

are being caused by this in all East European countries in the Financial Times 29 Jan 2007 p.15.

12. As everybody knows Archbishop Stanisław Wielgus resigned the See of Warsaw and admitted to being a long term Communist agent. There are all kinds of rumours that the Vatican knew this full well before they appointed him which has attracted some gossip: http://www.polskieradio.pl/polonia/article.asp?tId=46315, one of many Polish bishops and clergy who were communist spies apparently: http://www.traditio.com/comment/com0703.htm .

13. Speech by Gerard Batten MEP to the European Parliament :
"Mr President, I should like to pay tribute to my constituent, Mr Alexander Litvinenko. Alexander was fearless in exposing the political gangsters that now run Russia, and the creatures of the KGB and FSB that still hold political office in Europe. For his bravery, he paid the ultimate price.
In April, I made two speeches in this Parliament repeating allegations made to me by Alexander that Romano Prodi had been an agent of some kind of the KGB. Alexander told me that the key figure to understanding Mr Prodi's alleged relationship with the KGB in the 1970s was a man named Sokolov, also known as Konopkine, who worked for TASS in Italy.
Since Alexander can no longer testify to this effect, as he was ready, willing and able to do, I am pleased to provide this service for him posthumously."
(Speech made on Wednesday 29th November, Brussels
http://www.ukip.org/ukip_news/gen12.php?t=1&id=2765 .)

Batten says that Litvinenko was told this by Colonel-General Anatoly Trofimov, a former deputy chief of the FSB the successor organisation to the KGB.
"Alexander Litvinenko was known to want to testify about allegations regarding Russian intelligence links to European political leaders and Russian intelligence involvement within organised crime in Europe prior to his assassination. "(http://kavkazcenter.com/eng/content/2006/11/27/6559.shtml see also http://www.ukip.org/ukip_news/gen12.php?t=1&id=2055)

14. The Kathy Sinnott quote is from http://forumoneuropepodcast.org/audio/podcast-2008-02-15-53335.mp3 at 110 and the Bukovsky one from http://www.brusselsjournal.com/node/865 . He describes how he got access to these archives here: http://bukovsky-archives.net/buk-intro.html .

15. Just to take a few examples:
Armand Hammer
Some say a billionaire, he was certainly extremely wealthy, he was one of the biggest oil magnates in the US in the 20th century and yet even his name comes from the Soviet flag! "Politically, Hammer was a staunch supporter of

the Republican party", with high up White House connections, a close friend of Al Gore and his father and, believe it or not, knew both Vladimir Lenin and Ronald Reagan. His father, a friend of Lenin's since 1907, was the founder of the Communist Party in the US and it was discovered later that Armand himself was a Soviet agent. (http://en.wikipedia.org/wiki/Armand_Hammer , http://www.theforbiddenknowledge.com/hardtruth/armand_hammer.htm   and http://www.amazon.com/Dossier-Secret-History-Armand-Hammer/dp/0786706775).

Viktor Rothschild
Another business person worth looking at is the incredibly wealthy Viktor Rothschild. As a socialist he joined the Cambridge Apostles while at University, a secret society of a 'mainly Marxist' hue. This has led to much speculation that he in fact was the fifth man in the Soviet spy ring along with his close friends Burgess and Blunt etc. During and after the war he was a senior, if unofficial, figure in the UK intelligence world, for decades friendly with the heads of MI6 and 5, head of research for Shell Oil, ran an influential 'Think Tank' in 10 Downing St under Ted Heath, and was security adviser to Margaret Thatcher.
(http://en.wikipedia.org/wiki/Victor_Rothschild,_3rd_Baron_Rothschild ,
          http://users.cyberone.com.au/myers/perry.html   and http://www.savethemales.ca/001411.html)

Nelson Rockefeller
The CIA Director, Walter Smith, warned Eisenhower that Nelson Rockefeller was a Communist spy. Obviously the Rockefellers are among the richest, and most influential, banking families in the US. (Stephen E. Ambrose, *Ike's Spies: Eisenhower and the Espionage Establishment* (Jackson, 1999), p.170.)

John Reid the current UK Home Secretary.
This is a quote from Craig Murray, the former UK diplomat: "For those who don't know, it is worth introducing Reid. A hardened Stalinist with a long term reputation for personal violence, at Stirling University he was the Communist Party's "Enforcer," (in days when the Communist Party ran Stirling University Students' Union, which it should not be forgotten was a business with a very substantial cash turnover). Reid was sent to beat up those who deviated from the Party line."
(http://downwithtyranny.blogspot.com/2006/08/looks-like-bush-found-soulmate-in.html)

Here is a bit of gossip picked up by W. Cleon Skousen, formerly of the FBI and Chief of Police in Salt Lake City, in discussions with a former senior official in the US Communist Party: "Dr. Dodd said she first became aware of some mysterious super-leadership right after World War II when the US Communist Party had difficulty getting instructions from Moscow on several vital matters requiring immediate attention. The American Communist hierarchy was told that any time they had an emergency of this kind they should contact any one of three designated persons at [New York City's] Waldorf Towers. Dr. Dodd noted that whenever the party obtained instructions from any of these three men, Moscow always ratified them. What puzzled Dr. Dodd was the fact that not one of these three contacts was a Russian. Nor were any of them Communists. In fact, all three of them were extremely wealthy American capitalists!"(http://www.natall.com/american-dissident-voices/adv030594.html)

Skousen is also the source for a list of aims of the Communist Party in the US, read into the Congressional Record in 1963: http://kentroversypapers.blogspot.com/2006/02/forty-five-communist-goals-to-take.html .

16. http://www.lewrockwell.com/kwiatkowski/kwiatkowski128.html .

17. http://www.newswithviews.com/guest_opinion/guest65.htm .

18. http://www.ihr.org/jhr/v13/v13n5p26_Martinez.html , a fuller quotation from the document is given in Piers Compton, *The Broken Cross* (St. Helier, 1984), (http://www.walkinthelight.ca/the_broken_cross_part_three.htm). The document is numbered as JR1022 and I think was first revealed in Richard Harris Smith, *OSS: The Secret History of America's First Intelligence Agency.* (Berkeley, 1972). See also Fr Luigi Villa, *Paul VI...Beatified?* (Brescia, 1998), (available at http://www.sheddinglight.info/archives_paul_vi.beatified.pdf) for a further description of this document.

The latter book describes, in elaborate detail, the allegations that Pope Paul VI was both an OSS and a KGB agent. For more of the OSS links see the radio interview with Attorney Jonathan Levy on 27 Feb 2006 http://mp3.rbnlive.com/Greg/0602/20060227_Mon_Greg1.mp3 and http://mp3.rbnlive.com/Greg/0602/20060227_Mon_Greg2.mp3 . Also http://www.maebrussell.com/Bibliography%20Sheets/346347s1.html , http://www.spiritone.com/~gdy52150/betrayalp5.htm and www.cia-on-campus.org/yale.edu/henwood.html .

The KGB allegations:
"Then in 1954 he was suddenly 'dismissed' to Milan under circumstances which have never been entirely clear. Myra Davidoglou documents the following facts: In July of 1944 Montini offered his services without the knowledge of Pius XII to the Soviet Union through the offices of his childhood friend Togliatti (then head of the Communist Party in Italy). The details of this sinister affair were exposed to the Pope by the Archbishop Primate of the Protestant Church in Sweden who was a state official and as such had access to governmental intelligence reports. This information came as a shock to Pius XII. An enquiry was made and among other things it was found that Montini's private secret[ary], the Jesuit Tondi, was a Russian agent and the man responsible for giving the Soviets the names of Catholic priests who were

being sent into Russia. This explained why they were all being immediately caught and executed. The upshot of this was that Montini was exiled to Milan without the traditional red hat." (http://www.wandea.org.pl/giovanni-montini.html)

19. For more curious tales from the Cold War I think another look at the Solidarity movement might be in order. The new revelations in Poland about extensive secret police infiltration of the Catholic Church are I think impacting now on most peoples understanding of that movement. Many are now wondering about how genuinely free of Communist influence it really was. This is an example of that type of speculation:

"Last month the headlines from Eastern Europe reported that Lech Walesa, the anti-communist Soldarity leader and former Polish president, had been accused of working for the secret police by Piotr Naimski, former head of the Polish secret service. Naimski claims to have seen Walesa's file, which lists the former Gdansk shipyard electrician as a secret agent of the communists, recruited in the early 1970s, code-named Bolek. Walesa denies the charges, which have been officially dismissed on more than one occasion. But if Walesa was an agent of the communists from the start, who is to say the communists haven't been calling the shots all along? As it happens, the stories about Walesa go way back. Ten years ago Dr. Wojcieck Myslecki, former managing director of Warsaw's Technical University, told me that Solidarity was a communist front. He called it a "controlled opposition movement." Myslecki also told of Lech Walesa's pro-communist activities before being elevated to a starring role in Poland's liberalization process. Myslecki was quite clear in making his allegations: Walesa was an agent of the secret police, who helped the communists infiltrate and control Solidarity for many years.

Myslecki's testimony is of particular interest because it agrees with the analysis of KGB defector Anatoliy Golitsyn, who wrote of Solidarity's role in his 1984 book "New Lies for Old." According to Golitsyn the communists were using organizations like Poland's Solidarity to attempt "previously unthinkable stratagems" such as "the introduction of false liberalization in Eastern Europe and, probably, in the Soviet Union. ..." Golitsyn wrote that the West did not understand communist strategy and disinformation. The appearance of Solidarity in Poland, he explained, "has been accepted as a spontaneous occurrence comparable with the Hungarian revolt of 1956 and as portending the demise of communism in Poland." But one has to question Solidarity's credentials, warned Golitsyn, pointing out that the French, Italian and Spanish communist parties "all took up pro-Solidarity positions."

Golitsyn further pointed to evidence that Poland's emerging democratic movement "was prepared and controlled from the outset within the framework of bloc policy and strategy."... Even Zofia Gryzb, who sat in the politburo, was a leading Solidarity figure. But none of these people were expelled from the party of Marx and Lenin for anti-socialist agitation.

Golitsyn and Myslecki would argue that Poland's democratic movement was orchestrated and guided by the communists from the start. According to their

252

way of thinking, Solidarity was one of many superficially anti-communist organizations built by the communists. Those who worked closely with the secret police -- like Walesa -- received special publicity. Cameras were put on them. Their faces were broadcast around the world. Such people would build popular organizations under communist control, especially organizations that would be accepted as "liberal" in the West. But the communist bloc would remain in existence, as always, beneath the surface."

The publicity given to this Solidarity Movement must have overshadowed what was said to have been a more authentic opposition group:

"Look at what happened to Farmers' Solidarity," says [Andrew] Suda. "It was a genuine grass roots organization."

As it happened, the Polish secret police could not allow Farmers' Solidarity to survive under Warsaw's controlled democracy. Therefore, in short order, Farmers' Solidarity was afflicted with a rash of mysterious deaths, accidents and arrests -- until that organization ceased to matter."

(By J.R. Nyquist for WorldNetDaily.com in 1999 and 2000, http://www.aisjca-mft.org/suda.pdf).

At the same time everybody agrees that the Solidarity movement was backed enthusiastically by the West, especially the CIA, as even Time magazine acknowledged:

"Now comes Time with a cover story on the "holy alliance" between President Ronald Reagan and Pope John Paul II--their intimate and active collaboration to keep the Solidarity labor union alive in Poland after Brezhnev's henchmen imposed martial law in 1981.

It is a dramatic and even glowing investigative account--under the byline of red-diaper baby Carl Bernstein, no less--detailing how the Church operated as a vast network shielding and nurturing Solidarity's underground activities inside Poland; how the Vatican and the United States Government constantly exchanged information and coordinated many of their actions; and how the United States, especially the CIA and the National Endowment for Democracy, along with the AFL-CIO, provided another lifeline of vital resources."

(http://www.findarticles.com/p/articles/mi_m1282/is_n5_v44/ai_12037629)

Food for thought on the goings on of the Cold War? Are both sides conspiring to hoodwink the people of Poland? Here are two further sources in the same vein:

Red Symphony is the name given to the transcript of the interrogation of Christian G. Rakovsky, onetime Soviet ambassador to Paris, by Stalin's agents in Moscow in 1938. (http://users.cyberone.com.au/myers/red-symphony.html)

Anthony Sutton, *The Best Enemy Money Can Buy* (http://reformed-theology.org/html/books/best_enemy/index.html) is an academic work detailing the astonishing assistance given to the Soviet Union by the West during the Cold War. See also *Wall Street and the Bolshevik Revolution* by the

same author at http://www.reformed-
theology.org/html/books/bolshevik_revolution/index.html .

20. http://www.thetruthseeker.co.uk/article.asp?ID=9202 .

CHAPTER 8

Is Martin McGuinness a British Agent? The new revelations considered.

Maybe it is true then that during the Cold War the general public, both in the East and West, were being treated to a virtual puppet show? Politics was no more than a theatrical production, an artificial left and right split with secretly both groups, at a high level, cooperating against the interests of the overall public? If so it might be mirrored by another conflict closer to home because unfortunately suspicions of British Intelligence agent provocateurs and devious political tricks have led many to believe that the Troubles were all along a similar kind of artificial conflict.

About a year ago there was an upsurge in revelations about British intelligence agency infiltration of (some would say control over) the IRA. This has culminated in a definitive statement from a former British army intelligence officer and handler that Martin McGuinness, widely considered the most powerful IRA figure of the last three decades, is a paid agent of the British government. It came from a former warrant officer in the Force Research Unit who uses the pseudonym Martin Ingram. His real name is well known, he is personally also known to and friendly with many Irish journalists so there is no real doubt about his identity or the fact that he really did serve in the British Army's Intelligence Corps in various places in Northern Ireland in the mid-80s. (The Force Research Unit is sort of a special Irish unit of that Intelligence Corps). In particular he served in Derry and was the handler for Frank Hegarty who infiltrated the Provisional IRA on his behalf during c.1984 and its the story of what happened to Hegarty that seems to confirm for Ingram that McGuinness is in fact a British agent. So basically he was told by his superiors to use Hegarty to get close to McGuinness and that is what happened the thing being that Hegarty rose suspiciously fast in the local IRA hierarchy even though he wasn't all that well known to McGuinness. In a space of only a few months he knew enough to pinpoint a huge arms dump held locally for example. So it seems that Ingram feels that Hegarty rose through the ranks so fast because he was an informer, in other words that McGuinness knew that and was systematically assisting the FRU in its task of infiltrating all ranks of the IRA. Hegarty after a while fled to the UK and was watched by FRU minders until he received word from McGuinness inviting him back to Ireland where he was ultimately to meet his death. The crucial point in this episode is that Ingram says that it was the commander of the FRU who "thought Frank to be a security concern and his depression was a potential problem for the FRU." So according to Ingram no great pains were expended in delaying him in the UK and his return and subsequent death seem to have been designed to solve that problem from the FRU's point of view.

So sure for most people its a conspiracy theory too far to say that McGuinness is a British government agent but the fact is that we now have a person in the know in the British intelligence community in Derry who is saying just that and his opinion must carry some weight. It is not the only reference that points this way and I thought I would point out a few more references for people to mull over before they dismiss this theory out of hand:

1) This is an account of a conversation between the former O/C of the Southern Command of the IRA (while being simultaneously a Garda agent) Sean O'Callaghan, and Brendan Dowd, discussing the opinions of the senior IRA figure Brian Keenan while they were both held in Full Sutton prison in England:

> " 'Does he [Brian Keenan] really think he was set up?' I asked Dowd. Dowd just smiled and said 'He thinks it was McGuinness.' 'He must be off his head,' I said, while at the same time being perfectly aware how Keenan came to such a conclusion. Keenan had been arrested at a security force roadblock just outside Banbridge in County Down, in March 1979. McGuinness was arrested at the same roadblock, but in a different car. Keenan maintained to Dowd that shortly before his arrest McGuinness, who was driving a car that may well have been known to the security forces, waved him down to tell him something that he, Keenan, regarded as unimportant. Keenan was adamant that the car he was in was clean and unknown to the security forces. He thought it possible that McGuinness, spotting that he himself was under surveillance, decided to take the opportunity to get rid of Keenan, who he knew was wanted on specific charges relating to the British bombing campaign. Waving down Keenan's car, he maintained, could have been McGuinness's way of pointing out to the police that there was another 'interesting' car in the area. Even Keenan, paranoid and untrusting as he was, couldn't

really believe that McGuinness was an informer...[goes on to say that the Marxist Keenan was against the Catholic Adams and McGuinness]...

Whether or not there is any substance in Keenan's belief that he was set up by a member of the Army Council, or in Dowd's allegation that Keenan blamed McGuinness in particular, it is certainly true that following Keenan's imprisonment Gerry Adams and Martin McGuinness assumed a degree of control over the republican movement that they could not have dreamed of while Keenan was around...

If Keenan really believed that he was set up by McGuinness, he has done nothing about it since he was released from prison four years ago. Was he simply speculating, thinking out loud? But if that was the case why did he send such a definitive message out of the jail: 'I was set up by a member of the Army Council. I know who it is. Wait until I get out.' "[1]

2) I believe it was Andrew Hunter, the then conservative MP, who stated once in the Sunday Times that he had heard that one of the British army units stationed in Derry in the 70s was given strict instructions to leave McGuinness alone.

3) One book that some claim has spurred a lot of the new thinking on British government control over the IRA is 'The Secret History of the IRA' by the experienced local journalist Ed Moloney. Here are a few quotes from a review of this book in the Telegraph (Oct 12 2002 p.3) by Toby Harnden:

"Is Martin McGuinness a high-level informer who has been working for the British for the past two decades? ...[This is one of] the tantalising questions raised by this important and compelling work, which slices through many of the convenient untruths that have been peddled by the political elites of Belfast, Dublin and London.

...

Moloney also offers remarkable insights into such men as Martin McGuinness, who he says held nearly every senior IRA rank but did much to undermine the organisation.

...

Although the book does not name the high-level informer who was apparently working for the British, there is a strong implication that McGuinness is the most likely "tout". As with a good mafia thriller, the reader is soon guessing which of the protagonists is wearing a wire for the Feds. If Moloney knows, he is not saying. But when he writes that "no one ever suggested Martin McGuinness or any other senior figures at his level were passing on information to the British", one suspects that this was not meant to be taken at face value."

Yet if this was true I respectfully submit that the accepted interpretation of the troubles has to go out the window. Basically its obvious then that the Republican paramilitary groups were just as much in the pocket of the British intelligence agencies as the loyalist groups and yet if that is the case then clearly those agencies, and indeed the occupying British army, had to be there for some other reason than the suppression of terrorism because the 'terrorism' was all along their carefully nurtured baby. My tuppence worth on that question is that the troubles were an Irish version of the Italian 'strategy of tension'. This strategy was so called by the Italian Prime Minister Giulio Andreotti and describes the reason why the Italian intelligence agencies, in alliance with those of the US and the UK, sponsored terrorism in Italy in the 70s and 80s. Basically they wanted to scare people into supporting those agencies and accompanying draconian security legislation etc. Again the story unfolded for the Italian public in much the same way that it has for us here in that first people began to realise that the right wing groups were really just the security agencies out of uniform and then they were later to find out that the left wing Red Brigades, ostensibly the latter's enemy, were also run by the security forces in alliance with the CIA and the P-2 masonic lodge.[2]

But I think furthermore that this revelation, if it is true, that McGuinness is a British agent must in fact also make people think about the whole structure of Irish civil society and not just the paramilitaries. What I mean is that the same intelligence agencies from the UK and the US (and working no doubt through domestic agencies as well, North and South) obviously also attempt to control political parties, media outlets, trade unions, police forces and judiciary etc and the question is have they had as much luck controlling those entities as they have the paramilitaries? Bear in mind they bring a lot of power and money to the table to do this. Ingram says that in the mid 80s he knew of one offer of £50,000 cash being offered to an IRA figure as an initial sweetener to persuade him to inform. If Tom Gilmartin's revelations about some Irish politicians are anything to go by then you have to wonder what you could buy with that kind of money in those circles. Of course those agencies also have huge information sources that they can use to blackmail people with as well and in fact Ingram says that Denis Donaldson was blackmailed when the RUC Special Branch found out that he had been caught stealing on a covert Marks and Spencers security camera.[3] Just look at the recent leadership contest in the Lib-Dem party in Britain and imagine how you could manipulate that race if you had access to the sort of information that modern agencies have access to by electronic and other means.[4]

Ingram provides a glimpse of that kind of infiltration of civil society when he talks about RUC Special Branch running senior agents within the Official and Democratic Unionist Parties where "they could and would be able and willing to exert influence." He says likewise that as regards the UK intel agencies' relationship with Irish government ministers and the Gardaí that "the level of penetration was high including Gardai commissioners." So maybe its sensible for Irish people to ask some hard questions sometimes about the various elements of Irish civil society and without being paranoid maybe we should be cautious if there is too cozy a consensus between this 'establishment' and the policies of the UK or US governments. I include the US because its obviously the home of the most powerful of those agencies as this reference in the Guardian to the CIA's role in the UK illustrates:

> "Indeed, in 1991 journalist Richard Norton-Taylor
> revealed the existence of a list of something like 500
> prominent Britons, including around 90 in the media,
> who were in the employ of the CIA, and paid through
> the old friend of the intelligence services, the BCCI."[5]

There are a lot of rumours out there of course and for example the Phoenix has this to say about Minister for Justice Michael McDowell who is particularly distinguished in criticising the Republican movement including McGuinness:

> "In the present climate of dirty tricks, the Stormont
> controversy and other manoeuvres by shadowy people
> in Britain Intelligence, one is entitled to ask if the same
> people are pulling [Lord] Laird's strings - as well as
> McDowell's."[6]

Without adding or detracting from the obvious implication of the Phoenix's remarks you cannot help thinking that if this was true, taken together with the story on McGuinness, it implies that much of Irish

259

political discourse is a kind of Punch and Judy show with the participants no doubt sharing a great joke at the gullibility of the Irish public as they wait for their checks from the one 'puppet master' !

Further thoughts in the light of more intelligence leaks

One simple point that is worth bearing in mind is that it is apparently accepted among Irish journalists that Sean MacStiofain was an agent of the Gardaí, possibly from 1969.[7] But if that is accepted then why not the allegations against McGuinness since MacStiofain's role and status in the IRA in the early 70s would be directly analogous to McGuinness' for the late 70s and since? Also does that not call into question the people selected by MacStiofain to attend the Cheyne Walk conference in 1972, which includes McGuinness. Presumably he would be expected to select other government agents in order to assist his handlers in controlling the IRA?

In any case it might be worthwhile to summarise where we are in this ongoing controversy. On Sunday 28 May 2006 the northern edition of the Sunday World and the Sunday Tribune revealed a document that Martin Ingram received from a member of RUC Special Branch which it is felt proved that Martin McGuinness was an agent for MI6. It was a transcript of an intercepted phone conversation between McGuinness and his handler, it is a short document reprinted in full here:

"J118: As I said, Patsy (SA3) was all for it, Tommy (SA1) was ready to go, he said he would have no problems asking the crew for their support.

G: Do you think there will be any problem with it?

J118: I know our fella (J119) has everyone geared up for it, he (J119) thinks it is his idea.

G: I think you should push this along as quickly as possible.

J118: Murray (B328) is pushing, starting to ask a lot of questions about Belfast Command.

G: Don't worry, we will look after things in that department, you just concentrate on the checkpoints.

> G: We must have another meeting next week. In the
> meantime you can use the number I gave you in
> updates on the progress of things."

The numbers clearly correspond to computer or file index reference numbers that identify each person of interest. In other words if anybody reading the document wanted to get background information on the person mentioned then they could just punch those numbers into a computer terminal and get the info. The point is that these are not codenames as such, they don't prove that anybody is an agent. G is said to be the MI6 handler, J118 Martin McGuinness, J119 Martin's brother Willie McGuinness, and B328 Sean 'Spike' Murray, Operations Director for Northern Command. It is reported to refer to planning for the 'human bomb' attack on the Coshquin checkpoint in 1990 and that it shows the MI6 handler was the prime mover in that incident. Obviously its a confusing document standing on its own but Martin Ingram says that he has checked it with other sources in the intelligence community who have authenticated it. The document he got also had various intelligence codes and jargon attached that proves its authenticity but which he cannot reveal for fear of compromising his source. The Sunday World newspaper followed the story up the next week reporting that it had a second security source, albeit anonymous, which confirmed the information and added that McGuinness' codename was 'Fisherman'.

So the bottom line is that a lot rests on the interpretation of the document by Ingram - and his sources - but the fact is that Ingram has already been proved right and trustworthy over Stakeknife and quite a number of other issues. Personally I think he has to be authentic when you see this kind of line being put about against him from some security sources who are briefing Jim Cusack:

> "Many [British Intelligence officers who served in the
> North] suffered from high stress levels and nurtured
> suspicions ...Since the ending of the Troubles these
> tensions have evolved into bitterness and anger among
> former members of the intelligence community who
> now wish to reveal the fact that deaths were allowed to
> occur...Many of these police and military intelligence
> officers suffered breakdowns after the Troubles ended
> as a result of the pressure they had been placed under.
> The decision by some to begin to talk about what they
> did and knew is - according to other former senior
> police - a kind of "therapy"."[8]

Frankly once you hear that kind of talk made against Ingram then you know he is cosher. The intelligence agencies are always looking for their slander angle and the 'mad' or 'Walter Mitty' one is particularly popular. I think they are trying to discredit Peter Preston the same way.[9]

More details emerged later about the source of the document. Martin Ingram received it (and other documents not yet revealed, he stated in the radio interview) in a dead letter drop from a member of RUC Special Branch approximately two years ago and apparently at the same time as the DUP received similar but not identical documents which show McGuinness as a British agent. In passing it might be worth pointing out that when Martin McGuinness responded to these allegations he said that it was part of a DUP plot against him. That's as opposed to blaming the British security forces or intelligence agencies which maybe was a little unusual. You might speculate that he did that to anticipate the DUP, preventing them from releasing their documents, because if they revealed them at that point it would look too much like the plot that he was talking about. Its also interesting to note that two years ago there was quite a lot of upheaval in PSNI Special Branch after the head of Special Branch, Bill Lowry, had been sacked.[10]

Martin Ingram also says that during the testimony he gave to the Saville Inquiry the British government seemed particularly anxious that he wouldn't name any agents. He reckons this was because they were nervous that he would name McGuinness at that time three years ago.[11] In any case McGuinness came well out of the Inquiry having fortunately secured the services of Dermot Gleeson (a leading Irish lawyer and one time attendee at Bilderberg meetings) to represent him.

Anyhow for a few weeks this was the topic of the day (although the big media outlets in the Republic were strangely mute for a few days after the story broke and played down the story after that) and this threw up two important voices that agree with the claim that McGuinness is an agent:

1) Raymond Gilmour was an RUC Special Branch agent in the IRA in Derry in the early 80s and he is now on record saying that he feels McGuinness protected him because he was also an agent:

> "I could never understand how I was allowed to run so
> long and do so much damage. Now I suspect that
> McGuinness was looking out for me."

Gilmour in his book also points out how he was advised not to give evidence or implicate McGuinness during his supergrass trial and this apparently wasn't the only time that happened:

> "Statements by another supergrass, Robert Quigley,
> implicated McGuinness in organising IRA activity, but

he was never charged."[12]

2) Fr Denis Faul who, among other things, was at one time chaplain to the Republican prisoners in the Maze, also believed that McGuinness (and most of the IRA leadership?) were British agents:

"Faul often would tell them [warning his pupils], "it will sooner or later emerge that your commanding officer was a tout, and that his commanding officer was a tout too. And whilst you're rotting away, they will be getting off scot-free." If only more imams in Britain today spoke like that to young Muslims tempted by jihad.

Faul's warning was only mildly hyperbolic. He was vindicated when it emerged that two leading Provisionals, Denis Donaldson and Freddie Scappaticci, had been on the British payroll — the tip of an iceberg. And he would have been unsurprised by allegations that Martin McGuinness was a British agent: he had claimed as much to me more than five years ago. "One thing about the Brits," he would say. "Just remember, they play cricket. Nice and long and slow."

This observation brought him little pleasure: he felt that though the British State was clever, it had cynically sold out the ordinary decent Catholics..."[13]

Two further points might be made by way of corroborating what Ingram has said. The first is the point that his handler was said to be from MI6 which is interesting because there have always been rumours of MI6 communication with, and closeness to, the IRA in general and McGuinness in particular e.g. from Liam Clarke:

"Some links to MI6 were even approved by the IRA. McGuinness had a so-called "back channel" to Michael Oatley, a former head of MI6's anti-terrorism operations. Oatley negotiated an IRA ceasefire in 1974-75. After it broke down he left open a secret channel of communication with two intermediaries in Derry, Brendan Duddy and Denis Bradley. This allowed messages to be passed to the IRA and McGuinness...His [McGuinness'] political value, underlined by his hotline to a senior MI6 officer, may be sufficient to explain why McGuinness has often seemed a protected species." [I wonder is that hotline an example of 'hiding things in plain sight'. !lol][14]

From Ed Moloney:

"Perhaps the most surprising aspect of last week's rocket attack on the London headquarters of MI6, apparently by the Real IRA, is that this is the first time that its headquarters, or indeed any building belonging to Britain's foreign spy agency, has been the acknowledged target of an attack by a Republican paramilitary organisation. One possible reason why serves to highlight intriguing aspects of the odd relationship that has existed between the various leaderships of the Provisional Republican movement and members of Britain's Secret Intelligence Services over the years of the Troubles...[the article hints at the closeness of the relationship, and ends:] All this may give a cogent explanation as to why the Provisional IRA never targeted Michael Oatley's colleagues."[15]

From the Phoenix Magazine:

"[Michael Oatley] He first met McGuinness in 1972 in Cheyne Walk, Chelsea, when he was a highflyer at MI6 headquarters in Century House. A year later he became second in command at British Secret Service (MI6) headquarters in Northern Ireland at Laneside, Craigavad. Since then, McGuinness and Oatley have got together regularly over the years in secret, and at one time (during the 1981 hunger strike) met on an almost daily basis. More recently, Oatley and McGuinness met in Donegal in 1990. It was that meeting which sparked the ongoing peace process of the Hume-Adams talks, a Downing Street declaration, and speculation about a peace deal. Officially, Oatley retired as a Controller (one of the highest ranks in the Secret Service) in 1991 on reaching the age of 56. However, never a man to let friendships die, he kept in regular contact with Martin - with consequences which we are now reading about."[16]

By James Casbolt – Former MI6 Agent:

"...many organised crime and terrorist groups and these groups like the IRA are full of MI6 agents."[17]

The second point of corroboration as it were concerns the question of whether or not it was remarkable and suspicious that Frank Hegarty was promoted so rapidly and given access to great secrets despite being known as indiscreet and even known for earlier giving information to the army while he was in the Official IRA. Liam Clarke seems to accept that Ingram's account of this is agreed in Republican circles:

> "IRA veterans agree with Gilmour that McGuinness often promoted suspected informers to positions where they could do most damage. One example was Frank Hegarty, an agent who worked for Martin Ingram. He was suspected of being an informer, but McGuinness personally put him in charge of hiding newly imported weaponry from Libya."[18]

Barry, one of the most distinguished and knowledgable indymedia.ie commentators, in one of his comments has also said that that is the feeling in Derry while during the radio interview Ingram cleverly extracted the same opinion from Eamonn McCann, a friend of Frank Hegarty and neighbour of Martin McGuinness, who admitted that he was "astonished at Franko's progress in the Provisional IRA." Eamonn conceded that Hegarty was "absolutely absolutely" not a discreet or particularly intelligent person, in fact Eamonn says that he was indiscreet "in a way I have never encountered in anybody else" among paramilitaries and that he was "not up to the job" of being an IRA/FRU agent. This then obviously corroborates Martin Ingram's view that his rapid promotion in the IRA was suspicious.

Now for the speculative bit! I was just wondering about one phrase that Ingram used in the radio interview when he said that he doesn't think that McGuinness was motivated by money (he is usually said to be religious, a Catholic figure) and this has got me thinking about what could have caused him to become an agent. While this is just pure speculation I just wonder whether or not he might have succumbed to another weapon in the intelligence agency armoury which is known as the 'false flag' operation. To explain how this works imagine some target called X living in Ballydebob who an intelligence agency wishes to recruit. Say for the sake of argument that he isn't motivated by money, is not the sort that would be easily intimidated and is suspicious and unsympathetic to intelligence agencies and the security forces in general. But a survey of his loyalties and lifestyle has thrown up the fact that he is a diehard supporter of the local stamp collecting club, hypothetically speaking !lol. So what the agency might do is that it will get him to work for them under false pretences in that it will encourage him to do some act thinking that it was for the good of the stamp collecting club rather than the agency. They would do this either by re-cruiting his superior or colleague in the club or by using somebody from the international stamp collecting club who is on their books. (Philip Agee in his book on the CIA, *Inside the Company*, says that the CIA control a huge list of international organisations like that, trade uni-ons, student bodies etc). Of course after a period of time if the guy has done anything illegal then they will blackmail him, threatening to charge him over the illegal act or expose him to irate colleagues, and this blackmail will keep him working for them after he has discovered that he was conned.

This has got me thinking about the problems in the Catholic Church and I would just like to say at the outset that I, a Catholic, derive no pleasure from pointing out these issues. Unfortunately it is increasingly obvious that some corruption in the Catholic Church has been around since the time when the Troubles started and possibly involved Vatican relations with Ireland at some point. Consider this kind of statement from Fr Brian d'Arcy:

> "This is the man [head of the Legionaries of Christ and the subject of 'well founded' accusations of child ab-use] who accompanied John Paul II to Mexico in 1979, 90 and 93. Despite knowing that these accusations had been made against him, Pope John Paul gave a public tribute to him calling him, "an efficacious guide to youth." And as late as 2004 John Paul II congratulated him for, "intense, generous, and fruitful priestly min-istry."...[earlier in the article:] If you want to find out why the sex abuse scandals were handled badly by the church that's the reason. The clerical club, right to the very top, closed ranks and destroyed the credibility of our precious church."[19]

Clearly a serving Catholic priest is not going to write that in a mass cir-culation newspaper unless he feels strongly that there is huge corruption at the Vatican level of the church. It is this background that must be considered when you hear that a former member of US Army Counter Intelligence in Italy in 1947, William Gowen, in a deposition given as part of a court case earlier this year, has apparently claimed that the then Monsignor Montini, the future Pope Paul VI, was considered by the Americans to be an OSS/CIA asset. Possibly an agent of none other than James Angleton.[20] While I believe this to be definitely a false charge it nonetheless could have been characteristic of the close rela-tionship that the OSS and then CIA thought they had with the Vatican at that time and since. It also ties in with the many stories of cooperation between the Vatican and the CIA e.g. in relocating German political refugees after WWII and in Poland in the 80s. It also might be linked with the many other allegations of shady dealings at the Vatican made by people like the Kerry Jesuit Fr Malachi Martin.[21]

Fascinating, I hear you say :-), but how does that fit in with Ireland and the IRA? The point is that the former personal secretary of this Cardinal Montini, Archbishop Alibrandi, as the Papal Nuncio to Ireland from 1969-1989 was very close and supportive of the IRA leadership [22] and was lobbying the Irish government on Ulster politics as early as 1970.[23] Other stories circulate which must have involved the Papal Nuncio in 1970:

> "Take a look at the Timewatch programme on this shown on BBC2 in 1996. They had witnesses who said the CIA had a meeting with the Provo high command to be and leaders of the Catholic hierarchy in Co. Fermanagh in 1970."[24]

So I know its speculation but I would suggest that if the CIA are the close colleagues of MI6 in this destabilisation, as e.g. the former UK Defence Minister Enoch Powell stated,[25] then it was probably done through their agents in the high ranks of the Catholic Church.

And you thought the Republican Movement had problems!lol

Footnotes

Martin Ingram's recent revelations are contained in an article at cryptome (http://cryptome.org/ingram-spies.htm), an interview with Radio Free Eireann in New York (http://archive.wbai.org/files/mp3/060114_133008rfeireann.MP3) and a long discussion at the slugger o'toole website (http://www.sluggerotoole.com/index.php/weblog/comments/4431/P0/). The later radio interview mentioned is at: http://irishfreedom.net/RFE/radio %20free%20eireann.htm (Radio Free Eireann, New York, 3/6/06), the other article on indymedia: http://www.indymedia.ie/article/76319 , and the Sunday World story: http://cryptome.quintessenz.at/mirror/mcguinness-spy.htm .

1. Sean O'Callaghan, *The Informer* (London, 1998), p.264.

2. You can read a more elaborate discussion of the strategy of tension in the Irish context in Brian Nugent, *Orwellian Ireland* (Co.Meath, 2008), Chapter 4 available at http://oireland.tripod.com , with many international comparisons in the Appendix.

3. He was working as a security guard on contract for them at the time.

4. Even Tony Blair was an agent of MI5 before he became PM: http://tinyurl.com/d9b32 which is the Bristol 'Evening Post' of 13 September 2005. This is from David Shayler who reviewed his MI5 file, see http://www.bilderberg.org/sis.htm#agent .

5. http://www.cpa.org.au/garchve04/1181miners.html Guardian May 5 2004.

6. The Phoenix Dec 16 2005.

7. http://saoirse32.blogsome.com/2005/11/26/sean-mac-stiofain/ noting Liam Clarke's article of the Sunday before Mac Stiofain died and Jim Cusack in the Sunday Independent 21 Dec 2003 http://britishcollusion.com/monaghan14.html .

8. Sunday Independent 4 June 2006.

9. http://www.indymedia.ie/article/76492 .

10. He was interviewed here: http://www.phoblacht.net/lowry1.html . He seemed pretty tight lipped about it all saying at one point: "Were they [the IRA] extensively penetrated? The former RUC man smiled, but refused to be drawn. 'Penetration of all terrorist organisations was good.'"

11. http://www.martiningram.blogspot.com/ .

12. Sunday Times 4 June 2006 p.5.

13. The Times 23 June 2006 http://www.timesonline.co.uk/article/0,,6-2239124,00.html .

14. Sunday Times op. cit.

15. Sunday Tribune 24 Sept 2000
http://www.bytecenter.com/members/bbs/RepublicanAlternative/index.cgi?
read=3406 .

16. 14 Jan 1994 quoted in Brian Nugent, *Orwellian Ireland* (Co.Meath, 2008),
beginning of Chapter 3, available at http://oireland.tripod.com .

17. http://www.thetruthseeker.co.uk/article.asp?ID=4540 I know this article
stands on its own in the sense that there is no way to prove that Casbolt was
genuinely in MI6 but at least as part of a pattern surely you cannot ignore
sources like this. Incidentally there is no reason to shy away from his
statements about the drug trade, books like Rodney Stich, *Drugging America*
(Alamo, 2005)
(available free at http://www.defraudingamerica.com/list_of_books.html)
show that he is not alone in claiming that MI6 and the CIA have an
undocumented but powerful role in that area.

18. Sunday Times op.cit.

19. Sunday World 11 June 2006 p.71.

20. radio interview with Attorney Jonathan Levy 27 Feb 2006
http://mp3.rbnlive.com/Greg/0602/20060227_Mon_Greg1.mp3 and
http://mp3.rbnlive.com/Greg/0602/20060227_Mon_Greg2.mp3 .The
background to the courtcase is at www.vaticanbankclaims.com .

21. Malachi Martin was from a Republican family in Ballylongford in Kerry, a
brother of the UCD historian and conservationist F.X. Martin
(http://www.historyireland.com/magazine/features/feat5.html). For his
shocking insights into corruption at the Vatican see e.g. the reviews of the his
books on Amazon (like at http://www.amazon.com/gp/product/customer-
reviews/0385492316/002-7249638-6075210) and an interview with William H
Kennedy, a friend of Malachi's, at
http://mp3.rbnlive.com/Greg/0605/20060502_Tue_Greg2.mp3 . A Dominican
friend of his, Fr Charles C. Fiore, says that: "He knew the Popes from Roncalli
to Montini to Wojtyla, and on several occasions met secretly with John Paul II,
to whom he gave a copy of *Keys of This
Blood*."(http://www.unitypublishing.com/newswire/fiore1.html) Fr. Fiore
himself has been trying to highlight the type of abuses that we have seen in
Ireland: http://www.worldnetdaily.com/news/article.asp?ARTICLE_ID=26940
There are though also disturbing allegations made against Malachi Martin here:

http://angelqueen.org/forum/viewtopic.php?t=14932 .

22. http://en.wikipedia.org/wiki/Gaetano_Alibrandi and
http://www.findarticles.com/p/articles/mi_qn4161/is_20051002/ai_n15645885

23. http://gazette.ireland.anglican.org/150202/panorama150202.htm .

24. http://www.indymedia.ie/newswire.php?story_id=72419 .

25. Brian Nugent, *Orwellian Ireland* (Co.Meath, 2008), Chapter 4 footnotes
111 and 114 available at http://oireland.tripod.com .

CHAPTER 9

Crisis and Corruption in the Catholic Church

"A Vatican-based bishop observed somewhat ruefully, 'these rules [on the paedophile scandals] are going to give the appearance of a "cover-up". That's because they are a cover-up.' "

This chapter is just an attempt to describe in more detail these allegations of corruption in the Catholic Church and to speculate on how the Vatican intends to juggle the competing interests of the two streams of thought within the Church.

There is obviously right now two wings or instincts within the Catholic Church, one traditionalist and one modernist. Obviously modernists feel that the church should build on the openness and reconstruction of the Vatican II period ('glasnost' and 'perestroika'!) and continue to modernise those old and traditional practices like the unique role of male unmarried priests and opposition to contraception etc. Maybe it could also be said that modernists feel that the church should move with the times and be in step with its flock even if the latter is outside the normal parameters of traditional Christian teaching.

Until maybe the last year or two the traditionalist wing wasn't as well known and might be worth looking at in more detail. It might seem a strange way to approach this but I think the easiest way to see how the traditional movement looks at things is to see their religion as in a kind of permanent state of war against Satan and Satanism, which would be I think in contrast to the modernist approach. In the same way that Satanists use symbols, language, colours, feast days and elaborate rites the traditional church tries to use the exact words, symbols etc in their rites that were handed down over the centuries since biblical times. (Just to digress in case people don't believe that Satanists - and followers of Pagan or esoteric religions which I apologise in advance for lumping in together here, just for the sake of simplicity [1] - use symbols etc quite a lot I would point out the use of: hand signals, like the horned hand, and 'V' shapes [2]; monuments, like obelisks and obelisk type structures especially with lights on top because Lucifer is considered the light bearer; colours, like a Black and Red combination according to the experienced journalist Piers Compton anyway [3]; feast days, Equinoxes, Solstices, Lammas (1st Aug), Walpurgnis (1st May)

271

etc; geometric shapes, like star shapes (especially if upside down of course) and triangles (including a small triangle made from three dots); phrases, like reborn or regeneration and symbols associated with that type of rebirth (like butterflies and the Phoenix); and numbers like 666 obviously.) In a way there is an ancient spiritual war going on here that the wider public is not much aware of. Its interesting too that Satanists often use Christian institutions or rituals and twist them around so as to mock them (like the upturned cross) showing again the importance of symbols and words in this ancient war. Therefore traditional Catholics want to feel armed in this battle with all their symbols and rites that traditionally aided them, for example what they consider the true rite of the mass,[4] the myriad symbols and images in old churches [5] and the true apostolic succession from biblical times.[6]

Again I appreciate that's not exactly the normal way of looking at this modernist/traditionalist split and I'm not trying to minimise the importance of other things to traditionalists like e.g. the well known, and not symbolic, teachings of old catechisms etc its just that the above description captures the atmosphere of this split better than any other way of looking at it? Traditionalists feel more comfortable looking at it as a kind of supernatural phenomenon than modernists I think. Maybe Irish people in general have always looked upon it like that too, in Ireland its always been a kind of supernatural fight over souls like this, with great traditions about holy wells, high crosses, pattern days, Marian shrines, and ancient prayers and sayings (like 'Dia dhuit' and 'Dia 's Muire dhuit') helping to fight off evil rather than the purely scientific and rational approach that maybe was more common elsewhere. Every turn of the page of Irish history brings out some English commentator complaining about the priest ridden superstitious Irish, about their supposed lack of reason and practicality about these things, but the Irish people always ignored them and stuck to the religion that St Patrick brought to them all those years ago at Tara. This way of looking at it then explains maybe things like traditionalists insisting on male celibate clergy - celibacy being one of the traditional cardinal virtues in the Catholic Church - because that's the only true way the rite of the mass was to be performed according to ancient tradition while the modernist group might talk about inclusiveness and practical issues like loneliness among the clergy.

The Catholic Church in the Vatican is now being assailed by both these viewpoints. On the one hand the modernists, and most of the establishment in the West, are pressing for the advent of things like women clergy and married priests while the traditionalist movement, which rejects this position, is growing increasingly influential. Like

Gaul - as traditionalists will recognise! lol - the Catholic traditionalist movement can be divided into three parts:

1) Independents. There are small organisations, and many individual priests, who celebrate the old mass completely outside the orbit of the Vatican and who do not recognise Benedict XVI as a legitimate Pope. This includes organisations like the SSPV - which broke off from the SSPX in the US - and IMRI and a few others. Its hard to generalise but many of these groups believe in a 'sedevacationist' position which means that they recognise no Pope, that the seat of the Papacy is vacant.

2) Indults. At various times since Vatican II the Catholic Church has authorised some groups to continue to say the old Latin mass, a permission that's known as an indult. In some cases there are Latin masses held in dioceses with the permission of the local bishop (e.g. Cardinal O'Connell gave permission for such a mass to be held at St Audeons in Dublin, before Archbishop Martin handed over that well attended building to the Polish church) as indult masses - and are served by the local clergy or normal religious orders - as well as masses held by special indult orders like the FSSP. Now of course there is much talk that the Pope's Motu Proprio has granted a kind of universal indult, but this is much disputed [7] and anyway its clear by now that it has not led to any great enthusiastic embracing of the Latin mass by the established dioceses or Orders.

3) The Society of St Pius the X (SSPX). This is a group that was founded by Archbishop Lefebvre in Switzerland and is one of the oldest and by far the biggest of the traditional groups. In practice, and cutting through a whole pile of complications!, this group falls somewhere between the other two positions. It is not officially part of the established Catholic Church - Archbishop Lefebvre and the four SSPX bishops were excommunicated by the Vatican - but in truth cordial enough relations seem to exist here and very significantly SSPX recognise Benedict XVI as a true Pope and pray for him in their masses. For these reasons it is treated with some suspicion by a few in the independent camp, and anyway regularly comes under fire for what its critics consider its dictatorial disciplinary atmosphere.[8]

It would be nice I think to write an article speculating how the holy Cardinals in the Vatican were going to conscientiously navigate their flock around these conflicting positions in the years ahead, but my heart isn't in it. Speaking for myself I think that the current leadership of the international Catholic Church is being badly assailed by corrupt forces. I apologise for being so blunt but that's the only conclusion that I can arrive at anyway, based on the experiences of the last few years. (And I absolutely and genuinely mean no disrespect to the very many good priests, religious, bishops, Cardinals - and all recent Popes - that are out there.)

Look at their relationship to the mafia for starters. The Vatican bank, which is totally controlled by senior Curia officials - known as the 'Pope's piggy bank' ! [9] - for decades now has been part and parcel of mafia operations worldwide. This is described here by Tony Gambino from the famous mafia family in New York, and a grandson of Lucky Luciano:

> "The Vatican officials, federal judges, top politicians all used to get regular pay-offs from the Gambino Family and, in fact, the Vatican and U.S. government make more money off the illegal drug trade than we did.

> That is why I am talking after just getting out of jail after 20 years. I am talking because people need to know the U.S. government and the Vatican are more dangerous and corrupt than the Mafia ever was.

> For example, I know for a fact the Cardinal in Palermo runs the Sicilian mob and former Cardinal Spellman of New York was considered the Vatican's American God-father since he pulled the strings and had his hands deep into organized crime." [10]

Also a recent book by the highly respected David Yallop elaborates further on these type of connections:

> "The 'privileged citizens' [who had Vatican bank accounts] also included the Mafia family Corleone. Their bagman to the Vatican bank was the 'Puppet Master' himself, Licio Gelli. Francesco Mannoia, the chief heroin-refining expert for the Corleone family, was one of a number of the family who learned of this arrangement from the then Godfather of Sicily, Stefano Bontate. He would later testify to this further link between the Mafia and the Vatican bank." [11]

It is furthermore very difficult to make excuses for the Vatican leaders with respect to these scandals because after all there is pretty much only one international bank based in the Vatican and it was headed by Archbishop Marcinkus, John Paul II's former bodyguard and, it was claimed, close friend. For decades this Pope kept him on as head of the bank and refused to hand him over to answer the numerous court proceedings taken against him in the US and Italy. Incidentally it goes without saying that throughout this time the mafia were involved in a full range of horrible goings on like murder, kidnapping, torture, prostitution, loan sharking, drug dealing etc etc., and this must have been well known to everybody at the Vatican. Unfortunately, maybe the only logical way of looking at this blind eye approach by the Vatican officials is to consider that they were also corrupt?

Then you have the huge paedophile scandals that everybody knows about. Considering the incredible scale of these scandals it is surely a mystery how the church authorities couldn't have rooted out this abuse long since, as the Belfast priest Fr Patrick McCafferty remarks:

> "The institution of the Catholic Church is - in so many ways - sinful, sick and dysfunctional. ...
>
> Those predators who happened to be priests and religious - along with their conspiring and conniving superiors and bishops - have actually abused and betrayed Christ Himself in the persons of His little ones.
>
> Jesus is very explicit in what He thinks of those who have scandalised "any of these my little ones". (Matthew Ch. 18:5-6 and verses 10-11). How could so many cardinals, archbishops, bishops, priests and religious have behaved so scandalously in the face of innocent suffering?
>
> How could they have so negated the essential message of the Gospel - both clerical abusers and those in positions of authority who sought to cover up their crimes - by the way they behaved towards the victims?"[12]

Again how could this have gone on so long and at such a scale without the protection of senior Church officials? I would suggest that only people like the Papal Nuncios and the heads of important congregations in Rome could have had the power to protect those paedophiles over the years, maybe because they themselves were guilty of that type of activity? Of course we are told that there were administrative failures etc that have all been ironed out now e.g. by the Catholic hierarchy in Ireland appointing a special Child Protection Office to deal swiftly with these cases. But it turns out that not long ago a Village article [13] described how the Director of that office, Paul Bailey, systematically covered up details of the abuse of Peter McCloskey, so you'd have to wonder at how sincere these changes really are. In the US meanwhile the Catholic bishops in 2002 set up a National Review Board to oversee their treatment of these issues chaired by the former Oklahoma Governor Frank Keating, only to find that the latter resigned the following year calling the bishops: "a Mafia, a criminal organization, not my Church."[14]

My guess is that the position of the Papacy in the West mimics what happened to the Orthodox church in the East under Communism. At that time obviously the Soviets were oppressing the Christian religion, and confiscating their churches, but at the same time they managed to infiltrate the Orthodox church and it is well known now that many of the Russian Orthodox patriarchs were secretly KGB agents. The KGB's control over the church became such a scandal that Russian emigrants were forced to launch a schism in order to try and preserve a true and authentic Orthodox church, a schism which has only now been healed in the last few years. Clearly the Vatican commanded a very strategic position during the Cold War and just like the Orthodox church must have become the focus of efforts by intelligence agencies to try and control it. There is quite a lot of evidence out there that the church was infiltrated like this at a high level starting from around the 50s and continuing especially since Vatican II.[15] Don't be fooled by their public opposition to Communism during the Cold War! There is even talk of a secret agreement between the Vatican and the USSR signed at Metz in France before Vat.II and anyway all you have to do is look at the treatment of Cardinal Mindszenty in Hungary to see the real instincts of the modern Vatican.[16] As Det. Jim Rothstein points out (quoted in the last chapter) these Cold War intelligence agencies - from East and West - had a vested interest in fostering these scandals - financial and sexual - because it helped them in blackmailing church officials and in the long run discredits the church which might also have been their aim. In any case for what its worth that is this writers opinion on why some of those church leaders were so negligent in allowing those scandals to occur, because at a high level - but not the highest! - some had succumbed to the prevailing corruption.

I think too that the actions of uncorrupt forthright church leaders would look a lot different to the current atmosphere. For me such a person would be bending over backwards to expose all these scandals and fire out of the church anyone remotely guilty of such horrific activities. Its interesting in that regard to see the short papacy of Pope John Paul I. There have been countless well informed reports [17] that that Pope was on the verge of clearing out corruption in the Vatican bank, sacking all church figures connected to Freemasonry - traditional enemies of the Catholic Church and currently said to be very powerful in the Vatican [18] - before his highly suspicious death only 33 days after taking office. Its now said as well that this Pope was in contact with a priest in New York who was trying to expose some of the paedophile problems. The Pope was reported to have personally telephoned the priest begging him to step up his activities and promising him indulgences if he did so.[19] While individual Popes cannot be responsible for everything in such a huge Church nonetheless is there not a gulf here between that type of leadership and what we sometimes have seen from modern Church leaders?

Hence this writer's tuppence worth is that the modern Catholic Church is to a depressing extent a paid up member of the corrupt global forces that are so powerful and so evident in the modern age. It emphasises things like climate change, see for example the importance Trocaire put on this in its Lenten campaign [20] - which is very much part of the globalists agenda because it provides an intellectual excuse for a world government; it has been accused of aggressively encouraging migration inflows - an aim of the globalists because it weakens the internal cohesion of nation states - into the US [21] and is quite prominent in supporting the big influx into Ireland especially from Poland, for example with suspicious speed it set up 125 regular Polish mass sites and established Polish chaplaincies in all dioceses.[22] The instinct then of some of the leaders in the Vatican seems to be not to preserve those truths that Irish people have been so attached to for centuries but rather to crush them in order to create an oecumenical world religion. Even the current Pope, while a Cardinal, was advised by some to be a member of a mysterious oecumenical group in Switzerland that even included Neil Bush the brother of the US President! [23] This process has progressed quite a bit too since Vatican II as Catholicism has begun to resemble Protestantism. The new mass after all very much resembles an Anglican service and the new reordered Catholic churches are indistinguishable from their Protestant counterparts. (This however is not to dispute the noble aspects of the oecumenical movement that Pope Benedict rightly favours.)

But now they have a problem. You see up to this the Catholic Church could safely ignore the traditionalist leanings of many of their congregation because basically those people had no where to go to if they were unhappy with the Church. The traditional Catholic movement, up to very recently, was minuscule when compared to the size of the official Catholic Church. It is hard to get exact figures, or survey data, but I would suggest that the whole traditionalist movement worldwide, until about the mid 90s, was probably smaller than a mid sized Irish diocese in terms of numbers of priests etc.[24] Think of a flea buzzing around an elephant and you get the general idea! But this is now changing dramatically because all the traditionalist groups continue to grow, some exponentially some by bits and pieces, while the established Catholic Church is almost collapsing, in the first world at any rate. For example to compare the two you could take the Florida based Most Holy Trinity Seminary which was established in 1995 by about 4 traditional priests led by Rev Sanborn. Although still quite a penniless group - they are currently housed in trailers as they build a proper seminary - they nonetheless ordain about 1 or 2 priests a year and now have 19 seminarians and five more to join next year.[25] Even this very small group could then be compared very favourably to the whole Archdiocese of Dublin which, to service its 200 parishes and 1 million people, ordained only 16 priests in the 8 years from 1999 to 2006, including none at all in 2005 for the first time in its long recorded history.[26] Again looking at this rapid contraction in the Catholic Church consider that in the US in 1965, at the time of Vatican II, there were 49,000 seminarians studying for the priesthood and in 2002 there were only 4,700.[27] Meanwhile in Ireland in 1965 there was 1,375 ordinations [28] while the current situation is that:

> "In 2005, 199 Irish priests died, whereas only eight priests were ordained (Intercom magazine, July/August2006). And this does not take into account clergy who have left the active ministry. These statistics are catastrophic. And they will get only worse...And the other tragedy for the church is that there is no short or medium-term solution to this crisis. The number of seminarians in training is tiny and, unless something entirely unexpected happens, will not increase any time soon."[29]

Compare that to the growth of the traditionalist movement, breaking it down into the three categories noted above:

Independent

The Instituto Mater Boni Consilii, or the Institute of the Mother of Good Counsel, which broke off from SSPX in 1985 starting with four priests now "the Mass is celebrated in 15 different places in Italy (including Rome), 6 in France, 1 in Belgium, 1 in Netherlands and [an]other in Argentina."[30]

Congregatio Mariae Reginae Immaculatae (CMRI) headquartered at

Spokane, Washington State, founded between 1967 and 1970 with about 6 priests,[31] currently: "The Congregation of Mary Immaculate Queen serves 29 churches and chapels in the United States, Canada and New Zealand. They also operate a seminary in Omaha, Nebraska, while the Sisters' motherhouse is located in Spokane, Washington."[32]

Based originally in New York the Society of St. Pius V (SSPV) had 6 priests - including Kelly - in 1993 when Fr Kelly was consecrated a bishop.[33] Now they celebrate masses at some 23 locations across the US.[34] Most of these religious groups also have orders of nuns and brothers affiliated to them which have also expanded, like the Daughters of Mary attached to the SSPV which was founded in 1984 on 14 acres in the Catskill Mountains. They started with 3 novices and 7 postulants and now have 49 members based in 3 locations.[35]

In the late 1970s three traditional priests formed the Union Catholica Trento in Mexico sometime before 1976. Later known as the Priestly Society of Trent they founded a seminary in 1985 with 5 seminarians and are now said to have "around 30 priests, 20 seminarians, 50 sisters, 12 priories and 20 churches and many more missions served on an irregular basis."[36]

Indult

The Priestly Fraternity of St Peter (FSSP), headquartered in Fribourg, Switzerland, started with 12 priests in 1988 and in 2005 it was reported to have "194 priests and 115 seminarians in 50 dioceses spread among Australia, Austria, Benin, Canada, France, Germany, Great Britain, Italy, Nigeria, Poland, Switzerland, and the USA".[37]

The Institute of Christ the King Sovereign Priest, based near Florence, was originally started by only two priests in Gabon in 1990 and now their website boasts that they have:

> "Thirty-five houses in ten countries, fifty priests, and over sixty seminarians in fifteen years are perhaps sufficient proof that the Institute is on the right path within the Church."[38]

SSPX

In 1977 SSPX had some 40 priests in one seminary, Écone in Switzerland,[39] while

> "today, the society has six seminaries and more than 500 priests in its ranks worldwide. It is active in 60 countries, including Ireland, and claims more than a million followers. In Ireland, the society has churches in Athlone, Dun Laoghaire and Cork, and its priests

celebrate regular Masses in six other chapels."[40]

Bottom line is that the established Catholic Church is almost collapsing in some areas while the traditionalist groups are, in places anyway (especially France), growing at a dramatic rate. This means that in the last few years the Vatican has felt the need, for the first time, to address the wishes of the traditionalists firstly for fear that their whole flock could disappear in that direction. Secondly, and more importantly, they need to crush the traditionalist opposition before they can turn wholeheartedly in this globalist direction that they are headed in. Put simplistically what they are doing, I think, is stamping out the opposition, and potential opposition, coming from their right before they can safely turn to their left. What they might hope for is that the SSPX could deepen their control over the independent traditionalist camp and that then in time the Society could rejoin the church, bringing this group under the control of these, unfortunately sometimes, corrupt powers. Once they are safely back under the Vatican's control corrupt officials can always destroy the ancient liturgy and practices by a thousand bureaucratic cuts and edicts like some say they are already doing to the FSSP via Rule 1411.[41] After all the Motu Proprio mass has only been used for a few months and has already been changed (the Good Friday prayers) to accommodate oecumenical sensitivities and anyway this rate of change is all of a piece with a church that has recently abolished Limbo (which dates from St Gregory Nanzianzus of the 4th century) and updated the seven Cardinal Sins (unchanged since Pope Gregory in the 5th century). Looking at this it is surely a stretch to say then that all the Church leaders are following Pope Benedict XVI's genuine traditionalist leadership? Maybe some hope to manipulate it to pull in the SSPX which again would leave traditionalist Catholics with no home to go to if they opposed any new changes that the church might be considering? [42] The Catholic congregation, and maybe some priests, could not then leave the church in response to any dramatic changes that might be in the offing because there would be no, large anyway, organisation that they could join? So maybe that is the plan of some, i.e. that some officials are more interested in controlling the SSPX than the positive religious aspects, which is certainly what motivates Pope Benedict.

Such are the woes of the Church. But there is no more Lazarus institution in the world than the Church in Ireland which is well known to have preserved the faith even when the whole of Europe had lost it at the end of the Barbarian invasions. Elizabethan executions and laws, Cromwellian devastations and 18th century Penal laws didn't wipe out the Catholic Church in Ireland so it remains to be seen if corruption and an anti-clerical world view can flatten it this time! This writers tuppence worth is that ordinary Irish Catholics will have to start looking a lot more sceptically about the activities and motivation of the leaders of this Church, and what they are being asked to do with respect to updating old churches for example, if they want it to survive for much longer. I thought I would close with this quotation from a French nurse that treated a high up Communist agent in the Vatican and who was inspired in part by the famous adherence of the Irish to their old faith:

"Which, for example has kept the Irish Catholics in ghettos for four centuries, where laws pretending to be legitimate and sacred acted as a barbed wire fence.

Not that I am Irish ...But the Irish, without being aware of it, have helped me to show some courage...
No, the very holy virtue of obedience is today the extremely powerful weapon that our enemies, who pretend to be our friends, make use of against what we were, to put up in its stead, what they have decided to have us become.

In short, this word "become" can be described, because it is known; it already has four centuries of existence, and it is called Protestantism.

There it is: We are invited bit by bit, little obedience by little obedience, from false humility to false remorse, from deceitful charity to deceptive ambiguity, from words disguised as a double-edged word, of which "yes" is "no" and "no" is "yes" - we are invited, I say, to pretend to remain good Catholics all the while becoming perfect Protestants."[43]

Footnotes

The quote at the beginning is from David Yallop, *The Power and the Glory* (London, 2007), p.315.

1. Again I don't wish to cause offence by this but I think traditional Catholicism would see itself at war with all these disparate esoteric and pagan religions which is why it makes sense to put them together here, even though its really too simplistic to group them like this.

2. http://www.truecatholic.org/pope/car-200412.htm#hands quoting mostly from Dr Cathy Burns, *Masonic and Occult Symbols Illustrated* (Mt Carmel, PA , 1999). For a description of occult star shapes see Fr Luigi Villa, *Paul VI...Beatified?* (Brescia, 1998), appendix II available at http://www.sheddinglight.info/archives_paul_vi.beatified.pdf .

3. http://www.catholicvoice.co.uk/brokencross/PartTwo.htm .

4. For a description of how the new Catholic Church is systematically stripping out those old symbols from Irish churches see "reorganisation and destruction of irish catholic churches" at http://www.archiseek.com/content/showthread.php?t=4691&page=153 , which is an article with 153 pages, and http://blogs.telegraph.co.uk/ukcorrespondents/holysmoke/august2007/stjosephs church.htm .

5. As regards the doctrinal and liturgical criticisms that traditionalists make against the new mass see e.g. the statement by the SSPV in 1984: http://www.geocities.com/orthopapism/sspv.html , the letter of Cardinals Ottaviani - the then head of the Vatican's Holy Office, the office in charge of protecting the faith - and Bacci written to the Pope on 25 September 1969: http://www.stjosephschurch.net/OttavianiIntervention.htm , and the Easter 1982 statement signed by 25 priests in Campos, Brazil http://www.geocities.com/SSPXCath/campos.html , and here the modern mass is compared to the Anglican Service: http://www.geocities.com/Athens/Rhodes/3543/novus.htm . Another important critic of the post Vatican II church is Dr Rama Coomaraswamy, one of his articles is available here: http://www.wandea.org.pl/arianism.html , and also you can see these articles by Bishop Sanborn: http://www.catholicrestoration.org/faq.htm . See also Fr James F Wathen, *The Great Sacrilege* (Rockford, 1971), available at http://www.dailycatholic.org/2004tgs.htm and Patrick Henry Omlor, *Questioning the Validity of the Masses using the New, All-English Canon* (Reno, 1968), available at http://www.novusordowatch.org/omlor/index.htm , and also see the writings of Fr Paul Trinchard like this one: http://www.dailycatholic.org/issue/07Apr/apr22tre.htm . For ongoing commentary from the traditionalist perspective see http://www.novusordowatch.org/archive.htm , and

http://www.traditio.com/comment/com0710.htm .

6. http://www.rore-sanctifica.org/texts-in-english.html .

7. For a critical look at the Motu Proprio see the article on it by Rev Kevin Vaillancourt in The Catholic Voice September 2007 http://www.strc.org/September%202007.pdf and Fr. Basilio Meramo, *Under the Appearance of Good, the Devil Poses as an Angel of Light* (Orizaba, Mexico, 13 Dec 2007), available at http://www.traditio.com/comment/com0802.htm .

8. The fact that it recognises Benedict XVI clearly puts it in an awkward and maybe self contradictory position. This is in contrast to the other two groups who can more easily shrug off the charge of schism: the independents see the existing Catholic Church as usurped by some anti-Catholic group (its fre-quently said to be the Freemasons) and generally recognise no Pope after Pius XII as legitimate and hence they aren't in schism with a church that they don't recognise anyway; while the indult groups recognise, and are in full accord with, the established Roman church so their position is very clear too. But SSPX see Benedict XVI as the true Pope and yet still do not consider them-selves in schism despite the fact that their bishops are excommunicated and they don't abide by Papal edicts. You cannot help thinking that this position makes them overly anxious to reach some accord with the Vatican. In recent times it has led to considerable drama within the SSPX as it tries to work its way through these contradictions.
(This 1997 letter by a former SSPX priest shows the contradictions in their position: http://www.catholicrestoration.org/library/letter_neville.htm . This is also Bishop Sanborn's view: "Many Catholics have accepted their line of recognizing Wojtyla as pope, but at the same time acting as if he does not exist. This is not a Catholic position, and it induces people, especially the young, to have a contempt for the Roman Pontiff....the principles upon which Archbishop Lefebvre founded the SSPX lead ultimately to their reunion with the Novus Ordo [meaning the Catholic Church as governed from the modern Vatican]." (http://www.catholicrestoration.org/newsletter/02_may.htm .)

According to Fr Michel Marchiset, a former SSPX and now independent priest, Bishops Fellay and Williamson are now involved in a good cop bad cop routine as they both aim to bring SSPX into the Vatican's orbit, the latter operating un-der cover of claiming to do the opposite (http://www.virgo-maria.org/D-Mgr-Williamson-leurre/index_mgr_williamson_leurre.htm). Maybe in the long run the much maligned Archbishop Thuc - the brother of the Vietnamese leader Diem - could emerge as an equally important figure in the Traditionalist move-ment as Archbishop Lefebvre (for Thuc see http://www.dailycatholic.org/issue/06Jul/jul26ttt.htm).

9. As stated by Attorney Jonathan Levy who was interviewed on the

Investigative Journal on 27 Feb 2006
http://mp3.rbnlive.com/Greg/0602/20060227_Mon_Greg2.mp3 .
He is taking a case against the Vatican representing the government of Ukraine, and others including many from Croatia, relating to gold taken at the end of WWII. He describes there the origin of the Vatican bank as "the perfect money laundering machine." The CIA also uses the Vatican bank according to him. He describes how "some people say Satanists" have even infiltrated the Vatican.

10.   http://www.arcticbeacon.com/articles/26-Sept-2007.html   and
http://firstamendmentradio.com/mp3/GSIJ_WED2.MP3 . Det Jim Rothstein had many run ins with Cardinal Spellman when he was working for the NYPD and he concludes that that Cardinal was "probably the biggest criminal I ever ran into."
(Jim Rothstein interviewed by Greg Szymanski on the Investigative Journal Monday 15 Oct 2007.)

11. Continuing the quotation:
"This mutually convenient arrangement came to a dramatic halt in 1981 when police officers raided Gelli's palatial villa in Arezzo and his office at the Gio-Le textile factory. What they found was a pandora's box of corruption and scandal. In Gelli's safe were the names and Masonic codes of 962 members of P2. There were also numerous dossiers and secret government reports. The list of P2 members was a veritable Who's Who of Italy: fifty generals and admirals, present and past Cabinet members, industrialists, and journalists, including the editor of Italy's most prestigious newspaper 'Corriere Della Sera' and several of his staff. There were also thirty six parliamentarians, pop stars, pundits and police officers and members of every single Italian Secret Service. It was a state within a state.

Many have said that Gelli was planning to take over Italy. They are wrong; he had taken over Italy." (David Yallop, *The Power and the Glory* (London, 2007), p.118.)
Another reference from the same book p.34:
"According to the terms under which the Vatican Bank was created by Pius XII during the Second World War, the accounts should have been very largely confined to religious orders and religious institutes. At the time Karol Wojtyla gave the green light to 'business as usual' only 1,047 accounts came into this category. A further 312 belonged to parishes and a further 290 to dioceses. The remaining 9,351 were owned by diplomats, prelates, and 'privileged citizens'. Among the privileged citizens were criminals of every hue.

The exalted personages included leading politicians of every political persuasion, a wide variety of members of P2 (the Italian Masonic Lodge), industrialists, reporters, editors, and members of such Mafia families as the Corleone, the Spatola, and the Inzerillo. Also included were members of the Neapolitan crime organization, the Camorra. All of them used the Vatican bank for recycling the profits of their various criminal activities. Licio Gelli [head of P2] assisted the Corleone family with their Vatican investments and members of the Magliana gang serviced the Vatican bank accounts of the Mafia's chief financial operator Pippo Calo. The Santa Anna Gate was a very busy thoroughfare as suitcases of money representing profits from the illegal narcotics industry went in past the Swiss Guards and up the stairs to the Bank. A number of the Mafia were traditionalists. They did not trust electronic transfers."

For a more detailed description of Catholic Church/mafia connections in Sicily see http://www.illuminaticonfessions.webfriend.it/ under 1/3/2008.

12. http://www.amazon.com/gp/cdp/member-reviews/A10BJO5EFZ6YJ6? ie=UTF8&sort%5Fby=MostRecentReview .

Fr McCafferty has said that he was abused by three different unconnected people as he was growing up. In his opinion the "Catholic Church had shown 'wicked contempt for survivors of clerical abuse'. He said that when he had tried to highlight it through the pulpit he had been regarded as a troublemaker by certain ecclesiastical grandees, who had refused to be influenced."
Later he gave more details of his experiences:
"Fr Paddy alleges that the abuse took place while he was a seminarian. In 2003, he wrote to his bishop, Patrick Walsh of Down and Connor diocese, and told him that a priest still in pastoral ministry within his diocese abused him repeatedly. The bishop did not reply to his letter. Two months later, Fr Paddy wrote again; this time he copied a letter he had just sent to the alleged abuser. The bishop replied and requested a meeting. Fr Paddy was given the impression by a senior priest that the police were informed of the allegations. But he has not been contacted by the police in the three years since; indeed, he claims, he has been "blanked" and ignored by those in responsible positions within the church. The alleged abuser is still a priest under the authority of the diocese, but is currently not in active ministry. Fr Paddy wants the church to laicise the priest; he would also like to know if the police were informed about the allegations three years ago -- and, if not, why not? "
(The first quote is from http://www.rte.ie/news/2002/1216/abuse01.html
                and   the   second   from
http://www.bbc.co.uk/blogs/ni/2006/09/a_scandal_within_a_scandal.html .
   See also http://news.bbc.co.uk/1/hi/northern_ireland/3295077.stm . He was interviewed on RTE radio at the time of the publication of the Ferns report, during which he outlined that much of this abuse was by Catholic priests, both during and after he was in the seminary.)

You can read about a similar case in the Scottish seminaries as related by Fr Steven Gilhooley:
"I went public [over the abuse] at great personal cost to myself, and reported my abuser to the police. He was given a jail sentence. Led by Cardinal

Ratzinger, Rome's response was to deliver a threat to my archbishop that if he didn't silence me, they'd discipline him.

"I was treated as the perpetrator rather than the victim. You can imagine how prayerful I found Cardinal Law's Mass on the eve of the conclave!"
Cardinal Law was given the much prized honour of saying that mass despite the fact that very serious allegations are made about him with respect to these paedophile scandals.
(http://news.scotsman.com/topics.cfm?tid=174&id=616882005 and see under 7 June 2005 at http://www.traditio.com/comment/com0506.htm) . Also David Yallop's book op.cit. details countless examples of where detailed descriptions of this abuse were put directly in the hands of John Paul II (and also the then Cardinal Ratzinger) who did nothing whatsoever to stop it.

13. Village magazine 20th April 2006 p.5.

14. http://www.traditio.com/comment/com0705.htm . He offered no apology later for comparing the church to the mafia, rather he said it was 'deadly accurate' as you can see from a cbs article here: http://www.cbsnews.com/stories/2003/06/13/national/main558594.shtml   .
From his resignation letter:
"As I have recently said, and have repeated on several occasions, our Church is a Faith institution. A home to Christ's people. It is not a criminal enterprise. It does not condone and cover up criminal activity. It does not follow a code of silence. My remarks, which some bishops found offensive, were deadly accurate. I make no apology. To resist grand jury subpoenas, to suppress the names of offending clerics, to deny, to obfuscate, to explain away; that is the model of a criminal organization, not my church."
(http://www.usccb.org/comm/archives/2003/03-128.shtml)
If you would like to read about some very serious allegations of corruption in the Vatican see "Shroud of Secrecy" a recent exposé book published in Italy: http://www.trosch.org/bks/rvw/millenari.html . That book even describes how Black Masses and Satanism are apparently practiced in the Vatican which is also alleged in David Yallop's best selling book *The Power and the Glory* op.cit.:
"There is even evidence that Satanism is alive and well within the Vatican."(p.456-7) and
"Satanic masses have happened regularly with hooded semi-naked participants and porn videos have been shown to very carefully selected audiences."(p.464)

There is actually a shocking comment too at the end of this article on indymedia from Mark in the Donegal Gaelteacht who discusses Vatican corruption: http://www.indymedia.ie/newswire.php? story_id=68750#comment209926 . I wish him the best of luck whatever happens.
As regards even more mysterious political goings on it still remains an

unexplained fact that someone in the Vatican strategically edited a wikipedia article on Gerry Adams:
"The site [that tracks wikipedia contributors IP's] also indicates that Vatican computers were used to remove content from a page about the leader of the Irish republican party Sinn Fein, Gerry Adams.

The edit removed links to newspaper stories written in 2006 that alleged that Mr Adams' fingerprints and handprints were found on a car used during a double murder in 1971.

The section, titled "Fresh murder question raised" is no longer part of the main online encyclopaedia entries."
(http://news.bbc.co.uk/2/hi/technology/6947532.stm)

More curious wikipedia changes by someone in the Vatican include this paragraph on Cardinal Tomas O Fiaich:
"The appointment was credited to the Papal Nuncio in Ireland, Archbishop Alibrandi, a controversial figure whom the Fine Gael and Labour National Coalition had already sought to have removed due to his perceived closeness to Irish republicans."
Which was changed to:
"The appointment was credited to the Papal Nuncio in Ireland, Archbishop Gaetano Alibrandi, a noted exponent of political dialogue with all sides and none in the heated Irish politico-cultural context of the 1970s and 1980s. Dr Alibrandi's efforts were not always appreciated by Garret Fitzgerald and the less democratically minded elements of the former Irish fascist party, Fine Gael, and Labour."
(http://en.wikipedia.org/w/index.php?diff=prev&oldid=29793555)

15. See the last Chapter infra footnotes 1-3.

16. The Metz agreement of 1962 is described at http://www.traditioninaction.org/HotTopics/a007ht.htm and for Cardinal Mindszenty see http://www.trawlr.com/items/2507840 .

17. See for example David Yallop's earlier book *In God's Name* (London, 1984).

18. For the question of Freemasonry in the modern Catholic Church see these two articles by John Kenneth Weiskittel, *The Bugnini File,* available at http://www.novusordowatch.org/bugnini.pdf , and *Freemasonry in the Catholic Church,* located at http://www.novusordowatch.org/freemasons.pdf . See also the list of Freemasons in the Catholic Church leaked in 1976 and published in the "Bulletin de l'Occident Chrétien Nr.12, July, 1976" available at http://www.aculink.net/~catholic/masonlst.htm . For allegations that the church was taken over by Secret Societies at the time of the Second Vatican Council

see Piers Compton, *Broken Cross* (St Helier, 1983), passim available at http://www.walkinthelight.ca/the_broken_cross_part_one.htm .
This Piers Compton was a well travelled 83 year old former editor of the 'Universe'. He wrote this book in 1983 and had been born c.1900 so he probably had known personally many of the early 20th century figures that he mentions. The editor of that Catholic weekly for some 14 years he clearly knew a lot of the gossip in the Vatican and he was also a poet and the author of numerous histories on subjects like the French Revolution, Queen Elizabeth I and the Crimean War. A short bio on this curious character, the author of a pretty shocking book:

"Piers Compton's first book was published before he was twenty. Since then he has spent his life writing, but he has interspersed this with a remarkable number of sidelines.

He was a copywriter and "ideas man" for American humour strips and films; was a "ghost writer" for eminent medical specialists; he spent five years on the stage in London and the provinces, and acted in the last of the silent films.

After becoming a Catholic he tried his vocation at monasteries in England and France; he was a political propagandist for different Parties in turn (and says, as a result, "wild horses would never drag me to a polling booth."); he soldiered abroad in anti-Communist causes. For several years he was Literary Editor of the Catholic weekly 'The Universe'.

His biographical studies, in which the military element has been marked, have always aimed at presenting popular but authentic historical reconstruction. He is at present working on a book dealing with Victorian social life.

Piers Compton is married, has a son Blaise and a young daughter Venetia, and lives at Marlow, Bucks." (Piers Compton, *The last days of General Gordon* (London, 1974), dustjacket.)

Here are a few quotes from his book on the curiously favourable media reaction that the later Popes have received (previously Popes were usually ignored or slandered in the British and US media), starting with the election of Pope John XXIII:
"Seasoned Catholics could not account for the warmth and admiration that greeted him as journalists, correspondents, broadcasters, and television crews from almost every country in the world swarmed into Rome. For very little had hitherto been known to the outside world about Angelo Roncalli beyond the fact that he was born in 1881, had been Patriarch of Venice, and that he held diplomatic posts in Bulgaria, Turkey, and France. As for his humble background, there had been peasant popes before. The Church could absorb them as easily as it had her academic and aristocratic Pontiffs.

But the secular world, as evidenced by some of the most 'popular' publications in England, insisted that something momentous had happened in Rome, and that it was only the promise of still greater things to come; while informed Catholics, who for years had pleaded the Church's cause, continued to scratch their heads and wonder. Had some information gone forth, not to them who had always supported religion, but to those who have served up snippets of truth, or no truth at all, to titillate and mislead the public?

An Irish priest who was in Rome at the time said of the clamour for intimate details regarding Roncalli: 'Newspapers, and radio, television, and magazines, simply could not get enough information about the background and career, the family and the doings of the new Holy Father. Day after day, from the close of the conclave to the coronation, from his first radio message to the opening of the Consistory, the remarks and the activities of the new Pope were dealt out in flamboyant detail for all the world to see.'"
(http://www.walkinthelight.ca/the_broken_cross_part_two.htm)

The calling of the Second Vatican Council:

"The same measure of unexampled publicity that marked the election of John XXIII, welcomed the plan. It was made to appear a matter of moment not only to the non-Catholic world, but to elements that had always strongly opposed Papal claims, dogma, and practice. But few wondered at this sudden show of interest on the part of agnostics; still fewer would have suspected a hidden motive. And if a small voice expressing doubt managed to be heard it was soon silenced as preparations for the first session of the Council went ahead."
(http://www.walkinthelight.ca/the_broken_cross_part_three.htm)

"The same voices that had eulogised the Rosicrucian John XXIII now clamoured for Montini, Montini of Milan. Anglicans, who had no time for a Pope of any or of no policy whatever, agreed that Montini was the man."
(http://www.walkinthelight.ca/the_broken_cross_part_three.htm)

On the subject of Masonic Lodges I guess a lot of readers don't see that much wrong with their being located in the Vatican but this goes against 100s of years of strongly held Catholic dogma as you can see in these pretty fierce quotes from Pope Leo XIII's Encyclical *Humanum Genus*:
"At this period, however, the partisans of evil seems to be combining together, and to be struggling with united vehemence, led on or assisted by that strongly organized and widespread association called the Freemasons. No longer making any secret of their purposes, they are now boldly rising up against God Himself. They are planning the destruction of holy Church publicly and openly, and this with the set purpose of utterly despoiling the nations of Christendom, if it were possible, of the blessings obtained for us through Jesus Christ our Saviour.
...
    In consequence, the sect of Freemasons grew with a rapidity beyond

conception in the course of a century and a half, until it came to be able, by means of fraud or of audacity, to gain such entrance into every rank of the State as to seem to be almost its ruling power. This swift and formidable advance has brought upon the Church, upon the power of princes, upon the public well-being, precisely that grievous harm which Our predecessors had long before foreseen. Such a condition has been reached that henceforth there will be grave reason to fear, not indeed for the Church - for her foundation is much too firm to be overturned by the effort of men - but for those States in which prevails the power, either of the sect of which we are speaking or of other sects not dissimilar which lend themselves to it as disciples and subordinates.

For these reasons We no sooner came to the helm of the Church than We clearly saw and felt it to be Our duty to use Our authority to the very utmost against so vast an evil. We have several times already, as occasion served, attacked certain chief points of teaching which showed in a special manner the perverse influence of Masonic opinions. Thus, in Our encyclical letter, Quod Apostolici Muneris, We endeavoured to refute the monstrous doctrines of the socialists and communists; afterwards, in another beginning "Arcanum," We took pains to defend and explain the true and genuine idea of domestic life, of which marriage is the spring and origin; and again, in that which begins ''Diuturnum,''(11) We described the ideal of political government conformed to the principles of Christian wisdom, which is marvellously in harmony, on the one hand, with the natural order of things, and, in the other, with the well-being of both sovereign princes and of nations. It is now Our intention, following the example of Our predecessors, directly to treat of the masonic society itself, of its whole teaching, of its aims, and of its manner of thinking and acting, in order to bring more and more into the light its power for evil, and to do what We can to arrest the contagion of this fatal plague.

...

For, from what We have above most clearly shown, that which is their ultimate purpose forces itself into view - namely, the utter overthrow of that whole religious and political order of the world which the Christian teaching has produced, and the substitution of a new state of things in accordance with their ideas, of which the foundations and laws shall be drawn from mere naturalism.

...

Again, as all who offer themselves are received whatever may be their form of religion, they thereby teach the great error of this age-that a regard for religion should be held as an indifferent matter, and that all religions are alike. This manner of reasoning is calculated to bring about the ruin of all forms of religion, and especially of the Catholic religion, which, as it is the only one that is true, cannot, without great injustice, be regarded as merely equal to other religions.

...

To wish to destroy the religion and the Church which God Himself has established, and whose perpetuity He insures by His protection, and to bring back after a lapse of eighteen centuries the manners and customs of the pagans, is signal folly and audacious impiety. Neither is it less horrible nor more tolerable that they should repudiate the benefits which Jesus Christ so mercifully obtained, not only for individuals, but also for the family and for civil society, benefits which, even according to the judgment and testimony of enemies of Christianity, are very great. In this insane and wicked endeavor we may almost see the implacable hatred and spirit of revenge with which Satan himself is inflamed against Jesus Christ. - So also the studious endeavour of the Freemasons to destroy the chief foundations of justice and honesty, and to co-operate with those who would wish, as if they were mere animals, to do what they please, tends only to the ignominious and disgraceful ruin of the human race.

...

Yea, this change and overthrow is deliberately planned and put forward by many associations of communists and socialists; and to their undertakings the sect of Freemasons is not hostile, but greatly favours their designs, and holds in   common   with   them   their   chief   opinions." (http://www.vatican.va/holy_father/leo_xiii/encyclicals/documents/hf_l-xiii_enc_18840420_humanum-genus_en.html)

19. As described by Detective Jim Rothstein (he overheard the phonecall) in an interview   on   the   Investigative   Journal   27   March   2007 http://www.republicnewsradio.com/station/archives/17?page=2   .   The   priest was Fr Bruce Ritter O.F.M. who ran a homeless shelter in New York. Like a lot of dissidents he was later accused on false charges of being a paedophile himself.   (http://query.nytimes.com/gst/fullpage.html? res=940CE0D81139F931A15753C1A96F958260)

20. Note how remarkable it is that environmental issues feature as one of the new deadly sins, see also http://www.msnbc.msn.com/id/20548340/ . For speculation that globalists are looking to exploit this issue to advance their agenda   see   http://www.oldthinkernews.com/Articles/oldthinker %20news/global_warming_hysteria_serves_a.htm   , http://www.taipeitimes.com/News/editorials/archives/2006/02/21/2003294021 and   AFP   12   March   2007 http://www.oldthinkernews.com/Articles/brown_wants_new_world_order.htm .

21. http://lonewacko.com/blog/archives/004408.html . The attorney Jonathan Levy has also said that the famous investigative journalist Gary Webb exposed some of the Catholic Church's sponsoring of illegal immigration to the US: "Illegal immigration [into the US] ..financed in part by the US bishops conference."   (The   Investigative   Journal   on   27   Feb   2006 http://mp3.rbnlive.com/Greg/0602/20060227_Mon_Greg2.mp3 .)

22. http://www.polish-chaplaincy.ie/index.php?lang=en&site=msze .

23. The Foundation for Interreligious and Intercultural Research and Dialogue

in Geneva (http://www.oilempire.us/pope.html).

24. A history of the post Vatican II Catholic Traditional Movement can be read online in Griff Ruby, *The Resurrection of the Roman Catholic Church* (http://www.the-pope.com/library.html).

25. http://www.mostholytrinityseminary.org/buildingproject.htm .

26. http://en.wikipedia.org/wiki/Archdiocese_of_Dublin_(Roman_Catholic) and http://www.abc.net.au/rn/religionreport/stories/2006/1690305.htm .

27. http://cmri.org/vatican2_stats.html .

28. http://www.irish-association.org/archives/david_stephens10_03.html .

29. Article by Fr Gerard Moloney in the Irish Times 20th Nov 2006 http://www.ireland.com/newspaper/opinion/2006/1120/1163947706546.html .

30. http://www.sodalitiumpianum.com/index.php?pid=1 .

31. http://www.the-pope.com/church06.html .

32. http://en.wikipedia.org/wiki/Congregation_of_Mary_Immaculate_Queen .

33. http://www.geocities.com/orthopapism/mendez.html .

34. http://www.traditio.com/comment/com0701.htm .

35. http://www.daughtersofmary.net/about.php .

36. http://www.angelqueen.org/forum/viewtopic.php?
t=11275&highlight=&sid=7046c5f81d86dc6a23c7284a43d22b20 , founded by Frs Arriaga, Zamora and Carmona. See http://en.wikipedia.org/wiki/Joaquin_Saenz_Arriaga and also see the two articles by Father Daniel Perez Gomez available at http://www.wandea.org.pl/priestly-society.htm and http://www.wandea.org.pl/church-mexico.html .

37. http://en.wikipedia.org/wiki/Priestly_Fraternity_of_St._Peter .

38. http://www.institute-christ-king.org/getToKnow.html .

49. http://www.the-pope.com/church07.html .

40. Sunday Business Post 16th Sept 2007 http://www.sbpost.ie/post/pages/p/story.aspx-qqqt=NEWS+FEATURES-

qqqm=nav-qqqid=26659-qqqx=1.asp . As pointed out accurate figures are hard to come by, this article is the only one that attempts to 'very roughly' look at the numbers for the congregations:

"There are estimated to be around one billion Catholics worldwide today, meaning Catholics make up around one sixth of the planet. Recent official Vatican figures estimated support of the Society of St. Pius X to be at around one million. Very roughly, would suggest that the entire Roman Catholic traditionalist world must number somewhere around the six or seven million mark. The biggest groups are indult and independent [meaning mostly SSPX I think], which collectively make up about four fifths of the traditionalist movement as a whole, Sedevacantists [what are called independents in this article] and other groups make up the remaining fifth."
(http://www.geocities.com/catholic_traditionalist/)

41. http://www.latinmassmagazine.com/articles/articles_1999_FA_Woods.html
.

42. As regards what they might be about to change next its curious that Cardinal Hummes, the new head of the clergy congregation in Rome, said:
"Celibacy is a discipline, not a dogma of the church. ... Certainly, the majority of the apostles were married. In this modern age, the church must observe these things, it has to advance with history." Although he 'clarified' all that shortly after he took up the job in Rome its still curious that he was given that post despite holding those opinions.
(http://www.cwnews.com/offtherecord/offtherecord.cfm?
task=singledisplay&recnum=3963). It is noteworthy too I think that Cardinal O'Brien of Scotland is in favour of married clergy:
http://www.scottishchristian.com/news/catholic/2005_05_01_archive.shtml .
Here is a good site on the question of women priests which could be in the offing in the long run: http://www.womenpriests.org/welcome.asp .

43. Marie Carré, *AA-1025: The Memoirs of an Anti-Apostle* (Rockford Illinois, first edition 1972 this 1991), first quote p.xi, the next from p.xiv.

CHAPTER 10

Irish Immigration, a state or EU conspiracy?

In the last chapter I made reference to the Catholic Church supporting immigration inflows which might have seemed an unusual criticism to make but this issue is clearly very serious, and divisive, and it might be helpful to look at it in greater depth.

I won't bore you with the basic issue, obviously people opposed to large scale immigration feel it might I guess overwhelm Irish culture and heritage, and in the event of an economic downturn lead to great resource pressures, while those in favour would emphasize that everyone is made equal, regardless of race colour etc, and is entitled to civil rights including the right to live and work where they choose. Or something like that, I am sure everybody is acquainted with the arguments. In any case it certainly is a bitter debate even now in Ireland, as demonstrated by the opposition to Justin Barrett, and it shows every sign of going downhill from there! Unfortunately some people from the pro immigration side of the debate Imho tend to be quite liberal with phrases like 'fascist' and 'racist' and the other side I think responds by talk of national treachery etc.

To cut to the chase I think it is fair to say that most people who are concerned about immigration, in any country, tend to be concerned that large numbers of strangers can change the character of an area, and that the delicate and unique cultural, social and political balances of a country can potentially be lost forever in a wave of 'multiculturalism' which is sometimes seen as a kind of McDonalds of a social order. In other words the dream of multiculturalism, that people would gain from interaction with other races, is sometimes felt to give way to a bland international type environment where every street corner is like inner city London or New York, and where the local unique character of the people is sometimes lost. To look at it another way, imagine a sort of traditional Irish kind of pub, say as featured in some film like the 'Quiet Man' or whatever. Picture the scene where you get an interaction with the people from the mountain, and the 'Great Glen', like the Thorntons or whoever, great people who originally came from Carrick at the time of the famine, or whatever the folklore is. Now obviously this is idealistic, and yes not very common right now anyway, but I would state that it is not true that it never existed or doesn't exist still in parts of Ireland. You would be amazed at the kind of memory and traditions that really do survive in parts of Ireland and that community spirit is I don't think completely unheard of, if now rare.

Now picture the scene say 15 years later. The pub is gone replaced by a shiny hotel with a motorway system to match. And of course it is under some outside management who employ a large number of people from all over the world. Obviously the question of the environment, and all these motorways, is a separate issue but is it the case that the community has lost something by this sudden influx of large numbers of outsiders? You can picture some local talking to people in the hotel and trying to interest them in some obscure folklore about the O'Gradys from the back of the hill. These stories are usually interesting to locals because having lived there they know the area and the odds are that they would be related to the O'Gradys 'going way back'. That is obviously not true of outsiders. Hence I think you can see that if a large number of that local's audience, as he relates his story, are from abroad it just isn't the same and the chances are he won't bother relating it.[1]

I think it is therefore pretty clear that there is some theoretical point where immigration can 'swamp' - as I the guess controversial phrase is - the local culture. In theory instead they will be doing the Latvian version of the Morris dance!lol But I don't know if that kind of corresponding cultural input ever really happens? I know people opposed to immigration have maybe cried wolf on that point in many countries, but that still doesn't mean that it is impossible, if I suppose the rate of immigration is large and sudden enough. And there is some evidence that the immigration that Ireland is now experiencing is of an unprecedented scale in size and speed. One commentator, David McWilliams, is saying for example that Irish people are expected to move out of the island's city centres by about 2020.[2] A look at some census information is interesting as well. In 1990 the percentage of foreign born residents in Ireland was 2.3, comfortably less than the UK at 4.2, and France at 5.6.[3] This is obviously not very surprising with the big retreat from empire that affected both countries migration patterns in the 50s-70s. Then in 2002 the Irish figure has gone to 7.1 while the corresponding UK and French figures are at 4.7 and 5.6 respectively. Therefore by 2002 we now had a significantly higher rate of immigration than both those countries where it is so controversial. And as you can see from the latest CSO graphs the rate of immigration has increased pretty exponentially from 2002.[4]

So why does everybody want to come to Ireland? It isn't the weather anyway :-) I know you will be told that its the Celtic tiger and there is gold on them there streets but this observer remains unconvinced on that point. I suspect that a lot of people who live here wonder how much that phenomenon has been exaggerated, even as regards employment statistics. Certainly throughout this time you always hear many stories of Irish people finding it very difficult to get employment in Ireland, and that's true of nearly all sectors. So if not a genuine overwhelming demand for labour then what was it? The theory I will put before you is that the increased immigration coming to Ireland since the 90s is in fact as a result of a strong co-ordinated government policy to encourage immigration at all costs.

I contend that the government, presumably in part pressured by some employers to act to counteract any wage inflation in an increasingly expensive country, has in practice gone all across the world trying desperately to encourage any and all to come to Ireland. I will rest my case on inter alia a speech given to a conference this year in Latvia by a FÁS economist.[5] In this presentation he talks about the huge FÁS (the Irish government employment and training agency) campaign to attract immigrants, who he sees as the engine of the Celtic tiger, using PR companies, ads in papers etc:

> "One of the big resource-intensive methods that we used were recruitment fairs - we used to get the companies to come over and we went to diverse places as South Africa, India, America of course, and across Europe, and we'd bring the companies over and they would recruit there and then. And we often got political involvement, we got our minister and the ambassador to open the conference and that covered over any sort of local resentment there might be to recruiting farm workers.

> And by and large it was successful. In six months, the website www.jobsireland.com [recte, was written www.jobireland.com, drawn up by FÁS to assist people living abroad find work in Ireland] had 20 million hits on the site and there were over 400,000 people who attended the fairs, and a lot of people did come back.

> One comparative advantage that we had was that we were the only country at the time when skills were at a shortage throughout the world. At a premium, we were the only country that had a designated task force to bring back skilled workers and to bring in foreign skilled workers.

> [Referring to a new FÁS campaign to assist Latvians

etc in coming to Ireland:]
Just briefly... I just want to mention an initiative that
FÁS have also developed to help workers from foreign
countries who are coming to Ireland, primarily from the
EU-10 who are coming to Ireland, and who are in
danger of being exploited.

...

And that's why FÁS is promoting this, what we call
"Know before you go" campaign, and basically we
have a CD and an information pack on the correct
procedure when you are coming into Ireland and its in
Latvian, it's in all the different languages, and get it on
your TV and on your newspapers.."[6]

There are two important aspects to this speech, which throughout
reflects FÁS' strong preference for immigration. The first spin that is
evident is that the whole immigration effort was almost entirely focused
on getting ex Irish emigrants to return back. But notice the reference to
India and farm workers? Is that likely to be where those emigrants were
to be found? Notice that in this advertisement for one of the many job
fairs they point out they are looking for 'Russian Nationals':

"Jobs Ireland Opens in Moscow

Over 15 Irish Employers and Agencies are represented
in Moscow, and Jobs are on offer across all industry
sectors with special emphasis on Information
Technology, Telecommunications, Retail and
Electronics.

Tom Kitt, TD, Irish Minister of State at the Department
of Enterprise Trade and Employment in Ireland will
open Jobs Ireland at the new Manege Centre in
Moscow on Saturday 31st March at 11am.

Ireland's rapid economic growth of recent years has
utterly transformed the employment situation. Ireland
now has the best job-creation record of any OECD
Country. Emigration has now been replaced by
immigration. Instead of people leaving Ireland in
search of jobs there are now labour shortages.

As a result of strong interest shown from Russians
registering on www.jobsireland.com. Russian nationals
interested in living and working in Ireland can now
meet the employers face to face at the Expo. The Jobs

Ireland Expo is part of the drive to attract suitably skilled and qualified Irish and Russian nationals to come to live and work in Ireland.

According to Gregory Craig, Director of Jobs Ireland "Labour is becoming increasingly globally mobile, particularly in the I.T. and Telecommunications Industries, Jobs Ireland is offering the opportunity of experiencing life in Ireland. Not only are there jobs on offer at the show but there is also a re-location village offering practical advice to those wishing to move."

www.jobsireland.com has thousands of jobs listed on site. Registration is free and it is the fastest route to working in Ireland. Advice is available online on living and working in Ireland, taxation, housing, banking, education and healthcare entitlements."[7]

The other spin, that is also evident in the above advertisement, is that with respect to foreign nationals at least they are only looking for important skills and highly qualified people to plug any hi tech gaps in the skill base of the emerging Celtic Tiger. But this is not really the pattern of Irish immigration, in practice most of the immigrants are employed in low skilled jobs, as in evident in this summary of Irish immigration patterns by Martin Ruhs of TCD and Oxford:

"Laissez faire policies until April 2003 [After 2003 the immigration has been primarily from other EU countries who don't require work permits]
– Labour market test only "constraint" on size and composition
– Rapid increase in number of permits issued
– 3 out of 4 migrants employed in low-skilled occupations
– Great diversity in migrants' countries of origin"[8]

And another reference from a report prepared for the NESC:

"The Consultants do suggest that Ireland's openness to admitting migrant workers for employment in a variety of jobs, including low-skill labour,"[9]

In case you are wondering, as you can see from the above references, most immigration into Ireland is via perfectly legal work permits issued as part of the "very liberal" immigration policies that the Irish government pursues.[10] This is true of immigrants from all over the world, three quarters of them for simple manual labour. You have got to get out of your head this idea of illegal asylum seekers which is the big issue in America. Here legal immigration outnumbers the illegal type by at least two to one.[11] Large scale immigration is considered desirable and pretty much encouraged at all levels, in order, we are assured, to feed the voracious employer demands of the Celtic tiger. It is described here for example:

> "The current immigration system's flexibility and responsiveness to employer demand for migrant labour has undoubtedly generated benefits for individual employers and the Irish economy overall. For instance, it is widely agreed that with the domestic labour pool drying up, immigration has played a critical role in meeting significant labour shortages at both the high and low-skill labour market segments. This has clearly helped maintain Ireland's rapid economic growth since the mid-1990s. Immigration is also considered a key requirement to maintaining high levels of economic growth in the future."[12]

Does that mean that FÁS are only filling jobs that Irish people don't want to do? Not necessarily, the report goes on to say:

> "In late 2002, FÁS carried out an internal comparative analysis of the available data on the potential labour supply (including the number of people on the Live Register and others registered with FÁS for the purpose of finding employment), vacancies notified with FÁS, and work permits issued across the various occupations. The striking finding of this analysis was that, in late 2002, the majority of work permits had been issued for work in unskilled occupations for which there appeared to be a sizeable supply of local labour."

This report by the International Organization for Migration, for the National Economic and Social Council, points out ominously that:

> "Ireland's policies to manage labour migration were designed in the context of a rapidly growing economy and a significant demand for migrant labour. As a result, there was little concern about distributional issues, such as the potentially adverse impact of immigration on the employment prospects of local (i.e., Irish and other EEA) workers.
>
> ...
>
> The lack of effective policies and thinking to protect

the employment prospects of local workers in a less favourable economic environment is, therefore, a serious weakness in Ireland's current labour immigration system."

This laissez faire non EU immigration policy has changed somewhat dating from 2003. It is now reported to be more difficult for new workers from outside the EU to get work permits. (The exception to this are spouses of current EU immigrants who I think were recently given work permits.) But of course since 2004 the main source of immigration has been from the enlarged EU who's citizens do not require that documentation. The EU has obviously expanded by adding on ten new nations on 1 May 2004 and added two more on the 1st January 2007. All told it has increased by some 104 million people. At one level you would have thought that this didn't matter very much since these countries are on the other side of Europe and any pro rata increase in immigration to Ireland would surely not affect us profoundly? And that assumption has proved to be very wrong. Ireland, although with only 4 million people one of the smaller republics in Europe, has attracted a remarkable proportion of this new wave of East European immigration e.g. about 50,000-100,000 Lithuanians have come,[13] about half of emigrating Latvians come to Ireland,[14] and about 200,000 Poles are said to have settled here.[15] Can I just say that on a personal level, as far as I am concerned, they are all genuinely welcome, but whether Ireland's transport, healthcare, housing and other infrastructure has sufficient extra capacity to handle this migration is a different question. Last I checked most of those services were in a ramshackle state not at all able to cope with the population already here, so why then does the government push so much to increase the immigration levels? Because that is what they are doing as you can see from this advertisement of another job fair this time in Poland:

"Considering working in the Construction Industry in Ireland? Visit the Jobs Ireland Poland Exhibition and find out more.

With representatives from the Irish Trade Unions and Construction Industry Employers Federation in attendance find out more about opportunities, conditions of employment and requirements of the Irish construction industry. Also in attendance will be some of Ireland's leading Construction Companies who are actively recruiting for a wide range of vacancies."[16]

This campaign by FÁS to encourage immigration from Eastern Europe is run in cooperation with the EURES (European Employment

Services) agency of the EU ("In Ireland, the Eures system is based within FÁS") [17] which was created "by the European Commission to facilitate the free movement of workers."[18]

Since as you can see FÁS operates very much under EU principles they don't distinguish between EU and Irish citizens and are actively encouraging other EU citizens to come to Ireland, as many commentators have noted e.g.:

> "The first is that the Department of Enterprise, Trade and Employment, which has responsibility for economic migration policy, is actively encouraging employers to recruit low skilled labour from within the European Union."[19]

The interesting thing about this is that the same EURES agency operates within the national labour organisations of the East European countries. In other words they are at both sides of the equation, and apparently one of the EURES partners, NVA in Latvia, is very aggressive in pushing emigration out of that country into places like Ireland:

> "Also, the state employment agency, Nodarbinatibas Valsts agentura (NVA) provides information about job vacancies abroad. Comments have been made in the media that the NVA is more concerned with finding jobs for people abroad than in Latvia."[20]

The information on jobs abroad must come from the advanced EURES systems, so presumably European Union policy is to encourage this migration flow.

It is a migration pattern that is doubly ironic too, in the case of Latvia, because that country had to face huge forced immigration flows from other parts of the Soviet Union. The thinking of the Soviets, apparently, was that if they could inject enough immigrants it would cause Latvia to lose its unique identity, and so weaken Latvian nationalism which might otherwise threaten the Union. So that after this immigration had taken its toll, in 1985, the Soviet governor in Latvia was openly talking about how people would have to adjust to the new reality and "come to terms with the limitations of nationality".[21]

One person incidentally who has taken a keen interest in Irish immigration is Peter Sutherland the Special Representative on Migration for the UN Secretary-General. He has praised the liberal immigration system in Ireland, which has "seen far faster change here than anywhere else" across the globe.[22] Now he feels that in response to these changes that "Irish people will have to adapt their sense of nationality", to better reflect living in a country that contains so many people who have not experienced the familiarities of the Irish identity:

> "We have to learn that our identity has to be adapted to recognize that we are becoming, and will be, a society with others in it. It is a big challenge...We have a challenge to change people's mentality. And it's a European challenge."

Anyway he feels that Irish people have no choice in the matter because

> "opting out of a multicultural society was not an option in an increasingly globalised world."[23]

So my tuppence worth is that the question of Irish immigration involves far more long term issues, and consequences, than just the economy's short term quest for cheaper labour. And that those who argue for less immigration are entitled to this opinion, and should not be referred to as 'fascists' or 'racists' for holding it. I will leave you with a long quote from Ashley Mote, who is also talking about identity and is not afraid to accuse the EU, whose Parliament he is a member of, of doing to the UK exactly what the USSR did to Latvia:

> "Blair's cabinet was warned by its own officials in 2000 that British national identity was in "permanent decline". The same document admitted Britain was being eroded by the EU.
>
> ...
>
> Immigration is not about the cost of lettuce. It is not even about caring for the sick. It is about an invidious invasion that threatens to overwhelm. It is about the looming destruction of our identity as a sovereign nation. It is about the eventual obliteration of our culture and the British way of life.
>
> ...
>
> Over the centuries we have developed a distinctive lifestyle, a culture and values which are now the glue which holds us together. They define who we are.
>
> ...
>
> If present trends continue, our nation of migrants will not be a nation at all. Our essential Britishness will be beyond repair. A serious breakdown in our social fabric is already apparent, and not just in the cities. Law and order is everywhere under threat. Gated communities are springing up as people fear the future. Others leave in despair and take their Britishness with them. Migrants form their own ghettos, living parallel lives isolated from each other and from the British way of

life that attracted them in the first place. Mistrust abounds.

...

Meanwhile, mass migration remains a form of corruption. It is a corruption of the nation state and - even more importantly - a systematic dilution of national identity. It is a deliberate destruction of a natural unit of stability in an unstable world.

Why?

The answer lies in the activities of the European Union, with the connivance of successive British governments since the Maastricht Treaty of 1992. They seek the creation of a single country called Europe by the free movement of people within the (now) 27 countries. For every migrant who arrived in Britain before the Masstricht Treaty was signed, 12 more have arrived since.

Such an upheaval has little to do with improving people's lives. It has everything to do with control - political control by an unelected elite. Stalin invented the idea in the totalitarian USSR. He used it ruthlessly to dilute national identities across the Eastern European countries which the Soviets controlled behind the Iron Curtain. Such criminal irresponsibility lasted for half a century.

How long will the EU's contrived invasion of Britain by deceit last? How long will it be tolerated by those whose lives are being turned upside down and who gave neither their approval nor authority for such a profound change in the British way of life?

In days gone by, those responsible would have faced charges of treason, and rightly so. Indeed, if the EU's headquarters had been in London, and their near total control of British government being more obvious, the commissioners now micro-managing our lives and destroying British identity would long since have fled for their lives.

303

...

Essentially the powerful elite who run the European Union have set themselves the awesome task of trying to weaken, if not destroy, the very fabric that holds communities together - sameness. Human groups with similar cultures have always protected themselves against outsiders.

...

Yet it is our own government that is today the greatest single source of terrorism. Theirs is the terrorism of state control - the erosion of fundamental British values and their replacement by a regime of oppressive laws ostensibly designed to prevent acts of violence against the British. But the practical effect is a 'reign of terror' not unlike that which followed the French Revolution of 1789.

Britain has become a self-imposed police state. There are more surveillence cameras here than in any other country in the world. The government encourages neighbour to spy on neighbour. Publicly expressed opinions can be against the law. Thinking about what is or might be an illegal act can, of itself, be held illegal. Anyone can be arrested and imprisoned for something they might do in the future. DNA from tens of thousands of innocent people, including children, is held on police databases indefinitely. And all supposedly to make us more secure." [24]

Footnotes

1. Liam Mullen reckons that something like that has happened in one of the old Dublin hotels http://www.indymedia.ie/article/75606 .

2. http://www.davidmcwilliams.ie/Articles/view.asp?CategoryID=-1&CategoryName=&ArticleID=378 .

3. http://epp.eurostat.cec.eu.int/cache/ITY_OFFPUB/KS-NK-06-008/EN/KS-NK-06-008-EN.PDF .

4. http://www.cso.ie/releasespublications/documents/population/current/popmig.pdf .

5. As another example you can see the big campaign organised to bring in nurses from all around the world outlined on p.9 here http://www.aph.gov.au/hansard/joint/commttee/J7003.pdf. The Irish government mobilised to get nurses from the Philippines, Spain, India and Pakistan, Australia, New Zealand, and (via FÁS) the EU. This was mainly in response to a decision to increase the nurses training term from three to four years. Surely there could have been another response to such a short term bottleneck?

6. http://www.policy.lv/index.php?id=103070⟨=en .

7. http://www.fas.ie/information_and_publications/press_releases/pr_2001_6.html .

8. Martin Ruhs, *Managing the Immigration and Employment of Non-EU nationals in Ireland* (Dublin (TCD) and Oxford, 2005), p.12. (http://www.compas.ox.ac.uk/publications/papers/Martin%20Ruhs%20-%20BW%20Launch%20of%20BP%20(19%20May%202005)%20(2).pdf)

9. http://www.nesc.ie/dynamic/docs/Full%20NESC%20report.pdf p.143.

10. The quote is from a recent report of the NESC quoting a report by the International Organization for Migration. http://www.nesc.ie/dynamic/docs/Full%20NESC%20report.pdf p.143.

11. This was pointed out some time ago by an African immigrant on Questions and Answers, who was frustrated that Irish people don't seem to realize that the question of asylum seekers only refers to a small fraction of the overall population of immigrants in Ireland.

"First, although asylum-seekers probably constitute no more than 10% of all

305

foreign immigrants to Ireland since 1995, they have been the subject of considerable media coverage, some of it negative."(written in 2001 http://migration.ucc.ie/irelandfirstreport.htm).

"Moreover, the great majority of migrant workers have been legally employed in relatively low-skilled occupations..."
(http://www.migrationinformation.org/Profiles/display.cfm?ID=260)

Gerard Hughes and Emma Quin, *The Impact of Immigration on Europe's Societies: Ireland* (2004), p.37:
"While there will continue to be a need in the future for research on issues relating to asylum the bulk of immigrants in Ireland are migrant workers and their dependants."
(http://www.esri.ie/pdf/BKMNEXT057_Impact%20of%20Immigration.pdf).

12. p.41 http://www.nesc.ie/dynamic/docs/Full%20IOM%20report.pdf . What follows is also from this report.

13. "It is estimated that 50,000 to 100,000 Lithuanians are currently living in Ireland, of whom about one third are planning to settle here."
(http://en.wikipedia.org/wiki/Lithuanians_in_Ireland).

14. Julianna Traser for the European Citizen Action Service, *Who's still afraid of EU Enlargement* (Brussels, 2006), p.34
http://www.ecas.org/file_uploads/1182.pdf .

15. Polonia article on Wikipedia and
http://www.drakkart.com/eire2/category/polish-emigration/ .

16. http://www.fas.ie/poland/index.html .

17. Eures particularly helps employers get "Access to 000's of unemployed" prospective immigrants in places like Poland.
(http://www.fas.ie/eures/Jobcentre_Plus_the_First_Group_and_the_Polish_Re cruitment_Fair.ppt).

18.
http://www.fas.ie/services_to_jobseekers/Know_Before_you_go/english/home. html .

19.
http://www.politeia.net/newsletter/politeia_newsletter_42_june_2006/labour_m igration_within_the_european_union_an_irish_perspective .

20.
http://www.eiro.eurofound.europa.eu/2005/12/FEATURE/LV0512104F.HTML

. Shows that NVA is also a EURES partner: http://www.nva.lv/eures/ .

21. "The Soviet government's policy of diluting the ethnic Latvian population through the forced immigration of non-Latvians, however heinous that policy may have been,..."
(http://www.hrw.org/reports/1994/WR94/Helsinki-14.htm).
"The vast numbers of workers who immigrated to Estonia and Latvia (less to Lithuania due to its predominantly agricultural structure) throughout the Soviet period caused serious alarm in these republics, where it was feared that the indigenous nationalities would soon become minorities... Moreover, it was seen to be a deliberate attempt on the part of the central authorities to drown out the Balts in their own republics.
...
In late 1985, the First Secretary of the Estonian communist party, Karl Vaino, still openly displayed strong pro-Russian attitudes in emphasising that "the Estonian people's historical destiny has indissoluble links with the (---) Soviet state (---) and the Great Russian People." With accelerating pace, events were to show that his calls to "come to terms with the limitations of nationality" went unheard in Soviet Estonia."
(http://ethesis.helsinki.fi/julkaisut/val/yhtei/pg/kauppila/ch1.html)
With respect to Lithuania: "Though the percent of the native-born population in Lithuania has not altered since 1940, even it saw agitation against what has been described as secret Soviet directives to reduce the native element to 60 percent of the population in the republic and 40 percent in the capital."
(Gershon Shafir, *Immigrants and Nationalists: Ethnic Conflict and Accommodation in Catalonia, the Basque Country* (1995), p.174 (footnote 200).)

22. Irish Times 8/07/2006
http://www.ireland.com/newspaper/finance/2006/0708/2300961266BWSUDS.html .

23. Irish Times Sept.26 2006
http://www.ireland.com/newspaper/ireland/2006/0926/1158591060155.html .

24. Ashley Mote MEP, *J'Accuse* (2008), p.4, 5, 6, 7, 8, 36, 37.

CHAPTER 11

How to create a Value System in a population to make Political Control easier.

But what was Peter Sutherland, a very important internationalist, really talking about when he was referring to identity in that quote? And how does it tie into the question of immigration? And what was Ashley Mote MEP referring to when he defined 'the terrorism of state control' as:

> "the erosion of fundamental British values and their re-placement by a regime of oppressive laws.."

To explain all this we end up where this book began, talking about how the value systems in modern society are creating conditions which allow conspiracies to flourish, and in particular are fostering subservient citizens who are allowing these globalists to walk all over them.

Hospitality as one example of an element in a Value System

First of all though I will take a simple example which hopefully will clarify what I mean by value systems. I think it is fair to say that up to maybe 10 years ago in the country in Ireland hospitality, and welcome towards strangers, would be considered a very important thing. A stranger coming into a house would be offered a cup of tea etc because it was the done thing, it was a kind of instinctive value system that was ingrained into society. Now if you look around you today its obvious that a generation of people are coming forward who have been bred up implanted with a lot of media and government campaigns which have encouraged virtually the opposite state of affairs. 'Don't talk to strangers', 'stranger danger', 'you cannot have enough security' and household electronic gates is the new atmosphere, far removed from the famous 'open house' of the Irish countryside. Also when people meet strangers in a public place much the same atmosphere prevailed. In tight knit rural, and urban, communities the chances were very high that a stranger you would meet would know somebody you'd know or even be a distant relation and so you wouldn't want to treat a person badly in case word would get around. This has been replaced by a practice of not even giving your surname to strangers and phrases like 'what are you looking at' and 'what do you want to know that for' have replaced the friendly open hearted conversations of only a short time ago. Ireland has definitely become a poorer place for the loss of these old values and it might be instructive to analyse what has caused this change. It is easy enough to figure out what is behind these developments, for example the decline of:

- religious feeling is an issue, because this partly underlined the sense of hospitality, people would remark that Joseph and Mary were turned away at the Inn and they would not like that to happen again;

- family pride, which would clearly motivate a lot of people to hold onto a good reputation for hospitality;

- local pride, much discussion would circulate about how a person was treated in a particular area and a Cork person or a Wexford person etc would not like to feel that they let down the reputation of their locality;

- and national pride, especially in their treatment of foreigners Irish people in the past would make sure to be hospitable in order that the outsider would come away with a good opinion of Ireland and her inhabitants.

There are obviously lots of other factors involved, such as the overwhelming power of the modern media and its capacity to change the ethos of the public, but I think it is clear enough that those issues are certainly a factor. Apart from the church influence, you can see how this element in a person's value system, hospitality, is just one side of the coin of a person's identity and pride. It ties in with how a person views himself. The stronger he feels in his identity - the more family, local and national pride he feels - the stronger these values will be in him and then in the country at large. Hence when you read this chapter you can see how identity and value systems mean much the same thing, and in particular you need to knock out of people their identity in order to change the value system. What follows is an attempt to see how the powers that be might be doing this, how they are deliberately changing the value systems in society to make political control easier.

Stripping out Traditional Values

This is a bit like joining the marines, firstly you have to strip out of people their previous identity and values, and almost deliberately break them down as it were, then build them up again using a new set of values. The first set of numbers below are the value systems to be knocked out of people, followed by those to be implanted:

309

1) Religion. Firstly you must burn out of people their religious identity and value system. This is definitely priority number 1. Clearly the main churches, Christian, Moslem and Jewish, teach people a comprehensive set of values and moral teaching, some of which have stood the test of two millennia, which make it impossible for a new value system to be imposed on top. Like Stalin then the first cry is that religion is bunkum, 'the opium of the masses', established religion has been people's oppressors for centuries, cause of all wars etc, blame them for everything except the weather!

There are also more subtle ways of discrediting religion, and of setting world religions against one another in order to destroy each in turn:

a) Islam. Maybe it might be possible to hype up a totally false virtually charicatured version of Islam, where so many virgins get to comfort a suicide bomber and where you get your hand chopped off for doing nearly anything. Don't forget that this extreme version of Islam comes from places like Saudi Arabia and among the Moslem fighters against the USSR in Afghanistan, both groups which are or were closely allied to the powers that be in the US and the UK. Then maybe you can embarrass and humiliate Moslems themselves with this kind of exaggerated Islam as well as use it to cause disquiet in the Christian world.

b) Judaism. Some would say that a clique which claims to be Jewish (but actually are not but are rather followers of ancient Babylonian pagan religions, including those involving the Cabala, as well as Jewish heresies like Spinozans, Frankists etc) are in powerful positions worldwide which in turn understandably infuriates the citizens of places like Russia, the US and Palestine who feel oppressed by this clique. This then serves to discredit Judaism in general and likewise creates tensions between them and the other great religions. After all if you think about WWII you cannot help but be struck at how this always powerful clique did very little to help the mass of the - real - Jews when they really needed it.

c) Christianity, in particular Catholicism. There is actually evidence out there that Communists, and others, deliberately infiltrated into senior positions in the Catholic Church and then no doubt did nothing to stamp out the emerging corruption which has done so much to discredit Catholicism in Ireland and around the world.[1] According to Det Jim Rothstein of the New York Police Department, who personally handled agents in the Vatican and the UN as part of major investigations into worldwide paedophile rings, the US and USSR intelligence agencies

310

both targeted the Vatican, because maybe both had a vested interest in seeing it discredited:

"There was a concerted effort by...both intelligence communities, the Americans and the Russians, to infiltrate the Catholic Church and subvert what they were doing. And that's how the paedophilia really got started."[2]

These networks run so deep that some quite erroneously felt that even Pope John Paul II,[3] and earlier Paul VI,[4] were Communist agents! But if senior figures in the Vatican (definitely not including any recent Popes) were compromised at any point this would certainly explain why the Catholic Church has been so ill led in recent times, not least in Ireland. The Catholic Church is particularly vulnerable to this kind of infiltration because it is so hierarchical. If you can control the Curia you can destroy everything, you can then even get the church officials to destroy the teaching in the seminaries and the priests the church interiors.

In the long run it might be hoped that all these religions would kill each other off in a kind of 'Clash of Civilisations' - which would include Moslem v. Christian clashes on the streets of Western Europe - which in turn would allow the powers that be to tell us that all wars are created by religions which we should then take care to stamp out. In the meantime you can always play them off against one another. For example if you wanted to stamp out Christian symbolism in the Gardaí or the schools or wherever you would highlight the use of Islamic scarves or Sikh turbans, get Christians infuriated at their presence or potential presence in Christian countries, and then use that outrage to pass laws which ban religious symbols in general. These laws can then be used to crush Christian symbols mostly, because they are after all more prominent in Ireland and other Western countries.

Anyway you have to destroy religion before you can really mess with people's minds and impose a new value system, its absolutely critical. If people must learn some religion at school then subtly destroy the catechisms taught there. (Caitlín Ó Seighin in the Rossport book describes how the new catechisms taught since the 70s are completely different from the traditional teachings of the Catholic Church. She regards this change as being crucial to understanding what is going on now in modern Ireland and the attitudes of the people.[5]) In the long run though it would be much better to destroy religious education totally, if at all possible, say its been modern and tolerant and all that! lol

2) Nationalism. This area again can provide a kind of yardstick by which people judge their actions, and a sort of pride that would cause

people to pause before they would do something very terrible. Think of Hacker in 'Yes Minister' and the way he would square his shoulders and quote Churchill when he would do something heroic for the good of the people (and not just for his own political self interest). For political control purposes we don't want anybody doing anything heroic! Its easier to control people if they are only motivated by the unheroic! We want people to think its all about the money or the job etc, that's the spirit if you want to keep people in a kind of open prison camp.

Irish nationalism and patriotism has over the years motivated people to do genuinely unselfish acts, and survive, with their values intact, everything the state could throw at them. While I know this is a minority viewpoint :-) I actually think, if you were to be fair minded, that you could see genuine idealism and courage in the face of state oppression in the actions of Irish leaders as diverse as Eoin O'Duffy and Brendan Hughes, and with many people in the - wide! - gap in between. Both of them could be relied upon to stand up to the state when they needed to.[6]

Nationalism puts a kind of backbone into people I think, it frequently causes them to strive above themselves and do the best they can for their country. A 'backbone' is exactly what you want to strip out of people if you want them to be passive sheep in a controlled state! As well as this nationalism can provide a way of uniting people and this is also bad news for our putative prison guards. Its obviously much more of a threat to the system if a number of people can unite against it at the same time, rather that individuals acting alone. This is another reason why national identity must be stripped out of people in a controlled police state type of world. How they do this is the interesting thing, basically they mess with people's minds and seek to root out the pride people have in the achievements of their country:

a) If, like most places in Western Europe, the country has a colonial tradition then it is said that the whole nation was one slave driving mass oppressing gang of fascists! Its very hard to play this card on the Irish nation, but you can always try e.g. by claiming that Irish people were willing oppressors in the British Empire etc.[7]

b) Cast doubt on the origins of the country and the genuineness of its borders, how historic they are etc. For example you sometimes hear that Belgium is a country just cobbled together from the remnants of post Napoleonic Europe, without any great claim to unity or historic identity. This is surely unfair though because Belgium is a recognisable and unique stretch of land going as far back as the 16th century, when it was already distinguishable from Holland and France. One writer on Bangladesh, Mohammad Zainal Abedin, who says that RAW - the Indian intelligence agency - controls 90% of the officials of the state television there, states that the latter intelligence agency tries to cast aspersions on the circumstances of that countries independence in the hope that this will drain the country of its sense of purpose and morale:

> "Now to over run a country an aggressor cripples its citizens psychologically...Though the country seems to be independent outwardly but psychologically and culturally its people are made subservient. They become imitative. Their cultural identity and exclusiveness and their spirit of nationalism gradually die down. A day then comes when they fail to perceive the significance and necessity of protecting independence and sovereignty. RAW relentlessly has been endeavouring to create such a situation in Bangladesh."[8]

You can get a little whiff of this creeping into revisionism in Irish history. We are supposed to have been conquered by the Romans - and hence not unique in Western Europe - the Celts didn't exist at all really, and anyway the Celts of Tara and the Gaelic lords of the Flight of the Earls were just the usual clique of oppressing horrible aristocrats that we are supposed to be well shut of.

You can compress historical periods in order to create the impression that all nations are just haphazard collections of passing migrants and not, and were never, a united mass. For example you can try that in Ireland and say that those Irish people descended from the Vikings or the Normans are just the same as the 'new' Irish from Poland or wherever ignoring the fact that the Normans have been in Ireland since 1170, a long time ago and for at least 500 years of that they were not considered Irish. It wasn't until the 1660s that they qualified as 'new Irish' (see for example John Lynch's *Alithinologia*). You have compressed the time period so that the centuries of shared history is forgotten.

Waves of revisionism can descend on the narrow shoulders of your historians, knocking the 'myths' that give a country its nationalistic pride. In Ireland's case we have been told over the last few years that Tom Barry was sectarian, that Oliver Cromwell was a good guy if a little misunderstood, that the Penal laws never really happened or were at least wildly exaggerated etc etc which thankfully our underpaid and overworked amateur historians have managed to beat off in time, not least on indymedia.

c) But the main way to destroy national identity is via mass migration.

Effectively a country loses its historic sense of itself if most of its citizens - or at least a large proportion - just don't identify with the traditional unifying ethnic make up of a country. In a recent interview in the UK:

> "Cardinal Murphy-O'Connor, the leader of the Catholic Church in England and Wales, said that government promotion of multiculturalism has destroyed the unity that used to hold British society together."[9] [... Referring as well to the UK's Christian heritage he is reported as saying that with this immigration flow] "people lose their bonds of belonging and sense of identity. He says this is already beginning to happen."[10]

The likes of Hacker quoting Churchill 'we will fight them on the beaches', or talk of the 'ancient liberties of a free born Englishman' will die out because all this means nothing to a person of Pakistani, or African or Chinese descent.

Its no good thinking you can get people to pass some exam as a citizenship test or some other such proposal that increasingly desperate administrators and citizens in countries like Denmark, the UK, Holland and France are increasingly dreaming up. You cannot graft onto a people some new artificial identity like this, it will never work, most migrants (and the descendants of migrants if they are of a different ethnic background to the host nation) just do not, and never will - or at least not for some 500 years - feel the sense of identity to their new country which is necessary for genuine patriotism and nationalism to exist. This is no doubt why mass migration flows seem such a feature of the modern world, maybe they are quite deliberately sponsored by the powers that be to create this effect of stripping out the nationalist identity from people. Although we are late to the game this is no doubt slated to be the fate of Ireland as well.

The only thing people are left with then is a sense of belonging to an ethnic group that is probably a minority in the country where it used to be the majority. In other words a white English person night derive his sense of himself from being around other people of the same ethnic group and background and history within England, even if the country itself no longer has that identity. They might end up similar to countries that never had, or live outside, a traditional state like the Basques who live in Spain and France, or the Irish of the UK and USA or even north of the Border. Like some in Belfast people might end up identifying with others on the basis of their appearance, or surname - or even first name - rather than the state, and ethnic identity and nationalistic pride could survive that way. But the powers that be have thought of that, they are ready for you there! They call that racism and are going to extreme lengths broadcasting constantly and educating people that that is totally unacceptable.

Hopefully then, from their point of view, in time nationalism and ethnic identity will collapse, to be Irish will just mean having a letter on a car number plate or a passport, it wont mean anything at all more than that in a bland globalised world of completely mixed up races and nationalities.

3) Communities. Another value system, and 'backbone', can come to people from strong communities, not just those at a national level. I think in places like working class Limerick a person would refuse to become some evil prison guard, or whatever, because their mates would kill them! (That's metaphorically speaking for everywhere outside Belfast :-) only kidding..) A certain code of behaviour exists in those places I think and this community spirit gives people strength which is again bad news to the powers that be. Hence those places will just have to go, bulldoze them to the ground on some excuse. After a while, as those people begin to live apart, they wont know who they are and will all the more readily give in to the system.

4) Families. This can also be a source of pride and a value system for some people. Maybe you wouldn't do anything that would make you feel ashamed in the eyes of your children or your parents or your grandparents or whoever. This could be the kind of bedrock values that a person has, he/she might have in their mind's eye what their father or mother would have done in a particular situation, so providing a kind of ongoing value system.

I'm afraid this is for the chop then too! Spread around Restraining Orders like confetti in legal proceedings! At least try to have children brought up by only one parent, so they lose half that value system (and get rid of grandparents and extended families out of children's lives too.) Do whatever it takes to bring them into the divorce courts, encourage adultery, whatever. Teach constant repetitive sex education classes. Never mind the fact that it bores the pupils and embarrasses the teachers hopefully it will highlight sex in such a way that long term monogamous relationships become impossible. Promoting that kind of lifestyle can also be useful in controlling society by simply distracting people away from focusing on political issues, a trick that the Romans called bread and circuses, as Aldous Huxley relates in his preface to a 'Brave New World':

"As political and economic freedom diminishes, sexual

> freedom tends correspondingly to increase. And the
> dictator will do well to encourage that freedom...it will
> help to reconcile his subjects to the servitude which is
> their fate."[11]

Hopefully this will drive people further away from religion as well, helping to destroy that other identity.

Maybe in some cases family pride can even extend to some historical references, a family might claim to live in such and such an area for centuries, and were always 'decent people' who wouldn't stoop to some low evil act. Ban or discourage history teaching while you are at it then! (Which is useful for stripping out national identity too.) By hook or by crook then people will no longer know about their family history and will not have that pride to guide them. In time maybe half the population will be illegitimate children who possibly never knew both their parents at all, and this then is the right material for the powers that be to work on.

Implanting Subservient Values

Ok then now you are ready for the next step. Imagine a line of people lined up like the Marines with their heads shaven, their identities stripped from them. All types are lined up intermixed, black, white, Asian, whatever without any groups formed that could interfere with the imposition of a new value system. They all now speak the one language too, a kind of unaccented bland broken English, the only language a mass of different races can use to communicate with one another. They have nothing to grasp at now that would cause them to stand up to their prison guards, no pride that could give them that inner fire to resist. But not to worry, we will now give you all new identities that will make our control over you all the easier.

1) Law. Its often been said that the origin of most law in the UK and Ireland derives from centuries of seeking to curb the arbitrary power of the state and providing inalienable rights and privileges that the latter cannot trample on at will. This might be true, by and large, of the Irish constitution as well as the ancient common law type of rights and principles like trial by jury, right to silence, innocent until proven guilty (actually CAB proceedings in the Irish courts work exactly the opposite way now), that a person cannot be convicted on just one man's word against another (a dead letter now if the other person is a Garda or state expert), that when you did your punishment under the system then you

can start afresh, that you cannot be tried again if acquitted of a crime (double jeopardy) etc. The point is that if you look around you today you can see that these ancient privileges are quietly being abolished.

Take one principle for example, the right to public justice as opposed to some private or secretive inquiry by some state body. It has always been clear under time honoured legal principles that justice must be public to be fair, for a whole host of reasons not least because parties can lie through their teeth in private proceedings and not face any consequences for doing so, because most people in a position to know the truth will not have access to their testimony, and also it can allow people to say one thing in public and an entirely different thing privately, a fantastic facility for a corrupt politician! As the philosopher and jurist Jeremy Bentham (1748-1832) noted:

> "Publicity is the very soul of justice. It is the keenest
> spirit to exertion and the surest of all guards against im-
> probity. It keeps the judge, while trying, under trial."[12]

Look at the Irish legal system now in that light. Michael McDowell changed centuries of Irish legal tradition when he created the Morris tribunal which for the first time can hear and report on a mixture of secret and public testimony. He claimed that was not to prejudice future legal proceedings, supposedly in the interests of the McBrearty family, while what has happened of course is that families like the McBreartys have been grilled mercilessly in the public hearings while senior figures like Garda Commissioners and Justice ministers have been put on the stand only in the secret portions of the tribunal. The inquiry into Clerical child abuse allows the various religious bodies to issue a public statement, frequently casting doubt on the full force of the allegations against them, and then the actual evidence from the victims is heard in secret. (Which allows rumours to circulate to the detriment of both the innocent clergy and many of the victims.) The recent inquiry into the death of Brian Rossiter in Clonmel has been held in secret which, one suspects, is precious little use to this family in their quest for justice. The whole Irish family law system is buried under layer upon layer of secrecy with only now and again horrifying tales of legal corruption and state aggression emerging into the public domain.

Another example of a time honoured legal protection could be the Coroner's courts. These were established in Ireland as long ago as the 12th century as a way of hearing public on the record testimony about the circumstances of a person's death, and are, and always were, particularly called into being if there are any unusual or suspicious circumstances surrounding that death. If you read newspaper accounts from the 19th century, for example, you can see how much interest there was in these courts. Frequently there would be a report of a suspicious death and then the general public would await the Coroner's court to find out the real circumstances and facts surrounding the case. Then if the court found that a person died in a suspicious way a murder investigation might be launched. It makes perfect sense to arrive at a verdict as to how a person dies and then possibly arrive at future court cases to determine who might be responsible for foul play. Nowadays the way it works is that the media, using selected Garda leaks - from the Garda Press office or inspired by government bodies you can be sure, not the initiative of individual Gardaí - pump out a particular version of events quickly, frequently fingering some person for the crime without the slightest hesitation. (For instance look at the media coverage of the Sophie du Plantier killing, or Rachel O'Reilly, or newspaper reports of the tragic house fire at Omagh.) After a while, after the media version has sunk into everybody virtually brainwashing the public with this official line, then the Inquest comes along and the same Gardaí close it down claiming that it might prejudice a future court case. Even the Garda Ombudsman's Office closed down an Inquest while the verdict was being considered by the jury, again on the basis of some will o' the wisp future never ending investigation. This then ensures that the public get a version of events which is not backed up by open testimony in a court setting, what that means is that they can make up any facts they like in these media leaks and don't have to take an oath and stand over their word given in public. The Omagh bombing is interesting to look at in that regard. The media story was burned into people's heads very quickly after the bombing but when the RUC were pressed for the hard facts at the Inquest, held a long time later, they actually refused to testify on the grounds that they might incriminate themselves.[13] Then in the only other forum where the hard facts needed to be put on the table, during the two trials held North and South, it turns out that the judges themselves flatly accused the state of manufacturing evidence.

Anyway the point is that the legal system now is not at all the ancient way of protecting the citizen, those old rights are being brushed aside with contempt and all we are left with is statute law, realms of it, creating new criminal offences at an enormous rate.[14] Statute law right now effectively is the rule book written by Bertie Ahern who has ruled over us either as Taoiseach or senior minister for well nigh a generation. If you think he is somewhat dishonest then don't be too surprised if the statute laws that you and I abide by right now have some other purpose than the stated ones! The English MEP Ashley Mote puts it succinctly:

> "The law was once championed as a shield for the protection of the common man. In the hands of today's rul-

ing elite it has become a weapon of the state. It is now
much to be feared. It is used ruthlessly to destroy opposition, however modest, wherever it is perceived."[15]

It isn't surprising then that the powers that be are very comfortable in
this new legal set up, and they would like you to feel the same way. The
law has now been established as the first and most important of the new
values in this police state.

We want you now to quote the law in all your transactions, we want
you to measure good and evil, and all your actions, according to this
yardstick. This is now your new religion and identity, learn to love it,
learn to hate those that infringe on it in any way. Now as you go around
the prison camp you can quote from the law (which is just the prison
camp rule book, drawn up by the prison governor) whenever you see
some poor fella eating an apple as he cycles along between the prison
huts, or read the riot act to some guy who pulls on a cigarette in a re-
stricted area. Just get into the habit of judging your fellow inmates by
this yardstick, be judgemental don't be afraid to aggravate your neighbours with every pointless subsection in every regulation in that manual, even if it is patently the wrong thing to do. You don't question the
law, you abide by it and criticise anybody who doesn't or hasn't abided
by it with the same full intensity. There is also a full set of organisations
to complain to if you see anybody breaking the law, with confidential
phone numbers advertised everywhere for you to inform on your fellow
prisoners. (Don't give me that Irish tradition of not informing, don't you
know there is no such thing as being Irish? What did it ever mean exactly? I don't want you quoting 'traditions', myths, scientific untruths!
Haven't you been to the re-education classes, don't you know nationalism - aka racism - is wrong? - This just proves again how you must burn
out nationalism in order to control people properly.)

Then some laws come down to you like Star Trek 'from the Federation', with even less likelihood that you had any say in drawing them
up. Don't question the merits of that law that requires the school huts to
pay for water when the very thing seems to come down in buckets constantly! Excuse me you don't do that, when the law asks you to jump
you ask how high, don't ever question the laws we give you ever again,
is that understood?

2) Tax. Another set of values, related to the legal one, is tax. Again paying tax is hyped up as the end all and be all, a crucial yardstick in
judging your fellow man.

This is because the prison is actually an open prison, people work
outside it so its very important that when they come back they give the

319

prison authorities all their income. After all that's what funds the whole prison system, if they didn't have that where would they be? Of course you are told that the taxes are to pay for the prison health service etc but if you look around you carefully you might notice how that service, and nearly every other one, goes to rack and ruin while every corner of the prison now has new shiny CCTV cameras, and the prison guards and officials seem to always get higher pay and perks. Also its important for the prison system to track all the money transactions made by the prisoners, that way they can police them easier and the tax system facilitates this surveillance.

3) Work. Or rather work work work to give it its official title:-). We want to burn this into your soul, work is what we will allow you to do to gain self respect and dignity and all that. We want you to work constantly and judge people by the amount of work that they do. This is the next most important value system. If people are completely obsessed with work, as some people accuse Americans of being, then they will all become lovely worker ants without any spark of life in them or with enough time to look around and see the creation of the prison system around them.[16] As well as creating a value system that puts work above almost all other human activities it might be possible to increase the rate of growth in a country which can itself compel people to work harder, in order to keep afloat of an increased cost of living.

Communism, in the former USSR for example, always strove to install the work ethic as one of the great values that people should have by giving awards to great workers and other similar schemes. (Don't forget that this modern obsession about work in the West is quite a new thing, about 100 years ago the exact opposite was considered to be the right qualities of a gentlemen. While I suppose a conscientiousness in doing work, and supporting families, was always valued to a certain extent nonetheless at that time being honest, well read, having cultural talents etc would be much more highly prized in a person, and society, than just working for works sake which is where we are now really.) The USSR authorities obviously knew that if they could keep their citizens busy with their heads down working constantly, or travelling to work, then they could more easily control them.

Furthermore a workaholic type culture can have the effect of coarsening society, which in turn makes it less cohesive and therefore will help to kill off that community (or family) type value system as described above. What I mean is that in non workaholic environments society functions with towns and villages full during the day, with some people knocking around who aren't all the time working. (Or indeed just not taking their work so seriously that they couldn't stop for a chat now and again.) Also families will clearly function best if there is somebody there to talk to etc. Clearly if everybody is at work all the time then family structures and village life collapses.

If you think about it too you can see that cultural aspects of a society usually depend on people who don't have a regular job. Irish culture heavily depends on its penniless poets like Patrick Kavanagh, or ill paid musicians, or actors, or historians, or even people who could be relied upon for a long conversation during the day. In a workaholic culture often the cost of living drives these people to abandon their pursuits and they could even just get fed up meeting people who pester them with questions about when they are going to get a 'proper' job. This kind of bleak social landscape is the inevitable by-product of a workaholic culture.

Hence now we want you to develop that boiled eyed insensitivity and constant resentment of the workaholic. See that guy protesting over there, go over and ask him will he grow up and get a job, go on that's the spirit! We want you to work work work, think workhorse with blinkers on, that's you! Don't think, you're not paid to think! In fact in education we want you to be focused on what your future employer wants. We don't want dreamy spires with philosophers thinking about the world around them. Coming to think of it it would be helpful if the cost of living or fees were so high that students had to work full time while trying to study. That's the spirit, no time to read things, you're just there to regurgitate what you're told. We don't want these student types with time on their hands able to go to demonstrations or whatever, better to have an economic necessity so that for them its work work work too!

Now having burned this work value system into your soul, at times, when we need to, we might pull it away, or threaten to, and collapse your sense of yourself or your standing among your peers. To a remarkable degree the powers that be now have the capacity to deny the possibility of work to those they dislike. Most jobs now are either on government contracts, frequently short term without any job security, or require some kind of tax certificate or state licensing permission e.g. you cannot even apply now to be a nurse on the CAO form without going through a Garda vetting process. (This increasing job insecurity is not necessarily an accident, this itself might be a control mechanism in society. Probably the powers that be would like teachers, judges, doctors, Gardaí, solicitors and barristers to have no jobs for life and instead be dependent on the state for their livelihood. One way of doing this could be for the state to seize control of the independent professional bodies, like e.g. the Medical Council so they can easily sack any doctor that gets in their way.) Royston Brady has come forward recently to say that he was directly threatened by a senior Fianna Fail figure that if he didn't stop speaking out in the media:

> "I would find it very hard to get work in this town. It is a small town."[17]

He doesn't say who this senior FF figure was but in all probability it was Bertie Ahern, who is described as Royston's mentor in FF, and you can see that with so much employment resting on the say so of state agencies, which obviously he ultimately controls, it is a very real threat in the modern age. Frances Cahill, the daughter of Martin Cahill 'the General', has described in elaborate detail how none of her family were ever allowed to take up normal employment, even though many of them had nothing to do with criminal activities. The Gardaí went to enormous lengths to sabotage any attempts that Frances made to find work, even as a shop assistant. The threat of losing employment is held over all who might threaten the system, and this threat is greater when work - and to a certain extent the money derived from it - is hyped up as the ultimate in human endeavour.

Sin a bhfuil ar aon nós, my tuppence worth on the type of values that make political control that much easier in our modern world. I know this probably seems like a surprising list of implanted values, no doubt many people feel that the law, tax and work are good things, and indeed they are in some respects. After all most of the important laws are still based on old Christian principles and this writer is definitely not advocating that people should start killing or stealing or breaking laws for the sake of it. Also some sort of taxation is surely necessary and good. The same is true of the work that many people have put in over the years to rear families etc. But everything can be twisted and brought to ridiculous extremes and I think that's where we are now. Those values are held up - especially in the US - as the end all and be all of human existence, the height of praise you can bestow on anybody is to say that such and such a person was always law abiding and hard working who always paid their taxes. The same person might have been hopelessly discourteous to his fellow citizens, say in back seat driving putting great store in the minutae of the motoring laws, never helped out people in his community and contributed to family life only by constantly haranguing his children/spouse with endless questions about when are they are going to get a job. The point is that those values are actually pretty poor yardsticks to judge people by, and in the long run can devalue rather than enhance societies.

And, in this writers humble opinion anyway, it absolutely is true that the powers that be are twisting and hyping these values to suit themselves. Anybody who attends Irish public meetings or protests cannot but be struck at how ill attended they are even in populous places like Dublin city. In practice most people are simply working all the time and therefore cannot contribute to political campaigns, a fact that the government, you can be sure, is well aware of and pleased about. While it might be painful for some to face up to this, the truth is that right now the law in Ireland is becoming just a set of rules written by a number of corrupt politicians to suit themselves (as regards that corrupt claim I would point to the testimony of Tom Gilmartin), and they are simply outlawing all genuine political opposition to their position. Consider that recently politics.ie, the largest Irish political website, closed down all discussion whatsoever of any matters relating to the Taoiseach based on their interpretation of the libel laws.[18] Public Order offences meanwhile are being used to crush all protests against the state, for example the community at Rossport woke up one morning to a line of hundreds of Gardaí who had orders to crush their ongoing opposition to a Shell gas refinery. As I say in practice we are at the point now where real political opposition to the powers that be is simply illegal, and then what are people going to do if the law has been held up as a kind of new religion? Presumably many will now docilely accept this new situation because they know no other morality than the law, hence this law value system creates subservient citizens.

Meanwhile those old values were, and are, much more of a threat to the powers that be. To clarify look at it from the perspective of a British administrator in modern Ireland for example. From his point of view if he could burn out of people their historical memories and nationalism (what you are trying to kill off is the memory that Ireland had been united and that the British had stolen Irish lands in the Ulster Plantation) and their religious identity then that's how you can make Ireland as British as Finchley as the saying goes! That gets to the heart of the resistance in a way, without those values every place becomes a sort of bland suburban landscape where the established hierarchy and laws are submitted to without question. If, for example, you had some map of the troubles and you were trying to figure out again the 'roots of resistance' what you would notice I think is that people will stand up to the state in those working class areas where many people are related to one another and where there is great solidarity, and in rural areas where there is great historical memory and pride (the type of place where they could point out to you the bog they had to live in when Cromwell confiscated their estates) everywhere else you will find no serious resistance. In particular if you could look at such a map now and see the large amount of middle class suburb type areas, where different ethnic groups live together, you can see that no serious rebelliousness would ever come from there. They get their values from the media, which emphasise things like the above, and anyway they couldn't unite because they have nothing in common with their neighbours. If you were such an administrator plotting a plan of political control then what you would do is bulldoze out of existence those tight knit urban areas - they call that urban regeneration! - and drive out of rural areas the original inhabitants - say by various planning things, collapse of rural services, transport nightmares, the ruination of the agricultural economy etc - and this will cement political control both now and into the future.

While no doubt most people would not agree that the powers that be in this country are that powerful or clever enough to contemplate these things my guess, as detailed in Chapter 1, is that they can be cleverer than people think, and some prominent international power structures have indeed thought through long term planning of things like this.[19]

Necessity to crush the sense of history

Incidentally one crucial point to be made here is that in the process of supplanting values it helps if true historic memory of the past is crushed, and if change and modernism is held up as almost a value in itself. To give a simple example of how this works, imagine if you were some devious banker who plotted to encourage a whole generation to ruinously borrow money beyond their means. What you would need to do is encourage a kind of 'brave new world' atmosphere, so that your borrowers to be would be comfortable borrowing vastly more money than their parents and grandparents did. In otherwords if you can persuade that generation that their forefathers lived in some very simple primitive world, unlike the sophisticated wealthy successful world that the new generation inhabits, then lending that money becomes much easier, the new generation will not stop to think about how much greater they are in debt when compared to their parents. Also it might be helpful to blot out the historical memory of the various economic bubbles in history (like the South Sea bubble, the Tulip bubble, housing bubble in early 90s UK etc), because obviously if that generation knew this history well enough they would see the comparison to their own era.

The point is that it is very helpful to crush historical memory when trying to replace peoples values. In fact it may be possible to go further and foster a kind of change for changes sake kind of atmosphere which will clearly help you in scrapping old values and replacing them with new ones. Hence if you can fill the air with talk of 'change', 'progress', 'in this day and age' etc then people will unconsciously feel the need to scrap old values and replace them with new ones.

In Ireland meanwhile it is particularly important to crush historical memory, because Irish history contains so many parallels to what is occurring today. The British government made enormous efforts, over centuries, to stamp out the Catholic religion in Ireland knowing that it promoted a set of values that they couldn't control. (And of course they pushed the Anglican religion instead, an 'established' church which not accidentally was headed by the English monarch and had its bishops appointed by the British Prime Minister.) Another time honoured trick of theirs was to establish plantation schemes where they would try and attract immigrants into Ireland who would supplant the natives. They hoped by this to create a more amenable, hard working, law abiding, less rebellious society, with long term consequences that are still being felt in Ulster. They always kept a beady eye on, and frequently executed, Irish poets and harpers knowing full well that if they could root out the cultural sense of Irishness out of the people then they could more easily be able to psychologically take over the country. Then having done that they used the education system and the media to quite deliberately spread around the notion of British fair mindedness and the fruits of liberty sealed by a 'Glorious Revolution.' Colonel Maurice Moore accused them of this when he wrote his account of the Irish Volunteers:

> "It is not only the vanity, but also the policy of the English people to spread these fallacies, and they certainly have had considerable effect, by dint of hearing them repeated, people believe to a certain extent in their truth...[but after 1916 Irish people] began to consider history more carefully; they remembered that ...'Perfide Albion' represented the European view of her diplomacy."[20]

Daniel Sheehan, an Irish Parliamentary Party MP, describes the same policy:

> "Through the whole of the nineteenth century it had been the malign purpose of England to destroy the spirit of nationality through its control of the schools. Just as in the previous century it sought to reduce Ireland to a state of servitude through the operations of the Penal Laws, so it now sought to continue its malefic purpose by a system of education "so bad that if England had

wished to kill Ireland's soul when she imposed it on the Sister Isle she could not have discovered a better means of doing so" (M. Paul Dubois). And the same authority ascribes the fatalism, the lethargy, the moral inertia and intellectual passivity, the general absence of energy and character which prevailed in Ireland ten or twelve years ago to the fact that England struck at Ireland through her brain and sought to demoralise and ruin the national mind."

Then the atmosphere in Ireland changed dramatically after the Irish Ireland movement started:

"In giving to the young especially a new pride in their country and in their own, great and distinctive national heritage, it did a great deal to strengthen the national character and to make it more independent and self-reliant. It started the great work of rooting out the slavery which centuries of dependency and subjection had bred into the marrow of the race. Mr Arthur Griffith has admitted that the present generation could never have effected this work had not Parnell and his generation done their brave labour before them, but considered in themselves the achievements of the Gaelic League can only be described as mighty both in the actual revolution it wrought in the moral, intellectual and spiritual sphere, in the reaction it created against the coarser materialism of imported modes and manners, and in the new spirit which it breathed into the entire people."[21]

Hence at a high level they can really do this, with control over the media, and other institutions, they can mould the ethos of a whole population to suit their aims of long term political control.

The Open War of Ideas

I suppose what's absent in this analysis though is how exactly are they doing this in modern times? Again the issue of control over the media (mentioned in Chapter 1) and the education system are maybe key elements here but there is also a wider question I think about the way that the globalists exert great influence in modern society. Maybe the way to look on this is that you have a kind of open clash of ideas in society and that the globalists are winning this battle hands down. Its not a secret kind of influence necessarily, its a public open genuineish debate that this corrupt clique is winning. What is happening I think is that this clique has elaborately thought through their intellectual and philosophical positions, maybe over decades before they actually adopt them, while the rest of the population receive a kind of vocational and functional education and are ill equipped - and have little time - to think through the contradictions and self serving element in the globalists viewpoint. If you look at modern Ireland today I think you might agree that many opinion formers in society tend to be trained in accountancy or have business degrees etc while the extent of knowledge of history, theology or philosophy - apart from Marx and Engles - is very poor, which makes them easily influenced by the globalists in these intellectual battles. After all we live in a democracy, this means that political power rests ultimately on the opinions and attitudes of the wider public. Therefore to control society you need to win the intellectual war, control the public's opinions and you control the country, and in this intellectual war maybe we are less well equipped than ever before.

I apologise that this might sound a bit wafflish :-) but look at the immigration issue for example and maybe you can see where I am coming from. Is there some vast secret conspiracy to encourage the public to lose their Irish identity as a process of integrating immigrants? No there is a public and open intellectual debate going on with one side, the opponents of immigration, completely overawed (and possibly intimidated by verbal abuse) by the liberal arguments put up by their opponents. They might instinctively think what is happening is wrong but they lack the intellectual ammunition to fight back? This again might be no accident, the chances are that the globalists know exactly what points to make to entrench their position (and they know that a lack of knowledge of history etc among the wider public helps them), they probably thought it through decades before unleashing these global migration flows and are well acquainted with the arguments that worked well in other countries.

To give a concrete example of how a group can win an intellectual argument by thinking through in advance their position consider the role of 'tolerance' in modern intellectual debates. Certainly to be tolerant to another person is normally a sign of strength and confidence and human decency, a characteristic of a nice guy and usually altogether a good thing. The same might be said, to an extent, of society in general. Surely being tolerant of one's neighbours foibles is healthy and leads to an harmonious society. That 'extent' word is the key point though, I think, brought to ridiculous limits it can actually destroy society. To illustrate this picture a guy who decides to jog around Dublin in his un-

327

derwear!lol There are some parts of the city where probably people will stand and stare but wouldn't say anything because live and let live is the philosophy, who are you to judge what other people get up to etc, and then there are other parts, usually old Irish working class areas, where he would be teased mercilessly and probably run out of the place. The interesting thing is that those areas which were tolerant of him, you will find, are the same areas where he could be dead for a week before anybody would notice! The 'tolerant' areas are the same places where there isn't a sense of community at all. If you think about it, minding your own business and tolerating everything everybody else does is pretty much the definition of a community less society. Being able to draw attention to differences in people, and to a degree teasing a person so much that they discard their difference, or even just verbally talking about it so much that it no longer matters any more, are how communities are formed? If you feel you shouldn't, or even legally cannot, mention to a person that he is walking around in his underwear then you can be sure no friendship or community feeling will ever form between you and our liberated jogger.

Look at tolerance in action in family structures as another - and maybe more real world :-) - example. Irish society, up to I guess the 90s, has been accused of intolerance in the way that it treated people outside the normal family structures. For example it has been said that women who got pregnant outside marriage were virtually imprisoned in Magdalen laundries because of the social stigma attached to their position. Maybe again you can see some merit in this criticism, after all some were treated very badly in those laundries, treatment that you wouldn't wish on your worst enemy. Now there is no such stigma, and therefore partly flowing from this you have huge rates of illegitimacy, family breakdown and the energies, and even the wealth, of large numbers of Irish people are tied up in endless heartbreaking family court dramas. The point is that if you are going to be tolerant of everything then family structures, and many other institutions, will inevitably collapse?

Consider what would happen if you made 'tolerance' the end all and be all goal of a simple institution like a football team. Say the manager of the team was a very tolerant person and the board and fans put great store by this. Again no question this has definite merits to a degree. There are probable plenty of good footballers who only need an encouraging word now and again from a manager who might overlook some small foible in their person or game. But picture the scene if this is brought to ridiculous limits. Say the manager is tolerant and understanding when the players arrive in late all the time, he is sensitive and has no harsh words to say when the team balloon the ball wide every game, he never takes action against any player who might be too young or too old or unfit etc because he is being tolerant and inclusive. Obviously if this was the only criteria for a manager then the team would go to rack and ruin in no time, the point is that 'tolerance' is only one aspect of any institution or society, if it is highlighted too much then efficiency and purposefulness will collapse.

Maybe you can see that effect when you view Irish political discourse as it applies to family structures. Most Irish politicians and media commentators are proud that Ireland is now a 'tolerant' country where anything goes in family life, not like those dark ages where terrible intolerance ruled. Tolerance, and inclusiveness which is much the same thing, is the only criteria they use to judge the state of family life. I think that if they looked upon it more broadly, and asked themselves what would be a good or bad picture of Irish family life taking into account the majority of people and Irish life as a whole, I think they would have to conclude that the current set up is disastrous, far worse than the family structure that existed in the recent past.

Furthermore, as pointed out in the value systems above and in footnote 19, destroying family structures is actually one of the aims of the globalists and so this lamentable picture is possibly not the accidental outcome that people might presume it to be. The Catholic Church, over centuries, accused Masonic orders of deliberately manipulating and twisting the concept of tolerance in order to achieve their aims of destroying current institutions (particularly Catholic teaching itself).[22] In other words the accusation is that this modern concept of tolerance, and its effect in destroying the efficiency and purpose of institutions, is actually deliberately used and highlighted by some of these globalist groups as a way to achieve their ends.

This then is maybe an example of how the globalists work, not by secret conspiracies in dark corners but by a kind of open conspiracy. They have thought through their intellectual position, and what parts of the picture they wish to show to the general public, while the population are left bamboozled by all these twists and turns and generally fall into their traps and end up enthusiastically agreeing with the globalists agenda because they have been out gunned like this in the war of ideas. It might be useful too to go back and analyse when this sort of thinking became popular in Irish political discourse, at what time did Irish opinion formers abandon any concept of the efficiency of family structures and instead talked only of tolerance? When did this all begin anyway? I think most people would agree that this began in the early 80s with the Constitutional Crusade of Garret Fitzgerald and his sidekick, and legal expert, the then Attorney General Peter Sutherland.[23]

Public Policy set by a small clique worldwide

This highlights one final point about conspiracy theories. A lot of people say about these theories that they have to involve a huge number of people operating in a coordinated secret fashion to work, and since this is felt to be implausible hence conspiracy theories usually do not happen. But sometimes if you observe the drifts of public policy you can see the same names cropping up again and again. Its not all businessmen or all politicians or all academics that influence society, and hence have to be part of some given conspiracy, its usually just a small number of key people that make the real difference in public policy nationally and even internationally. I think that real power is exercised by an apex of key people around the world, who could – and I am not making specific allegations – cooperate in achieving some specific goal.

The aforementioned Peter Sutherland's career possibly highlights this. Just like in the case of family structures and tolerance, maybe it might be interesting to try and trace to their source the origin of the Irish and international public policies listed above and throughout this book:

- Possibly if you were to speculate on when this practice of interfering with Coroner's Courts started you might point to the closing down of the Inquest into the Dublin and Monaghan bombings in the mid70s as an early, and particularly glaring, example of this phenomenon. This was done on the recommendation of Peter Sutherland then working for the government as a young barrister.[24]

- If you were to take up the phrase that Fr Fahey, quoted in Chapter 1, made about the money power controlling political parties and tried to analyse that in modern Ireland you might point to the serious allegations that Tom Gilmartin has made about the role AIB played in his affairs, and in that banks great influence over the political machinery of Ireland at that time.[25] Peter Sutherland was the chairman of AIB all this time.

- Say you were to take that analysis to a global stage and ask yourself how bankers exercise power internationally your gaze would probably alight on the Bilderberg group (eg even Charlie Haughey, as quoted in Chapter 4, was suspicious of the influence 'these international bankers' of the Bilderbergers exert over the political process worldwide) and the

Trilateral Commission (note the allegations quoted in Chapter 7 by a leading Russian dissident) where senior politicians, bankers and media personnel seem to cooperate in influencing public policy. Peter Sutherland is an important world banker, the chairman of Goldman Sachs, and he is also now the European chairman of the Trilateral Commission and on the steering committee of the Bilderberg group.[26]

- Maybe after reading Chapter 7 you might have wondered how these big oil companies exercise so much influence internationally, and how is it that in normal economic academic circles this role of currencies, and the incredible artificial wealth the Western oil companies made out of the oil shocks of the 70s and the present, seems to be little heard of and down played. Speculate you may but I might point out that Peter Sutherland, a leading international oil magnate as the chairman of BP, is on the advisory board of countless international economic think tanks and universities, like his fellowship of Oxonia,[27] the leading economic study group attached to Oxford University, and his membership of the advisory boards of the School of Business attached to UCD,[28] of the Instituto de Empresa in Madrid [29] of the IESE in Pamplona [30] – the two leading business universities in Spain – , of the School of Business and Economics of the University of Exeter, of the Nyenrode business university in the Netherlands and is now Chairman of the Court of Governors of the London School of Economics.[31]

- If you were to try and analyse who is behind the recent immigration flow into Ireland it might not be irrelevant to point out again that Peter Sutherland is the UN Special Representative on Migration and one of the leading figures in convening the Global Forum on Migration and Development.[32] As pointed out in the quote at the end of Chapter 10, he takes a keen interest in Irish immigration and links this back to the question of identity. It was actually said in the Seanad in 2005 that he thought Ireland should double its then rate of immigration. He is also a benefactor, member of the board and president of the International Advisory Council of the Institute for International Integration Studies located in the Sutherland centre in TCD.[33]

- As regards globalist use of legal trickery it strikes this observer that one of the ways that supra national organisations are now beginning to control nation states is the use of competition laws to justify intervening in a whole host of areas that traditionally remained the competence of national governments. Again trying to trace that to its source you might point to the very serious modern WTO competition rules and requirements and in the EU you could point to a time in the late 80s when the European Commission built up a lot of case law giving it power over member states where commercial competition was concerned, and which now seems to extend into virtually all areas of national life. This was done when the Commission competition portfolio was held by a lawyer, one Peter Sutherland, who also was the first head of the WTO and later chaired an important Consultative Board of that body.[34]

- Finally Peter Sutherland has now been appointed one of the leading financial advisers to the Vatican (and nicknamed 'God's banker') which is an exciting position in the light of some of the revelations highlighted in Chapter 10.[35] (I hasten to add that his appointment post dates the scandals mentioned in that chapter.)

So hence, and as pointed out I am not making specific allegations, maybe the moral of the story is that the real strings in political life are pulled by only a tiny number of key people, therefore its not necessary for a large number of people to know about a given conspiracy, only these few powerful opinion formers and decision makers need to know about it. Which added to the many other points made in this book might perchance cause a rational person to pause before dismissing allegations of conspiracies wherever they may be!

Footnotes

1. As corroboration of the general topic of the changes in Irish society, the weakening of the community value systems etc, there is this quote from boards.ie:

"There's very little sense of community in modern Ireland. In the 80s and even the first half of the 90s there was much more emphasis on community, people knew most people who lived near them, there was a common bond etc.

I'm from Wicklow Town and in the late 80s the town's biggest employer ended up with its staff striking. The rest of the people in the town bought groceries etc for the families struggling during the strike. That's what Ireland was. Nowadays almost every strike the country sees is criticized for how it will effect the individual.

Ireland's a greedy country now, far too caught up in its SUVs, iPods and designer fashions. Communities barely exist anymore because people only care about themselves.

Thats the death of old Ireland IMO. Moneys all that matters to people now." (http://www.boards.ie/vbulletin/showthread.php?t=2055212230&page=2).

For communists in the Catholic Church see for example Marie Carré, *AA-1025 : The Memoirs of an Anti-Apostle* (Rockford Illinois, 1972), passim and the statements of Bella Dodd, the Attorney General Designate of the Communist Party in the US, to the US Congress in the 1950s quoted in Hamish Hyde, *Church Infiltration,* Hibernian Magazine Jan 2007 issue 9 available at http://www.hibernianmedia.com/ , and from http://www.tldm.org/News6/VaticanII-1.htm :
'"In the 1930s we put eleven hundred men into the priesthood in order to destroy the Church from within." Twelve years before Vatican II, she said: "Right now they are in the highest places in the Church". She also predicted changes in the Church that would be so drastic that "you will not recognize the Catholic Church."
Dr. Alice von Hildebrand recalled, during an interview with Latin Mass magazine, that "Bella Dodd told my husband and me that when she was an active [Communist] party member, she had dealt with no fewer than four cardinals within the Vatican 'who were working for us'." (Latin Mass magazine, Summer 2001)'

2. Jim Rothstein interviewed on the Investigative Journal 27 March 2007 http://www.republicnewsradio.com/station/archives/17?page=2 .

3. See for example the article by Fr Michel Marchiset, a former SSPX priest, in translation from the French here: http://www.virgo-maria.org/articles_HTML/2007/002_2007/VM-2007-02-28/VM-2007-02-28-A-00-Compromission_communiste_Eglise_conciilaire.htm , and this from Fr M

E Morrison of San Francisco:
"On June 27, 2007, the roof blew off one long-time Newchurch cover-up. A special commission chaired by Newchurch Archbishop Slawoj Glodz, of Poland, publicly presented the results of its investigations, which found that one out of ten Newchurch bishops in Poland after Vatican II were spies for the Communist Secret Service (SS). Twelve of them are still living. Glodz passed over the delicate question of whether Karol Woytyla, later JPII, was one of these spies."(http://www.traditio.com/comment/com0707.htm)

You can see where they are coming from if you mull over two simple, and I think widely accepted, facts:
a) The Communist authorities in 1956 had won the right of veto over appointments to the Catholic hierarchy in Poland. As an example of widely respected authorities that prove this I will quote from two academics, and note as well the phrase 'traditional protocol' in the Yallop quote below:
"After Gomulka came to power in 1956...a 1950 agreement accommodating Church activities was renewed, with the added provision that granted the state veto power over Church appointments." (Arthur J Wolak, *Forced out: The Fate of Polish Jewry in Communist Poland* (Tucson, 2004), p.104.)

"This found expression in a resumption of interference in ecclesiastical appointments in 1958. Until then, the government had not exercised its right of veto under the terms of the 1956 agreement.. ...Wyszynski testified that on several occasions during the 1960s he had changed the list of candidates for ecclesiastical positions following state interference."
(Hanna Diskin, *The Seeds of Triumph: Church and State in Gomułka's Poland* (Budapest and New York, 2001), p.163.)

b) Approx. 20 per cent of the Catholic clergy in the Krakow diocese are thought now to have been Communist agents. See for example:
"As a result of the presbyter's investigations into the documents of the National Remembrance Repository, opened after the fall of the Communist regime in 1989, implications also arose about how much Krakow's former Newchurch archbishop, Karol Woytyla, later JPII, himself cooperated with the Communist Secret Police. Polish historians have concluded that up to 20% of Woytyla's diocesan clergy were involved in collaboration with the atheistic Communists. Was he himself?" (http://www.traditio.com/comment/com0712.htm referring to Fr Tadeusz Isakowicz-Zaleski and citing Source: Catholic World News)

Actually the percentage varies in some reports but even where it is a little smaller it is agreed that in the urban university cities like Krakow the rate would be much higher than in rural areas:
' "There is a sort of unholy alliance in Poland that has been present for many years, but is fully visible only recently, that is based on a culture of mendacity," said Andrzej Zybertowicz, professor of sociology at Nicolaus Copernicus University in Torun, the heart of the Polish church's most conservative camp.

He argued that there were three elements of this alliance: former members of the secret police and the Communist Party who are now active in business and politics; apologists who wanted to forgive and forget past collaboration; and an influential part of the hierarchy of the Polish church.
...
Poland's current primate and archbishop of Warsaw, Cardinal Jozef Glemp, told an Italian news agency last year that the overall percentage was 15 percent. The percentage was likely to have been much higher in major cities and university towns, some historians say, where surveillance was heavier.'
(New York Times 10 Jan 2007
http://www.nytimes.com/2007/01/10/world/europe/10poland.html)

The obvious next step is put those two facts together and conclude that presumably the Communist authorities would use their right of veto to get appointed their own agents as bishops? An easy thing to do since we now know that so many of the clergy were Communist spies? David Yallop in his uncomplimentary but highly respected biography of John Paul II relates this anecdote on the appointment of John Paul II as Archbishop of Krakow:

"Acting on the traditional protocol, Cardinal Wyszynski submitted three names to the Polish Government. All three had previously been approved by the Pope. Wojtyla's name was not on the list. Months later the list came back to Wyszynski with all of his candidate's rejected. The files of the Polish secret police and additional information from former Communist-Party members reveal a wonderfully ironic tale - independently confirmed by papal biographer George Weigel [footnoted as "Witness to Hope"]. A bemused Primate retired to his study and eventually a further three names were sent to the Vatican for papal approval, which was forwarded to the Polish Government. After a further three months the second list came back to Cardinal Wyszynski; again the regime had given the thumbs down to all three names.

During the late autumn of 1963 Father Andrzej Bardecki, the ecclesiastical assistant on the Catholic Church-financed paper, Tygodnik Powszechny, had a visitor at his Krakow office. Professor Stanislaw Stomma headed a minority Catholic Party in the Polish Parliament. With a maximum of five members it was in reality no more than a rump yet it served many useful purposes, not least as a conduit between the Communists and the Catholic Church. The professor quietly invited Father Bardecki to join him for a stroll around part of the city. As the two men walked, Professor Stomma recounted a conversation he had recently had with Zenon Kliszko, the Communist number two. Kliszko had asked him who would be the best candidate for the vacancy in Krakow. 'I told him, firmly and categorically that Wojtyla was the best, indeed the only choice.'
Kliszko beamed and replied, 'I've vetoed seven so far. I'm waiting for Wojtyla and I'll continue vetoing names until I get him.'... [This was a hint to be passed

on to the Catholic authorities:] Kliszko's tactics worked a charm. When he had received a further nomination from the Cardinal, the list contained the name 'Wojtyla'. It is not every Communist leader that can claim to have been instrumental in the making of a Pope."
(David Yallop, *The Power and the Glory* (London, 2007), p.11-12. While the specific points in the text are not footnoted the bibliography includes:
"Polish State Files on Karol Wojtyla, including Sluzba Bezoieczenstwa (SB - Secret police) reports covering 1948-1978, Krakow and Warsaw archives. This includes one document dated 5 August 1967 entitled in English: 'Our tactics regarding Cardinals Wojtyla and Wyszynski.' This document is described by Yallop on p.15:
"The recommendation was that Wojtyla be given every support even to ensuring that he should be handled very gently... ..the Communists planned to keep maximum pressure and discomfort on Wyszynski [the senior Polish cardinal] who, they believed, would eventually erupt as he saw the young man being granted every conceivable privilege and respect...So the old man was to be humiliated and hemmed in at every turn while 'we should act positively on matters of prestige that would improve Wojtyla's self-esteem.'")

4. See Chapter 7 footnote 18 infra.

5. Mark Garavan ed., *Our Story: The Rossport 5* (Magheramore, 2006), p.81-82.

6. Obviously a lot of people don't think that about Eoin O'Duffy but I include him because I can find precious little genuine evidence of horrible Hitler like anti semitic actions that he is supposed to be responsible for. As I see it all he did was lead a group of people who tried to stand up for free speech in the face of intimidation from the state intelligence services - the Broy Harriers - and then lead them to Spain to stand up for the Catholic Church, showing, like Brendan Hughes, the courage of his convictions. I'm just trying to be fair minded to all strands of Irish nationalism, and to note that bravery and genuine unselfishness (and abuse in the popular media!) is to be met with everywhere in the Irish nationalist tradition.

7. Consider these comments for example in a recent edition of Studies:
"Ireland did not have an empire, but the Irish helped administer one and, in doing so, inevitably imbibed beliefs about racial inferiority than justified Western imperialism. ... Republic of Ireland, all this suggests, came into being with the software of Western racism preloaded. This might, for instance, account for the experiences of recent African immigrants, noted in survey after survey, of very high levels of racist incidents.The software kicked in when they arrived.
A recent effort to conceptualise Irish racism, After Optimism? Ireland, Racism and Globalisation, by Ronit Lentin and Robbie McVeigh, falls within this school. Their core argument, using a concept developed by David Goldberg, depicts the Republic of Ireland as a racial state in the process of becoming a ra-

cist state...

Here the duty of the civilised liberal is to be intolerant of intolerance. A new insistence upon Western cultural superiority seems to underpin opposition to multiculturalism within a number of Western states.

...

In The IRA and its Enemies the historian Peter Hart documents disproportionate killings of Protestants and Travellers as 'informers' in West Cork during the war of independence. Travellers, the 'tramp class', had been ordered to leave the county in early 1921 by the North Cork Brigade. Cork, incidentally, was the location of Frank O'Connor's fictional Guests of the Nation. Hart's evidence suggests that any real informers were unlikely to be from these minority groups:

Not all executed 'spies and 'informers' were strangers or deviants and some of those who were, were in fact guilty of helping the authorities. Nevertheless, these were exceptions. The great majority of suspects – and, it seems, most informers – were respectable Catholics, but the great majority of victims were not. They were killed not for what they did but for who they were: Protestants, ex-soldiers, tramps and so on down the communal blacklist. Their deaths were not the consequence of political heresy, but of a persecution that went beyond the immediate hunt for informers. Guerrilla war transformed them into the unwanted enemy within.

The hostile reception to Hart's research by non-historians, such as the literary critic Luke Gibbons suggests that ethnic-nationalism, anti-colonialist or otherwise still has a hard time coming to terms with real exclusions, past and present. Gibbon's 2005 Village article "Memory without Walls: from Kevin Barry to Osama bin Laden" exemplified the politics of memory (as distinct from actual history) at work here. Gibbons claimed, erroneously, that historians like Hart 'have sought to recast the guerrilla warfare of Tom Barry, Liam Lynch and others as "terrorism", "serial-killing" or "ethnic-cleansing" '. Yet, 'ethnic-cleansing,' a term popularised after the break-up of former Yugoslavia, might not be inappropriate to describe sectarian burning-out and forced land sales between 1919 and 1923 in both parts of Ireland.

Gibbon's article ends with a discussion of an iconic photograph of two African women walking past the shutters of 16 Moore Street (first published in The Sunday Tribune), the building where the rebel leaders of 1916 surrendered. Real immigrants, the new guests of the nation, can only be bit players in such post-colonialist pageants. The exclusions they experience may have much to do with racism, but they also have something to do with longstanding local identity politics. In this context to insist blithely that the Republic of Ireland is a racial state serves to mask a broader potential mechanics of exclusion." (Ryan Fanning, *Against the Racial State*, March 2007 Studies http://www.studiesirishreview.ie/j/page78)

8. http://usa.mediamonitors.net/headlines/raw_and_bangladesh_one , http://usa.mediamonitors.net/content/view/full/23249 and http://usa.mediamonitors.net/headlines/raw_and_bangladesh_final . One of RAW's aims is "To

mount malicious propaganda about founding principles and ideological basis of the country and create favourable public opinion for merger with India." The TV reference:
"Ninety percent of the officers of BTV [state owned bangladesh TV] have close links with RAW. These officers receive regular monthly allowance from RAW (Weekly Sainik : July 17, 1991)."

9. http://www.independent.ie/world-news/europe/sharia-law-comments-leave-bishop-in-hot-water-1286301.html .

10. Cardinal Murphy-O'Connor Sunday Telegraph 10 Feb 2008
http://www.telegraph.co.uk/news/main.jhtml?
xml=/news/2008/02/10/nsharia110.xml&CMP=ILC-mostviewedbox and
http://www.telegraph.co.uk/news/main.jhtml?
xml=/news/2008/02/10/nsharia210.xml&page=2 .
Some people are saying this about Ireland as well:
"Ireland's Identity from what I remember has certainly deteriorated over the last 15 years, I remember most fondly the times when you would hear the usual exchange of dublin wit and respectful slagging between friends on the bus or elsewhere.

Even when I was a young fella there was always the hype about visiting the "Fun Factory" near Stillorgan and when travelling down the country, you'd hear the locals chattering amongst themselves about the GAA Match or village gossip with musicians playing traditional music in the corner.

The last 15 years of the so called "Celtic Tiger" has been nothing more of a curse... I remember tales of the markets in Moore Street and the traders shouting "5 Oranges for a Punt, already packed for ya missus!"... now they have been replaced by a barage of Restaurants and nobody there speaks english - or in any other main street in the North Side like Talbot Street.

Mass immigration has weakened our identity and is destroying what is left of it...

I associate Ireland with these traits:
Irish Language
Christianity & Tradition
Catholic Dominated but equally contributing Protestant population
GAA
Myths & Legends
Troubled yet interesting history
Good Education
Nationalism & Pride
Independence
MonoCultural - A land that has a populace with a single culture representing all

they stand for and practise.

The Ireland that is now abandoned all these wonderful traits for only false promises and Greed: There was No Boom only a Bank loan that was borrowed from dodgy people...who even lent money to the unemployed!!!! :evil: :evil: :evil: :evil:

The only way this Ireland can come back is if we allow those with Strong Ancestral & Cultural ties back into this country and offer them citizenship regardless of generation or location in the world.

The Irish-Diaspora like the people of Ireland never wanted this: cosmopolitan, multicultural, fake concept of everyone is Irish if you arrive to live in Ireland."
(DaBrow   at   http://www.politics.ie/viewtopic.php?
f=70&t=40582&st=0&sk=t&sd=a&start=24)

11. http://www.thetruthseeker.co.uk/article.asp?ID=8059 . Pope Leo XIII felt that some groups promoted this kind of lifestyle in order to weaken people's courage and resolve:
"For, since generally no one is accustomed to obey crafty and clever men so submissively as those whose soul is weakened and broken down by the domination of the passions, there have been in the sect of the Freemasons some who have plainly determined and proposed that, artfully and of set purpose, the multitude should be satiated with a boundless license of vice, as, when this had been done, it would easily come under their power and authority for any acts of daring."
(Humanum   Genus   Encyclical   of   Pope   Leo   XIII
http://www.vatican.va/holy_father/leo_xiii/encyclicals/documents/hf_l-
xiii_enc_18840420_humanum-genus_en.html)

In Peru Montesinos promoted much the same kind of bread and circuses philosophy:
"For the big national broadcasters that he intimidated, bribed, and then video-taped, Montesinos had some advice: keep politics off the air as much as possible, or else. Not just the opposition and its demands (that went without saying), but politics itself was suppressed, in favor of game shows, soap operas, and sports." (http://www.bostonreview.net/BR26.3/rosen.html)

"Brzezinski [the former National Security Adviser to President Carter of course] went on to say that our society "is now in an information revolution based on amusement focus, spectator spectacles (saturation coverage by television of sporting events) which provide an opiate for an increasingly purposeless mass."
(Dr John Coleman, *Conspirator's Hierarchy* (1992), p.26 quoting Brzezinski, *The Technotronic Era.*)

12.
http://www.lawlink.nsw.gov.au/lawlink/Supreme_Court/ll_sc.nsf/pages/SCO_s
pigelman200905 . In contrast the Irish family courts are mired in secrecy as
you can read at http://www.rate-your-solicitor.com/forum/viewtopic.php?
id=221&action=new .

13. http://www.indymedia.ie/newswire.php?story_id=68249 .

14. An example of this can be seen in the UK as described by Ashley Mote
MEP:
"For every single day that Labour have been in power since 1997 one new
criminal offence has been created - a scale of state oppression which surpasses
even the best efforts of Hitler and Stalin. The sheer number of criminal offences on the statute book today is double the number in 1997.
Criminal law now seeks to manipulate the attitudes and views of ordinary, otherwise law-abiding people...and has seriously undermined 800 years of British
freedom and our rights. It is a draconian piece of constitutional vandalism..."
(Ashley Mote MEP, *J'Accuse...* (2008), p.38.)

15. http://www.ashleymote.co.uk/topics.php?filter=&sec=article&art_id=474 .
For an example of how devious minds have thought through this question of
the law there is this from the Protocols of Zion (which should only be read
bearing in mind the caveats listed in the next footnote below):
"The word "freedom," which can be interpreted in various ways, is defined by
us as follows -

Freedom is the right to do that which the law allows. This interpretation of the
word will at the proper time be of service to us, because all freedom will thus
be in our hands, since the laws will abolish or create only that which is
desirable for us according to the aforesaid program."
(http://www.iahushua.com/BeWise/prot12.html).

16. "It has been commented on many times during the course of history that the
average person in most countries has little or no time to spare to think beyond
making a living, raising a family and holding down a job to make these
objectives possible. This leaves little or no time to attend to politics or matters
of economics or other vital issues, such as war and peace that affect their lives
and the life of the nation. Governments know this. So it seems, do highly
organized groups operating behind many different front organizations which
always have the edge over the citizenry."
(Dr John Coleman at http://coleman300.com/books.htm)

This apathy - or exhaustion - type effect has been noted before by devious
minds that hoped to control societies. For example you can see this in the
famous Protocols of Zion. I wish to strongly emphasise that I, like everybody
else, believe these to be forgeries in the sense that they most certainly do not

represent the collective agreed views of the Jewish people, but whoever drew them up, even if it was the Czarist secret police, seemed to have a great insight into how to manipulate societies:

"In order to give the goyim no time to think and take note, their minds must be diverted towards industry and trade. Thus, all the nations will be swallowed up in the pursuit of gain and in the race for it will not take note of their common foe. But again, in order that freedom may once for all disintegrate and ruin the communities of the goyim.

...

The intensified struggle for superiority and shocks delivered to economic life will create, nay, have already created, disenchanted, cold and heartless communities. Such communities will foster a strong aversion towards the higher political and towards religion. Their only guide is gain, that is Gold, which they will erect into a veritable cult, for the sake of those material delights which it can give.

...

What form of administrative rule can be given to communities in which corruption has penetrated everywhere, communities where riches are attained only by the clever surprise tactics of semi-swindling tricks; where looseness reigns: where morality is maintained by penal measures and harsh laws but not by voluntarily accepted principles: where the feelings toward faith and country are obliterated by cosmopolitan convictions?

...

The principal object of our directorate consists in this: to debilitate the public mind by criticism; to lead it away from serious reflections calculated to arouse resistance; to distract the forces of the mind towards a sham fight of empty eloquence. In all ages the peoples of the world, equally with individuals, have accepted words for deeds, for they are content with a show and rarely pause to note, in the public arena, whether promises are followed by performance. Therefore we shall establish show institutions which will give eloquent proof of their benefit to progress.

We shall assume to ourselves the liberal physiognomy of all parties, of all directions, and we shall give that physiognomy a voice in orators who will speak so much that they will exhaust the patience of their hearers and produce an abhorrence of oratory.

In order to put public opinion into our hands we must bring it into a state of bewilderment by giving expression from all sides to so many contradictory opinions and for such length of time as will suffice to make the GOYIM lose their heads in the labyrinth and come to see that the best thing is to have no opinion of any kind in matters political, which it is not given to the public to understand, because they are understood only by him who guides the public. This is the first secret."

(http://web.archive.org/web/20060206040834/http://bookcase.kroupnov.ru/pages/library/Waters/index.htm)

17. Sunday Independent 27 Jan 2008 Living section p.4.

341

18. The reference to Frances Cahill is from Frances Cahill, *Martin Cahill, my father* (Dundrum, 2007), passim. The politics.ie closing down discussions of the Taoiseach is from http://www.politics.ie/viewtopic.php?t=33182 .

19. See the Appendix at the end of this chapter.

20. Col. Maurice Moore, *History of the Irish Volunteers,* Irish Press 25 Feb 1938.
He gives as an example of British duplicity:
"The Union of England and Ireland had been obtained by promising the Protestants a continuation of their ascendancy and the Catholics emancipation from the penal laws, but both were betrayed when it suited the policy of the English Government." (Irish Press 25 Feb 1938.)
Most of the time he referred to the conduct of the British troops in Dublin in 1916:
"Every house occupied by the troops was robbed...Even officers of the new army joined in the pillage."
While in contrast:
"A lady of my acquaintance in Leeson St. (a unionist), whose house was occupied [by the Volunteers in 1916], left 36s 6d on her desk in the hurry of her flight; it was untouched on her return, and a note was left regretting the necessity of occupation, and saying that the drawing room had been swept out before the house was vacated." (Irish Press 26 Feb 1938.)

21. Daniel Sheehan, *Ireland since Parnell* (London, 1921), available at http://www.gutenberg.org/files/13963/13963.txt .

22. That this emphasis on Tolerance is originally a Masonic concept you can see from:
"And yet since 1717, when the first Speculative Grand Lodge was formed in England, Masons, both operative and speculative, have been taught tolerance of religion politics and other ideals. Because of these ideals, we have been condemned by extremists on all sides of the many struggles. The lesson of tolerance learned through long years of experience has made an indelible impression on the philosophy of the Masonic Lodge, and this philosophy was and is an important motivation for men of every country,sect,and opinion to join our Fraternity.
...
There is no principle in the ancient teachings of Freemasonry that has been more prominently advocated than the doctrine of toleration.
...
As such Masonry is indeed the "Mother of Tolerance" and we can honestly say that Freemasonry is simply the current evolution of a brotherhood formed at the dawn of humanity."
(http://www.lodgeroomuk.net/bb/viewtopic.php?pid=144)

"Throughout the remainder of his Masonic career, the Mason will receive countless additional instructions about the relationship of brotherly love to the concept of tolerance, especially the concept of religious tolerance." (http://www.masonic-symbolism.com/sample.html)

That Catholic writers have accused Masons of deliberately twisting this concept of tolerance to destroy institutions you can see in some of the statements by Pope Leo XIII in footnote 18 Chapter 9 infra, and also see this quote from Fr Denis Fahey:
"The formation in "tolerance" given in the Lodges aims not merely at that negative mental state which puts religious truth and error on the same level, treating them both with indifference; it aims at the production of a positive hatred of what it calls the "intolerance" of the Catholic Church, namely the Catholic Church's insistence on the Divine Plan for order. The formation in Masonic "tolerance", then, is really a formation in hatred of the firmness and strength of the Catholic Church, in standing for the Supernatural Life and order of the world. This is the ultimate reason why Anglo-Saxon Masonry, ostensibly so conservative, has constantly favoured movements towards the Left, opposed to the true order of the world." (http://realnews247.com/fr_fahey_best_introductions.htm)

23. http://historical-debates.oireachtas.ie/S/0097/S.0097.198203260012.html .

24. http://www.dublinmonaghanbombings.org/press2003oct17.html .

25. "On the night of February 15, 1991, developer Tom Gilmartin claims he was inundated with phone calls from county councillors alleging a plot by bankers to subvert the democratic process.
Allied Irish Bank wanted the councillors to withdraw a vote on Gilmartin's plan to build the future Liffey Valley shopping centre in west Dublin, according to Gilmartin.
"I had councillors ringing up all evening,wanting to know what they would do," he claimed, "because the bank and Mr [Owen] O'Callaghan wouldn't allow them to put the zoning in until I conceded control of my company to them."
The country's biggest bank "literally blackmailed me all evening until I signed the heads of terms", according to Gilmartin."
(Barry O'Kelly in the Sunday Business Post 28 March 2004 http://archives.tcm.ie/businesspost/2004/03/28/story656910893.asp .)

26. http://en.wikipedia.org/wiki/Peter_Sutherland .

27. http://www.oxonia.org/whoweare_people.html .

28.
http://www.smurfitschool.ie/aboutsmurfit/advisoryboards/ireland/peterdsutherl
andsc/ .

29. http://www.ie.edu/documentos/IE_Basics_051104_eng.pdf .

30. http://www.iese.edu/aplicaciones/news/view.asp?id=863&lang=en .

31. For Nyenrode see http://www.nyenrode.nl/nyenrode/iab.cfm, Exeter
University is at http://www.sobe.ex.ac.uk/about/advisory_board.php and as
regards the LSE see http://sinclairsmusings.blogspot.com/2007/01/peter-
sutherland-for-chair-of-lse.html . By the way this is just a small fraction of the
posts that Peter Sutherland holds in the general area of business and
economics. He is also on the Hong Kong Chief Executive's Council of
Economic Advisers, Chairman of the Ireland Fund of Great Britain, Chairman
of the Board of Governors of the European Institute of Public Administration
and on the Advisory Board of the European Journal of International Affairs
(http://www.europeanjournal.org/advisory.htm), President of the Federal Trust
for Education and Research in London (http://www.fedtrust.co.uk/), Director of
the European Insitute (USA) and a member of the Helsinki Process on
Globalisation   and   Democracy
(http://www.helsinkiprocess.fi/HelsinkiGroup/members.asp), on the advisory
board of the Centre for European Reform in London ("A think-tank with an
increasingly influential role in the shaping of official policy"-Financial Times)
(http://www.cer.org.uk/about_new/about_advisoryboard_new.html),   and
Chairman of both the General Assembly and the Advisory Board of the
European   Policy   Centre   in   Brussels
(http://www.epc.eu/PUB/PDF/AR2005.pdf). As well as that he is on numerous
company boards eg. he is a director of Ericsson, Royal Bank of Scotland and,
formerly, Delta airlines.
As regards his political influence consider this:
"Cheney bypassed Turkey on his visit to the region but found time to attend the
secretive Ambrosetti Conference in Cernobbio on Lake Como in Italy, where
he accused Russia of arming "terrorists." Cheney met in Cernobbio with Israeli
President Shimon Peres, Spain's former neo-fascist Prime Minister Jose Maria
Aznar, BP's chairman Peter Sutherland, Italian Foreign Minister Franco
Frattini, and President Giorgio Napolitano of Italy."
(http://www.thetruthseeker.co.uk/article.asp?ID=9307)

32. http://www.gfmd-fmmd.org/en/press-release/155-united-nations-member-
states-mark-closing-inaugural-global-forum-migration-and-dev .

33. Seanad debate:
"Mr. Peter Sutherland seems to think that we will not need 45,000 immigrants
annually but almost double that figure to fulfill our economic requirements."
from http://historical-debates.oireachtas.ie/S/0179/S.0179.200502220007.html

and for TCD see http://www.tcd.ie/iiis/documents/documents/Global %20Development%20Conference%205-6%20July%20final.pdf and http://www.tcd.ie/iiis/pages/iiishome/governance_board.php .

34. http://www.rieti.go.jp/en/events/bbl/06032301.html .

35. http://www.encyclopedia.com/doc/1G1-177652433.html .

APPENDIX

Sources that describe the planned change in values mentioned in the previous chapter

Soviet Psychopolitics

To show that serious and powerful groups have indeed thought through these kind of theories on a global scale consider this from a manual on Soviet psychopolitics. Psychopolitics is defined as the 'the art and science of asserting and maintaining dominion over the thoughts and loyalties of individuals, officers, bureaus, and masses, and the effecting of the conquest of enemy nations through "mental healing."' The manual begins with a foreword by Beria and goes on to say:

"A continuous hope for prosperity must be indoctrinated into the masses with many dreams and visions of glut of commodity and this hope must be counter-played against the actuality of privation and the continuous threat of loss of all economic factors in case of disloyalty to the State in order to suppress the individual wills of the masses.

...

It is not enough for the State to have goals. These goals, once put forward, depend upon their completion, upon the loyalty and obedience of the workers. These, engaged for the most part, in hard labors, have little time for idle speculation, which is good. But, above them, unfortunately, there must be foremen of one or another position, and one of whom might have sufficient idleness and lack of physical occupation to cause some disaffecting independency in his conduct and behaviour.

...

In rearranging loyalties we must have a command of their values. In the animal the first loyalty is to himself. This is destroyed by demonstrating errors to him, showing him that he does not remember, cannot act or does not trust himself. The second loyalty is to his family unit, his parents and brothers and sisters. This is destroyed by making a family unit economically non-dependent, by lessening the value of marriage, by making an easiness of divorce and by raising the children whenever possible by the State. The next loyalty is to his friends and local environment. This is destroyed by lowering his trust and bringing about reportings upon him allegedly by his fellows or the town or village authorities. The next is to the State and this, for the purposes of Communism, is the only loyalty which should exist once the state is founded as a Communist State. To destroy loyalty to the State all manner of forbidding for youth must be put into effect so as to disenfranchise them as members of the Capitalist state and, by promises of a better lot under Communism, to gain their loyalty to a Communist movement.

Denying a Capitalist country easy access to courts, bringing about and supporting propaganda to destroy the home, creating and continuous juvenile delinquency, forcing upon the state all manner of practices to divorce the child from it will in the end create chaos necessary to Communism.

...

If we could effectively kill the national pride and patriotism of just one generation, we will have won that country. Therefore, there must be continual propaganda abroad to undermine the loyalty of the citizens in general and the teenager in particular.

...

The role of the psychopolitical operator in this is very strong. He can, from his position as an authority on the mind, advise all manner of destructive measures. He can teach the lack of control of this child at home. He can instruct, in an optimum situation, the entire nation in how to handle children -- and instruct them so that the children, given no control, given no real home, can run wildly about with no responsibility for their nation or themselves.

The mis-alignment of the loyalty of youth to a Capitalistic nation sets the proper stage for a realignment of their loyalties toward Communism. Creating a greed for drugs, sexual misbehavior and uncontrolled freedom and presenting this to them as a benefit of Communism, will with ease, bring about our alignment.

...

The first thing to be degraded in any nation is the state of Man, himself. Nations which have high ethical tone are difficult to conquer. Their loyalties are hard to shake, their allegiance to their leaders is fanatical, and what they usually call their spiritual integrity cannot be violated by duress. It is not efficient to attack a nation in such a frame of mind. It is the basic purpose of Psychopolitics to reduce that state of mind to a point where it can be ordered and enslaved. Thus, the first target is Man, himself. He must be degraded from a spiritual being to an animalistic reaction pattern. He must think of himself as an animal, capable only of animalistic reactions. He must no longer think of himself, or of his fellows, as capable of "spiritual endurance," or nobility.

347

...

[As part of this process of degradation of the sense of 'nobility' in a populace it was also apparently a Communist aim to destroy beautiful vistas, art and buildings in case they tended to enrich and strengthen people, this is from a list of Communist aims entered into the record of the US House of Representatives on 10th Jan 1963:

"- Continue discrediting American culture by degrading all forms of artistic expression. An American Communist cell was told to "eliminate all good sculpture from parks and buildings, substitute shapeless, awkward and meaningless forms."

- Control art critics and directors of art museums. "Our plan is to promote ugliness, repulsive, meaningless art."

http://kentroversypapers.blogspot.com/2006/02/forty-five-communist-goals-to-take.html]

...

As it seems in foreign nations that the church is the most ennobling influence, each and every branch and activity of each and every church, must, one way or another, be discredited. Religion must become unfashionable by demonstrating broadly, through psychopolitical indoctrination, that the soul is non-existent, and that Man is an animal. The lying mechanisms of Christianity lead men to foolishly brave deeds. By teaching them that there is a life here-after, the liability of courageous acts, while living, is thus lessened. The liability of any act must be markedly increased if a populace is to be obedient. Thus, there must be no standing belief in the church, and the power of the church must be denied at every hand.

The psychopolitical operative, in his program of degradation, should at all times bring into question any family which is deeply religious, and, should any neurosis or insanity be occasioned in that family, to blame and hold responsible their religious connections for the neurotic or psychotic condition. Religion must be made synonymous with neurosis and psychosis. People who are deeply religious would be less and less held responsible for their own sanity, and should more and more be relegated to the ministrations of psychopolitical operatives.

By perverting the institutions of a nation and bringing about a general degradation, by interfering with the economics of a nation to the degree that privation and depression come about, only minor shocks will be necessary to produce, on the populace as a whole, an obedient reaction or an hysteria. Thus, the mere threat of war, the mere threat of aviation bombings, could cause the population to sue instantly for peace. It is a long and arduous road for the psychopolitical operative to achieve this state of mind on the part of the whole nation, but no more than twenty or thirty years should be necessary in the entire program. Having to hand, as we do, weapons with which to accomplish the goal.

...

Because its [psychoanalysis] stress is sex, it is, itself, adequate defamation of character, and serves the purposes of degradation well. Thus, in organizing mental health groups, the literature furnished such groups should be psychoanalytical in nature.

...

We have battled in America since the century's turn to bring to nothing any and all Christian influences and we are succeeding.

...

Movements to improve youth should be invaded and corrupted, as this might interrupt campaigns to produce in youth delinquency, addiction, drunkenness, and sexual promiscuity.

...

The degradation of populace is less inhuman than their destruction by atomic fission...The psychopolitician has his reward in the nearly unlimited control of populace, in the uninhibited exercise of passion, and the glory of Communist conquest over the stupidity of the enemies of the People." (http://www.geocities.com/Heartland/7006/psychopolitics.html and http://www.geocities.com/Heartland/7006/psychopolitics-pt2.html)

Yuri Bezmenov

For some later analysis of Communist thinking it may be well to quote from Yuri Bezmenov. Born in Moscow in 1939 the son of a senior Soviet army officer he served later in Novosti, a KGB front media organisation, mainly in India and defected from there to the West in 1970. During his time with the KGB he learnt the tactics of brainwashing whole countries: (He particularly talks about a process of 'demoralization' by which he means not lack of morale but a process of stripping out morals from people, as one commentator has pointed out:
"We wanted to keep the term "Demoralization" in the framework of quotation marks in the subtitles. It must be heard [as]...: "loss of morality" or "loss of values.""")
"Interviewer:
Well, you spoke before about "ideological subversion" and that's a phrase that I'm afraid some Americans don't understand. When the

Soviets use the phrase "ideological subversion" what do they mean by it?

Bezmenov:
1. Ideological subversion is the process which is [a] legitimate, old word, and open. You can see it with your own eyes. All American mass media has to do is to "unplug bananas" from their ears, open up their eyes, and they can see it. There is no mystery.

It has nothing to do with espionage. I know that espionage intelligence gathering looks more romantic. It sells more deodorants through the advertising. That's probably why your Hollywood producers are so crazy about James Bond types of films. But in reality the main emphasis of the KGB is NOT in the area of intelligence at all.

According to my opinion, and the opinions of many defectors of my caliber, only about 15% of time, money, and manpower is spent on espionage as such. The other 85% is a slow process which we call either ideological subversion, active measures, or psychological warfare. What it basically means is: to change the perception of reality of every American that despite of the abundance of information no one is able to come to sensible conclusions in the interest of defending themselves, their families, their community, and their country.

It's a great brainwashing process which goes very slow and is divided into four basic stages.

The first stage being "demoralization". It takes from 15 to 20 years to demoralize a nation. Why that many years? Because this is the minimum number of years required to educate one generation of students in the country of your enemy exposed to the ideology of [their] enemy. In other words, Marxism-Leninism ideology is being pumped into the soft heads of at least 3 generation of American students without being challenged or counterbalanced by the basic values of Americanism; American patriotism.

Most of the activity of the department [KGB] was to compile huge amount / volume of information, on individuals who were instrumental in creating public opinion. Publisher, editors, journalists, uh actors, educationalists, professors of political science. Members of parliament, representatives of business circles.

Most of these people were divided roughly into two groups: those who would tow the Soviet foreign policy, they would be promoted to positions of power through media and public manipulation; [and] those who refuse the Soviet influence in their own country would be character assassinated OR executed physically, come Revolution.

...

Simply, because, you see the useful idiots; the leftists who are idealistically believing in the beauty of Soviet or Communist or Socialist or whatever system; when they get disillusioned, they become the worst enemies. That's why my KGB instructors specifically made the point, "never bother with leftists, forget about these political prostitutes - aim higher" this was my instruction. Try to get into, uh, large circulation, established conservative media. Reach filthy rich movie makers, intellectuals in so-called academic circles. Cynical, ego-centric people who can look into your eyes with angelic expression and tell you a lie. This are the most recruitable people; people who lack moral principals - who are either too greedy or too, uh, suffer from self-importance, uh, they feel that they matter a lot. Uh, these are the people who KGB wanted very much to recruit.

...

So basically America is Stuck, with demoralization; and unless, even if you start right now this minute; you start educating new generation of Americans - it will still take you 15 to 20 years to turn the tide of uh, ideological perception of reality; uh back to normalcy and patriotism.

The result? The result you can see -- most of the people who graduated in the 60's, dropouts or half-baked intellectuals, are now occupying the positions of power in the government, civil service, business, mass media, and educational systems. You are stuck with them. You can't get rid of to them. They are contaminated. They are programmed to think and react to certain stimuli in a certain pattern [alluding to Pavlov]. You can not change their mind even if you expose them to authentic information. Even if you prove that white is white and black is black, you still can not change the basic perception and the logic of behavior. In other words [for] these people the process of demoralization is complete and irreversible. To rid society of these people you need another 15 or 20 years to educate a new generation of patriotically minded and common sense people who would be acting in favor and in the interests of United States society.

...

2. The next stage is destabilization...

...

It only takes 2 to 5 years to destabilize a nation. This time what matters is essentials; economy, foreign relations, [and] defense systems. And you can see it quite clearly that in some... sensitive areas such as defense and [the] economy, the influence of Marxist-Leninist ideas in the United States is absolutely fantastic. I could never believe it 14 years ago when I landed in this part of the world that the process will go that fast.

3. The next stage of course is crisis, which may take only up to 6 weeks to bring a country to the verge of crisis. You can see it in Central America now; and after crisis, with the violent change of power structure and economy, you have the period of so called "normalization" [which] it may last indefinitely. Normalization is a cynical expression, borrower from Soviet Propaganda. When the Soviet tanks moved into Czechoslovakia in 1968, comrade Brezhnev said "Now the situation in brotherly Czechoslovakia is normalized". This is what will happen in [the] United States if you allow all the shmucks to bring the country to crisis.

To promise people all kinds of goodies, and the paradise on Earth. Uh to destabilize your economy to eliminate the principal of free market competition; and to put a big brother government in Washington D.C.; with benevolent dictators...who will promise lots of things - Never mind whether the promises are fulfilled or not. ...he will create false illusions that the situation is under control.

Situation is NOT under control.   Situation is disgustingly out of control.

Most of the American politicians, media, and educational system train another generation of people who think they are living at the peacetime. False. United States is in a state of war; undeclared, total war against the basic principles and foundations of this system. And the initiator of this war is not Comrade Andropov of course - it's the system. However, ridiculous it may sound, [it is] the world Communist system, or the world Communist conspiracy. Whether I scare some people or not, I don't give a hoot. If you're not scared by now, nothing can scare you. You don't have to be paranoid about it. What actually happens now; that unlike myself, you have literally several years to live on unless United States wake up. The time bomb is ticking. With every second the disaster is coming closer. Unlike myself, you will have nowhere to defect to, unless you want to live in Antarctica with penguins.

This is it, this is the last country with freedom and possibility.

...

[Notes from a lecture by Bezmenov:]
Stage one: Demoralization. Preparatory period 10 to 30 years

Here subversion goes on simultaneously on various "levels" of national and human activity: level of consciousness (ideology) level of authority (socio-political power and administration), and level of material wellbeing (economy).

Level of consciousness (ideology)

Infiltration into mass media, educational systems, organized religion and religious groups, cultural and professional groups and organizations. The main goal: psychological change of national and individual perception of reality to such an extent that majority of a nation does not perceive any danger emanating from totalitarianism, moreover the hostile system is ultimately accepted as non-belligerent and even in certain aspects desirable, in any case -- functional as an alternative to the present one.

The most efficient methods of demoralization is semantic manipulation of population, or word pollution, whereby the normal true meaning of the words and traditionally accepted meanings are being gradually replaced by Orwellian type surrogates, partly or totally opposite to the reality. Example: "Patriotic Front Guerillas" -- Moscow trained and armed regular force, practicing mega-mass murders and terror against defenseless population of their own country. Example: "United Nations" a forum for ideological war between life-time bureaucratic representatives of various elites and Juntas, most of them not related to any nation at all (Belorussia, Ukraina, GDR etc. "ambassadors" to UN). Example: "World Peace Council" -- Soviet sponsored propaganda front, supporting localized military conflicts, as long as they are directed against the Western (USA) interests. Example: "Free medical aid" (anything "free") -- a government-subsidized service, financed from taxation of the population, and extended to population disregarding the real needs, capabilities or merits of individuals. etc...

Level of authority

Subversion on this level requires infiltration into domestic institutions of a nation as well as into her foreign policymaking bodies.

Domestically the aim of the subverter is to weaken the home defences, such as security services, police, army, civil service, other public services (transport, post office, hydro - if nationalised, etc). The methods - discreditation of the administration of the most vital national services. Investigations of "wrong doings", corruption affairs, sex scandals - implication of the national leaders and politicians in fraudulent or dubious affairs, smear tactics in media etc. Ridicule everything "patriotic" as psychotic. Describe every effort to reveal the activity of subverter (KGB et al) - as "paranoid". Discredit everyone, who can testify to public, media and parliament the true nature of subversion (immigrants from Communist regimes are shown to a nation as "emotionally unbalanced". Solzhenytsin "arrogant prophet and a profiteer" etc).

Stage 2 Destabilization (2 years to 5 months)

Encouragement and provoking of labour unrest...creating inflation...propaganda of "strong government" and necessity of "controls" - militarisation of the "grass roots" movements and minority groups...and sidetracking of the public attention to the non-issues...Propaganda of gun control...thus, rendering a nation helpless and defenceless in the future event of political terrorism; breaking down of democratic institutions (parliaments to city halls) and replacing them with a number of centralised government appointed bodies, people can not re-elect or get rid of otherwise; breaking down of national unity (ethnic, racial, religious, linguistic etc).

Stage 3: Collapse, Explosion (2 weeks to a month)

Interrelations between parts of economy break down; general strike; growth of terrorism and crime; total discontent; currency crisis (gold rush); collapse of the government and import of an alternative "exile" government; power concentrates in the hands of the militant "revolutionary" group, who will be disposed of later on. The nation is ripe for the final act of subversion: "invitation of a communist occupational army (Cuban, Soviet etc).

What to do about it? Is it possible to prevent subversion?

Yes. It takes a unified national effort. Any democratic nation should cultivate attitudes as devotion to one'e country, patriotism, moral strength, working ethics, resurrection of all national traditional values." (Notes of a lecture by Yuri Bezmenov (alias Mr. Thomas Schuman) at the News Word International correspondent's seminar Feb. 22 - 24 (1979?): http://www.scribd.com/doc/3832917/Demoralization-of-America-by-KGB , and an interview in a 1984 documentary by G. Edward Griffin called *Soviet Subversion of the Free Press: A Conversation with Yuri Bezmenov*: http://www.crossroad.to/Quotes/brainwashing/2007/bezmenov.htm . The clarification of what he means by 'demoralization' is from http://www.notanotherconspiracy.com/2008/10/demoralizationdestabil-izationcrisisnorm.html .)

Jean D'Eau

That this Communist atmosphere is now reflected in the approach of the Western media can be seen in this comment by Jean D'Eau in Hungary: "For your American readers, I would like to say that the one bitterness of life which is perhaps particular to nowadays Eastern Europe is the double brainwashing most people have been submitted to. To put it simply, most Eastern Europeans and particularly Hungarians belong to one of two "living dead" categories: the ex-communist and the "modern" living deads.

The first category is composed of those who became adults in the communist regime and thus are largely devoid of religious, moral and patriotic sense; they are often alcoholics too and, due to the poor quality of their inner world, very prone to psychological depression as well as all kind of illnesses.

The second category is composed of those who were children or not yet born when the communism collapsed, eighteen years ago; most of these people were raised up by the worst violent/pornographic American-Talmudic entertainment industry which took control of the East European -but particularly Hungarian- mass media during the nineties; these people are even more lacking of moral values than those of the first category and are moreover often obsessed by sex and violence; they are also often addicted to various kind of drugs and count a great number of homosexuals/lesbians in their ranks." (11 March 2008 http://www.savethemales.ca/index.html).

Vasili Ivanov

The Russian historian Vasili Ivanov explicitly links this type of Communist tactic to Masonic thinking (as does Jüri Lina in his elaborately researched *Architects of Deception*):
"In order for the masonic ideals to triumph, it was necessary to kill the soul of the Russian people, remove the people from its God, obliterate its national character, trample its mighty history in the dirt, dull the intellect of its young generation and raise a new kind of people without a God or a native country: two-legged wild creatures who, after being trained, would obediently place themselves in the masonic cage." (The Russian historian Vasili Ivanov writing in A. Balabukhi, editor, *The Occult Powers of the Soviet Union* (St. Petersburg, 1998), p. 358 quoted by Jüri Lina, *Architects of Deception* (Stockholm, 2004), p.314.)

Jüri Lina

The aforementioned Jüri Lina, the former Estonian dissident who had to flee from the KGB, compares Communism to the new Globalism:
"Instead of Communism, which really is a terrible ghost on the loose in Europe causing spiritual rabies wherever it goes, there is now mondialism (le monde = the world) which involves an even greater danger. It is a new ideology, which is to uphold and justify the build-up of the European Union. Igor Shafarevich's revealing book "La setta mondialista contro la Russia" / "The Mondialist Sect against Russia" was published in Parma in 1991. The main goal of the mondialists, according to this book, is to eliminate the sense of nationality; destroy the minds of young people with hard-rock music, violent films, pornography and drugs; imitate the American way of life in its worst form; blot out historical memory; mix the races by means of mass immigration... The subject of mondialism, which is pure Illuminism in a new form, has hitherto been avoided in Sweden. The goal of the mondialists is a world government."
(Juri Lina, *Under the Sign of the Scorpion* (Stockholm, 2002), p.410.)

Dr John Coleman

The results of research by the former MI6 agent Dr John Coleman:
"The United States is being transformed from One Nation Under God to

a polyglot of nations under several gods. The U.S. is no longer One nation under God. The framers of the Constitution have lost the battle. Our forebears spoke a common language and believed in a common religion Christianity, and held common ideals. There were no aliens in our midst; that came later in a deliberately planned attempt to break up the United States into a series of fragmented nationalities, cultures and beliefs. If you doubt this, go down to the East Side of New York, or the West Side of Los Angeles on any given Saturday and look around you. The United States has become several nations struggling to coexist under a common system of government. When the floodgates of immigration were opened wide by Franklin D. Roosevelt, a cousin of the head of the Committee of 300, the cultural shock caused great confusion and dislocation and made "One Nation" an unworkable concept. The Club of Rome and NATO have exacerbated the situation. "Love thy neighbor" is an ideal that will not work unless your neighbor "is as yourself." To the framers of our Constitution, the truths they laid out for future generations were "self evident"--to themselves."

...[From a list of the aims of the globalists:]

"To bring about the utter destruction of all national identity and national pride, which was a primary consideration if the concept of a One World Government was to work.

To engineer and bring about the destruction of religion, and more especially, the Christian Religion, with the one exception, their own creation, as mentioned above.

...

To encourage, and eventually legalize the use of drugs and make pornography an "art-form", which will be widely accepted and, eventually, become quite commonplace...

...

To weaken the moral fibre of the nation and to demoralize workers in the labor class by creating mass unemployment...The youth of the land will be encouraged ... to rebel against the status quo, thus undermining and eventually destroying the family unit.

...

To export "religious liberation" ideas around the world so as to undermine all existing religions, but more especially the Christian religion. This began with the "Jesuit Liberation Theology", that brought an end to the Somoza Family rule in Nicaragua, and which today is destroying El Salvador, now 25 years into a "civil war".

...

To give the fullest support to supranational institutions such as the

357

United Nations, the International Monetary Fund (IMF), the Bank of International Settlements, the World Court and, as far as possible, make local institutions less effective, by gradually phasing them out or bringing them under the mantle of the UN.

To penetrate and subvert all governments, and work from within them to destroy the sovereign integrity of the nations represented by them."
(http://www.apfn.org/apfn/300.htm)

Dr Henry Makow

This is the opinion of Dr Henry Makow, the experienced journalist, author, inventor of the board game 'Scruples', and formerly Professor of English Literature at the University of Winnipeg in Canada:
"The bankers' first precaution is to buy all the politicians. The second is to buy the major media outlets in order to promote the illusion politicians make decisions and represent our interests. The third precaution is to take control of the education system, ensuring that people stop thinking at an early age.

Then the bankers use the government and media to convince us that religion, nationalism and nuclear family are unfashionable, and we want what they want.

We "want" world government ("globalization"). The bankers need to eliminate nation states, freedom and democracy in order to consolidate their power and streamline their business. The UN, the IMF and World Bank -- glorified loan sharks and collectors -- will make the laws.

We "want" diversity. Countries are not allowed to maintain their national identities or traditions. Last Christmas, my provincial Premier tried to rename the Christmas tree at the legislature a "multicultural tree." Diversity is respecting every culture but European Christian.

Every nation must be heterogeneous as a box of Smarties – no one in a position to challenge the bankers.
...
People – stunted, love-starved, sex-obsessed – without family, religious or national identity, are easy to control. (They'll join anything; they're looking for a family.)"
(http://www.thetruthseeker.co.uk/article.asp?ID=8997)

Alta Vendita

Tactics deployed by members of the Alta Vendita (a Masonic group in Italy in the early 19th century), as detailed in some of their captured letters:
"The essential thing is to isolate a man from his family, to cause him to lose his morals.
...
It is of absolute necessity to de-Catholicise the world.
...
When you shall have insinuated into a few souls disgust for family and for religion (the one nearly always follows in the wake of the other), let fall some words which will provoke the desire of being affiliated to the nearest lodge.
...
Catholicism has no more fear of a well-sharpened stiletto than monarchies have, but these two bases of social order can fall by corruption. Let us then never cease to corrupt. Tertullian was right in saying, that the blood of martyrs was the seed of Christians. Let us, then, not make martyrs, but let us popularise vice amongst the multitudes. Let us cause them to draw it in by their five senses; to drink it in; to be saturated with it; and that land which Aretinus has sown is always disposed to receive lewd teachings. Make vicious hearts, and you will have no more Catholics.
...
It is corruption en masse that we have undertaken: the corruption of the people by the clergy, and the corruption of the clergy by ourselves; the corruption which ought, one day to enable us to put the Church in her tomb... The best poniard with which to strike the Church is corruption. To work, then, even to the very end."
(Fr George Dillon (ed. Fr Denis Fahey), *The War of Antichrist with the Church and Christian Civilisation* (London, 1950) chapters XIV and XV available at http://www.catholicvoice.co.uk/dillon/text.htm#14)

Domenico Anghera

For some further references to Masonic thinking there are:
"The following quotations from the speech made by Domenico Anghera, Grand Master of the Supreme Council of Scottish Rites when

conferring on General Giuseppe Garibaldi the 33rd degree and administering his oath of allegiance [c.1870], are here of interest in view of the connection of the two masonic powers in France:

" . . . Our first step, as builders of the new temple to the felicity of human glory, must be destruction. To destroy the present social state, we have suppressed religious teaching and the individual rights of persons...

' I swear to recognize no fatherland but that of the world. I swear to work hard, everywhere and always, to destroy frontiers, borders, boundaries of all nations, of all industries, no less than of all families. I swear to dedicate my life to the triumph of progress and universal unity and I declare to profess the negation of God and the negation of the soul'. "

And now, Brother, that for thee, fatherland, religion and family have disappeared for ever in the immensity of the work of Freemasonry, come to us, illustrious, most puissant and very dear Brother and share with us the boundless authority, the infinite power that we hold over humanity. " The only key of progress and happiness, the only rules of good, are thy appetites and instincts "

(Lady Queenborough [Edith Starr Miller], *Occult Theocrasy* (1933), p.340 quoting Domenico Margiotta, *Le Culte de la Nature dans la Franc maçonnerie Universelle*, p. 45 et seq.)

Masonic document paraphrased by Fritz Springmeier

Here is a paraphrase from the French of another curious Masonic document that was prepared in the past for those involved in the Rite of Mizraim and the Prieure de Sion:

"The Mass Media creates the thoughts of the people. It tells the people what they need, it allows the people to voice their complaints, and to express discontent. By using the power of the Press secretly we have also made much money. We are leading the people from one disenchantment to another. They will even tire of our rule and welcome the King/Priest dictatorship of the House of David that we have been preparing for centuries.

Agents tell the people that in order to secure liberty, the international brotherhood of all, and their equality of rights they need to abuse their national governments. This is to be accomplished by a unification. But we do not tell them who will rule the unification.

Who can overthrow an invisible force? Freemasonry remains a mystery to the public and serves as a screen for us.

It is critical to undermine all faith, destroy the principle of the Godhead, and replace it with materialism and mathematical calculations. Keep the public busy, put industry onto a speculative basis, and foster a desire for consumerism and wealth.

We will slowly increase the centralization of government.

We have created a class of specialists from our administrative branch that have developed the manipulation of the public into an art. This skilled manipulation uses theory, verbiage, regulations and other items and quirks which the public can't comprehend. The principle object is to debilitate the public's mind by criticism, and lead it away from serious reflection of what is really going on. These distractions along with sham fights will prevent resistance. We must bring them into a state of bewilderment by allowing and promoting so many contradictory opinions, that people will lose their heads in the labyrinth, and come to believe the best thing is to have no opinion of any kind in politics. Sow discord, dislocate the forces against us. Discourage sincere personal initiative. A man with genius and initiative is more dangerous to us than millions of the public.

In order that the real meaning of events are not realized they will [be] masked with economic theories. We will manipulate government through public opinion, which we can create by the power of the Press.

We will create tenor [recte terror presumably]. We will harness the anarchists, the socialists, the Utopian dreamers so that they will bore away at the last foundations of the established form of order. We will not give them peace until the New World Order is in place.

In order to carry out struggles, money is needed, and all the money is in our hands. We have fooled, corrupted, bemused, amused the youth with principles we know are false. We have created laws that are an incomprehensible tangled web.

Should any city dare oppose us, we can terrorize it so that even the bravest will be intimidated. The subways, sewers, and other subterranean corridors can be mined and the city blown into the air along with its government, records, and service systems.

We will be saviors to the mobs, who will vote us into power. We have everyone regardless of qualifications voting, because otherwise it will be difficult to get our consensus from a properly educated group of people.

We set up republics with constitutions. And then use the press to condemn the rulers and make them impotent and inactive, and in effect they become useless and superfluous. We put into power presidents from the masses, who can be blackmailed. The people in government are often not our own people, but our puppets who we can blackmail and destroy if they don't follow orders.

In order to create conditions so that people will want a world government, every kind of trouble and discord must be promoted, including the inoculation of diseases, starvation and drug use.

Secret Masonry is not known, and the aims are not even suspected by the cattle. They are attracted to us by our show lodges which serve to throw dust in the eyes of their fellowman. Any attempt to attack us by the press on its own will be stopped. But note that we ourselves will attack ourselves in the press—at predetermined points. Not a single pronouncement will reach the public without our control. The International News agencies are already ours, and use what we dictate to them. The masses look at events of the world through the glasses we provide them. We will neutralize the influence of the privately owned press. If ten privately owned presses are permitted, we will have 30, and so on. But the public will never suspect this, because our journals will be the most opposite in appearance, opinions, and procedures. The official publications are guarding our interests. Then come the semi-official publications. Then will come what appear to be the organs of opposition to us. Our real opposition at heart will accept this stimulated opposition as their own and will show us their cards.

Like the Indian god Vishnu, we will have a hundred arms— publications of all possible complexions.

Our false attacks on ourselves will convince the public that all organs that oppose us lack substance to their criticism. Our opponents will lack the ability to give full expression to their views because of the lack of their media power. We can ignore them.

The masses must be retrained and given new employment periodically. Keep them further distracted with amusements, passions, games, sports of all kinds, art competition. They will grow less and less reflective, and adopt more and more our way of thinking. We will continue to direct their minds with all kinds of fantastic theories, new and apparently progressive. Progress, like a fallacious idea, serves to obscure truth, so that none may know truth but us.

We have stage managed so many people over the years in many institutions. Our belief will not be examined, but the shortcomings of the various beliefs of the masses will be discussed by our experts.

In countries called progressive we have created senseless, filthy literature, to direct the masses to learn what knowledge we want them to know.

Whenever we come into power, even into the New Order, Masons that know too much will be eliminated.

We are facing only two major powers, the Russian Czar and the Papacy. The curious join the Masonic Lodge. Using their vanity they can be

brought into a total state of slavish submission. Their conceit allows us to bring them into a state of naivete. Masons who know too much are executed when required by a normal kind of illness. This action prevents any opposition from within Masonry itself."
(Fritz Springmeier, *Be Wise as Serpents* (1991), p.653.)

Cornelia R. Ferreira

This modern Catholic author describes here how she feels that many modern social changes are being 'engineered' deliberately by an elite according to Masonic principles, particularly in the US education system:
"Let's look at how some of the main tenets of this education are being implemented.

First is the destruction of loyalty to parents, Church and nation, as this loss of loyalties is necessary before one can be a world citizen. In 1889, Freemasonry deemed ...that, in order to advance its universal socialist republic, "freedom of thought and conscience of the children has to be developed systematically in the child at school and protected, as far as possible, against all disturbing influences, not only of the Church ..., but also of the children's own parents, if necessary, even by ... moral and physical compulsion."
...[quoting here John Dewey, the 'father' of the modern US educational system:]
"the marvelous development of progressive educational ideas and practices under ... the Bolshevist government to foster the required collective and cooperative mentality ... The great task of the school is to counteract ... the influence of home and Church ... Thorough-going collectivists regard the traditional family as exclusive and isolating in effect and hence as hostile to a truly communal life ... The institution of the family is being sapped indirectly rather than by frontal attack ... Our special concern here is with the role of the schools in building up forces and factors whose natural effect is to undermine the importance and uniqueness of family life ..."
...
In 1946, Brock Chisolm (head of the World Health Organization and close friend of Communist Alger Hiss) outlined these goals, which are the same as those of psychotherapy. In the journal Psychiatry he wrote that "a program of re-education [Comment by Ferreira: note the Communist term for brainwashing] or a new kind of education" was

necessary whereby

"the science of living should be ... taught to all children ... Only so ... can we help our children to carry out their responsibilities as world citizens ... To achieve world government, it is necessary to remove from the minds of men their individualism, loyalty to family tradition, national patriotism, and religious dogmas ... We have swallowed all manner of poisonous certainties fed us by our parents, our Sunday and day school teachers, ... our priests ... The re-interpretation and eventual eradication of the concept of right and wrong which has been the basis of child training, the substitution of intelligent and rational thinking for faith in the certainties of the old people, these are the belated objectives of ... psychotherapy. Would they not be legitimate objectives of original education?"
(http://www.trosch.org/msn/cfn_new-age-edu1.html)

Fr Brian McKevitt O.P

The ('barely managing' !lol) editor of the *Alive!* magazine in Ireland is another Catholic writer who feels that the modern preassures on the family and church value systems, in Ireland anyway, are being deliberately engineered. His name is Fr Brian McKevitt O.P., from Dundalk originally but now of St Mary's Priory Tallaght, here writing about the role of the EU and the UN in Ireland:
"Changes in society are being engineered
Last month Alive! reported on a trip by Irish officials to meet the UN Human Rights Committee in Geneva. They went to report on how Ireland is advancing the agenda set out in the Covenant on Civil & Political Rights.

According to the Iona Institute the UN Committee then "recommended that Ireland cease favouring the family based on marriage, it criticised the preponderance of denominational schools here, and it told us to legalise abortion."

Here we got a brief glimpse into the way the UN and the EU are being given a profound role in reshaping Irish social and religious life.

When we talk about the major changes that have taken place in our society in recent decades we usually attribute them to economic growth, the media, scandals in the Church and so on.

Rarely do we examine the way many of these changes are being engineered. What happens is that the government signs up to a new nice-sounding convention or treaty, like the Convention on the Rights of the Child.

Usually these conventions are a means to advance the left-wing secular agenda. But we have no public debate about what is at stake, and the signing is done with little fanfare. Everything is played down.

Next comes an international committee to monitor how countries are enforcing the convention. These committees are usually packed with left-wing radicals with their own extreme agenda.

Under this kind of pressure our government firmly but quietly pushes the left-wing agenda, through education, social policy, the lobby groups it funds, conditions attached to 3rd world aid and so on.

But it is time this ended. The government must stand up to the abuse of power by these committees, and defend our Christian values. It could start immediately by publicly repudiating the above recommendations by the UN Human Rights Committee."
(Alive! Oct 2008 Editor's Jottings)

Serge Monast

Serge Monast (1945-1996), a Quebec based investigative journalist (inter alia he worked with the Los Angeles Free Press in the 1980s and later North American correspondent of Agence Internationale de Presse Libre - North America (AIPL-NA), a press agency founded in France and sometimes known as The International Free Press Agency), published some pretty scary documentation on what he felt were the longterm aims and plans of many of the powerful international elites. In 1994 he stated that their goals were:
"1. To abolish all Christian traditional religions in order to replace them with a one world religion based on the cult of man.

2. To abolish all national identity and national pride in order to establish a world identity and a world pride.

3. To abolish the family as known today in order to replace them with

individuals all working for the glory of the new one world government.

4. To destroy all individual artistic and scientific creativity to implement a one world government, one-mindset."
(http://educate-yourself.org/cn/projectbluebeamintoandnworeview.shtml)

Monast also published a document from French intelligence that was stated to represent minutes, or protocols, of a meeting of 18 leading global businessmen, a group who Monast considered the top echelon of Anglo-Saxon masonry. These were the 6 heads of the largest banking corporations, alongwith the largest food and energy companies meeting in Canada in 1967 and later in 1985. I guess there is no way to verify this information but he appears to have been a highly respected journalist and these documents are certainly very interesting. He published the text, which he called the Protocols of Toronto, in French and I apologise that what follows is from a machine translation into English but which hopefully is reasonably clear:
""PANEM AND CIRCENSES" [The title of the document, from the Roman phrase 'Bread and Circuses']
All historical periods that led to the decline of civilizations were marked, without exception, with "the spirit of wandering Men". Today, we must ensure that the "Spirit" is translated into a "World Leisure Company" in all its forms. This "leisure" must consist of [sex], the [drugs], the [Sport], the [Travel / exotic], and [Entertainment] in general, but accessible to all strata of society. The man must come to believe that he is "Modern" and that its modernity is composed of its capacity and its ability to enjoy widespread, and now everything that surrounds it.

To achieve this objective, it is imperative to infiltrate the media (radio, television, newspapers), circles the "Mode" and "Culture" (circles of New Music) by which we influence, certainly All strata of Western society. So taking under the thumb of "Sense" young people (adults of tomorrow) we will therefore proceed to infiltrate and change in depth, without being harassed, political, legal and Education, which we will change to the course, the future direction of Societies covered by our "Plan".

The people we know, have no historical memory. They tirelessly repeat the mistakes of the past without realizing that these same mistakes had led their fathers before them, the same disqualifications they live in

366

worse before the end of this century. See, for example, that their grandfathers had lived at the beginning of this century thanks to the hard work of our predecessors.

After without limits, the release of manners, the abolition of morality (in other words, the wandering of the mind), they experimented the "economic crisis", then "War". Today their grandchildren and their children are going rights to a similar conclusion, even worse because this time, we will finally establish our "New World Order" without any of them are able to see, they are too preoccupied to meet all their needs overly sensual the primary.

...

In principle, we know, the exception proves the rule is contrary to it. But in our vocabulary, the exception is what should be imposed on all. We must make sure to make "Exceptions" in different spheres of society, as being new "Rules" applicable to all, a primary objective of all future social protests led by Youth Nations.

Thus the exception becomes the detonator by which all historical society will collapse on itself in a confusion shortness of breath and unprecedented.

The foundations of "Western society", in essence, come into line, the Judeo-Christian heritage. It is precisely this legacy that made the "Family", the "Knot", the "cornerstone" of the current social structure. Our predecessors who had financed the revolutionary writers of the late nineteenth century and early twentieth century understood the importance of dividing, and then to break this "vital core" if they wanted, Russia, to achieve up the new "communist system" of the time.

...

To succeed with certainty to the construction of a world government, [A New World Order Community] where everyone, without exception, will be subject to "global status" of the "New Order", we must, first instead, to remove the "Family" (which will, in turn, the disappearance of traditional religious teachings), and second, leveling all individuals by removing the "social classes", in particular, the "Middle Classes ". But we must proceed so that all these changes appear to be from the popular will, that they have the appearance of "Democracy".

Using isolated cases, but by amplifying the extreme with the help of student protests noyautées by us, journalists favorable to our cause and purchased politicians, we will be able to set up new bodies with all appearance of "Modernity" as an "Office for the Protection of Children" protected by a "Charter of Rights and Freedoms."

For the success of our "Global Plan [The Red Plan]", we need to implement in all Western societies of the 70s', the 'Office for Child Protection', whose staff (young intellectuals without experience, fresh out of universities which highlighted our global principles), will comply to the letter, without discernment, the "Charter of the Rights of the Child." Who dare oppose it without at the same time be identified to medieval barbarism?

This "Charter" painstakingly developed in our "Loges" we will finally negate any parental authority in breaking the family individuals opposed to each other to protect their personal interests. It will encourage children to report parents too authoritarian because too traditional and too religious. It will thus contribute to parents to submit a "Collective Psychosis of Fear", which inevitably cause, generally in society, a slackening of parental authority. Thus we have succeeded, as a first step, to produce a society similar to that of Russia of the 50s' where children denounced the State their parents, without anyone noticing.

By transferring to the State "Parenting", it will be easier, subsequently, to capture one by one, all the responsibilities that had been, to date, the sole responsibility of parents. Thus we can take it all as an abuse against the child, religious traditional Judeo-Christian origin.

...

Understand this: "Our goal is not to protect children or anyone else, but to cause the break, then the fall of Nations which are a major obstacle to the implementation of our" New World Order. "That is why the "Office of Child Protection" must be invested with absolute legal authority. They must be able, as they see fit, but always under the pretext of child protection, to remove them from their original family environments, and place them in family environments foreigners or government centers already committed to our global principles and religions. Therefore, will be completed and the final breakup the Western family." Without the protection and monitoring of their original parents, these children will be permanently handicapped in their psychological and moral development, and represent, therefore natural prey easily adaptable to our referred globalization.

...

In this sense, we must infiltrate the "System of Education" of Nations

368

to make under the cover of" Modernity "and" Evolution ", the teaching of religion, history, from Decorum thinner while at the same time under an avalanche of new experiments in the field of education, the language and mathematics.

In this way, by removing the young generations, and any basic moral boundary, any knowledge of the past (and therefore any national pride), so any respect, any power by knowledge of language and science (thus the reality), We will help build a youth largely willing to all forms of delinquency. In this new world fragmented by fear of parents, and their abandonment of any responsibility for their children, we have the way to train, in our own way and according to our primary objectives, a youth or arrogance, disrespect, the humiliation of others will be considered as the new basis of "self-assertion" and "Freedom".
...
For complete breakdown of the education system and thus society in general, it is essential to promote "sexual freedom" at all levels of Western society. We must reduce the individual, so the masses, the obsession to meet their primary instincts by all possible means. We know that this step represents the culmination by which any company will eventually collapse on itself. Does he not been of the Roman Empire at its peak, and like all civilizations throughout history?
...
This "sexual liberation" will be the ultimate means by which we will be able to remove the "People's Conscience" any reference to "good and evil." The collapse of this barrier religious and moral will to complete the process of the false "human liberation of the Past", but which in reality is a form of slavery that will benefit our "Global Plan ".
...
It is well recognized by all that man, once having secured its basic needs (food, clothing and shelter), is much more likely to be less vigilant. Let him sleep while his conscience to guide our own spirit by creating pure play, favorable economic conditions. So during this period of 70 years where our agents infiltrate across the different spheres of society to accept our new standards in education, legal rights, and the Social Policy, we will spread around him an economic climate of confidence.
...
In this sense, we will make nation-states, new "parents" of individuals. Through this trust which our "International Agents" have done everything necessary to avert spectrum of global war, we will encourage "Centralization" excessive for the state. In this way,

individuals can acquire the impression of complete freedom to explore while the legendary burden of personal responsibility will be transferred to the State.

...

On the other hand, this machine [the new larger centralised government] will give a cold and insensitive of government, this complex machine and how useless in many of its functions, will serve as a screen and protection against the people. Who dares venture through the maze of such a maze in order to assert his personal grievances?

...

In the same vein, and to ensure the profitability of our influence with the people, we will control all news media. Our banks will therefore fund only those who support us as they oversee the closure of more recalcitrant. This is expected to pass almost unnoticed in the population, they are absorbed by their need to make more money, and entertainment.

...

The rural owners, for their economic independence, their ability to produce the staple diet of States, is a threat to us and our future plans. In crowded cities, they will be more dependent on our industries to survive.

We can not allow the existence of independent groups of our "Power". So eliminate the landowners by making them obedient slaves Industries is under our control.

...

Across the state, do we attach to highlight the "Respect" mandatory diversity of "Cultures","Peoples", "Religions", "Ethnic" groups which are ways for us to get the "Individual Freedom" before the concept of "national unity", which will allow us to better divide the peoples of nation-states, and thus weaken their authority and their ability to maneuver. Pushed to the extreme limits, but on the international level, this concept in future races push of different nations to come together to claim individually, each with its own share of "Power", which will complete ruin of nations, and will erupt in endless wars.

When the United Nations will be weakened by as much infighting, all based on the recognition of "Rights of Minorities" to their independence; that nationalists divided into different cultural and religious factions oppose blindly struggles without end, that Youth will be completely lost touch with its roots, so we can serve the United

Nations began to impose our New World Order.

Indeed, at this point, the "humanitarian ideals, social and historical" of nation-states have long broke under the pressure of internal divisions.
...
Here is the detailed manner in which we will by 1998 to pave the road to the birth of our "world government".

- Increase the "leisure" which has been so profitable to date. By serving as the invention of "Video" that we've funded, and games attached to it, finish perverting morals of youth. Offer him the opportunity to meet all his instincts now. A being possessed by his senses, and slave to them, we know, neither perfect nor inner strength to defend anything. It is an "individual" in nature and is a perfect candidate that we can easily shape according to our desires and our priorities. Furthermore, remember the ease with which our predecessors could steer the entire German youth at the beginning of the century, using the latter disillusioned!

...
- To ensure at all costs the success of such an undertaking, let us ensure that our agents already infiltrated the Ministry of Intergovernmental Affairs and Immigration of the United States should change the laws of these ministries. These changes will focus on opening the doors of western immigration increasingly mass within their borders (immigration that we have indeed caused by having taken care to break here and there, new conflicts premises). By press campaign orchestrated well in public opinion in the United States targeted, we cause them a large influx of refugees who will, to destabilize their domestic economy and to increase racial tensions in the within their territory. We will ensure that groups of foreign extremists are part of the influx of immigrants, which will destabilize the political, economic and social conditions in the target nation.

...
- These changes will help us to social change in depth labor "police and military" of nation-states. Under the pretext of the exigencies of time and without arousing suspicion, we rid once and for all of all individuals having a "Judeo-Christian Conscience". This "Restructuring and Military Police Corps" we will not dismiss a challenge, the older, as well as all elements are carrying our global principles. These will be replaced by young recruits devoid of "Conscience and Morality" and already all trained and supported the indiscriminate use of our technology networks."

(Only the first and last square brackets comments are by the current author, the rest is presumably added by Serge Monast http://nenki.com/conspir/protocoles_toronto.html)

Index

374

If you liked this book you might like to read some of the author's other works, including:

Orwellian Ireland

Inspired by the book Stasiland, this work is an attempt to see if some of the state practices that flourished in Communist Eastern Europe might be replicated in modern Ireland. It goes into the question of intelligence agencies, what agencies are active in Ireland, how they harass dissidents, their use of modern technology and their role in secretly supporting paramilitary groups in Ireland and around the world. It includes a lot of first hand testimony of state harassment, and even torture, which is on a par with what happened in countries like East Germany. Finally it concludes with some searching questions about the real government policies being pursued in Ireland.
978-0-9556812-0-2

The Toronto Protocol: the real Plan of the Global elite?

This short but explosive text was first leaked by Serge Monast in Canada in 1995. It is reported to be the plan of an elite group who are manipulating the general public and governments across the world to bring about their long term goal of a world government. They cover in this document a wide variety of areas including the question of parental rights as opposed to state rights over children, the overall media and economic climate which was planned to be favourable in order to lure into complacency the general public, etc etc. Could it be for real? You decide!
978-1471070020

Shakespeare was Irish!

As more and more scholars come to realise that the accepted story of William Shakespeare is untenable, this book tries to unmask the covert Irish influence on his work and the remarkable career of William Nugent, the only Irish candidate ever put forward for Shakespeare.
978-0-9556812-1-9

Slí na Fírinne

This English language book puts the traditional Catholic proofs of God's existence into a modern context. It covers most of the arguments raging in the theism v atheism debate and also includes quotes on the nature of God and his existence from c.80 philosophers and scientists.
978-0-9556812-8-8

The Irish Invented Chess!

For over three centuries a controversy has raged as to the exact origins of 'fidchell' – in modern Irish 'ficheall' – or Irish chess, a game played in Ireland from biblical times. This book argues that that game of fidchell, or brannaimh, was recognisably our modern chess.
978-0-9556812-6-4

www.ingramcontent.com/pod-product-compliance
Lightning Source LLC
Chambersburg PA
CBHW020654270326
41928CB00005B/109

* 9 7 8 0 9 5 5 6 8 1 2 2 6 *